BODY & SOUL

For thirteen convent years she had fed her mind and denied her body. Like a trained seal, it had been obedient because it knew no different. Normal urges had stirred it, when nature had rebelled at the sterile rule the vows imposed. But however strong the desire, it had been impersonal. The ache was for something never known, the longing for someone never seen.

She had always been a watcher, always apart. For all those years she'd hidden her body beneath draperies, her spirit behind bars. She had neutralised herself and her emotions, taken a perverse pride in the denial of human needs and satisfactions.

Even when Hal kissed her on the moor, even when they danced and she had noticed the solid triangle of wide shoulders and narrow hips – still she had felt remote: His youth and his strength were not for her.

All that had changed. They lay facing each other, laced together. *Look at me with the eyes of your heart.*

Marcelle Bernstein worked on the *Guardian* and the *Observer* specialising in profiles of people and places. She has written for many major international newspapers and magazines.

Her first novel – the bestseller *Sadie* – was followed by *Salka* and *Lili*. Her internationally acclaimed documentary book *Nuns*, for which she interviewed 500 nuns and was granted unprecedented access to strictly enclosed orders, provides the background for this new novel.

BODY & SOUL has been filmed as Carlton Television's first major drama series, screened across the ITV network in Spring 93. It stars Kristin Scott Thomas, Anthony Valentine, Amanda Redman, Dorothy Tutin, Patrick Allen, John Bowe and Madeleine Christie.

Marcelle Bernstein lives in Brighton with her husband, the writer Eric Clark, and their three children.

BODY & SOUL

Marcelle Bernstein

Mandarin

A Mandarin Paperback
BODY & SOUL

First published in Great Britain 1991
by Victor Gollancz Ltd
This edition published 1992
by Mandarin Paperbacks
an imprint of Reed Consumer Books Ltd
Michelin House, 81 Fulham Road, London SW3 6RB
and Auckland, Melbourne, Singapore and Toronto
Reissued 1993
Reprinted 1993

Copyright © Marcelle Bernstein 1991
The author has asserted his moral rights

The Ballad of Lucy Jordan by Shel Silverstein.
© 1975 Tro-Essex Music Ltd.
International Copyright Secured.
All Rights Reserved. Used by Permission.

A CIP catalogue record for this title
is available from the British Library

ISBN 0 7493 3610 2

Printed and bound in Great Britain by
BPCC Paperbacks Ltd

Member of BPCC Ltd

For Eric,
Rachael, Charlotte and Daniel

BODY & SOUL

BOOK ONE

I

She woke as always long before dawn. In the suspended space before full awareness she allowed herself a few moments of luxury, savouring the warmth of her body, protected from the day which lay in wait. The call would come soon, anyway.

As sleep slid away, she felt the ache in her back. They said the cold brought on arthritis but surely she was too young. And the thin horsehair mattress provided only scant protection against the slats of the bed. She shifted slightly and the narrow sides – it had not been built with comfort in mind – confined her movements. As she turned, the harsh wool blanket scratched her neck. In all these years she had never managed to accustom herself to them, nor the thick sheets which were washed once in twelve months. She realised further sleep would be impossible.

She opened her eyes. Skimpy cotton curtains stirred and lifted so she could make out the bars at the window. Some people had fitted cardboard shutters to keep out the worst draughts, only she hated the dense darkness that brought. Though even in pitch black she knew every inch of the cell she had occupied now for thirteen years. She could pace it out blindfold on the bare stone floor. Ten paces from door to window, seven across. Put out a hand and the washbasin was on her left. Put the other hand to the ugly bedside table with its stubby lamp, the dark orange shade faded from long use.

It was against the rule to switch on the lamp after nine o'clock, though she would have liked to read. Through the walls she caught the rumble of faint, familiar snoring. In the past the sound had soothed when she could not sleep, the reassurance of someone nearby when insomnia unlocked devils she could subdue in daylight. Now the uneven snuffles irritated. She sighed. Unkind thoughts were as heartless as cruel words.

Across the far end of the cell she had strung a makeshift washing line, so she could rinse out her own underwear. A sudden gust of wind jiggled the feet of her long wool stockings in a lunatic dance. She had spun the wool for them herself, and knitted them. They were warm, even with the open sandals they wore summer and winter alike. But they itched. She had said so once, and been told firmly that discomfort was not to be avoided.

And things used to be much worse. It was only five years ago that they had been permitted to use soap for laundering. They had to make it themselves but it was infinitely better than washing soda. She winced at the memory of her hands raw from water and cold. That was during the winter when they had painted their cells. Under the washbasin was a leftover Snowcem tin she used as a waste-bin. She had painted it white, but it was still an old tin.

In the last year or two she had become more and more conscious of the bleakness of her surroundings. For ten years she had accepted without question uncarpeted corridors, the stone-flagged kitchens and outhouses where they worked, upright chairs and rough wood tables. Then one day she had gathered a bunch of flowers from the garden – bluebells in March, their blithe colour and scent making her ache for something she couldn't name – and looked for a vase. In the end she had used a jamjar, her efforts reduced to a child's attempt at beauty. It had brought home how much she missed the small pleasure of looking at something which was more than functional, something decorative and unnecessary. She longed to see a picture or an ornament.

An agonised squealing jagged the darkness outside. Then it was sliced by silence. Sometimes, when she couldn't sleep, she would sit by her window and watch for the barn-owl to drop on invisible prey. Wide speckled wings beating slow. Cruel pale angel bringing a thousand tiny deaths. The quiet pressed against her ears: she could sense little bodies crouched flat with fright. She had been told there were two owls in the church tower of the village less than a mile away. She had never been there. She could never go now.

It must be almost four. Accustomed as she was to living one hour at a time, she had learnt to estimate it accurately without a watch. She had worn her neat Tissot on its lizard strap when she came here, but surrendered it along with all her other possessions: handbag and purse, lipstick and compact, the jeans and fringed leather jacket she'd worn to travel.

She thought with distaste of the clothes she would soon put on, the coarse wool garments. When she had worn them first they had seemed honourable, won by her own efforts. But lately she had caught herself thinking wistfully of something pretty. A ribbon. A touch of silk. Frivolities she would never enjoy again.

Such things were petty distractions, of course. They didn't matter. The clothes she wore were the same as they had been a hundred years ago, as they would be in a hundred years' time. They were meant to be simple, stark and sexless, without artifice or adornment. They did not even have safety pins – she had been shown how to collect berries and keep them in a tin till they hardened. The she would soak them in water, string them onto cords and knot them firmly into her garments.

She had described this once in a letter home. They were permitted to write each month now, instead of two or three times a year, but the letters were censored. It had been spotted and that page had arrived with the offending lines neatly scissored out. And to tell such things on visiting days were unthinkable. The double set of bars, the brief time allowed, made idle chatter impossible.

Over the years she'd found it best to keep to herself the wry amusement she felt at so much here. Everyone talked a lot about a sense of humour being important to survive, but it did not extend to discussing their lives with outsiders. This had the effect – as was surely intended – of distancing her from her family, cutting her off even more completely than stone walls and heavy wood doors, massive locks and keys, had already done. It was as if her previous existence belonged to someone else. Even her name had been taken away from her: she was Anna now only to herself and her family on those rare permitted occasions.

Her old name, her old identity. How eagerly she had relinquished them all those years ago. How willingly she had taken the leap into the unknown. And how traumatic the surrender had proved to be.

Blind obedience was exacted, fierce discipline exerted. She had been taught to carry her hands in a special way, clasped together at waist level, to walk on the ball of her foot. She must not speak without need and even then she should not look at the person she was addressing but keep her eyes carefully lowered. She was trained to respond with deference to those in authority, to move on the instant when a bell rang. If she was ordered to brush a corridor in a certain manner, that was how it must be done; any improvement was forbidden. If she broke a glass she had to admit to it, if she wanted an aspirin she must seek permission. Once she dropped a plate during a meal and had to kiss the ground.

As time went by, she became aware that she no longer possessed tastes or held opinions. It was as if her personality had been shrunk. There was scarcely anything about her, now, to mark her out from all the others. This painful piece of self-knowledge depressed her deeply: she felt diminished, destroyed, less than whole. For a long time – for years – she could not come to terms with it. She felt like a fly she'd seen once, trapped in a beautiful piece of amber, stifled and stilled by its surroundings.

Anna had told herself this would pass. She looked around and saw that her companions were either going through the same thing or had experienced it already. She had been down on her knees scrubbing the hall, her hands raw and smarting from the pure ammonia they poured into the water, when the woman beside her had whispered, 'Hope you're not wearing your Dior tights.'

'As it happens,' she'd muttered back, for they were forbidden to speak, 'I've left them tucked into my Guccis.'

They had continued to rub the floor in sweating silence, but Anna's spirits lifted. She was able to see the absurdity of her situation. She understood well enough what they were about, she realised that it was intended for her own good, that the words they had read to her were meant.

The victim must be consumed.

Dreadful words. Worse, perhaps, than the reality. And then the next week she had been told to sweep up leaves from the courtyard. It was March and a rain-laden gale rampaged outside. She had stared in genuine bewilderment, biting back the protests. Quietly she had put on wellingtons and gone outside with the unwieldy broom of twigs she had made herself, to stand helplessly as the leaves spun round her. It was too much to ask. It was impossible, ridiculous.

And then she thought, of *course* it's ridiculous. That's the point. She had smiled. If that's what they want, they can have it. I've nothing else to do. She had started to brush the leaves into a heap, not caring that they were instantly scattered, humming to herself. She had understood then that to question orders was useless. They existed not so much to be carried out as to be given: their purpose was to break the will. The process was intended to be destructive, it was hardship at some deep psychological level.

And in some strange way she couldn't define, it had made her stronger. Daily she discovered she could endure a little more. She found possibilities within herself and there was no going back to the soft girl she had been before.

In the veiled pre-dawn light, Anna stared round her cell. The single bookshelf, the stool, the piece of sacking she used each morning as a bathmat when she washed, for there was only one bathroom for them all. The small cross of palm she had pinned to the wall.

Odd to think how happy she had once been in this confined

space. How contented. The primitive labour, the petty restrictions – in her own cell these things ceased to chafe. The day was divided by bell into half-hour intervals and for each half-hour she was allotted a task. The relief of letting herself in here at night was immense.

She had never imagined how difficult it would be to live so closely with so many. She listened to the snores from beyond her wall, waiting for the rise and fall, the gurgle, the uneven pause. The rise and fall, the gurgle . . . she groaned. Damn, damn, damn. It was an intrusion, an infringement of the only privacy she had, a reminder that she was bound to these people, that nothing she used or wore or touched was hers alone. Even the food she ate was decided by others and there was no choice, ever. You ate what was put in front of you, like it or not. Better if you didn't, better if it tasted of gall and vinegar.

The thought of food made her long for a cup of tea. She wouldn't get one till she'd been up for over an hour. And lucky to have that. Until quite recently – only a few years before she'd arrived – tea was unknown and the only hot drink they ever tasted was sugared water. They still were not permitted coffee. She often thought if she'd known that, she'd have had another cup of the awful stuff they served at the station buffet on her way here. Was that really thirteen years ago?

When she had first arrived, puffing away on a last cigarette, she thought she had never been anywhere so remote. Those early impressions were still vivid: the grey stone lodge spouting smoke beside the gate, the winding drive overhung with dark trees and then the ugly, solid house standing high in its overgrown acres, surrounded by a ramble of rhododendrons. At one side of the house the ground fell away to reveal the plain below and distant mountains, humped misshapen Welsh giants.

She had over-tipped an appreciative taxi-driver without noticing, her eyes already fixed on the view. She had stood there for a long time, her bag on the gravel beside her, staring out across the valley where three rivers snaked silver through fields of jade. There was no sound but the dry clapping of leaves in the soft wind and the call of a reeling bird. Silence had belled around her, enveloping as a cloak.

Anna was accustomed to the aural assaults of a busy city: buses and pounding lorries, shouts and sirens, bursts of music from passing cars, whistling workmen, stammer of drills on building sites. Nothing in her life had prepared her for such deep peace.

Silence was the rule. Except for brief specified times, it was stringently observed. Day in, day out. Enforcing it became a fetish, so that even the accidental slamming of a door was an infringement and had to be reported on your knees.

Even that hadn't bothered her. For the first few years here she had loved it all: this was what she had chosen. There had been tremendous relief that her future was settled, a great security. When she was working the garden, hacking down undergrowth with a bill-hook, she would straighten up with a hand on the small of her back, and the vision of her valley would be as refreshing as cool water.

She had not minded the hard physical labour for she was young and strong. Gradually it had changed her, transforming the eighteen-year-old with a hint of puppy fat lingering round hips and thighs into a lean-bodied woman with a narrow waist and small breasts. She reflected ruefully that the food certainly didn't contribute to excess weight: many evenings she got up from the long tables still hungry. Last night it had been soup, cold fish with oil followed by a plate of cabbage, and a piece of gingerbread. You received enough food to get a certain amount of work from your body. She could have eaten twice the amount she was allotted. And she'd give anything to taste red meat. Funny, at home she'd almost become a vegetarian, so little did she like the idea of eating flesh, and here she was yearning for a steak. And chips.

It was the work, of course, which produced the appetite, repetitive tasks deliberately chosen to be performed mechanically. She not only did much of the gardening, she also looked after the hens, cleaning out the shed and feeding them as well as collecting eggs. The task she could not bear, that brought her awake in the night with apprehension, was to wring the necks of the old birds when they ceased laying. She tried to do it with closed eyes, like the owls at the moment of kill, but she hated the desperate last struggle, the wrench of tearing gristle, the glazed stare. Terrible to do that with her bare hands.

She inspected her fingers. Even in the half-light she could see ingrained dirt no amount of washing would remove, dark lines ridging her nails, feel callouses on her palms. They were the hands of a good workman, not a woman just over thirty.

They had been pretty hands when she first arrrived here, with scarlet varnish on her nails. Estée Lauder, the most expensive she could buy, a rare and final gesture of extravagance. She'd painted it on with infinite care before she left home. On her second day they'd politely requested that she remove it, gave her cottonwool and a bottle of acetone and that had been that. The varnish had remained in its elaborate bottle in her washbag. She had returned to her cell one evening to find the bag gone. She never asked why, nor was she ever told. The scented soap from her brother, the skin tonic she liked, talcum powder – all had been taken. Only her toothbrush remained and the tube of toothpaste. When that was finished, she used salt like everyone else.

It must be time for the call, surely. She lay snug, her nose just under the blanket so she didn't inhale the sharp air. Only September and she could see frost flowers on the glass from her breath. They were so high here, sometimes she would find summer plants withered by night frosts even after warm days. She had turned towards the window and the fastening of the soft bonnet they all wore at night pulled against her throat. She undid the knot and took it off, rubbing her hand over her head; it felt as curly and rough as the coat of the Welsh collie they used for herding the small flock of sheep.

She still remembered the afternoon when her brother had been allowed to bring his two little boys to see her. When she first arrived here, visitors were permitted only rarely. Exceptions would be made for emergencies such as illness or if some close relative died. A chaperone was always present. Now family members could apply once a month in writing for appointments. Other places, she'd learned, were far less strict. But she had wanted this.

Too oppressed by their surroundings to do more than mutter answers to her questions, the children had sucked their thumbs and leaned fidgety against Simon. As he led them away after an hour, Anna heard Jamie ask in his piercing treble, 'Have they cut off all her hair, Dad?'

Simon had hurried them out but she had felt terrible, some sort of monster. The truth was they *had* cut her hair. She had always worn it long, held back with a tortoiseshell slide or a velvet band. It had suited her, given her an even more youthful look with her shy smile and immature features. She'd once found a picture in a book about unicorns of a medieval princess who looked like her: pale skin, high rounded forehead, straight nose and oddly complicated mouth, the lower lip full and tremulous, the upper sharply cut, precise and almost prim.

She had brushed and brushed the golden-brown bush of her hair that last time, before she braided it into a long plait down her back and knotted it with an elastic band. They had cut it off in public and put it in a little rush basket: it had looked like a glossy animal coiled in sleep and she had been unable to resist touching it. Warm it felt, alive, and she had been seized by a terrible pang of anger and anguish. How primitive, how senseless, to make her do this.

But that was nothing to what she'd felt later when they ran a pair of clippers over her head, nipping her scalp as they shaved. She had known they were going to do it, of course, only she had not really thought it through. Chunks of hair falling on the white sheet round her shoulders, the realisation of how hideous she must look, shorn like a tennis ball, the strange chill of her head without its warm mane, the funny weightless feeling. She'd been grateful that she couldn't see herself.

Some of the women kept their hair like that, running a razor over their skin every three or four weeks. It was convenient, they said, and cool. Others, like Anna, just cut the ends, snipping at random with nail scissors when it felt uncomfortable. She had no mirror – none of them did – and she hadn't even seen one in thirteen years, so she had no idea what she looked like. Terrible, probably.

Anna smoothed what would have been a fringe if she'd let it, and wondered what colour it was now. Going grey for all she knew, though the bits she cut off were still dark enough. Darker than it used to be, in fact, for what was left was always covered and even when she worked outside the sun never got to it.

The sound of the handbell jerked her fully awake. It was five o'clock and all along the corridor she could hear the sharp rap at each door, the repeated words of the call she had listened to every morning for nearly thirteen years.

Almost here. She could make out the slip of sandalled feet and the pealing bell was strident. The woman next door answered, a few muffled words. Then it was her turn.

'Blessed be His Holy name.'

She made the unvarying response.

'Be for ever praised.'

Anna reached out and turned on the bedside lamp, the orange glow warm and welcoming. She pushed herself up and swung her legs out of bed, waiting a minute to ease the cramp in her back. She twisted sideways and dropped down onto all fours. She lowered her head and kissed the cold floor, aware of the suspicion of grit against her lips, the metallic taste of stone.

She sat back on her heels, bracing herself for the day. It never used to be like this. Not long ago she had started each morning in a flurry of anticipation, eager for any experience it would bring. The life had felt rich to her then. She had truly believed she had a mysterious contract with God, that she was an instrument to bring His love into the world.

It was hard to pin down the moment when this no longer seemed true. A great restlessness had begun in her, at first no more than a twinge like a pulled muscle. Unassuaged it had grown into a tight ball somewhere under her ribs so that sometimes at night she worried in case it was physical and something really was wrong. Nothing was, of course. She was never ill. Few of them were: no one came in from outside to bring even a cold and if their food was frugal it was also wholesome.

She washed her face, patting the cold water carefully round her eyes. When she was in college she'd read in some magazine this kept the muscles toned, and she'd always done it. Her one remaining vanity. Then she ran a bowl full of tepid water – the best available at this hour – and unbuttoned the top of her nightdress, slipping it from her shoulders with a shiver to bunch round her hips. Standing on the thin piece of sacking she washed with her flannel, round her throat, under her arms. Her nipples hardened at the touch of the cool water and she hurriedly wrapped herself in the worn towel and stepped out of her nightdress, tossing it onto the bed.

She soaped the flannel again. It was homemade from mutton fat scented with their own lavender, but it didn't produce much lather. She finished soaping herself vigorously, resting each foot in turn on the warm wood of the stool. In some houses, she had been told, they had to wear a shapeless black garment and wash themselves as best they could beneath it, not to see their own naked bodies. She had once asked naïvely; Why? The answer had been a brief lecture on the celibate state. 'Bodily passions,' she was advised, 'darken the mind and weaken the will. We must guard against such passions.'

Anna washed her hair every morning; she hated the sweaty feel she got when she worked hard and the white linen band of the head-dress pressed against her forehead. It took only minutes to towel-dry. Rubbing it briskly, she reflected that a celibate body was still a feminine body. She had thought, in the early years here, that she would somehow become like an angel, that physical satisfactions and happiness, if rigorously denied, would no longer be desired. Maybe she was a late developer or something, because she'd found it harder and harder to close off that area. Once or twice she'd attempted to discuss it but hadn't got very far. You were allowed to ask the mother prioress for a special permission to speak, if you needed spiritual help from another nun. The mistress of novices in her day had been the kind and conventional Sister Matthew who firmly believed that 'You never want what you've never had'. She'd added, obviously intending to relieve Anna's mind, 'I'm sure you're not oversexed, Sister Gabriel, you're not eccentric.' The innocence – the ignorance – behind that comment was shocking as cold water thrown in her face. When Anna in desperation had persisted, ('But why do I feel this way, then?') Sister Matthew masked embarrassment with uncharacteristic annoyance. 'Don't be morbid.'

She knew the theory of it, of course, and in theory it worked. Her chastity was supposed to free her, to clear her soul for union with God and make it possible for more than one person to have a claim on her love. In practice, she felt a freak. Outside these walls, any woman of thirty-one who remained a virgin must be either desperately unattractive or remarkably cold-hearted.

She wasn't one or the other, she felt pretty sure of that. Only she had conspired to believe what she was instructed: that virginity was the life of angels. A happy and easy sacrifice, they said, a *living* sacrifice. Dwelling in perpetual sweetness like the fly in the heart of the apple. A reminder that in eternity there will be neither male nor female.

She ran her fingers through her hair. Dry enough. Climbing into the decorous underwear, the flannel vest and pants, she thought that eternity was a long way off. It hadn't seemed so, once. When she was younger, secure in her new-found religious fervour, she had believed that life was short, that it would quickly pass, and that the afterlife would be for ever.

And how quickly time had passed for her, out in the world. How crowded the days had been, how noisy. The bustle of school, then college, the stress of work and the frenetic round of student activities. She had hung around on the edges, never quite part, always watching a little wistfully as other girls rode the Rag week float, or spoke in debates.

She had not been special in any way, and perhaps that explained the decision she had so dramatically and – in her parents' eyes – disastrously taken. The life she had chosen marked her out all right, had brought her a degree of glamour nothing else could have done.

At the end of the autumn term she had only told a couple of friends she would not be returning to college. They had pressed her to know why and like all secrets, it was sweeter for the sharing. She never knew which of them had broadcast it, and by the time she found out it was too late and her destination was common knowledge. That last night of term they had given her a party, 'something to remember the old place by' as someone had said, putting another drink in her hand. Which she drank. What she didn't have now she never would.

She had her first hangover the next morning. Weights had been attached to the back of her eyes and if she turned her head quickly she felt sick. The one comfort was that she wasn't going to feel like this again. Packing her trunk and addressing it to her parents' home, saying goodbye at college, getting the train: Manchester, Shrewsbury, then the branch line to Welshpool. Everything had been very slow, like swimming through oily water.

It was the hangover, of course, it would change. But oddly, it didn't. It was only after several weeks she realised there were two kinds of time. The time outside, punctuated by the demands of others, of classes, meals and phone calls. And time in here, drawn out, slow, full of the shadows of silence, the spaces of recollection. She learnt to use the time as it was meant to be used, listening for the voice of God. Sometimes she truly believed she heard Him, and she was filled with elation, knowing this was where she was meant to be. Everything had seemed right.

Anna pulled on the long woollen stockings and tightened elastic garters above her knees. She buttoned the long-sleeved bodice of double-wool and the thick tweed underskirt. The winter clothes were always handed out on the same date, and if there was a warm spell, you just had to live with it. She took the thick, dark grey robe off the hanger behind the door and buckled the leather girdle round her waist. Next the straight, sleeveless black scapular went over her head, reaching the ground back and front.

Receive the yoke of the Lord and bear his burden which is sweet and light.

Once those words had been true for her. She had wanted to give up the pleasures of the senses, she had chosen hard work and obedience, she had desired the silence the prelate had promised her 'from now until death'. The cloister was meant to be purgatory, for there would be heaven at the end of it. She wrapped the white band of the torque round her head and fastened the heavy black veil in place over it.

Place on my head, O Lord, the helmet of salvation.

Almost five thirty. Time for Lauds, then sung Prime. She took her long woollen mantle from its peg, checked the large pocket in her underskirt: handkerchief, pencil, paper, matches. She struck one and opened the glass front of the oil lamp which hung from a nail in the wall. She must remember to refill it. She turned off the bedside light, opened her door and waited.

The dark corridor filled with a stream of grey-clad women, each carrying her lamp, moving purposefully. Anna joined them, adding her small glow of light to the others, pacing the stone passages into the courtyard. Following the line she walked round the covered verandah which ran along three sides of the house and led into the ante-choir.

By the time she reached the carved wooden figure of Our Lady of Walsingham, she could already smell incense and the aromatic pine branches with which, two days before, she had decorated the walls of the chapel. Here, the heart of the community, the nuns gathered for prayer seven times a day and once at night in the pattern of homage unbroken since the sixth century.

Anna never saw this place, the hub of all their lives, without a small shock of pleasure: the long windows, stained glass subdued by dawn darkness, the polished stone, the simple altar draped in damask. A wide-meshed grille divided the nuns' choir from the public side of the chapel, where visitors and relatives could come for the rare, joyous events of their cloistered lives, for Clothings and Final Professions. Through a square opening the nuns were given communion, through it they reached to light the great Paschal candle in its brass and copper holder. Their side of the grille was cool and empty, with their seats in rows down both sides, high-backed chairs at the head for the mother prioress and the mother sub-prioress.

Anna bent her head. All around her the nuns stood in meditation, beginning their day as every other. They were enclosed and they could do nothing for the world but pray. And their prayers, they believed, caused strength to flow through them down to the world. They asked for no proof of the efficacy of their prayers; they knew they were helping.

As in the past, she had known. She still did, but something inside her had changed, something she didn't understand. She could see the beauty in the life, but it was no longer enough. All these women, each face illumined by a reading lamp, absorbed and content, lost in something beyond themselves – she used to find in this sight a feeling of total commitment, of unity, more important to her than anything on earth.

Anna closed her eyes tight, struggling to find that dim inner place where God and the soul meet. She spoke the words of the morning prayers softly, immersing herself in the timeless chants. If she didn't question, if she didn't think, it still worked for her.

Not until the first hushed hour in choir was over and the nuns made their way in procession to the refectory did the nagging little inner voice begin again, insinuating and ugly, repeating what she already knew.

I can't go on.

2

The lorry that had been pursuing him for five miles started to overtake on the long downward slope. It reared over the red Mini on four sets of double wheels higher than his head. To his left a deep ditch separated the twisting road from the sweeping Yorkshire moorland, on the other side a dry-stone wall held back the heathery hillside. He glanced up. *Doric Deliveries* was written in great red letters along the silver sides.

The deafening rumble reminded him of the Tube yesterday at St Paul's after his meeting at the bank: sweat prickled again on his forehead. He'd stood on the very edge of the platform as the train punched through the tunnel, stale air blasting on his face as he stared down at the metal threat of rails. He'd welcomed the press and push of bodies behind him: it would look like an accident. He wanted it – but not badly enough to die in front of two hundred strangers.

There were no watchers here. He eased his hold on the steering wheel, felt the little car drift dangerously close to the swaying, creaking hulk. He rested his right wrist on his thigh, held on with the tips of his fingers. Just a fraction further, just another moment, and the Mini would be under those mammoth wheels. Then the road curved to the left, the lorry fell back and a glance in his wing mirror showed the driver, leather-patched elbow protruding from the open window. Another bloke with a wife and kids. He gripped the wheel again.

The little town of Ingleton clings to the rugged West Riding hillside. He looked down to where the Twiss and Doe rivers flow together in spectacular countryside, but the view meant nothing to him. He'd been driving aimlessly since he left home that morning at seven thirty – his usual time, so as not to upset Lynn or Bax – and the sight of the main street lined with shops and cafés to serve the fell walkers and potholers reminded him that he could use a coffee. Until he remembered that he'd emptied his pockets in the bedroom that morning, leaving all he had on him – seventy five pounds and loose change – where Lynn would easily find it. Not much point in drinking coffee anyway, considering what he was about to do.

He pulled into the kerb near a letter box, between a baker's delivery van and an Escort with a toy faun on the rear shelf, its head nodding as a woman pulled out two small children and an assortment of prams and bags.

He lit a cigarette. Only one left. More than enough. For a moment he weighed the smooth, gold Dunhill lighter Dad had given him on his twenty-first; God, a lifetime ago. Then he dropped it into the padded envelope lying on the passenger seat. He glanced at his watch, the elegant Roman numerals, the lizard strap. Four twenty. He unbuckled it and put that into the envelope too, checked that the letter was inside, sealed it with the sellotape he'd brought with him.

Holding the neat parcel, he found himself recalling a similar envelope that had arrived at his parents' home in Bradford thirteen years before. No note, nothing – just his sister's watch, sent back by the convent. As if, his father had said in hurt bewilderment, she were dead. His mother had left it lying on the table. 'She's dead to us, isn't she?'

He wondered whether things would have been different if Anna had stayed. Maybe if she'd gone into the mill with him as Dad had wanted, if they'd shared decisions, he'd not have made such a God-awful mess of everything. He'd wanted to talk to her about his problems last time he went to Wales to visit: even as a kid, Anna had always been keen on the mill. But the figure behind the heavy double-grille and black veiling had been shrouded and remote. Too cut off from the world to comprehend his problems. He briefly regretted not having written to say goodbye.

The Escort woman was strapping her baby into its buggy: all he could see was a tight denim bum and suede boots. He waited till she straightened up, a pretty girl pert under a shiny fringe. She stared into the Mini, right at him, but nothing registered. That made him feel even worse, confirming that he was looking older than his forty years, his face furrowed by anxiety. His bathroom mirror showed how the blue had washed from his eyes, and the thick hair he'd always kept so well-cut had become thin and flat, the elegant touch of silver over the ears lost in encroaching grey.

No wonder the Escort girl wasn't interested. A year or two ago she – any woman – would have responded to his look, given him a considering stare, flicked back her hair, acknowledged that he was attractive. Trivial enough, but the sort of contact that kept you feeling part of the human race.

He gave a start: God, he must've been sitting here for half an hour at least, he was freezing. A car came towards him with sidelights on and he realised the day was already fading, the air tinged with blue. Melancholy soaked through him. It was always worse at night: in the last six months he'd learned to dread the evenings.

A couple of climbers approached, their skinny shanks emphasised by black nylon leggings edged in luminous yellow, woollen bobble hats absurd above bearded faces. Arguing about the height of Ingleborough summit and Whernside, they brushed past him without a glance. As if he'd already ceased to exist. With almost vindictive force he shoved the padded envelope into the scarlet gape of the old-fashioned letter box before he changed his mind.

As he drove off he was vaguely conscious of people going into shops, gossiping on the pavement. Women mostly, headscarves firmly tied against the wind, hauling dogs and shopping and responsibility behind them. He wondered if his own wife was doing the same thing. Thinking about Lynn was something he ought to do but his despair was by now so great nothing else mattered.

Misery crouched on his shoulders, weighted his movements, hollowed an ache beneath his ribs. For so long he'd pretended. Getting up, going to work, returning home. Days were stripped of colour, food devoid of taste. He stared at meaningless accounts, read pointless documents, signed a name less than his own. He resented the mill more than ever. He'd never wanted it but his youth and time had been swallowed up by its demands and in return he had nothing but debts.

Lately, even Lynn and his boys had seemed an intolerable burden. He wouldn't let himself acknowledge the coming baby; what should have been a source of joy instead increased his desperation. A huge heap piled on top of him, pinning him down, while he struggled to keep it all up. Well, not any more.

As the last houses straggled away behind him he accelerated, in a hurry now, anxious to get it over and done with. Lynn used the Mini as a runabout to ferry food and children; it bore numerous scars and baulked at starting in the mornings so they called it the Camel. An old joke. The sort they didn't seem to share these days.

He tried not to think how much had changed between them. Lynn seemed preoccupied with the boys and permanently tired: he'd said last night – only half-joking – 'I'm Number Five in this house' – and she'd snapped his head off. Later, lying sleepless in the early hours, he'd wanted to wake her, tell her everything, seek comfort in her warm familiar body. But he didn't. His desire for sex had waned as depression deepened, and when Lynn initiated lovemaking lately it was invariably disastrous, leaving both of them restless and unsatisfied. He wiped a hand down his face to expunge the memory of yet another failure.

Maybe it was his fault. Lynn had known the mill wasn't doing well, she could see he was worried, but whenever she raised the matter he refused to discuss it. His father never talked shop at home either. Then, on a surge of mad optimism, he'd borrowed more and more and even raised enough from the London people to buy new equipment. By then Lynn was pregnant and he'd let her think the money was his own: she'd been so happy for him.

He'd lied by omission and there was no way he could now admit the truth. And the truth got steadily worse. The new yarns didn't do as well as he'd so confidently predicted. It wasn't his fault, the whole of the wool industry was reeling from the state of the economy. All across the country people were losing their livings, their houses, small businesses were going bankrupt. People just didn't have the money to spend.

He'd failed. He'd got it all wrong. He felt himself sinking until he forgot how it felt to be happy. Even reading a story to Jamie was an effort: he'd get to the end of *The Giant Jam Sandwich* without remembering a single word or picture.

He undid his seat-belt. He had one hell of a headache: the Mini was raucous and rackety at speed, they never used it for long distances. He'd started out in the Jag that morning as usual. It had handled like the thoroughbred it was, instantly responsive, smelling richly of leather, and he'd turned round and driven home and put it back in the garage, unable to do to that fine piece of engineering what he was planning to do to himself. It'd fetch a good price, anyway.

Open country now, purple moors and bronze bracken. he was driving into veils of mauve rain. In the distance, threads of pale light poured from beneath rolls of dark cloud like a biblical painting. The beauty of the place made him feel used up and ugly. Slowing down, he lit his last cigarette from the stub of the first. He inhaled deeply, welcoming the smoke into his lungs. And they said it killed you.

From here he could watch the road dipping away in front of him, stone walls hugging close. Not a vehicle in sight. He took a last drag before chucking the cigarette out of the window and settling more comfortably into his seat like a man readying himself for a long journey. He changed up into fourth – too high for the twisting, slick surface – rammed his foot down on the accelerator and shut his eyes.

As soon as he felt the Mini go into a skid he lost his nerve.

He was normally an excellent driver but nothing now was normal. He stood hard on the brakes, every muscle rigid with effort. Sinews corded his neck and his eyes strained wide in terror. So he was able to see that it was too late.

3

'Sister Gabriel. Come to my office after Terce, please.' Mother Prioress paused in her stately passage towards her place at the centre of the top table.

Anna bent her head, acknowledging the summons. She was aware that a ripple of interest, quickly stilled, ran along rows of waiting women. After grace the nuns seated themselves and the heavy benches scraped on the stone floor.

'*Wot?*' Sister Dominic murmured beside her.

'I've won the pools.'

'C'mon.' Sister Dominic drawled out of the side of her mouth. 'Tell.' They were all opening the polythene bags which had been set out the night before, containing the crusty bread they baked themselves, a spoon and a napkin. There was a plate with a pat of butter and the godet, the handmade cup like a wide handleless bowl.

Beneath the rustle and movement Anna said, very low, 'They've decided it's time for a woman Pope and they want my advice.'

Sister Dominic turned a snigger into a cough. The teapot, passed from hand to hand along the narrow table, had reached Anna. She poured into the godet, gave it to Lis, and sat in accustomed silence. This promised to be a better day: on Saturdays the grim miles of the week were safely behind her. And there was honey on the table, she'd collected it herself with Sister Thomas à Becket. She loved going down to the seven hives in the herb garden, donning the mesh helmet and long white coat, lifting the conical roofs to reveal the tawny glistening rug of insects.

She pointed her forefinger in one of the many ritualised gestures the nuns used at meals and received the earthenware pot with a smile of thanks. She dripped honey onto her bread. Each table had to share a single knife in a custom which went back, like the design of their cups and much else in their order, to medieval France.

Anna – who had scarcely tasted sugar for thirteen years – relished the grainy sweetness on her tongue. And checked herself. Gluttony was a sin. In expiation she would forfeit a second cup of tea when the pot came round again. At the end of the main meal of the day, a scrap plate would go up and down the rows of sisters, collecting everything that could not possibly be eaten. An extra penance would be to take something from this dish and eat it squatting on the floor. It was a remnant of an ancient custom, intended to teach humility and mortify the spirit: sisters would beg from table to table that they be fed 'for God and Our Lady's sake'.

She would do that at midday. In the meantime, Lis was right. What could Mother Emmanuel want? She ran through the day in her mind. After Lauds, Mass and Terce she would collect the eggs before going to the sewing room. It was her turn to work on the winter petticoats, long-sleeved, round-necked garments made out of a scratchy hopsack material that was hard to stitch. In the afternoon she would work in the kitchen garden. Much of their day was spent in hard physical labour, repetitive toil deliberately chosen so it could be performed mechanically. It wasn't important. It was merely the exterior, the outer shell. What mattered was that their minds were free for God.

She glanced across at the square figure of the prioress in her dark grey robes, the white band round her face emphasising the pouched cheeks and determined mouth. An intimidating woman, her assessing gaze was fixed on the reader's desk. Anna always felt she was ageless, old as the order itself, a figure out of her time, whose features could have appeared in a sombre painting by Velázquez.

She had been prioress for the last twelve years, a testimony to her qualities of leadership. When this little Welsh community was so short of entrants it looked as though they would have to leave the house, the father-general of the order in Rome had allowed Mother Emmanuel to come to them as prioress on a permanent basis. Single-handed, she had managed to attract novices and revitalise the community. Her personality, her energy, held them all together: had she remained in the world, Anna had always thought she would have risen to the top of any field she chose. She'd said so once to Lis, who'd agreed. 'And I bet she'd have picked the police,' she added. Anna had to stifle a smile. Unlikely. But not impossible.

The prioress felt Anna's look and turned her head slightly. Her habitual imperious expression softened into one of grave concern that worried Anna more than the summons. Well, she'd know soon enough. And curiosity must be avoided at all times. She put her hand flat on the table and Sister Peter, on her right, silently passed the jug of goats' milk.

As she drank, Anna forced herself to concentrate on the reading that accompanied every meal. Since eating was so gross an occupation, the mind should be elsewhere. She listened to the rolling phrases from the Book of Daniel with satisfaction.

Sister Aelred, the reader, was a tiny woman with a huge sense of humour whose name in religion was that of an early Saxon bishop. You were supposed to emulate your namesake but she would roll her eyes expressively at the very idea. Almost all the nuns had men's names, ostensibly because the large number of women got through the available feminine names fast. But Anna suspected that the real reason, never stated, was to depersonalise them. When religious life was modernised in the sixties and seventies following the great meeting of bishops that was Vatican II, most orders dropped their use of men's names and nuns reverted to their own. Only Anna's and one or two of the other older and deeply ascetic

32

foundations decided to retain their old ways. She'd told her family what would happen when she entered, and her mother had gone white. 'Just like going into prison.'

Anna had vehemently denied this. But of course it was true. The taking of her clothes, the removal of all personal items – even her pretty leather manicure set – the life in common, the new identity. For a prisoner, a number. For a nun, the title Sister. Black nonentity. The loss of her past. Of her self.

The fifteen minutes allotted to breakfast were up. The mother prioress stood to lead the way back to chapel for Matins, and they were already in their places by the time the bell struck seven. This was Anna's favourite of the offices, she could almost see the unaccompanied voices of the women rising through early morning Welsh mists, making music that had remained unchanged for centuries.

Later, smoothing her bed and sweeping the cell, she wondered again about the summons. She brushed more slowly. Perhaps Reverend Mother had guessed her terrible secret, perhaps she knew.

Anna had been hugging unhappiness close for so long, trying not to let anyone see what she was going through. She had straightened her shoulders when she felt beaten into the ground by misery. When she woke in the early hours to find her pillow wet with tears where she'd cried even in sleep, she'd splashed her face with cold water and quietly gone to chapel. She'd struggled towards the belief that her suffering was valuable, endeavoured to become the willing sacrifice, the *living* sacrifice, she believed God wanted of her.

She hadn't been interested in an ordinary life, in the mediocre existence of other people. Only the extreme would do, only strict enclosure. But the truth was, the life she'd chosen was too hard for her. Too extreme. She couldn't sustain it. She had given it all she had and, day by day, she knew in her heart she was failing. She wasn't strong enough, she wasn't good enough, she wasn't humble enough.

But she didn't think Mother Emmanuel was humble either, and she had been an enclosed nun for forty years.

Forty years. Anna stood stock still, broom in hand. She could not envisage herself still here in thirty years' time. She would never manage it. The long littleness of the life would have driven her mad by then.

The prioress's office had been a linen room at one time, and two walls were almost entirely taken up with cupboards containing the bits and pieces with which the nuns supplemented their meagre income. Handmade candles of creamy wax, polystyrene models of cells, bags of dried petals from their heavily-scented, old-fashioned roses. The two remaining walls had been economically covered by the nuns with the sample squares of wallpaper from pattern books discarded by the DIY shop in Welshpool.

Mother Emmanuel always worked with her door open. ('All the better to see you with, my dear,' as Lis had observed after receiving one of her regular reprimands for running upstairs.) She glanced up at Anna's knock and pointed to a chair. Anna sat with some relief: if it was trouble, she would have been let stand. She waited for two minutes while the older woman finished her typing. This was a two-finger business, but the typewriter was a smart black model, a present from the community when the prioress had reached the fortieth anniversary of her entry into religious life. The whole day had been declared a holiday: they'd all taken a picnic down to a remote corner of their land and in the evening gathered in the community room to act out a play written by the Novice Mistress.

That had been a lovely evening. Mother Emmanuel had reminisced about the Ladbroke Grove convent where she'd entered at fifteen: the darkened room, the four gaunt figures draped in black waiting to receive her. Then Sister Louis had sung for them, unaccompanied, 'The Falcon hath borne my love away'. Her beautiful Irish voice soaring through falls and cadences, the words heart-breakingly poignant. And in the remembering silence when she finished, Anna had thought, we're all like a family of Victorian daughters, living our uneventful, chaperoned lives in the country.

It went deeper than that, of course. There'd been a time when she, too, had come near to feeling what one of the older sisters described to her while she was a novice. That Christ was her husband, that she could talk to Him about anything, that He really cared about her. That whatever she had given up, she was enclosed within a greater love. She crossed her wrists neatly on her lap and sighed. When had that conviction ceased to be true?

At the sound, Mother Emmanuel pulled the paper out of her typewriter and put it into a folder. Anna thought she was making herself very busy, as though putting off the moment when she must speak. It would have been nice to lean forward and inhale the scent of the bowl of pot-pourri on the desk. But the Rule forbade it. The *Manual for Novices on Mortification of Exterior Senses* said: *Do not smell fragrant herbs, fruit or flowers, much less bring them into your cell, or keep them for the pleasant odour.*

'Sister Gabriel. There's something I must tell you.' Unaccustomed kindness in the voice brought Anna bolt upright. It was going to be bad. She stared at the doughty figure in front of her, concentrating on two deep worry lines like quotation marks between the superior's brows. She was remembering with horrid clarity sitting here seven years ago, when Reverend Mother had told her about the car crash which had killed her parents. Her first desperate thought had been to turn time back, just a few hours, so that Mum and Dad could still be driving home from the Lake District, as they so often had, listening to John Dunne on the radio and . . .

'It's a family matter, I'm afraid. Your brother. Simon. He had some sort of attack yesterday afternoon . . .'

Anna opened her mouth to ask, but she knew already what was coming.

'They rushed him to hospital but I'm afraid he died early this morning.'

'No.' Anna stated it quite calmly. 'There must be a mistake.'

The prioress shook her head. 'No. No mistake, Sister. I'm so very sorry.'

Cold ran like water down her arms and back.

'He can't – he's only just forty! People don't die just like that!' She was on her feet and her voice cracked. 'It can't be true. They've mixed him up with someone else.' Oh dear God, make it not be true.

'It is true, Sister. It is. It was Simon's doctor who telephoned. He was with your brother when he died. There's no mistake.' She came round the desk. Anna stared down at the hands covering her own. They were gnarled with work and prominently veined, their grip strong as a man's. When Anna raised her head, the compassion in the dark eyes under their heavy lids told her there was no escape from this reality. She could hardly breathe, there was a gasping sound somewhere near her and then Mother Emmanuel speaking in the distance but she couldn't hear properly. She held onto the prioress's hands as if she were a rock in a wild sea.

'. . . down Sister. Sit down, there's a good girl.'

Anna obeyed, still clutching hold like a child in a fright. Oh God. Simon. *Simon.* Her mind blank. She heard the prioress telling her what little she knew: the name of the hospital, the time of Simon's death. Words that should have helped, phrases intended to console. None of it made any sense. If only it could be yesterday again.

Mother Emmanuel asked her a question and went out, closing the door silently behind her. Anna thought about Simon when she could first remember him, in the baggy grey school shorts and socks that wouldn't stay up, and that smelly glass-eyed monkey called Monkey he kept stuffed down the bottom of his bed. And later, bringing her home from school, insisting she walk in front where he could keep an eye on her without actually appearing to be with her, in case his friends saw them. The gap between his front teeth and the time he lent her a new sweater before he'd even worn it. He used to call her Bud.

That did it. Anna drew her knees up onto the chair, clasped

36

her arms round them, put her head down and sobbed. She cried for a long time. When she could breathe properly again she fished in her underskirt pocket for her white cotton square and wiped her eyes and nose.

It was only then she remembered Lynn. And the boys. How could she not have thought of them sooner? She was selfish, horrible, concerned with what Simon's death meant to her, when his wife must be in the most terrible state. And the little boys – how do you tell a four-year-old? She told herself she must pray for them all but she couldn't calm herself enough to formulate the words.

Mother Emmanuel tapped on the door before she opened it, scrupulous as always.

'Perhaps you'd like to go and lie down.'

Anna shook her head. 'I'll go to chapel in a minute. May I have permission to leave the sewing this morning, Mother?'

'Of course. And we will all pray for your brother and his young family. Which brings me to something else.' Unbelievably weary, Anna waited. She wanted only to be alone but could not say so in the face of the older woman's concern. She shut her eyes while her superior settled behind her desk. 'This isn't the moment for everything I have to say to you, Sister. But I've been worried about you for some time.'

Anna opened her eyes but said nothing. Mother Emmanuel went on quietly. 'Every nun experiences what you have been going through. God's silences are hard, especially for us contemplatives. In active orders people can perhaps bury themselves in the problems of others, or in their work. But we have nothing else. When there's no response from God, when your questions go unanswered, it feels pretty grim.'

Another time, Anna would have smiled at the choice of words, the curiously dated slang. Not today. 'I didn't think . . . I tried . . .'

'We've all been through the hours of despondence. Just like you. So you see, I recognised it all too clearly.' Anna made a small movement of protest and the prioress nodded. 'But even in bad times, He sends compensations, if you can look for

37

them. If you can believe, deep down, that nothing is going to pull you away from Him.' She stopped speaking and looked out of the narrow window. Her face bore its usual expression, as if life had confirmed her worst suspicions of it. 'I've chosen a bad time to say this. Your brother's death is going to be hard for you. Very hard. But it will be even harder for his family, they must learn to live with his physical loss also.'

'Yes.'

'Your family has asked if you can go home for the funeral.' Anna looked up, waited. 'Of course I had to refuse,' the prioress went on smoothly. Anna wasn't surprised. The role of constant enclosure here was strictly observed and it had not occurred to her, even when she was unable to attend her parents' funeral, to question it. She did not speak again, but waited till she was dismissed and could go alone to chapel.

It was a long night. Anna relived the days after the news came of her parents' death on the motorway. Simon had taken care of everything and afterwards had come to tell her about it. Not until months later did the realisation of what had happened really hit her, and then she wished she had been able to see them buried, to speak about them to people who loved them, to work through her grief. Thank God they hadn't lived to endure Simon's death.

For the first time in all her years here, she switched on the bedside lamp in defiance of the rules, unable to lie any longer staring into darkness, cold right through to her bones. She was up long before the call came, washed and dressed, her bed neatly made with hospital corners.

In chapel she tried to open to the silence. She was a nun, she was strictly enclosed, she believed that through prayer, she became an instrument, a conduit through which God's love could flow. In the past, she had found it. She'd turned inward, willing Him to possess her, heart and mind. And there had been answers for her.

This morning, she couldn't lose awareness. She was sharply conscious of the slip of sandalled feet on stone, the smell of damp they could never eradicate even in summer, the dry rasp of Sister Peter's cough. She shut her eyes tight, forced her way down through the folds of her soul to the still centre nothing could touch.

Anna didn't join in the singing. She heard with a shiver the words of the psalm, knowing they were meant for her:

'You sweep men away like a dream

Like grass which springs up in the morning.

Our life is over like a sigh.'

Images of Simon: at fifteen, saying, 'I've always wondered what this would feel like,' as he poured bottled ketchup over his head and let if drip down into his eyes. At sixteen, saving up to buy a car. It took him two years to afford an old Citroën which had to be towed to the house. He spent every free moment renovating it, working with a passion he displayed for nothing else. She had polished the burgundy-coloured seats for him: she could still smell the leather.

And now he was gone. His life over like a sigh. A sudden huge rage grasped her: how could You let it happen, how could You? Simon was barely forty, he had a wife and two little boys, people who needed him. She wiped a tear with an angry gesture.

If she felt this, how much worse it must be for Lynn. She hardly knew her sister-in-law: the marriage had taken place after she entered, and though Simon had brought his new wife twice to the convent, the visits had not been successful. Lynn had said little, intimidated by the grilles and veils. Anna knew only what she'd glimpsed of carefully disordered blonde hair, good clothes, narrow feet in expensive shoes, a voice surely too soft to be true. Once, as the couple were leaving, Anna had seen a quarrel break the surface, an argument clearly started before they arrived at the convent. Lynn had stopped short in the corridor outside the visitors' parlour, Simon had hustled her on.

It confirmed for Anna the hazards of married life. Her parents' marriage had been all recriminations and regrets, a repository of wasted opportunities. She'd determined not to repeat it – something her parents suspected but never mentioned. Simon had evaded matrimony for a long time, his boisterous bachelorhood continuing until he was over thirty. But then Lynn had been so clearly a catch for him: pretty, independent, with a life and a mind of her own.

The chapel bell pealed, rounded notes floating clear as bubbles across the valley.

Anna thought: After a time Lynn will be all right. She'll get over it, find someone else. People do.

Compline was at eight. In the dark chapel, the lamps of the women gleamed in pools and the altar light glowed red beyond the nuns' grille. They made their last prayers before the Great Silence fell on the house, not to be broken before the first prayers of the morning. On her way along the stone corridor which led to their cells, Anna was halted by Mother Emmanuel. The older woman was standing beneath a handwritten notice: PLEASE NO SPEAKING IN THIS PASSAGE. THE CELLAR STEPS FOR A QUICK WORD. FOR LONGER SPEECH THE LAMP OFFICE OR THE COMMUNITY ROOM. She beckoned and Anna followed her into the doorway leading to the cellar.

'You look better this evening, Sister.' Anna nodded, grateful for the kindness. The prioress watched her for a moment as if trying to reach a decision. 'There's been another call about you from Bradford.' She paused before adding, almost reluctantly, 'It appears there are – circumstances – which indicate that you should be allowed to go home.'

Anna heard her with amazement: she couldn't imagine what had changed since yesterday. 'I've thought about it carefully,' the prioress went on, 'and it seems clear that you should go. Just for a short time, a week or so.'

Anna was bewildered. 'But I hardly know my sister-in-law. I can't think why she wants me.'

'Apparently she is in a terrible state. It is an act of charity to help her.'

Schooled to taking orders without argument, Anna forced herself to ask, 'Surely I can't go out just like that.'

'This is a special case. We must not turn our faces away.' The prioress sighed. 'You are needed at home.'

She forced back the questions. She would be told what she had to know.

'Your sister-in-law has no one else, the doctor tells me. Her own mother's in a nursing home somewhere, no question of any help from that quarter.'

'What will the Bishop say?'

'In this case, a permission from him will not be necessary.' Mother Emmanuel's voice dripped acid at the implication that her authority was not absolute. 'Ten years ago, yes. But we are all trying to move with the times. It is in keeping with the spirit of renewal that you answer you family's needs. I shall send Sister Rosalie with you. She's a sensible girl.' She consulted a piece of paper. 'Your train leaves Welshpool at eight forty in the morning. You change at Shrewsbury and again at Manchester. That's more complicated, I'm afraid, you have to go to a different station, Victoria, for your connection to Bradford.' She handed over the paper with a frown. 'It's an awful journey but there seems to be no alternative. And you'll arrive just after one o'clock.' She paused. 'I should prefer if you didn't eat on the train.' Anna nodded. 'Well. You may pack tonight, keep your light on to do so. I will see you in the morning before you go. Good-night, Sister.'

Anna made her way to her own cell past the neat pairs of handmade sandals each nun left outside her door. It was unbelievable. After thirteen years, she'd see again the world beyond the enclosure walls that she thought she had left for ever. The prospect of coping with trains and stations was terrifying. She even doubted she could find her way to Simon's home – which of course she'd never visited – after so long.

A black plastic suitcase had been placed in her cell. Small as it was, she still had difficulty filling it. A fresh bodice, stockings, three clean linen bands. Four pairs of knickers. She would wrap her toothbrush in her flannel and put them in a plastic bag from the kitchen. The infirmarian had left on her bed a silver foil card of aspirin – items for which they normally had to ask a permission – and a pack of sanitary towels. She'd never have thought of that. And there was no way she could go into a chemist for such a purchase.

It was extraordinary to be packing a case again. Anna enjoyed it for the first minutes – until she remembered why she was doing it. Despite her sorrow, she couldn't entirely stifle anticipation at seeing the little boys again. She'd only ever talked to them from the other side of the grille with its formidable double grating. She envisaged herself reading bed-time stories.

These thoughts got her through the early part of the night, until exhaustion sent her to sleep despite her grief. And when she awoke at two o'clock, she was reassured by the fact that Sister Rosalie would be with her. As Mother Emmanuel said, she was a sensible girl. In the elaborate, dated hierarchy of monastic life Sister Rosalie was one of the order's two extern sisters. Until the sixties, they had lived outside the convent and never entered, taking care of 'their' nuns, shopping and acting as their hands and feet to the outside world. They would put provisions and letters inside a large wooden revolving cupboard and a nun inside the enclosure would swing it round: it was so designed that neither ever saw the other's face.

In the years since Vatican II – the great meeting of bishops to revitalise religious life – the differences between choir and lay nuns had blurred. The other extern sister was a sour woman who had resisted all attempts to integrate with the community. But Sister Rosalie – twenty-three, plump and practical with a happy smile – had welcomed the chance. She'll take care of me, Anna thought. It was a measure of the way she had been indoctrinated that she perceived only a small irony in the prospect of placing herself in the care of the younger woman.

She forced herself to concentrate in chapel that morning, to search for the still centre nothing could touch. Guide me and keep me, Lord. After breakfast she presented herself at the prioress's room.

'We have a problem, I'm afraid. Sister Rosalie isn't at all

well this morning.' Mother Emmanuel frowned at her thoughts. 'In fact, both extern sisters seem to have eaten something that disagreed quite violently with them. And Sister Thomas à Becket is sick, too.' She clicked her tongue. 'I thought the stew last night tasted odd. Did yours? Well, anyway, there it is. Sister Rosalie clearly can't go with you and there's no one else I can spare. You'll just have to travel alone, Sister. I'm sure you'll be all right. The taxi'll be here for you at eight o'clock.'

She held out her hands and the great carved amethyst of her office gleamed. Anna knelt and put hers, palms together, between them in the age-old gesture of fealty and homage. 'Come back to us safely, my daughter,' said Mother Emmanuel.

Anna was at the enclosure door fifteen minutes before the taxi was due, but the Turn sister was there already. Sister David directed a noncommital nod towards her as she struggled with the cumbersome iron key and pulled back the four massive bolts. She didn't approve of any nun going out, no matter what the reason. If she could have physically prevented Sister Gabriel from leaving, her actions said, she would have done so.

In the bare, wood-panelled outer hallway, Anna felt as if she'd been served with an eviction order. She balanced her bag on one of two upright chairs beside the carved dresser. On it were some hand-painted Christmas cards, hopefully for sale to visitors, and a pottery plate containing three stamped letters and another hand-printed card: PLEASE WOULD ANY KIND CALLER POST THESE LETTERS. THANK YOU! Anna slipped them into her sleeve to post at the station. Precisely on time a car with *Robert's Taxis* printed on the side came down the drive. She expected the middle-aged man who'd brought her here thirteen years ago but the girl who got out and stood regarding both Anna and the building with avid interest was no more than nineteen. She wore a miniscule denim skirt over long black-covered legs ending in what appeared to be very large workmen's boots. These items notwithstanding, the most riveting thing about her was a bright pink wig.

"Morning,' she said, and Anna was relieved that her voice at least was normal. 'Station, innit?' When she moved forward to pick up the case Anna noticed vivid blue stuff painted round her eyes.

'Hallo. I can manage, thanks.' She carried it herself. As she climbed into the back seat, she glanced up and gave a little wave towards the windows. She couldn't see anyone, but she knew Sister Dominic would be watching.

The girl chattered on, asking where she was going and would she be long, undeterred by monosyllabic replies. Anna alternately worried about the journey and the hair in front of her. It wasn't a wig, she concluded, though it was the colour and texture of candyfloss and stood up in spikes. Did many people have hair like this? And why?

She'd forgotten Welshpool was such a nice little town. It was evidently market day: plenty of horseboxes, cattle-trucks and Range Rovers crammed with muddy retrievers. Even at this hour, people were carrying bunches of Michaelmas daisies and vegetables in carrier bags. Woolworth's hadn't changed a bit though Boots had a new front. She caught sight of a charming shop, its latticed window packed with bright fabrics, a sign in curlicue script proclaiming Clover Connection with appropriate flowers. The car speeded up just then and she couldn't make out whether her wool was in the window. Almost single-handed, she thought with pride (though she shouldn't, pride was a sin), she contributed at least a thousand pounds a year to the convent's income through that shop.

At the railway station she didn't pay the pink-haired girl – they had a contract with the convent – but suddenly realised she had no change for a tip since Mother Emmanuel had given her a purse containing only notes. She'd counted them in the car, a hundred pounds. She couldn't imagine what Mother had been thinking of, and planned to take most of it back with her.

In the ticket queue a young man, little more than a boy himself, wore a baby strapped to his chest in a canvas sling.

When she looked at it in amazement the father beamed proudly back. The only other person there, a woman in her fifties in a maroon coat, stared with stony eyes. Anna remembered how many Welsh people disliked the nuns. Sister Rosalie had heard from a shopkeeper whose mother had watched the order arriving in Welshpool for the first time fifty years before. The child, glimpsing dark-clad figures in the gloom of curtained motorcars, had raced home terrified: *Mamgu, the nuns are coming!*

Anna asked for her return ticket and the man behind the glass tapped at a machine. 'That'll be twenty-one pounds fifty to you. Change at Shrewsbury, nine thirty-nine to Manchester Piccadilly . . .' She didn't hear the rest.

She said nervously. 'Sorry, but I only wanted third-class, please.'

'Third-class?' He peered out at her suspiciously, as if she were trying to make a fool of him. Then his face cleared as he worked it out.'From up the road, aren't you? Must be a long time since you went anywhere.' He leaned forward confidentially. 'They keep puttin' up the fares, see. Fuel costs more, servicin', rollin' stock. It don't go in wage packets though, an' that's a fact.'

Anna counted out ten-pound notes hurriedly: he could obviously continue for a very long time. The ticket she received was thin piece of card, nothing like the nice thick oblong she was expecting. On the platform a wrinkled man sweeping with a very long broom tipped his hat to her – how long since she'd seen anyone do that – and observed, apparently oblivious to the fine rain which had just started, 'Nice now, innit?'

The train in Shrewsbury might have been the one she'd arrived in all those years ago, with netting racks above the seats and leather straps to open the windows. It did not prepare her for Manchester's Piccadilly, for the bewilderment of platform signs, the hoardings advertising mysterious products: Novo, Metrocard, Betacom. She negotiated the bus journey to Victoria for her connection, trying not to look too hard at the parades of modern shops, hotel blocks, offices. How loud it was here, how brightly lit. The traffic moved too fast for her to do more than grasp the impression of slick, sharply-cut clothes in the windows, strained tight-faced people hurrying by. No one seemed to notice her, she was mercifully inconspicuous among the hodge-podge of humanity. Even on the platform at Victoria only a few people glanced at her, though she made a striking figure among the suits and denims.

Accustomed to waiting, she stood straight and absolutely still, enveloped in the heavy mantle of slate-grey wool. It gave her pleasure to know that their order's foundress would have worn the same garment in her day, in medieval France. Even the design of the metal clasp, with its curious pronged catch, was laid down in the Rule. It was one of the anomalies of religious life – and a source of both annoyance and pride – that the original, like the mother-of-pearl buttons on their nightdresses, had been the cheapest available, used by the common people. But now the order had to have them imported from France at considerable cost: scarcely, as the mother prioress tartly observed, in accordance with monastic simplicity. Still, they were beautiful and wore well, so they didn't need too many. Anna had inherited hers, and it had already lasted the religious lifetimes of two nuns before her.

And now she was glad of the mantle's warmth, the weight of rough wool intended as protection against unheated stone buildings. The soft Welsh morning had given way to driving rain and the quality of the light had changed, bringing the grey-mauve shadows of her Bradford childhood. It evoked windy streets and towering chimneys and Lowrie's matchstick people. It added to her unhappiness.

She didn't want to go back, and certainly not on her present tragic errand. During the last few months – no, be honest, it had been going on for three years at least – when she had allowed herself to think about other places, other lives, reality had played no part. She'd seen herself poised and aware in some unspecified but interesting role. Until now, standing amongst these preoccupied people, she hadn't considered what she had to offer the outside world.

It had never occurred to her that the world would have altered in her absence. She thought of the boy with his baby, the advertisements for goods she didn't recognise. People had changed, the world had changed. It had gone on without her, while she was stuck in her medieval time-warp in the Welsh hills.

She had no qualifications, no training. Nothing to offer that anyone outside would want: she could bake altar breads and drive a small tractor. There'd be no glossy office, no high-powered meetings for her. More likely one room with a gas-ring and washbasin in Leeds or Halifax, working in a canteen perhaps or sorting mail in some neon-lit nightmare.

A small child broke from a nearby group, tripped and fell wailing at Anna's feet. She bent to help her up, conscious of sticky clothes and runny nose. Twins squirmed and squabbled in a pushchair as the mother, an exhausted lank-haired woman, snatched the straggler with a muttered word of thanks to Anna, who watched sympathetically and wondered what state Lynn must be in. Poor Lynn.

When their train arrived Anna folded the pushchair for the mother and handed up bags. For a moment it looked as though she'd be asked to hold a child on her lap, till she handed it hastily back and found a seat in another compartment.

This train had tinted windows, fierce air-conditioning, bright striped velour seats that could be tilted back. Music oozed from hidden microphones, interrupted by an occasional voice announcing meals and arrival times. Stewardesses patrolled with trolleys of coffee and wrapped pastries: no wonder tickets were so expensive. Anna was beginning to feel as if she'd been gone a hundred years instead of just thirteen.

It was an hour to Bradford. She fumbled in her case for the book she'd slipped in at the last minute. The convent library was well-stocked – Classics, Language, Poetry, Popes, Lives of Saints, Memoirs of Lay Women, of Religious. There was a notable lack of what Mother Emmanuel scornfully described as 'religious literary trash' but plenty of fiction: well-read copies of *The Borrowers* and the Narnia series as well as Agatha

Christie and Rumer Godden. She couldn't really read those in public so picked Thomas Aquinas. She didn't feel like him at the moment but opened the book anyway, to avoid the possibility of anyone speaking to her, and gave herself up to thinking about Simon.

4

Kingswalk, Heaton, turned out to be a private, treelined road. The Pakistani taxi-driver who brought her from Bradford Interchange station shot her quick, curious glances in his driving mirror, as if he found it difficult to fit her into this setting.

Substantial Edwardian houses lay in groomed gardens with large cars parked in their driveways. As they stopped at number 52 she noticed a child's tricycle lying on its side in front of the garage. A small boy sat on the grass verge, spinning the front wheel disconsolately, his chin cupped in one hand.

He watched her approach. 'I can't mend it,' he said, as if justifying himself. 'I promised Jamie but I can't. Dad was going to do it. He said he'd definitely do it at the weekend.' His words, like his tone, were reasonable and matter-of-fact: he didn't sound like the eight-year-old he was. But there were smudges of dirt on his arms and his eyes were swollen from crying. Her voice cracked with emotion.

'Hello, Baxter.' She addressed him formally, though she knew no one called him that. She'd never been at ease with children, despite her best intentions, and now she struggled for something to say. She cleared her throat. 'Maybe I could help you, later on.'

He considered her with more interest until he remembered his manners and sprang up. 'Please come in.'

'Where's your mother, Baxter?'

'In bed. She's there a lot,' he added confidentially. He led the way round to a side door and started through it before standing back politely so she could go first.

The house had been gutted and redesigned. Even she recognised an immense amount of time and money had been lavished here.

The hallway was dark crimson with a floor of white marble. A shallow open-tread staircase of pale wood led to a galleried landing. A long white sofa stood against the main wall. On either side, doors of glass were ajar and spotlights in the ceiling gleamed on two trees in white tubs which flanked the sofa. The windows were covered in blinds of silvery stuff like aluminium.

She hadn't given a thought to how Simon and Lynn might live. She'd not been inside a private house for thirteen years, and had only the faintest recollection of her parents' comfortable suburban chintz and china. This carefully planned luxury was outside her experience. It was impossible to reconcile her Simon with the man who lived – the breath caught in her throat – had lived here. Simon, who only ever wanted old sports cars and pretty girls to put in them.

When she looked more closely, she saw flaws in the presentation. The sofa had grubby marks, the glass doors bore many handprints. The marble floor was littered with story books, it badly needed washing and a garageful of toy cars was strewn everywhere.

In the middle of the floor a small boy in dungarees with a yellow and red striped jumper was laboriously covering a large sheet of paper with scrawls of bright colour. He looked round at her over his shoulder and she found the cliché was true: her heart actually missed a beat as she saw her brother's face. His expression was Simon's, and even his movements as he scrambled to his feet reminded her of that lost boy. She wanted to put her arms round him and hold him safe, but of course she didn't. The habit of self-restraint was too strong in her now.

'Hallo, Jamie. Remember me?' It was a silly question, of course he didn't.

He shook his head.

'You came to see me in my convent in Wales . . .' She'd almost said: With your father.

He sucked his chalky thumb. 'Why are you wearing those funny clothes?'

'They're the same clothes I had on when you saw me.'

He squinted up at her. 'Does you head come off?'

'My head . . . Oh, you mean this.' Anna touched the folds of her veil. 'When I go to bed.'

'What about when you have a bath?' Bax put in. Then he glanced upwards. 'Hi, Mum. Look who's here.'

Lynn came slowly down the stairs, holding onto the rail as if for support. She wore crumpled cords and a man's shirt. That was all Anna noticed: the dark tartan stretched over the heavily-rounded stomach.

'Anna. Hallo.' The voice was colourless.

Anna couldn't take her eyes off the pregnancy. 'Lynn. I came as soon as I could. How are you?' She stared up at her sister-in-law. It was impossible even to glimpse the elegant, aloof woman she had known only through the convent grille. Lynn's feet were bare, the scarlet varnish peeling from her toenails. Her hair hung unbrushed round her face, her shoulders slumped in dejection, her hands hung loose, fingers open and hopeless.

Anna moved to the bottom of the stairs. The two women looked at each other. Close to, Lynn's face was unnaturally thin and the skin round her eyes was bruised and puffy.

'I'm so sorry. Lynn, I'm so very sorry about Simon.' She tried to communicate her intense sympathy. 'I can't believe it.' She wanted to say more, but the two little boys solemnly listening made it difficult. 'What a shock for you.' She searched for what comfort she could offer. 'But at least his suffering is over now. We must pray that he's at peace.'

'Yes. We must.' A flat, final note in her voice warned Anna off. The enmity she read in the other woman's eyes was puzzling.

'I'm so glad you asked for me. I'll do everything I can to help you. And the children.'

'Thank you.' Lynn added, making an evident effort, 'It's good to see you. Thanks for coming, I realise it was a lot to ask, but I do need help. You can see why.' She moved past Anna, pushed one of the glass doors and led the way into a room more sumptuous than Anna had ever expected. Her sandalled feet sank into creamy carpet. Wood and leather reflected light from tall lamps, thin black tubes with bowls like upturned glass flowers. At the windows, silver threads gleamed in the heavy curtains. Lynn let herself collapse into a leather chair, frail in its bulk.

Anna could see that the Lynn she remembered from visiting days – the cool, lacquered girl who smiled so rarely – would have walked out of such a house. It was harder to relate the scruffy figure before her with this carefully contrived luxury. Anna turned, trying to avoid her own image in the many mirrors. She must cut a strange figure: standing in this ultra-modern room, dressed for the Middle Ages.

Lynn pulled a packet of Silk Cut from her pocket. 'I know, I know,' she said, though Anna had not uttered a word. 'I'll stop next week. Maybe. Dr Barnes has been nice – he rang you for me – but he can't give me anything because of the baby.' She used a slim silver lighter. 'I wish this'd knock me out for a month. That's what I need.'

Anna saw with compassion the pallor of her skin, the way grief had hollowed her eyes. 'Have you slept?'

Lynn shrugged. 'If I fall asleep, I dream. I'd rather be awake, thanks.' She drew on the cigarette. She spoke without emphasis and this somehow made her words doubly affecting. 'We didn't go to bed at all, the first night. Well, you can imagine. I'm terrified of the nights, now. Everything seems so awful, I don't know how we'll get through this.' She sat hunched, her fingers trembling. She was in a far worse state than Anna had anticipated. A small figure rushed into the room to Lynn's side and pressed himself against her, whispering urgently. Lynn's free arm went round Jamie's waist and the two heads of streaky blond hair were close together. After a moment she hugged and released him with a kiss on the nose.

'Go on, then, Tum. I won't forget.' The child darted off and Lynn gave Anna a rueful look. 'Wish my frights would go away so easily.'

Anna nodded. She could see her sister-in-law had drawn strength from the incident. The brief physical episode with the child had reached through her misery. She thought how, during her own recent bouts of dark uncertainty in the convent, that had been what she missed more than anything – the simple human contact most people took for granted and which, it seemed at such times, she alone was denied. To touch a hand with warmth, to kiss a cheek in affection – these things, so small and unconsidered in the outside world, were forbidden to her now and always. Even in their brief times of relaxation, no nun must touch another, however casually. If ever she were alone in a room with only one other woman, the door must not be closed. And the rule that two people could not sit beside each other at recreation more than once discouraged intimacy.

As a family, Anna reflected, hers had not been demonstrative. Her parents never even walked arm in arm and the smallest public display of affection was discouraged once she left childhood behind. She could still recall her hurt when her mother flinched away from her attempted embrace on Bradford station before a camp holiday with the Brownies.

Only Granny had been different. Anna had always supposed it was because her sight was so poor that the old lady constantly sought to catch hold of a sleeve, to stroke hair or pat a knee.

She knew better now. Such small gestures were born of loneliness. They were an attempt to hold isolation at bay. Years of enclosure had taught her that. As they had taught her to school herself so rigorously that even now, when it would really have helped both Lynn and herself, she could not reach out. She had not given Lynn or the boys even a brief kiss of greeting. Not a touch to express her sympathy. It was, she thought bitterly, as if physical contact was a language she had forgotten how to speak.

Anna sat down opposite her sister-in-law. You were supposed to congratulate women who were having babies, to say how lovely. She considered phrases she might offer Lynn and decided against them. 'When is the baby due?'

'Eleven weeks.'

After a long silence Anna spoke again. 'Do you want a boy or a girl?'

Lynn stared at her, hostile through cigarette smoke. 'For God's *sake*.' She saw Anna wince. 'I just want a healthy baby. Ten fingers, ten toes. Not too much to ask, is it? I can't give the poor little sod a father, so I'd like to make sure it has everything else.'

Anna found herself saying, 'The Lord giveth and the Lord taketh away.' She almost cringed at the glib ease of the sentiment.

'Well, maybe the Lord giveth. I wouldn't know. But in this case, the taking away was not a divine decision.' Lynn's voice was dry and quiet.

Anna frowned. 'What d'you mean?'

'There's something I'd better tell you. Before someone else does.' Lynn drew so hard on her cigarette the end glowed red. 'It's about Simon. When Dr Barnes telephoned your superior he didn't quite tell her the truth: it wasn't his heart. He wasn't ill. It was deliberate.'

Anna had accepted the image she had been given, of Simon dying suddenly, taken unaware. She was thrown by this information. 'Deliberate? So there wasn't an accident?' It made no sense. 'I don't understand.'

Lynn watched her own fingers. 'He'd been . . . everything was going wrong at the mill, he was very worried.' Anna listened. She was remembering the last time Simon had visited her at the convent, seeing again the drawn face, the nervous movements of his thumbs, his unaccustomed silences. And she had said nothing.

Lynn looked up, her face stiff with the effort of telling it. 'I knew we had money troubles, of course I did, but he didn't tell me how bad it was. I don't think it *was* that bad, really.

But perhaps if he'd told me, if we'd shared it . . . Anyway, it's too late now.' She was quiet for a while, staring at her trembling hands, reliving it yet again. When she did speak it was disjointed, full of sentences that dropped unfinished as if she was too worn to tidy them up.

'We didn't mean to have another baby, it was too . . . sorry.' She wiped her eyes with her fingers and glanced apologetically at Anna. 'We hadn't planned it, but when it happened of course we – I – was pleased. But I think perhaps Simon . . . It was another responsibility for him. Simon didn't like responsibility much, you know.' She looked up in appeal. And Anna nodded, remembering her brother in his early twenties, sliding gracefully out of commitments, getting her to answer the phone or the door to girlfriends he considered had grown too possessive. She could see him now, hiding out of sight of the anxious caller, convulsed with laughter while she dutifully stammered out some excuse. She – at fourteen, fifteen – would chide him for his adolescent behaviour but he shrugged it off, waited ten minutes, then drove to some out-of-the-way pub with a couple of mates. It had been a relief to Anna as well as her parents when he had finally announced his intention to marry. Anna, in the convent by then, assumed he had changed, would shoulder his responsibilities. Listening to Lynn, she realised how wrong she'd been.

'I worked until two months ago,' Lynn was saying. 'Only with these two, it was part time. Everything began to get on top of me, I couldn't keep the house straight . . . Well, you'll see . . . the worry made me ill. For a day or two it looked as if I was going to lose the baby . . . Simon insisted I stopped working, he said we owed so much, the bit I earned wouldn't make any difference.' She sniffed. 'He said he'd work twice as . . . and then he started getting so depressed. I couldn't cheer him up. We didn't even . . .' her eyes flickered at Anna. 'Well, anyway. I felt so useless. I knew he'd always hated the mill.' She was suddenly accusing. 'He never wanted to go into the business, you must have known that.'

'I knew.' Anna spoke very softly.

As if she couldn't hold it in any longer, words burst from Lynn. 'You got away from it all right, didn't you? Perhaps if you'd been here it wouldn't have happened, I'd not be sitting alone like this with . . .'

'Don't, please. I'm sorry, I'm so sorry, but I never dreamt . . .'

Drawn by raised voices, Jamie appeared in the doorway. 'When'll Dad be home, Mummy? I can't work my forklift.' Lynn flinched as if she'd been struck and Jamie immediately reacted with another wailed demand. 'Can I have a fairy cake Muuuuummy?'

Lynn stubbed out her cigarette and levered herself to the edge of the seat. 'You must be starving, I never thought. I'll get something to eat.'

'No you won't, Mum.' Bax was behind Jamie. 'I'll do it.' Lynn gave him a grateful smile and leant back in her chair.

'Thanks, darling. I'll be there in a minute.'

Anna helped Jamie with his garage, and then followed Bax to the kitchen. The floor was tiled in grey and the walls – what she could see of them – were silver. Against them were banks of cupboards, rows of shelves, all in what seemed to be dark perspex. All the worksurfaces were grey-veined marble and on them stood white machines she didn't recognise. Beneath them were more machines, much larger, with knobs and dials and timers.

For a second, she thought of the convent kitchen with the ancient coal-fired Aga which heated water, warmed the vast room in winter and cooked slowly in two great ovens. On one of the iron hobs they kept a huge kettle, on the other a permanent stockpot into which they popped any suitable leftovers. On many days, the thick nutritious soup was their main meal.

If Lynn's kitchen was better-equipped than any she could have imagined, it was also appallingly dirty. Used plates and cups stood on the window ledges, on the black ash table. Many held uneaten food: baked beans, tinned spaghetti, half-consumed cereal. There were chips lying on a spread newspaper and half-full mugs of dark liquid, a thin scum of milk coating the surface. A tin-opener stuck out of a can of evaporated milk, the lid still caught in the wheels. A grill-pan coated with congealed fat was upended in one of the two sinks and it looked as if someone had tried unsuccessfully to make porridge: a glass saucepan contained a wooden spoon standing upright in blackened mush.

Anna took it all in with increasing dismay. She looked for a tea-towel, but the only one, with several holes burned it it, lay under a casserole dish on the floor containing a chicken carcass which a half-grown grey cat was eating. A bag of flour lay on its side, contents spilled on the floor-tiles, and as Anna moved to pick it up sugar scrunched beneath her sandals. It would take her half a day to tidy up.

'I've been doing a lot of cooking lately.' Bax had one of the perspex cupboards open, which turned out to be a refrigerator. He and Anna gazed into it. It was full, but closer inspection revealed that the packs of yoghurts were long over date. She'd throw them away tomorrow. The cheese looked all right, Cheddar and Edam in sealed packs, plastic and unappetising compared to the rich cheese they made themselves in Wales. The old utensils in the cool stone-floored dairy, sieves and paddles, stone moulds and skimmers. It was a slow, peaceful process in which she took much pleasure. They sold quite a lot to the organic foodshop in Welshpool along with their surplus eggs. For it was laid down in their ancient constitutions that they must not eat of the bread of the poor unearned.

'Cheese on toast?' She consulted Bax seriously. His eager expression faded.

'Oh, crumbs. Real crumbs – I used up all the bread. I burned a lot of it making toast.' He gestured towards a heap of his failed attempts. 'Sorry.' He didn't appear to notice the rest of the mess. He looked earnestly up at her. 'I'm getting really good now.'

She could have hugged him. 'That's . . . excellent.' She stared into the fridge.

'Let's have fish-fingers an' chips an' peas. Jamie's favourite.'

He opened another cupboard which was a freezer. The one item in the place, she thought, with which she was familiar. They had recently acquired one in Wales, a huge chest they kept in an outbuilding. They would never have permitted themselves such a luxury but one of the nuns had it left to her by a relative, and the community decided they could freeze so much produce for the winter that it would be a real economy for them. It was full of fruit and vegetables, sliced and washed. Lynn's contained Sarah Lee's Blackcurrant Cheesecake and Moo Lai's Stir-Fry Dim-Sum.

'Fine.' She held the chilly boxes and looked around. 'Where's the stove?'

He stared at her with pitying disbelief at her incompetence. 'What's a stove? We've got a special thing. A catastrophic hob.'

'Very appropriate. Where is it?'

He showed her. 'Mum says it's lethal. I tried to make porridge on it an' now I mustn't.' He demonstrated the wall-mounted oven with a control panel that could have piloted a plane.

Later, when he and Jamie had gone to bed and the women were drinking coffee, Lynn explained. 'Ceramic. It's a ceramic hob. All the latest mod cons.'

Anna said carefully, 'You've got some lovely things.'

'Sure. No expense spared.' Her tone was thin and bitter. Anna, who was trying hard to like her sister-in-law, bit back the retort that presumably she had bought them. 'There's almost nothing you could think of that we haven't got,' Lynn went on. She wasn't boasting: it was more a weary recounting of mistakes. 'We must own every damn gadget known to man. Simon loved gadgets. We've got an electric trouser-press and a special iron that cost an arm and a leg and practically does your shirts for you. We've a waffle-maker and a sandwich-maker and a chip-fryer and a food processor.' Her gesture took in the machines that had defeated Anna. 'Then Simon's got a personal computer and the house is fitted with smoke-detectors and humidifiers. Outside there are tungsten halogen lamps that turn on if you cut across their beam, so the lights come on before you get in at night. There's a special timer thing to water the plants . . .' she laughed '. . . though you'd never guess it to look at some of them. We've two televisions – three if you count the portable – and a music centre. Simon got rid of all his records and replaced them with CDs.'

Anna listened in a daze: she'd no idea what half the items might be. Lynn got up and pulled down the door of yet another machine, in which she stacked the dishes and cutlery. 'I only run it at night now,' she said. 'And only every other day. There's an electricity bill I can't pay, to go with all the other bills. For weeks before Simon . . . we'd been turning hot water and heat on just for a couple of hours in the evening to put the boys to bed. Simon says . . .' she faltered. 'Simon said it didn't really save much, but at least I feel I'm trying. I go up while it's still warm.'

Still, Anna thought, a dishwasher. The nuns washed up in water heated on the stove, in an ancient teak bowl. The old sink was so high the nun who was doing it had to stand, wrapped in the oilcloth apron, on a block of wood to reach. A different world.

She glanced at the oven-timer. It read 20.19. She worked it out in disbelief: she always went to bed at nine, after Compline. The exhaustion and emotion of the day had caught up with her: even in her thick habit she was very cold. She longed to be by herself. But there was something she had to know first.

'You didn't finish telling me about Simon.'

Lynn was bending over the dishwasher. 'There's nothing more to tell.'

'You said something about deliberate.'

Lynn scraped bits of fish-finger onto a saucer. 'That'll do for the cat. Or the hamster.'

'I still don't understand what happened.'

Her sister-in-law slotted the plates into their racks with exaggerated care. '*You* don't understand,' she said, her voice muffled. 'Let me tell you, *I* don't understand.' She straightened up, one hand supporting the small of her back. 'He killed himself. The bastard.'

5

Anna knelt by the window for a long time but her prayers were jumbled and difficult. The tight white headband bit into the pain above her eyes. All she could think was that Simon had committed a mortal sin, that he would not be allowed to lie in hallowed ground.

Her head still throbbed with Lynn's whispers. 'He seemed all right when he got up. Much better. He went off about the usual time. The only strange thing, he came back straight away and took my car, the old Mini. He said the Jag had a flat. I looked at it later and it was fine. It's as if he couldn't bear to hurt that damn car.' Her hands had quivered as she lit another cigarette. Anna couldn't move, frozen by the terrible telling. 'He didn't turn up at the mill and Peggy – you remember Peggy in the office? She rang about midday to ask where he was. At tea-time we started to get really worried. Then someone . . .' her voice dropped even lower, 'someone reported a crashed Mini near Ingleton. God only knows what he was doing over there.' Lynn didn't bother to wipe her eyes.

'How did you . . .?'

'The police were very good. They got in touch with our doctor and he came round and told me.' She pressed both hands against her face as if trying to hold herself together. 'That wasn't the worst, believe it or not. The worst thing was he sent me a letter. It came the next morning. It dropped through the door with the rest of the post, with the bills. Can you imagine how it felt, seeing his handwriting? I couldn't bear to open it.'

Anna waited while her sister-in-law drew a breath rasped with tears. 'He explained why he was doing it. That he'd brought the business to bankruptcy and it was all his fault and he couldn't face the failure. That he loved us.' Lynn's harsh whisper had ceased at last.

Anna had been so shocked she knew it would take a long time to come to terms with the facts. But she'd tried, for Lynn's sake, to be positive.

'Try not to brood too much,' she'd advised. 'That's all behind you now. We've just got to get you through the next few days and you'll be all right, you'll be fine.' She'd repeated this soothingly, as if she were talking to the children. But Lynn had listened with an expression both grim and sarcastic and Anna couldn't blame her; whatever awaited this woman over the coming weeks, being fine would not be part of it. Going upstairs, she'd made one last attempt to console. 'Something will come along, you'll see.'

Lynn had paused with her hand on her bedroom door, her face turned away. 'If you believe that, Anna, you'll believe anything. Good-night.'

Anna sighed and got to her feet with an effort. She was in Jamie's room, a cheerful little space. Pale wooden furniture on a small scale – bed, wardrobe, miniature desk – set against wallpaper covered with cartoon cars in primary red, yellow and blue. The bed linen carried the same pattern and so did the curtains.

It was almost midnight. She went next door to the bathroom. It was large, apricot-tiled, with a separate shower cubicle. But it was the bath she stared at: round and sunk into the apricot-carpeted floor, enclosed by glass panels. Beside it, a curved shell designed to hold soap contained a lot of marbles, two plastic ducks and a flannel decorated with Thomas the Tank Engine.

The sight of that bath made Anna's skin itch beneath her clothes. She'd never felt so tired and grubby. She went over and leant down to turn on the tap. Hot. She thought of her strip washes on the sacking mat in her cell, of the rare occasions when it was permitted to bathe under a lid of wood with a hole cut for the head at one end. Other orders washed whilst still wearing a long black garment. To hell with it.

When she put out the light and released the long window blind it was possible to see well enough to bathe in the dark. She turned on the taps and adjusted the temperature, waiting while the hot water foamed into the tub.

She unpinned the veil and with a sigh of relief undid the serré-tête, literally the head-grip, the tight inner bonnet. She rubbed the indentation above her brows where the band pressed.

Undressed, she glanced at the glass wall behind the bath, knowing it would be too steamed up to see herself. In the darkness – tinged yellow from the streetlights – she could just make out a pale shape, blurred and indistinct, so slight it scarcely looked like a woman's body. How thin she'd become. Simple food and hard work had probably done that. She put her hands protectively over her breasts. Poor little things.

The bath was so huge she floated free. Never had she experienced anything so voluptuous; the hot water, the silence, the darkness. She was quite sure such physical indulgence was wicked and she didn't care.

A glass bottle stood on the shelf beside her, half full of crystals. Swirling them round, she released familiar heavy sweetness; gilly flowers in the enclosure garden, where they grew many old-fashioned plants. She sniffed with the intense concentration of a child.

The soap smelt the same and lathered richly. How different from the hard blocks they made themselves at the convent. She scrubbed her scalp, as if she could clear away all the misery of the last few days. Then she tipped back her head to wash it off, lying almost submerged in the perfumed water. Occasionally she lifted out one foot for the delight of putting it back into the heat. She had stopped thinking now. All her sorrow and anxiety – Simon, Lynn, the boys, her own situation – had floated away, dissolved in steam. The tension had gone from her muscles, the ache behind her eyes had disappeared: she was nearly asleep.

A car hooted somewhere in the road. She soaped her flat stomach and thought of the hard bulge of Lynn's pregnancy under the tartan shirt. Simon's child. Her hand slowed and stopped. She'd love to see the baby, but it would be weeks yet and she'd be back in Wales. She, who had no experience at all of children, had spent little time with them before she entered, had believed at seventeen that she longed for a baby. Her imagination had never gone beyond that point, had never reached as far as a growing child. It was a warmly swaddled little figure she envisaged, helpless and dependent, loving only her.

She was very still in the warm water. Exhaustion and emotion played tricks so that her mind looped memory like an old film, playing back scenes she thought she'd forgotten. For the first time in many years, she recalled her family's reaction when she'd announced she wanted to be a nun. The Summers family were Catholic in name only, so that while Anna and Simon had been baptised, none of them had set foot in a church for years.

At first, her mother had listened absently. 'Yes dear' and gone on with her ironing, taking it no more seriously than she had all those other declarations over the years that her daughter wanted to be an acrobat or a vet. With Anna's persistence came disbelief. 'Don't be silly, you don't know what you're talking about. Girls like you don't go into convents.' Her father had laughed, told her not to be a little idiot and gone off to the golf-club.

A month later she raised it again, over Sunday lunch. Her parents had glanced at each other with a unity rare between them. Her mother had said smoothly, 'You're really too young. Hardly seventeen. That isn't old enough to choose a life like that. And why, for heaven's sake? It's not as if we've ever encouraged that kind of thing.' Anna's hurt face had softened her. 'It's just an adolescent phase,' she said comfortably. 'You'll grow out of it.'

63

'Next week it'll be some fella you've set your heart on,' her father added. 'Wait and see.'

Uncertain of her ability to assert herself, accustomed to accepting their decisions, she had allowed herself to be enrolled in a secretarial course. She hadn't been interested but the head of her 'good' comprehensive had persuaded her parents it would suit her. The brisk, no-nonsense voice decisive against her doubt. 'We all realise Anna isn't an academic but she's intelligent and practical. She'll do very well.'

Anna had hated it from the first. The shorthand symbols were ridiculous and typing lessons drove her mad, thirty girls pecking out letters in unison. Only Simon had listened when she told him she was unhappy and even he had no practical advice to offer. Poor Simon. It was no better for him. He'd never wanted to go into the mill. His dream had been to part-own a garage, to work with sports cars, but he lacked funds for such an investment. Looking back, she hadn't understood. It was just a fact of life that men worked in mills. Her father had done so, her grandfather. Summers had always been yarnspinners in Bradford.

She stirred the water thoughtfully with her foot. She'd been in the grip of obsession in those days. She had not been brought up in a religious environment: the only time she attended church regularly was as part of her Brownie pack. But at just sixteen, she read a poem by Gerard Manley Hopkins:

'But you shall walk the golden street
And you unhouse and house the Lord.'

That had begun the great experience of her life. Through the poetry she had discovered a deep love of God. It had been as devastating and all-consuming as a first love affair – and equally private and self-regarding. It was almost as an after-thought that she started going to a Catholic church and that she did so at all was an accident. A schoolfriend's younger sister was to be confirmed and Anna was invited. The ceremony had been charming: White dresses, flowers, upturned faces of girls glowing, the party afterwards. A group of nuns was seated near her, severe in full-length black and white. She watched their still hands and tranquil faces, the warmth of their smiles.

So Anna found herself in a convent for the first time almost by chance. The nuns were from a nursing order in Huddersfield and she and the schoolfriend were invited over for tea. A few months later she spent a weekend with them in retreat. This time, she was taken beyond the formal sitting room of the convent. She went to chapel with them, slept in a small whitewashed room they called a cell.

The order had a house magazine to give their far-flung sisters nursing in Africa news of each other. Several issues carried articles on 'My Call'. Anna read them at first casually and then with concentration. They were personal accounts of the way each woman had discovered her vocation. The striking thing was their similarity – they all insisted it was not something they had decided for themselves.

God picked me up by the scruff of the neck,' wrote one. 'I didn't choose,' according to another. 'I was chosen.' Anna had puzzled over these remarks but when she mentioned them to one of the sisters, she had laughed. 'Well, I'd have to suggest the possibility that that explanation shifts the initiative of their choice. The religious equivalent of being swept up by a knight on a white horse.' She'd seen Anna's disbelief. 'You know you must marry a man, that it's right for you to be joined with him and bring new life into the world. It is the same for us. All of us do have a very strong conviction that this is where we're meant to be.'

'The motives for entering are as different as the entrants,' added Sister Morag. 'No two are the same. The varieties of call are like the stones of the sea.'

The stones of the sea. Anna had thought about that for a long time afterwards. Almost to her surprise, she realised how happy she felt. And then an awful thought struck her: only God could give such happiness. Perhaps she ought to give it back?

The very idea was absurd. Not her. She put it out of her head. After service one Sunday she was asked, with the rest of the congregation, to an ordination for young men entering the priesthood. The priest smiled at her as he spoke. 'You must come along.'

It hadn't crossed her mind for a fortnight. But maybe more than chance took her to that part of Bradford on the Wednesday. Walking home across a park she saw the church on the far side of the road. The ceremony had already begun when she slipped into a pew. Three figures in white had their backs to the congregation. It was only when they turned that she saw how young they were. In their very early twenties, and giving their whole lives to God.

Anna had wept. She didn't see how she could escape it now.

She told the nuns in Huddersfield how she felt, and how frightening she found it. 'I don't think I want this,' she'd said to Sister Morag. 'I'd like just ordinary things. A job and a nice flat. And I just thought sometime I'd get married.' It was difficult to find the right words 'It's not what I want, but I think about it anyway. I don't understand.'

But Sister Morag had understood. 'It was like that for everyone here. Fear and desire are the first signs of a vocation. Every woman invariably feels both, no matter who she is, how old she is. The first contact with God is disturbing, and the conflict is natural.'

Fear and desire. Now she'd heard the words, Anna experienced them with increasing intensity. She assumed she would join Sister Morag's order but something held her back. And then, one of the Sunday colour magazines ran a feature on a closed community of nuns in the hills of Wales, accompanied by photographs. There was an enduring quality about them, an atmosphere of contentment that pervaded the pages. Graceful grey-clad figures worked in calm rooms, white-coifed heads bent over the parchments they were decorating with gold-leaf. A smiling young woman on a wooden bench plucked the strings of a guitar. Two lines of nuns, habits billowing in the evening wind, made their way across a courtyard to the glowing lights of a chapel.

Anna scarcely needed to read the article to know. This was

it. This was what she wanted. Everything she learned fuelled her excitement. The simplicity, the serenity, the changeless pattern of life. Even the under-furnished, white painted rooms appealed to her, so unlike her cluttered home with its fussy wallpapers and patterned carpets. It wasn't until she was in her late twenties that she was able to perceive her motives, to admit that her decision was at least in part an utter rejection of her parents and their values. Two months later at the convent she had met a short, imperious woman who specialised in putting entrants in touch with communities that suited them. Anna told her how drawn she was to the life of the strictly enclosed contemplatives she'd been reading about. 'Do you realise how austere they are?' Mother David had asked her. 'Their Rule is that of a sixth-century saint. And their pattern of life was laid down in thirteenth-century France. They live exactly as their foundress did then. Sandals of leather and rope. Eating from pottery bowls, rising at night to pray for the world. Hermitages in the garden where they can go to contemplate God in even more peace.' She'd laughed. 'You have to be tough for that kind of simplicity.'

Mother David had told her how in American communities lengthy tests and in-depth interviews were conducted by clinical psychologists. 'The contemplatives here don't go in for that – yet. But they do need to be sure that you're not entering for negative reasons. Too great a need for emotional security, for instance. Fear of men and marriage.'

Was she afraid? Anna said candidly, 'I'm not involved with anyone. I just don't seem to be interested.' Behind the words, the picture of her parents' bitterness. Mother David had looked at her with tired eyes that had seen a great deal. 'You're very young, after all. Maybe too young – we don't now encourage girls to enter before they've seen something of life, you know.' So Anna had submitted to her parents' idea of commercial training. But seated at the ugly wooden desks and the office machinery she thought about the convent. She returned regularly to the Huddersfield convent for months of instruction and guidance, persisted through the questioning and then, finally, the written assessments.

Accepted by the order, she made all the arrangements herself and told her parents the date she was entering. Then her mother had used the last weapon she had left. Even in the warm water Anna felt cold with the memory of her contorted face and harsh words. 'Throwing yourself away, that's what you're doing. Wasting yourself. Wasting everything we've done for you. You won't have any of the things other girls have. You know that, don't you? You won't have a wedding, you won't have a baby. Anna, you won't even have children.' The pleading in her mother's voice had been harder to bear than the fury. 'You won't even have children. That's a tragedy and you can't see it.'

At barely eighteen Anna had been certain she alone was right. But she was too young, too lacking in self-knowledge, to appreciate that more than any single thing, it was a baby taking her into religious life. The rosy, smiling Infant in His mother's arms, the child who needed her love.

As He still did. Anna pulled the plug. The creamy towel she wrapped round herself was so thick she was dry almost immediately, not like the cold morning washes in her cell when her skin felt damp even after she was dressed. Still in the dark she pulled on her thick nightdress and buttoned it to the throat. She cleaned her teeth with Lynn's paste but her brush was so old and scruffy she was ashamed to leave it out and hid it in the nylon spongebag she had brought with her to the convent and which had been returned last night. And she thought about the old missionary nun who in her late eighties boasted she'd had only two possessions all her life – her umbrella and her toothbrush.

Fear and desire. Anna felt them still, after thirteen years. Only the source was different. Then, anticipation of religious life had induced them. Now it was the prospect of the world.

Anna must have slept – though she had not expected to – because a sound woke her with a start. For a moment she lay, not knowing what she had heard. The image of Simon was as clear as if she'd just been talking to him: the tall, slightly ungainly body, the face as she'd seen him last, hair noticeably greying at the sides, his habitual expression of gentle amusement only visible in brief flashes, the features heavier, tired.

Simon. Simon. She fumbled to switch on Jamie's lamp. It was an enchanted castle fashioned in painted pottery. Turrets and towers and tall pointed windows glowed from within and as she lay and looked at it, she noticed tiny animals inside – a dormouse in a red dress, a hedgehog in dungarees. She pressed her head into the pillow again, sniffing the sweet animal smell of a small boy.

When the sound came again she recognised Lynn's voice. She was up in an instant and on the landing. Lynn's door was ajar and she went in without knocking in case Jamie was asleep. He was, a round bundle under the covers. And so was Lynn, though Anna could see from her restless movements that she was dreaming and the dreams were bad. She stood undecided, watching in the faint light from the hallway while the woman in the bed tossed and whimpered. Was it better that she slept, however fearful the dreams, or woke to reality? Then she saw that even in sleep Lynn was crying.

'Wake up, Lynn. Come on, wake up!' She spoke louder, but her voice could not cut through confused sleep. She put out a tentative hand to Lynn's shoulder, drew it back. She could not bring herself to touch the smooth bare flesh: years of training rendered her incapable of the casual familiarity of such a gesture. She turned on the bedside light and spoke Lynn's name again.

Lynn sobbed 'Simon! Simon!' and when she opened her eyes they were wild with pain. She stared up at Anna as if she didn't recognise her.

'You were crying in your sleep,' Anna whispered. 'I was afraid you'd wake Jamie. Can I get you anything? A glass of milk?'

Lynn swallowed. 'No. Nothing. I didn't mean to wake you.'

'I'm used to it. We get up in the middle of the night always, to pray.'

'Just stay with me for a minute.'

The only place to sit was the edge of the bed. Anna hesitated, then chose the floor beside her sister-in-law. Everything in here was soft blue. The bedhead and the wall of fitted cupboards had a stippled finish like rough velvet. The curtains matched exactly and so did the carpet. The subdued luxury of the room intensified Lynn's dishevelled grief. Anna averted her eyes, embarrassed by the full breasts caught in lace, the satin stretched tight over the mound of the coming child, tendrils of blonde hair plastered to tear-streaked cheeks. Despite her weeping, Lynn looked the very essence of femininity. From her nightdress, from her skin, came a faint, evocative perfume.

Anna was acutely conscious of the contrast she presented in her garment of thick cream cotton, high collar and plain sleeves. With her flat chest and the ridiculous bonnet tied under her chin, she must look a figure of fun. A pantomime dame, sexless and comical. Scarcely a woman at all. Less than a woman. A line by Philip Larkin she'd read at school dropped into her mind: *unchilded and unwed*.

Lynn gasped, 'I can't see how I'm to manage it all by myself. It's just too much to face. How could he do it. How could he leave me alone with everything.' They weren't questions, but bleak little statements. 'He couldn't cope when there were two of us. But I'm going to have to survive alone. The children are so little. And the baby. Oh God, the baby too.' She pressed her hands flat against her belly in a protective gesture that made Anna's eyes blur.

'You cry.' She wanted to touch Lynn, but could not. 'You need to cry.' She was crying herself. 'When the baby's born, when you've got a new little one, you'll feel better.'

Lynn's head rolled on the pillow. 'I won't. With a tiny baby, you want to be protected. It's very primitive. If you haven't . . . I can't explain to you,' she finished helplessly.

'It's not something I understand,' Anna admitted. 'I can

only try to imagine. But God won't give you anything you cannot bear.'

'He gave Simon something he couldn't bear.' Lynn's flat statement was beyond argument. There was silence.

'Poor Simon,' said Anna at last, out of her thoughts. 'If only he'd asked for help.'

'He went to the bank, the day before he . . . He did ask for help, but he didn't get it.'

Anna digested this. 'You said there were money troubles. But if he had a bad patch, surely his bank wouldn't let him go under. Not a mill like Summers, after all those years.'

'It wasn't just a bad patch. We've already borrowed up to the hilt. Simon couldn't admit how badly the mill was doing. I guessed there were problems – he slept so badly, he was so tense and worried. But whenever I tried to talk about them, he put me down, told me I wouldn't understand, that everything was under control.' Her voice shook. 'He hid all the bills the way Jamie hides toys he's broken. I found them after . . . They're all over the house, I don't know how I'll ever . . .' She stopped speaking, eyes fixed on nothing. 'I was no help,' she went on finally. 'I just tried not to show how concerned I was, and hoped for the best. I thought: He'll be all right, he knows what he's doing. And I'm pregnant. I've enough to cope with.' She made a tight little sound in her throat. 'I didn't know what I had coming to me.'

Anna made soothing noises. 'We'll think of something, we'll get advice. Maybe you'll have to sell this house but at least that'd mean you had plenty of – '

'There's a second mortgage on it already.' Lynn's voice was weary. 'We talked endlessly about selling. But even if we had, the money would only have gone back to the building society and we'd have had nowhere to live.' She was crying again. 'He just wasn't any good at that damn mill. He hated it, his heart wasn't in it. He used to say it depressed him just going there. But what could I do? We've a family, he couldn't just walk away from a business. We had to live. We had to live,' she repeated tonelessly.

Anna started to speak softly so as not to wake Jamie. Out of her real belief in the love of God, she told Lynn that nothing, *nothing* happened which was not His will. 'Everything has a purpose and so does this, even if we can't see it now. His love encloses us all. He holds us in the palm of His hand.' She held out her own hand, palm curved upward. 'You will be safe. You will come through this. It will take time, but everything will come right. You'll see.'

After a while, her sister-in-law's breathing became calmer and her hands stopped their nervous movements.

'Will you sleep now?'

Lynn gave a tired sigh. 'Thanks. Thanks for coming out for me. And for listening.'

'It's what I'm here for.' At the door she turned. 'I'll leave it open in case you need me again.'

Back in Jamie's room she sat on the edge of the bed. She'd never sleep now. It occurred to her that if she wanted, she could make a cup of tea even at this hour.

Her bare feet – she owned no slippers – were cold on the tiles as she picked her way through the debris and it took her a few minutes to work out how to use the jug-kettle. There were only three tea-bags left. Unfamiliar with their use, she left it in the hot water too long. She'd telephone Reverend Mother, but it would probably be all right for her to go shopping in these circumstances. Taking her mug, she went to sit on the sofa by the stairs. On the opposite side of the dark red hallway a door swung and banged softly. She moved to close it, glancing in as she did so. The hall light was enough to show her a narrow room with cork-lined walls and a huge old roll-top desk in dark wood. This room, like all the others in the house, had been visited by the whirlwind. The desk was half-open and papers poured from every pigeon-hole. Drawers were pulled out, letters lay on the floor, on the old-fashioned swivel-chair with its padded leather seat.

Anna bent automatically to pick some of them up from the carpet. She gathered a sheaf in her left hand – she was still holding her mug of tea – and put them on the desk. As she did so, she saw even in the bad light the words printed in red capitals. FINAL DEMAND.

She took a deep breath. For the last thirteen years – almost all her adult life – she'd been taught that curiosity must be avoided at all costs. Years before, talking to the depositrix, the order's accountant, in her office, she had been reprimanded for allowing her glance to stray to the papers on the table. Vain, perverse and wandering thoughts must be guarded against. The accounts were none of her business.

And this was none of her business. Or wouldn't have been, before she'd listened to the desperate woman upstairs. She sipped her tea thoughtfully. Until this moment she had failed to appreciate the irony of her situation. She had taken a vow of poverty, giving up everything to identify with those who had nothing. And yet she had lived all this time free from financial worry and strain. Everything was provided for her: food and clothes, shoes and shelter. That their order must have no fixed income, no endowments or revenues of any sort was laid down in their constitutions. The mother prioress had explained it to the novices when they first came to the house.

'We can never be self-supporting,' she had told them, 'if we are to fulfil our time of prayer – what our life is primarily about. We must depend on divine providence and whatever we can earn with our hands to pay our way.'

Anna had been impressed by this. She was not a materialistic girl. When all her friends had spent Saturdays shopping in Bradford she'd gone to the museum, the art gallery, or just stayed home reading. Simplicity of life was just what she wanted.

A plump, pretty novice had asked anxiously, her fingers searching for the reassurance of the pearl necklace she had taken off for good a month before, 'What happens if there really isn't any money? Do we beg?'

'Some orders are permitted to ask for alms. But not ours.' Mother Prioress had smiled with, Anna could have sworn, a touch of the mildest malice. The novice blinked.

'But . . . what if there isn't any food?'

'Teresa of Avila, the great Teresa, once told her nuns dinner would be ready at six – if there were any by that time.' Mother Emmanuel had paused. 'She did not starve and nor do we.' She had touched the bundle of papers on her desk. 'Often, when the bills come in, I just don't know how I'm going to meet them. But the Lord has not failed me yet. He sees to it that someone sends a donation, or we get a tax rebate. Something always comes, just in time.'

Anna had been struck by the childlike confidence of this otherwise clever, managing woman. If Mother Prioress could look at bills, she could. Resolute, she switched on the antique brass lamp, cleared a space on the chair and sat down, pushing back the wooden top. She emptied each pigeon-hole methodically, scrupulously refraining from looking at any letters or personal documents. She found a couple of empty folders and put receipted bills – there were barely half-a-dozen – into one and the rest into the second, which bulged after fifteen minutes. These she sorted carefully. No sign they'd been paid: no ticks, receipts. She jotted down figures on a pad as she went and totalled the result twice, to be sure.

She was sitting back appalled at the result when she realised she had not touched those lying on the floor. When she'd added them, the list was daunting. Electricity, gas, water, rates: almost two thousand. Two dentist's bills, both over three hundred pounds, for Simon and Lynn. Thirty pounds for fluoriding the children's teeth. There were credit-card bills from American Express, Barclaycard, Access, Diners and a string of others she'd never heard of. How did Simon get hold of so many? They totalled almost four thousand. And then there were local store-cards from Debenhams and Rackhams. A bill from an off-licence for wines and spirits that couldn't be right: Simon and Lynn could not have drunk that much. Unless they'd had a party.

All these were family bills. The horrifying total – more than seven thousand pounds – didn't even include food. She put them back into the folder with a sigh. She must be behind the times – maybe everyone had debts like this now. Still, Simon must have had some sort of insurance. And the mill was still there for Lynn and the boys.

Really tired now, she started to pull down the lid of the desk, to leave it tidy, but it stuck halfway. She tugged harder to no avail. Then she noticed one of the drawers beneath the pigeon-holes was sticking out. She had tried one or two and found them locked, and not bothered with the others. She tried to shut this one but though empty it would not move. She could leave the desk open but Lynn might see the folders, and this was not the time for them. Anna fiddled with the drawer and on impulse pulled it out, to make sure nothing had dropped behind it. Her searching fingers found a knob in the narrow space. She pressed, thinking something had come loose, and one of the locked drawers slid forward.

The bills in here had obviously been kept separate. Kept secret, she found herself thinking as she examined them. Two – one dated from the summer, the other from last week and written in red – were for work on the Jaguar amounting to maybe two thousand pounds. The quality of paper on which the others were presented – the heavy linen weave, embossed lettering, in one case the amount owing handwritten in copperplate – showed these were not normal domestic items. They seemed to be from menswear shops in London with names even she recognised as exclusive. Sulka, New Bond Street, pyjamas. Turnbull & Asser, Jermyn Street, six shirts. Hermés, three silk ties. She looked for a long time at this, unable to believe that a tie – a tie! – could cost over a hundred pounds. Jogging shoes from Lillywhites, Piccadilly, for the same amount. A staggering three hundred and fifty pounds for a pair of handmade shoes from Trickers in Jermyn Street.

Well, she wore handmade shoes herself. The difference was, she made them with her own hands. With a sigh, she bundled up the bills and folded them. Altogether, Simon and Lynn appeared to owe around ten thousand pounds. She slipped the secret bundle back into its drawer and pushed it shut. This time, the desk closed smoothly and she switched off the lamp.

The pale marble was perilous under her weary feet. It was

not her place to judge Simon. She must not condemn him for the deception of those hidden drawers and secreted bills. She could not imagine the pressures he had had to bear, the worries. But she did know that a few hours ago she had felt nothing but pity for her dead brother. Now, there was only a bewildered anger.

6

'No.' Lynn pushed her cup away and folded her arms on the table, pillowing her head on them in exhaustion.

'But it has to be done.' Anna tried to sound encouraging. She succeeded only in imitating the brisk sergeant-major manner of the health visitor who had just departed after trying in vain to discuss the impending birth. 'The mill belongs to you now. It's your only source of income. Lynn, it's very important that you go in, if only for an hour.'

They had been arguing over this – or rather, Anna had been attempting to persuade, while Lynn had scarcely spoken – at intervals over the last three days. Now Anna contemplated the obdurate hunched back before her.

'It'd be easier for you to visit Nightingale Street now, while I'm here to look after the boys, than it will be in another few days. And I can't stay any longer. Reverend Mother insists I go back to the convent next Saturday.'

Simon had been dead more than a week, and Lynn ought to go in to the mill. There had been dozens of touching letters from the employees, many of whom had known him since his childhood. They had twice sent flowers to the house and there had been regular anxious telephone calls from Peggy in the office. They needed to be thanked, reassured, told that for the moment at any rate, the mill would carry on.

Anna looked at her sister-in-law's lank hair, at the crumpled clothes and bare feet. It would do Lynn all the good in the world to go, to see how much people cared, to take an interest in something beyond her own troubles. She had said as much, but Lynn merely retorted, 'All very well to say. I haven't got a single decent garment I can squeeze into, and anyway I don't feel like to talking to those people.'

Anna blurted on a burst of impatience, 'It doesn't *matter* what you wear. Put what you've got on through the washing machine and iron them. Just *do* something.'

Lynn's voice was muffled, 'Do it yourself.' After a moment she lifted her head. 'Well, I mean it. I'll go if you come with me.'

Lynn drove the Jaguar. Her competence behind the wheel, after the time Anna had spent with her, was astonishing. She handled the heavy car with a casual dexterity that made her seem a different woman from the grieving creature back at Kingswalk.

Anna commented on her skill and Lynn said, sounding genuinely pleased, 'I love driving. But I'm the world's worst parker, Simon always says.' Her voice dropped. 'Always said.'

Anna struggled to keep her away from that subject for the moment. 'I never knew what you did before you married.'

'Hertz receptionist. Delivering rented cars to hotels, airports, that sort of thing.' She glanced in the rear mirror. 'A poor man's air hostesss. We got to wear natty little black and yellow uniforms and sit in smart offices. Anna' – her tone had changed, she sounded panicky – 'what'm I going to say to them? I hardly ever went to the mill.'

'We'll take it as it comes.' Anna kept her voice calm to hide her own anxiety: the prospect of facing so many people was unnerving after her years of enclosure. She did not want to be involved: she had turned her back on worldly things, had made her decision and stuck to it. This was not of her choosing and she resented it. It had to be done, though, Lynn had to be supported.

The prosperous suburbs looked somehow darker than she remembered, diminished. As they neared the city centre these gave way to miles of terraced housing and then smooth swoops of concrete appeared where she expected red brick. Gleaming

glass instead of drab walls. And light winking welcome everywhere, on shopfronts, theatres, around a sign declaring BRAD-
FORD BOUNCES BACK.

At the outer edges of the square mile of the city centre,
dingy name-boards recalled the old trades that had been plied
there for generations: spinning and dyeing, carding and weaving, alpaca. They pointed to warehouses up cobbled alleys, to
high narrow buildings where stone steps rose steeply inside
open doorways.

Just before Nightingale Street a row of cramped Victorian
workers' houses stood unchanged. Anna dredged up recollec-
tions of front doors opening straight into crowded rooms, net
curtains looped over china Alsatians and crinolined ladies. The
corner newsagent where she and Simon used to buy jelly babies
and liquorice all-sorts from Mrs Clegg, who tipped them from
wide-necked jars into tiny triangular paper bags.

The shop was still there, but the name over the door was
Tisdall Nelson Nadi. The houses seemed smaller, more
grubby, walls sprayed with graffiti: 'Power to the Pakis' was
one, and 'WOGS OUT NF BASTARDS'. Dustbins stood on littered
pavements and a couple of Indian youths skidded past on
skateboards, bouncing on the cobbles of the wide yard in front
of Nightingale Mill.

The sign on the wall was unpainted as it had been last time
she saw it. J. E. Summers & Son Ltd Yarnspinners. Blue
letters grubby on the peeling board. The main door had always
been sealed shut to make a typists' office, and the side entrance
had served for the clerical staff. She followed Lynn through
the covered alley that ran beside the building, past packing
cases and discarded cardboard boxes. As she went through the
door, she brushed it at waist height with a searching finger.
She had scratched her initials twenty years ago and they were
still there, AS scored deep into the dull paint.

The offices she had never expected to see again were as
familiar as if she had walked out yesterday. Buff coloured
walls, dark brown lino, old-fashioned frosted glass partitions
separating the cubicles which housed the invoice clerk, the

cumbersome switchboard, the wages clerk. Across the passage was the larger office where her father had worked at his wide desk topped with faded morocco leather. In the far corner a smaller desk had belonged to the works manager. But that office was Simon's now. Only not any more. The sharp thought hurt so much she made a little sound, and her fingers went to the rosary at her waist.

Beside her, Lynn said, 'I'll see if Peggy's in,' and turned right. Before she reached the door Anna heard the warm greeting from the woman who ran the office.

'Mrs Simon, I'm right glad to see you. Come in, do, and sit yourself down. I'll get Mr Beattie.'

'Not for a minute, Peggy. Look who's with me.' Lynn stood aside so she could see Anna. The woman stood in the middle of the room, one hand out to take Lynn's, frozen in mid-gesture.

Peggy Dakins had known Anna from babyhood. She could remember her coming to the office with Mr Summers at five-years-old, at ten, her hair in braids or bunches, pieces of sticking plaster covering grazed knees, a brace on her teeth. Then the schoolgirl, awkward in adolescence. The college student, big scarf round her neck, man's sweater over short skirt. Peggy was not religious and though she had written to Anna in the convent, and had letters back, she had not tried to picture her now.

She saw a tall figure in long grey garments, wide sleeves concealing her hands. Beneath a black veil her head was wrapped in a white linen band that came down over her forhead. Her skin was not a girl's any more, but the lines were faint, drawn more by squinting against the sun than by anxiety. The blue-grey eyes were shadowed now by sadness over her brother. There was a feeling of calm about her. Peggy thought maybe it was the clothes and then changed her mind: it was the way Anna held herself, very straight and still. But when she smiled, it was the same girl she'd always known.

Peggy took two steps forward, put her arms around Anna, 'Hallo love,' she said, and kissed her.

Taken by surprise, Anna was stiff for a moment. And then Peggy's motherly bulk, her faint smell of talc and Tweed, the feel of her blue angora jumper – all apparently unchanged by the years – broke down all the inhibitions of her training: she hugged her warmly.

'Oh, Peggy, it's lovely to see you.' She stood back. The curly greying hair, the touch of lipstick – she looked smarter than Anna remembered, but no older. 'You haven't changed a bit.'

'Go on with you, love. I'd have retired years ago if they'd let me.' The smile disappeared. 'But I can't tell you how it saddens me to see you for this reason.' She turned to Lynn. 'It means a great deal to us that you've managed to come down here: the others will be so pleased.' She pulled a chair forward for her. 'Are you getting on all right now, you and the boys? You must tell me what we can do for you.'

Lynn glanced at Anna for support. 'I want to thank everyone who sent us letters and those lovely flowers. And I suppose,' her voice dropped, 'I suppose I ought to talk to Stan Beattie.'

Anna saw Peggy's eyes flicker and caught the hesitation.

'Yes. Yes, I expect you should. Why don't I get him now, and we'll maybe go round the workrooms after? You shouldn't do too much, not in your condition.' She went out, leaving the door open.

The gas fire hissed and Anna stared at the scratched metal tray with its picture of an owl on which stood an electric kettle, half a bottle of milk and five unmatched mugs. Above them, on the window-sill, a row of spider-plants in pots hung down almost to the level of the heavy old typewriter. When she was little, she used to write stories on it, during long empty Saturday afternoons when her father brought them in as a treat while he worked. It was the same in here as it had always been, even to the Dales calendar sent out by one of the big wholesalers, the glass-fronted bookcase piled with ledgers. And the smell. Wool and cardboard boxes and Peggy's scent and a thin rank whiff from the latest of the mill cats.

'D'you know, that's the first time I've seen you touch anyone. You don't even kiss the children.'

Lynn's remark was not rude, simply an observation. Anna looked away, hurt despite herself. It was true, of course but it had not occurred to her that anyone would notice. *Touch no one*, the *Manual for Novices* of her order insisted, *and do not allow yourself to be touched by anyone without necessity or evident reason, however innocent.* More than a decade of obedience to this rule had held her back when she longed to kiss the boys, to hug them. Obedience – and the fear that the children wouldn't like it, but wriggle away from her, embarrassed.

They heard a man's voice in the corridor and Peggy answering. Then Stan Beattie was in the doorway, and Anna remembered how much she had detested him.

He was older, of course, thicker. But the voice still the same, grating on her ears, and there was more grey than brown now in the hair that looked oiled smooth. He wore the khaki coloured cotton jacket he always put on to save his suit from machine-grease if he went into the workrooms, and beneath it his yellow tie was patterned with horses' heads.

'Morning, Mrs Simon. It's good of you to come down.' They shook hands and he turned to Anna to do the same. She kept hers folded and after a moment he realised his mistake, and angled his hand to his pocket.

'Hallo, Mr Beattie. How are you?' She was sorry for his discomfort.

He made some reply: she was only aware of his slow survey of her, from head-dress to bare feet in leather sandals. While he asked her how long she would be staying with Lynn, during the small talk while Peggy made coffee, she thought of what she knew about him.

He had worked first for her father as overlooker among the machines and when Simon took over the mill had become manager. There was a tired-looking wife and two small children who must be more or less grown-up by now. He used to possess the slick good looks of what her mother called a carpet Romeo: Anna somehow connected him with dance-halls and had been aware that the younger women in the factory disliked him. He would stand too close, his hands would accidentally brush a hip, a breast, he would feel their bottoms as he passed. More than once she had heard her father warn him about his behaviour, but he was too good an overlooker to lose.

Anna knew his appraisal of her was no more than the way he treated all women, but it disturbed her anyway. She had long ceased to behave like a sexual being. She had abandoned all the trappings of femininity and now her flattened breasts, her cropped head and heavy draperies all made her appear like some curious middle sex, without desires or physical needs, muted and bland. In the convent where all were alike, this presented no problem. Only now in the outside world was she conscious of being different. Odd. She didn't want anyone to look at her as Stan Beattie was doing now: it offended her. She kept her eyes fixed sternly on the coffee mug in her hand.

Peggy turned to Anna. 'You'll come round with us. The girls would love to see you.'

Anna spoke softly. 'I don't think so. Thank you.'

'Anna, you must. You said . . .' Lynn's voice dragged despairing. 'I won't go up alone. I can't talk to them by myself.'

Peggy sounded hurt. 'They're lovely girls, Mrs Simon. It's only you're not used to them all.'

Lynn shook her head and Peggy appealed to Anna. 'I think it'd be best . . . Could you, just this time?'

Anna thought; It's not much to do for her, is it? She said, as graciously as she could, 'Yes, all right, of course I will,' and stood up. Best get it over with.

The boundary between offices and mill was an old sliding door set deep in metal runners: on one side the floor was lino, on the other stone. Lynn gave a little shiver as, preceded by Peggy and followed by Stan Beattie, they crossed the covered packers' yard that divided the two halves of the building. Anna, in her woollen robes, did not even notice the difference in temperature.

The open tread stairs were bare wood, worn shiny and

bowed in the middle of each step from long use, and the handrail was splintery: when she was little, she'd refuse to hold on and someone would have to walk up behind her. Even before they reached the top they could hear the racket from the workroom: the clang and clutter of machinery, the music, the voice of Jimmy Young. And then the smell: as distinctive as that in Peggy's office, evoking her childhood more surely than photographs or songs. The mill produced almost exclusively artificial fibres now, but the scent of lanoline still hung in the air. Just inside the sliding door at the top of the stairs, a row of ancient but immaculate lavatories in narrow wooden cubicles smelt of disinfectant.

The girls, as they were always called, were not girls at all, but mostly elderly women. Many of them had spent all their working lives at the mill, and several had daughters employed there too. As a child, Anna had always been daunted by her visits upstairs, by the questions she had to answer, the jokes. They had been kind, though. There were always little garments beautifully knitted for her dolls, bonnets and legging and coats in crude pinks and yellows.

Peggy went in first and Anna, who was ahead of Lynn, saw that the vast low room looked just the same. The heavy old machines her grandfather had put in, strung with moving threads. Dark wood polished by time and long use. The air filmed with fine dust from the spinning threads.

'It's little Anna!'

At once heads turned towards her, all wound in scarves to keep their hair from the moving parts. The faces beneath the patterned squares were older but as familiar as if she had just stepped out for a moment: Betty and Leila, Marlene, Sylv – and there was Rene, hurrying forward, cheeks shiny with pleasure, metal curlers in ridges beneath her scarf.

The women beamed while Rene pumped her hand, holding her arm tight, then led her round the machines to say hallo to everyone, as tongue-tied and embarrassed as she had ever been at twelve. She glanced back at Lynn, who was going round quietly with Peggy, not saying much but clearly coping.

'It's good to see you both here,' one of the girls shouted above the din, offering her a strip of chewing gum, warm from her pocket. 'We've been right worried. How's she taking it?' She gestured with her head towards Lynn.

'She's in quite a state,' Anna admitted. Doris was one of the most intelligent of them, vociferous about everythng from women's equality to high-rise housing. No use pretending to her. 'We're hoping she'll feel better once the baby's born.'

'You're not hoping for much,' Doris modified her shout very slightly. 'On her own with three kids, she'll need more than your hopes.'

Anna nodded, started to say something but Rene hurried her on. She saw now that among the women were many she had never seen before, Indian and Pakistani women with gold studs in their ears and a diamond in one nostril, incongruously clad in smocks over their baggy trousers. She was introduced with unusual formality to the older women, Mrs Verma, Mrs Chandubhai, who made small bows, respectful of her veil. But the younger ones – Rani and Lila – smiled gaily in their bright tracksuits, slim brown hands deft among the threads.

'This is Shiraz,' Rene had reached a machine which was immobile while its operator, a dark beauty with hair in a plait down her back, read a brightly coloured magazine. The drawn comic characters were Asian, Anna noticed. 'And Hal's down there somewhere.' All she could see of Hal was a crouched figure beneath metal and wood with only blue running shoes visible. Rene shouted his name, but it was lost in the noise and she had to reach down and tap him on the shoulder.

After a moment he extricated himself and got to his feet: his movements were smooth and precise, athletic even in the confined space. In a single quick glance Anna was conscious of hazel eyes blinking gently as if the lights were too bright for him, curling gold-brown hair receding very slightly at the temples despite his evident youth. His strong eyebrows grew peaked in the middle, and Anna couldn't decide whether these or her appearance were responsible for his air of startled amusement. She smiled briefly and concentrated on Rene.

'Peter Hallam works under that Mr Beattie.' Rene's scorn for the foreman was famous. 'Nothing he don't know about machines, is there, Hal?'

Anna listened to the firm voice which was audible even through the noise of the room. He sounded north-country, but not from Bradford. Rene explained who she was, and added, 'Our Anna's Sister Gabriel now.'

'I can see that,' Peter Hallam replied. Anna flicked another glance at him, but he was staring at her bare feet. Not as Stan Beattie had done, with a kind of insolence, more as if he was too shy to look directly at her.

Lynn and Peggy had caught up with them now, and behind them Stan Beattie said with heavy jocularity, 'We'd best get these two ladies away so you can all go back to work.' He jerked his head towards the machines. 'It's too quiet back there for my liking. Where there's noise there's brass.' He deliberately broadened his accent to make a music-hall joke out of this announcement but no one laughed.

Peter Hallam said, 'Goodbye, Sister Gabriel' very quietly and the hand he lifted to her held a spanner and an oil-covered rag. He turned away and she watched him wriggle neatly back underneath the doffer-frame.

Back in the office – they used Peggy's, Lynn refused to go into Simon's big room – Stan Beattie's assumed joviality vanished. He said heavily, 'You must know the situation here. Things are going from bad to worse. There's bills we can't even try to pay. We can't afford our basic raw materials and young Hal's having to deliver as well as deal with machinery since Dawson went.'

'Old Joe Dawson retired recently,' Peggy said in explanation. 'Mr Simon decided not to replace him just yet, to save money. We don't really need a full-time driver, not with things as they are.'

Anna waited for Lynn to speak, but she said nothing, emptied by exhaustion.

'Mrs Summers will need to go to the bank. Perhaps she

should go with you, Mr Beattie. But in the meantime, just for a week or so, can you manage? Will you be able to pay wages?'

'If I don't pay anything else.' Beattie sounded grudging.

Anna went on swiftly. 'We don't know what the financial situation is yet, really. Mrs Simon' – she hesitated as she used the employees' name for Lynn, but she did not react – 'Mrs Simon and I have to talk to the bank manager. So if you could hang on for a bit?' She stopped, but Lynn turned her head away. 'Mrs Simon wants everyone to know she plans to keep the mill going. She doesn't want anyone to lose their jobs.'

'That's right.' Lynn made a visible effort. 'I need the mill to continue, and I'll sort something out. I'm selling the Jaguar for a start, and that should fetch enough to buy wool and whatever else you need. I hope that will tide us over.' She heaved herself out of her chair. 'I must go home. I'm sorry I can't stay longer.'

Stan Beattie said heavily, 'I'd best get back upstairs.' He shook hands with Lynn. 'I'll wait to hear from you, then. And Miss Anna.' He nodded at her, but did not offer his hand this time, 'I don't expect we'll see you hereabouts again. I'd just like to say I'm sorry about your brother. He's badly missed.'

'Thank you, Mr Beattie, That's kind of you.'

He went away and Lynn murmured, 'Won't be a minute,' and headed for the lavatory.

As soon as they were alone, Peggy closed the office door.

'Can I talk to you?' she asked. 'I mean, am I allowed to discuss financial matters with you now you're . . .' she gestured towards Anna's habit.

Anna made a little grimace. 'I've been worrying about Lynn's finances along with everything else. And I heard what Stan Beattie said about the situation here. It sounds pretty bad.'

'It's not as bad as he makes out.' Peggy's voice was bitter. 'He reckons if he piles it on, Mrs Simon'll sell out to him cheap.'

Anna was horrified. 'But Peggy, she can't do that. How will she live? She's no money of her own.'

'Little he cares, for her or anyone else. The way he sees it, he's been here so long, he's entitled to take it if he can get it.'

Anna sat down.

Peggy continued, speaking very softly, 'I know you never liked Stan Beattie and no more do I. Oh, he can be nice enough when he wants. We've worked together a long time and he doesn't bother me. There's been no animosity between us because there's been no cause for it, and it's best to rub along with someone you see every day. But I never trusted him.' She paused and then added, 'His eyes are too close together.'

Anna shook her head. 'I hope you've more reason than that for accusing him, Peggy. He can't help his eyes.'

'He can help where they go,' Peggy retorted, 'and he's not taken his off Master Simon's desk these days past. That's where he means to get and no mistake. And I don't intend to sit by and let it happen.'

'But has he *done* anything? Said anything, to make you believe this?'

'Hanh!' Peggy literally snorted and Anna almost laughed at the sound, as she had done years ago: she and Simon used to bet their pocket money on whether they could incite Peggy to make this dismissive exhalation. 'He's no need to, I can read him like a book.' She patted a pile of papers on her desk. 'Everything that comes into this mill, be it invoice, final demand, cheque or whatever, I open. I can read a balance sheet better than anyone and what I don't know about this business isn't worth knowing, though I says it as shouldn't. And I know that we've enough orders coming in, and enough material going *out*, to pay the workforce and leave enough over for Mrs Simon. We can't go on indefinitely like this, I'm not saying that. But it's not as desperate as he' – she jerked her head towards the door – 'makes out.'

Anna studied the intricate weave of the woollen sleeve she wore.

'Do you mean,' she asked very quietly, 'that Simon died for no reason? That things aren't as bad as he believed?'

Peggy looked stricken.

'No love, I'm not saying that. Your brother was in a terrible state, really low. I said to him over and again, why don't you go to a doctor, they can treat depression. But you know him, obstinate even as a lad, he wouldn't have any of it. No, he had reason for despair. The business is all downhill now, and when I think how it was in your father's day I could fair weep.' She sighed. 'But he wanted to live well, did Simon. He wouldn't cut back on anything. Not his car, not his expensive wines, not his clothes. He seemed to think no matter what happened, those things would be provided for him.'

Anna nodded. She knew all too well. Even before she had seen the house, even without the contents of the secret desk drawer, she was aware that Simon would not have changed since she lived at home and watched him spend money he did not have. In those days, of course, his needs had been fewer. He would borrow from friends for a night out, wheedle cash from their mother before a date, write cheques when he was overdrawn already. It hadn't seemed to matter, it had been the way he was, part of the relaxed, easy-going charm of his. She just had time to say to Peggy, 'Thanks for telling me. I'll think about it,' before Lynn appeared, white with tiredness in the doorway.

In the Jaguar, she huddled into her coat.

'Honestly, I can't face driving back. I've got such a head.' She leant back against the soft leather. 'It was awful in there, hateful. I kept thinking Simon was going to walk through the door. That it had all been a terrible mistake, and he was back.' She drew a long, shuddering breath. 'I'm never going in there again. Never, never, never.'

'Stop that,' Anna spoke sharply. 'Let's go home, please.'

'I can't drive this damned car. I'll ring the garage tomorrow and sell it. I keep thinking that he couldn't bear to drive it that day.' She stopped, eyes squeezed shut. Anna waited a moment. Lynn added, without opening her eyes, 'You can drive, can't you?'

'I . . . yes.'

'Well, you could get us home.' She spoke with weary impatience and Anna heard the words she did not say: Can't you do *anything?*

The truth was, Anna had been driving for the last ten years. She had passed her test before she entered. No one, she reflected could have failed to drive with Simon for a brother. He had taught her himself and she'd passed the test first time, just three months after her seventeenth birthday. That had been one of the things her parents had used to try and change her mind: 'We'll buy you a car. A sports car.' That had tempted her more than anything, but she'd resisted. She had never expected to sit behind a driving wheel again.

But after two years as a novice, after the initial training and the long hours spent over books, she had been given the kitchen garden to work. It had been neglected for years: until Mother Emmanuel arrived they had been an ageing community and no one had had the strength to do what was needed there. The convent employed one old man, a part-time gardener who remembered the house in the old days when it was owned by a Welshpool solicitor. Mr Dunbabbin was over seventy when Anna first met him, a stooped figure with hands knotted like weathered wood and an old hat he wore against sun and snow alike. The first time she had gone out to meet him, he had backed away nervously and held up two fingers: she had forgotten that he was only allowed to speak to the nuns when strictly necessary, and then only when two of them were present.

But he had kept his strength. Between them, they heaved rocks out of the ground to clear the land for the small tractor. This had been given to the order by the widow of a nearby farmer. They had accepted it gladly, but the older women were nervous of it. Even Anna had been wary at first. She wore thick gloves and looped her habit up with hooks and a leather strap called a lackey to keep it away from the engine. She had started off in the slowest gear, afraid she had forgotten her skill, but it had soon returned and the exhilaration of ploughing long furrows – forward and back, forward and back – in the wind became a high spot for her.

Still, she reflected, driving a tractor on a Welsh hillside wasn't quite the same as handling a Jaguar in the middle of a busy city. Beside her, Lynn slumped dejected over the wheel. On a wave of pity Anna opened her door. 'Move over then.'

She adjusted the seat to her longer legs and looked at the controls. She was used to three rudimentary gears and reverse. The endless dials, the knobs and switches, lights, arrows, wavy lines – she'd forgotten, if she'd ever known, what such sophistications were for. Well, she didn't need lights, and this must be the indicator . . . She switched on the engine, put the car gently into first gear and slid away from the kerb.

She drove with agonising care, waiting for long gaps before joining the traffic stream, allowing herself plenty of room on both sides, keeping wide spaces between herself and the vehicle in front. The car was alive under her hands, a powerful presence, purring darkly as they idled at traffic lights, responding smoothly as she accelerated away. She thought of the grinding tractor, the hard plastic seat, and a wide smile creased her face before she managed to compose herself: she was too absorbed in what she was doing to notice the startled glances of other drivers at the sight of a nun in full habit driving a signal red Jaguar XJS convertible.

Pride was a sin. But for the twenty-five minutes it took to drive back to Kingswalk, she was guilty of it.

7

The chapel was a place of velvet shadows: muted greys, deep blues, darkness embroidered by candles. A ribbon of incense unfurled from the swinging gold censer, rising with the sweet, unaccompanied voices of the nuns. Under her lashes, Anna looked at the face of the chantress beside her, absorbed in the plainsong:

Cum transieris per aquas tecum ero, et flumina non operant te.

When thou shalt pass through the waters, I will be with thee, and the rivers shall not cover thee.

Through the grille she could see the altar with its damask and candlesticks. Behind it the burdened crucifix; limbs of twisted gilt, drooping head on the slender neck, the pierced side, the pain. She bent her own head. Forgive me for leaving You. I have been away in body. But before that, I had deserted You in spirit. Her fingers were on the rosary, her mind quiet. She had been back inside the enclosure for just two hours.

Everything was as she had left it. The welcoming smiles of her sisters, the bells, the wind whipping round the courtyard as she hurried to her cell. She opened the door with trepidation, afraid two weeks in Lynn's house would make her own home appear shabby. But the little room was too austere even for comparison. It seemed larger than in her memory, more calm, a haven. On its hanger behind the door a fresh nighdress hung, and a clean headband was folded on the bed. Someone had placed a single bronze chrysanthemum in a medicine bottle on the window-sill to welcome her: that would be Sister Dominic. Lis. The thin curtains had been drawn and it felt warm. She said a brief prayer: Thank you Lord, for returning me safely.

It must be about almost six o'clock – she had five minutes before supper. Swiftly she unzipped the nylon bag and unpacked, anxious to be rid of all reminders of her journey. She put her clothes for washing beside the door, placed Thomas Aquinas on her bedside table: she had not opened him more than three times.

In the long refectory, there were quick glances and nods, though of course no one spoke. Mother Emmanuel led grace and added, 'We are happy to have Sister Gabriel back with us at last. At recreation, we will be able to speak with her.'

The meal started, as always, with soup made from anything left over from the previous day. Then an oval dish was passed along the table with baked eggs on it. She handed the dish on, accepted boiled potatoes and sprouts, drew a circle on the table with her index finger to ask Sister Aelred for the salt.

Looking with fresh eyes, convent customs she had always taken for granted seemed bizarre. The pattern of day and the pattern of their leather sandals, the design of their underwear with drawstrings and the way they polished the wooden floors to a fine finish on their knees. Even using a piece of bread as a spoon, and rarely drinking anything but hot water – all these things, like the stockpot of soup that always simmered in the cooking office, had their origin in the customs of medieval France. They had been laid down then in the Rule by their foundress, a determined woman with the heart and soul of a visionary and the practical mind of the landowner's daughter she was. Her nuns were to live as the poor lived. And they still did, Anna reflected, English women almost in the twenty-first century behaving as if they were French peasants seven hundred years before.

Sister Dominic brought round desert in earthenware bowls they made and fired themselves. Anna noticed she had an extra apricot floating in her hot milk, four where the others had three. She ate quickly, so no one would notice.

Sister Dominic was one of the youngest of the nuns. At first, the community had doubted she possessed the stamina even for the six months as postulant and two years as a novice. She looked too slight to withstand the arduous life, the long hours on her feet, the cold. Old Sister Godric was the only one who'd disagreed.

'The most successful enclosed nuns,' she had remarked, 'aren't the ones you'd think, the quiet, thoughtful types. The girls with outgoing personalities, the ones who never stop talking – they're the best material.'

She'd been watching Sister Dominic as she said this, Anna remembered. Some of the younger nuns had been decorating the community room for some saints day, and Sister Godric and Anna had come in silently to find Sister Dominic standing on a chair, drawing pin in one hand, a mass of pink and yellow paperchain in the other, laughing so hard she nearly fell off. Seeing them, she had made a tremendous effort to pull herself together, but irrepressible giggles kept bubbling up.

That was the first time Anna had really noticed her. The features emphasised by the white novice's veil were no more than conventionally pretty, the sort of face that might have advertised a chocolate bar, neat nose and nice teeth. But it was lit up by eyes that glowed with a suppressed excitement, as if she was bursting to tell some marvellous story.

The novice mistress, Sister Thomas à Becket, had at first been wary of accepting Sister Dominic – Elisabeth Down, as she was then – at all. 'Too excitable,' had been her verdict, but Mother Emmanuel had decreed otherwise, conscious that they had had only two prospective entrants in five years. The cautious Sister Thomas à Becket had fallen under Sister Dominic's spell like everyone else, charmed by her quick enthusiasm, her bright mind, her willingness to work: it was impossible not to become fond of someone who gave so much so freely.

It was typical of Lis to put a flower on her window-sill, Anna thought, walking upstairs in single file. She was behind Sister Dominic as they went into the community room.

'I found your flower. Thank you for the thought.'

'It was the last one in the garden. No more now till next year. But isn't it a wonderful colour? And don't worry, not much smell, so you can enjoy it.' Anna smiled.

Do not smell fragrant herbs, fruit or flowers, much less bring them into your cell, or keep them for the pleasant odour.

Even so, a large bowl of convent-made pot-pourri scented this room, the gathering place for the convent. Heavy shutters were fastened over the windows and the polished wood floor was bare. Round the wall hard-backed chairs were placed at regular intervals and the only colour came from a painting of Easter candles, which hung over the old-fashioned black sideboard. It was the work of one of the nuns. Anna had made a frame from the trunk of an ancient oak that had fallen in the gounds eleven years ago, learning to use a chain-saw to deal with it. The only other piece of furniture in the room was a table-tennis table. Anna had been amazed by this when she first arrived, but it had been explained that Mother Emmanuel had obtained permission to attend an auction when they needed beds, and the table had been part of a job-lot. They used it on feastdays for recreation, and kept the nets and bats in the sideboard along with a set of Monopoly.

Recreation took place for an hour and a half, three times a week. In the old days, the custom in their order was to sit in two rows with their workbaskets, always in the same place year in, year out, and speak only to their neighbour. Now they were able to choose any seat and talk freely, demonstrating that no one enjoyed a good chat more than an enclosed nun. They didn't gossip or the convent would have been a little hell, as Mother Emmanuel said, and she discouraged them from 'talking shop'.

Sometimes they brought out the old Dansette gramophone and their half-dozen records, a motley mixture of dated popular tunes from the fifties and religious music. Their elderly radio was kept under lock and key, but occasionally they used to listen to the afternoon play. They had stopped doing so some years ago when the plays had become too gritty in their language and situations for the taste of some of the nuns. The middle-aged ones, Anna had noticed. Sister Godric, for all her garrulous frailty, hadn't been bothered by the realism.

Now the mother prioress pointed to the chair beside her and Anna caught the soft indrawn sigh of annoyance as Sister Dominic moved away. She picked up her sewing but the superior put out a hand.

'Leave that, Sister, you've had a long day. But we'd like to hear about your trip – if you feel like telling us,' she added, with the scrupulous courtesy with which she always treated her 'family'.

When Anna had first entered, it had been Mother Joseph, God rest her soul, who had observed, 'If I am the superior, then you must all be inferior. I don't see it like that. Some orders did, my goodness, in the old days. Sisters had to bob a curtsey whenever the superior appeared. They were your subjects and no mistake.'

Glancing around, Anna thought again that the nuns resembled a family of Victorian daughters sitting demurely round the room. It took a closer look to dispel the impression. Several of them were very young. Sister Rosalie, the extern sister, was twenty-three and Sister Dominic twenty-four. Many were in their thirties as she was: Sister Louis, the slim Irishwoman with the exquisite unsexed voice of a choirboy, was thirty-five and the musician Sister Thomas à Kempis a year or so older. The novice mistress Sister Thomas à Becket was in her early forties like Sister Vincent, while Sister David and Sister Julian were forty-five. But in all religious orders, the majority of members were fifty or more and theirs was no exception. It was hard to believe the vigorous Sister Peter was fifty-two or Sister Matthew, with the great dark eyes of her Spanish mother, a year more. The prioress was sixty and Sister Aelred old enough to have forgotten. And Sister Godric would only admit to being somewhere in her eighties: she said she couldn't be bothered with dates any more.

But there was something about them all that Anna had not seen on any face during her weeks out of the enclosure.

In the world, she had found people looked kind or worried, cross or concerned; their expressions had matched their feelings. More and more she had found herself watching them, forgetting about custody of the eyes. Once, on the drive to the mill, she had glimpsed a youngish man, white, whippet-thin and vicious. Lynn's doctor was in his mid-forties, with a broad, jovial face Anna had only seen creased with anxiety. The policeman who had come to the house to talk to them about the procedure for releasing Simon's body after the post mortem had been too boyish for the weight of his task, chubby features stiff and solemn. And she'd seen bleak pain in the eyes of the people who had loved Simon, during the service in the crematorium chapel before the flower-laden coffin rolled behind curtains to the hidden flames.

The faces of these enclosed nuns had a strength borne of serenity. None looked harassed or worried, they were not worldly faces. The experiences that showed in the fine lines round their eyes, in the creases from nose to mouth, in the set of their lips, the expression in their eyes, were not the same as those on the faces outside. They knew, they were aware of the violence that went on beyond their walls. They prayed for the criminal as much as his victim: they were not shocked by the results of passions they had never known.

But for these women all experience was filtered through the gauze of faith. They retained even in their maturity a kind of innocence. Anna smiled at Sister Godric. Thick lenses over the near-blind eyes did not hide their blue beauty: she was wise, but she had never been hurt.

Mother Emmanuel was speaking. 'And how is your sister-in-law. And the children?'

Anna answered, sensibly and quietly, speaking practicalities, and all the time she could only think that Lynn was tethered by responsibilities, in a way those about her could not imagine. Until the visit to Lynn, she had never appreciated how free the nuns were of the shackles that bound most women. The endless repetitive small tasks of a family were not theirs. They did not have to prepare little meals, trudge to school, change nappies, wash clothes, give out sympathy and their time.

'And will Lynn be able to take care of the baby when it arrives?' Anna was taken aback. It had not occurred to her there would be problems and she said so. Mother Emmanuel tapped her teeth thoughtfully with her thimble.

'Well, you know her and I do not. But it sounds to me as though she will have quite a lot on her plate. Someone must watch for her interests at the mill, I imagine.'

Anna was filled with respect: she had done no more than mention the mill, had said something about not trusting the foreman. How little this woman missed.

'Could Sister Gabriel tell us of her journey, please?' Sister Rosalie, who had originally been going with Anna, blushed with the effort of speaking up in front of everyone. Anna willingly described everything from the taxi-driver with pink hair to the music on the Inter-City express. There were more questions: Was she scared, going around by herself? What was Bradford like?

Sister Louis asked, 'There are Muslims there now, aren't there? And Hindus?' with all the longing of someone who has only heard of fabled creatures. So Anna told them about the graceful girls at the mill with their gauzy trousers and nostrils pierced with diamonds.

Sister Thomas à Kempis inquired wistfully, 'What do they look like now, the youngsters – what do they wear?'

'Anything. Tiny little skirts and tights striped in bright colours. Or wide trousers to just above the ankle. Short leather jackets with their names on the back in studs. And their hair is amazing. I even saw a girl with the sides of her head shaved and the hair cut square' – she shaped it above her own head in illustration – 'and dyed purple. Boys with no hair except a great quiff like a crest in red or green. And they all wear enormous shoes, laced up, with heavy soles.'

'Even the *girls?*'

'Especially the girls. Some of them paint their faces white and their lips black.'

Sister Thomas à Kempis shuddered. 'They must look terrible. Like vampires.'

'I suppose they do.' Anna considered this. 'But they look beautiful, too, in an odd way.' She'd save for another occasion the fact that she had seen young men similarly decorated.

Sister David, the Turn sister who had watched Anna leave the convent, pursed her lips.

'Black,' she repeated with distaste. 'Oh no, I could never have cōped with that. In my day, girls used a touch of Coty pink lipstick and that was that.' Anna glanced across and tried, out of charity, not to see the little verticle creases that puckered Sister David's middle-aged upper lip.

Sister Godric lifted her head from her tapestry: her eyesight was so bad she had to use wide-meshed canvas and strong colours, like a child, where once she had produced the most delicate work. To her delight, she found she could achieve striking and original results, much prized among convent visitors. She observed mildly, 'Most of us here shave our heads. We claim we're doing it in the name of virtue, and to show we are dead to the world. Perhaps these young people do it as a sign of something too.'

'Hah!' The whole convent disliked Sister Vincent's easily provoked sneers, but since they always took the form of sharp exhalations which could have been annoyance with herself – this time, she'd just dropped a button she was sewing – no one ever protested. She had the profile of a bird of prey and a temper to match. She struggled to control it, but irritation with the other women made her every sentence abrasive as sandpaper.

There was silence, until from her seat at the far end of the room Sister Dominic, incorrigible as ever, asked, 'So did you go out at all? Into the city?'

'I drove through it several times.' Anna kept to herself the journey home behind the wheel of the Jaguar.

At once there was a clamour of questions: 'What was it like?' 'Were there wonderful new buildings?' 'Did you see many interesting people?'

Mother Emmanuel raised a stern finger for decorum and Anna caught Sister Julian saying, in a tone of real yearning, 'It must have been exciting. I used to love seeing shop windows all lit up at night. I should think it was all thrilling.'

Anna liked Sister Julian. She had entered the convent straight from school in the old way and regarded herself with painful honesty: she knew she was unimportant, that her only worth lay in what she could do for others and her God. Her round, anxious face had grown increasingly indeterminate over the years as her colouring and eyebrows faded so that her one good feature, her soft brown eyes, made her look like a currant bun. She flinched as Sister Vincent remarked tartly, 'I don't suppose Sister Gabriel went about at night; that would have been worldly.' She bit a piece of thread between her teeth with an audible snap. 'And I don't think we should discuss the pleasures of the life outside. It draws us away from our task and fills our minds with unnecessary thoughts.'

Anna sat back. Her mind, she thought, was filled with a mixture of amazement and amusement. A few weeks ago she would probably have said the same sort of thing. And yet how touchingly naïve the question had been, as if poor Sister Julian saw the world as a mysterious, enticing place, full of unimaginable distractions. She must be fifteen years older than Anna herself. And she talked like a girl of fifteen – no, not as knowledgeable as a girl of fifteen would be today.

'I agree. We made the Lord the gift of our freedom when we entered. So did you, Sister Gabriel.' Mother Emmanuel lifted her eyes from the darning egg on which she was mending one of the heavy winter stockings. 'We understand why you went to your family, and we are interested to hear about them. But all this talk of the world is an indulgence.' The sharp click with which she set down the darning egg was final as a full stop. Anna felt a quick anger she knew she should repress: *they* asked *me*, but Mother Emmanuel's expression told her not to bother.

Years ago, when she was sixteen, Simon had taken her to New York for a week. Her sole foreign trip, and she still remembered every moment of it. The heat of Fifth Avenue pavements and the blast of icy air-conditioning in Bloomingdales. Waffles and maple syrup for breakfast, hot pastrami in delis and dark cool bars where Simon spent too much time. They'd gone one afternoon to the Metropolitan Museum and beside a painting Anna had noticed one of the museum guards, a burly man in his early fifties, four-square in the doorway. He wore uniform trousers and shirt, carried a nightstick at his hip. He was alert and aware of everything around him and Anna could tell he would have preferred to keep the pictures under lock and key. His expression was sour and accusatory, as if he half-anticipated one of the visitors making off with a masterpiece.

The same expectation was on Mother Emmanuel's face now. Clearer than words, the elderly superior feared the effect the world might have on her nuns. Just then the darning egg rolled off the table and Sister Rosalie jumped to her feet and retrieved it. Without even looking, *knowing* it would be picked up for her, Mother Emmanuel held out a hand.

'Thank you, my daughter.'

Anna shut her eyes, suddenly conscious how tired she was. Perhaps she was experiencing culture shock. Returning to the convent, seeing it with fresh eyes, stepping back into their pattern of life, she'd thought it was Victorian. But it was feudal.

Outside, she had been forced by circumstances and Lynn's desperate state to make decisions, however small, to take charge, if only of the children. But here, it was laid down that she must allow herself to be moulded by the rules into the pattern of the order. She must give up her opinions and her tastes, respond with deference towards those in authority, move on the instant when summoned. In here, she was like a child herself.

She turned to Mother Emmanuel. 'If I might have permission to go to my cell early, Mother? It's been a long day.'

Released, she paced through the tranquil building. It was almost in total darkness, for they saved electricity whenever they could and kept table-lamps going on the lowest bulbs. Anna loved the convent like this. She moved slowly past the statue of St Joseph at the foot of the stairs, a pot of chrysanthemums placed before him; glanced through the open door to the kitchen where bowls stood ready in rows on the long tables, each containing a Weetabix wrapped in clingfilm. The courtyard was freezing as enveloped in her mantle she hurried round the three covered sides to the cells. There was rain on the wind tonight. In a few months, this enclosed space would gleam with narcissus she had planted, and the prospect pleased her.

Anna fell asleep thinking about the spring.

It was still raining five days later. She stood on tiptoe in the stone-floored cooking office peering out of the recessed window. Slanting spears of rain obscured the little courtyard: spring seemed very far away this afternoon. She moulded the lump of wax collected from chapel candles between her palms to warm it, and set to work greasing the cooking machine like a giant waffle iron on its high bench.

She liked making altar breads: a task chosen specially for the community because they could work on it alone. It was not too absorbing, but simple enough to leave the mind free for contemplation. It kept the monastery going financially, too, since they supplied religious retailers as well as Catholic and Anglican churches.

She thought about this as she mixed white flour and water to a soft paste by hand, the only way to get the texture right. With a practised touch she dropped a dollop onto the square, baking-hot metal plate. Using both hands she brought down the upper plate, into which she had fixed the crucifx design the Anglicans preferred. The heavy plate pressed the dough out flat and with a sharp knife she trimmed the edges and dropped them into a bin. The farmer down the road would collect it from the front entrance for his pigs.

The altar bread had to be timed precisely: two and a half minutes. The only clock in the monastery was in here, an ancient alarm, and she watched the minute hand until it was time to raise the plate and reveal the almost opaque white sheet. She lifted it carefully and placed it on one of the enormous trays to cool. She stirred the paste again, dropped the next dollop onto the hot metal plate, brought down the lid, waited.

She had filled eight of the great trays and her arms were starting to tire when she caught such a light knock on the door that she did not answer, thinking it had been imagination. When she opened on the second tap she found Sister Dominic outside, her arms full of tea-towels she had brought in from the line in the garden. She gestured with her head: Can I come in? Anna glanced along the empty corridor. It was against the rules but they had scarcely had a chance to speak since she returned.

Just this once she would break silence. You were allowed to ask permission to speak if a piece of machinery broke down, and she could deliberately let the cooking plates overheat. But she preferred to seek penance afterwards. Anyway, she could never resist Lis's eyes, grey and soft as a chinchilla rabbit she'd once owned.

The younger woman slid through the half-open door and leant against the wall, laughing quietly.

'Such a rush,' she whispered, 'I've only a moment, got to iron this lot.' She lifted the bright bundle in her arms. 'Anna, you were gone such ages, we missed you. *I* missed you.' She looked at Anna over the tea-towels, half pleading, half defiant. 'I longed for you. Did you miss me?'

'You wouldn't believe how busy I was.' Anna reproved her. 'I couldn't think of anything except what was going on there.' She saw the grey eyes darken and added more gently, 'But yes, I did. And it's marvellous to be home, you can't imagine.'

'You must tell me all about it, I want to hear everything. Not what you tell the others. The real things about outside, you know? How you felt, what you thought.' Her voice dropped. 'If you thought of me.'

'I told you, Lis. Everything is so ordered here, so timed, you forget that in the world there isn't any. No time at all. It's got worse, I'll swear it has, than when I left. Or maybe there's more time when you're younger. But every moment seemed to be full. No matter how hard I tried to keep space for prayer, I was always snatching it from something else. It was only quiet on Sunday morning, and even then I had to go to early Mass, to get away by myself.' She mixed the flour and water paste again with her hand, dropped another dollop onto the hot metal plate. Both women listened to the satisfying sizzle as she brought the upper plate down hard and clamped it shut. Anna ran her knife round the edges and added, her eyes on the clock, 'It's made me think though, going out, it's made me see what a tiny world we've made here. How protected we are. I thought when I entered I'd lead a life of poverty. And to an extent that's correct: I've nothing of my own. But on the other hand, I've everything I need, we all have. We're clothed and housed and will be all our lives, no anxieties about losing jobs and growing old, no question of being shoved into an old people's home. We work hard for our food, we make much of it ourselves, we grow the vegetables and keep the bees and the chickens, but we have all we want.' She lifted the upper plate and gingerly removed the hot, transparent sheet from the metal base.

'And you mean, that's not poverty?'

'Not by today's terms,' Anna answered. She stirred the paste again, watching her hand disappear into the soft dough. 'I know we send donations to charities, and offer our prayers for war-torn countries, for the children dying of starvation in Africa.' She dropped dough onto the hot plate, pressed down the upper one, clamped it shut. 'I tell you Lis, it's one thing hearing about it, being told by visitors and the priest. I cared, I really did: I thought I understood. I hadn't watched any television at all, I went out of the room when it was on, but Lynn was watching this report from Ethiopia.' She paused. 'I never imagined . . . There were pictures of this enormous encampment in the middle of a desert. They could have been people in the grip of a biblical famine.' She took the hot sheet out of the cooking machine and slipped it onto a cooling tray.

She looked down at it and instead of hot metal she saw hot sand and a woman endlessly braiding a child's long hair into tiny plaits. The child's face was pressed patiently into the woman's knees, thin arms linked with silver, dusty little feet. Sister Dominic waited silently.

'There was no colour anywhere,' Anna went on. 'Just the tones of their skin and the sand and their brown blankets. These beautiful people reduced to ghosts, their children so emaciated you could almost see through them.' She gestured round the room and added scornfully, 'This isn't poverty.'

Sister Dominic said, 'I've never heard you like this. You don't usually say such thngs.'

'No. Well, I'm not exactly here to talk,' Anna said soberly. 'But if I hadn't been outside, If I hadn't seen it, I would never have realised that by trying to make myself open to the world's suffering, I have successfully ensured my own comfortable survival. I feel ashamed for all the times at night prayers when I thought I felt hungry.' She shook her head. 'Poverty. Need. Abstinence. We don't even know what the words mean.' Her voice rang with scorn and Lis put a warning finger to her own lips. Anna paused, frowning. 'It wasn't only that. For Lynn, these last weeks have been terrible. She is so desperate, poor girl.' She glancd across at sister Dominic. 'I felt such anger against my brother that I frightened myself.'

Sister Dominic said in a small voice, 'You're crying.'

Anna sniffed. 'Am I? Sorry.' She sat down on the single chair and fished in her underskirt for the large white handkerchief. She failed to find it, and wiped her eyes with her sleeve. After a moment she said, 'All right now. It's just that I seem to have gone through more emotions in two weeks than I've had in two years here.' She glanced at the rainy window. 'I could do with a long walk, but in this I'd end up with pneumonia.'

'Maybe it'll be better tomorrow. If it is, I'll walk with you.'

'No. Thank you.'

The grey eyes darkened again, hurt. She was like a puppy, Anna thought, bouncing one minute, cowed the next. Now she turned to go, holding patterned tea-towels against her chest. 'You've changed. You're different.'

'I don't mean to be, but I am.' She dipped into the paste again. 'And I don't seem able to get back.'

Sister Dominic's fingers were on the door-latch, ready to lift it. With her back to Anna she asked, 'And me. How do you feel about me?'

'I don't know, Lis. I don't know anything at the moment.' She kept her voice deliberately calm.

The younger woman said fiercely, 'Well, I'll never be any different. I'll always feel the same about you, no matter what.' She turned suddenly, tea-towels dropping unheeded to the floor, face pale, hands outstretched. 'Anna, I . . .'

The door behind her opened inward and she visibly pulled herself together, collecting the tea-towels as Sister Peter popped her head round, and made a little bob, two fingers to her lips, the order's way of asking permission to speak during silent hours.

Anna said 'Benedicite'.

'Dominus,' responded Sister Peter, and as she came into the room saw Sister Dominic crouched on the floor. 'Whoops! Didn't mean to interrupt you girls.'

'Sister Dominic came in to bring me the cellar key,' Anna improvised swiftly, despising the lie.

'Good-oh. I'm here to do trays.'

Anna nodded and gestured towards them, showing she was almost finished. Out of the corner of her eye she saw Sister Dominic disappear in the direction of the kitchen to do her ironing. She trimmed the last sheet of altar bread and covered the trays with clean white cloths while she timed it. She was glad of the help: Sister Peter was a burly woman much given to the slang of her youth. Despite her size – or perhaps, Anna thought, because of it – those sausage-like fingers produced exquisite silverwork. She lifted four trays easily to Anna's two, and followed her down the steep stone steps to the cellar. By the single nightlight, they ranged them on wooden racks, moving in the gloom like nocturnal creatures, knowing every step without seeing it in this daily task.

'You'd best be wary with that young lady.'

'Sorry?' Anna was absorbed in the business of stacking the last trays.

'She's very . . .' Sister Peter searched for the word, 'emotional. It's silly to encourage her.' Sister Peter's tone was conversational, reasonable.

'I don't believe I do.' She was grateful darkness hid her alarm. What were they talking about?

'Well.' The older nun was noncommittal. 'If you say so, of course, but that's not how it looked to me.'

No one cares how it looked to you! But of course she didn't say that. 'I'd upset her,' Anna said quickly, 'I told her about some dreadful pictures I'd seen on television, famine pictures. It was my fault, I shouldn't have broken silence.'

Sister Peter sighed heavily, and her bulky shape moved towards the stairs. 'No, I shouldn't have spoken. It's not my task to offer criticism. I apologise for that.' She took hold of the stair rail. 'But one nun going out upsets the whole convent. It hasn't felt the same since you went. All your talk of travel and that, I don't know.'

So that was it. She felt a rush of affection for Sister Peter, with her sudden kindnesses and her many skills. 'I know. But I'm back now.' She added, 'It's all over.' But the words lacked conviction.

After Vespers Anna went out to check the animals. It was the only task in the convent performed so late, and she preferred it to all her others. With her feet in heavy galoshes and a plastic pixie-hood absurdly topping her head-dress, she tempted the geese into their pen with a pan of grain and bolted them in securely against foxes: she'd never forget the morning she had found nothing but a flurry of bloodstained feathers and a lump of red-brown fur caught on the wire.

Then she picked up her skirt and ran down through the kitchen garden to the long field, free for a few minutes, drawing deep breaths of cool air and relief. She had been back long enough to find irksome the pressure of community life, to remember how confined she had been before that telephone call had taken her out into the world. And then she had forgotten the sounds Sister Mark made when she ate. It wasn't her fault, false teeth slipped, but Anna found she was gritting her own teeth at that irritating click-click opposite her in the refectory. She had asked for patience in her prayers. Just a few hours ago in the Chapter of Faults the prioress had called on them to make full and clean confession of any wrong done. Lying face down on the floor with the others, arms by her sides, Anna had recited her faults: I confess to you, dear Mother and to you, dear Sisters, that I broke silence in the cooking office. And I had uncharitable thoughts.

She reached the long field where the small flock of Beulah Speckled-face were kept and counted a dozen stubby white shapes, pulled the gate to make sure it was secure. A young ewe wandered over and started rubbing its back against the wooden bars. She put a hand through and scratched the wide woolly forehead: the animal stared up at her, square sulphur-coloured eyes expressionless. She liked sheep – a one-way affection, she was sure. The coarse curls crisped under her fingers as she pushed deeper into the fleece, feeling the bony head move with the chomping jaws. Nice, stupid animals, requiring so little, giving in return their soft sheaths twice a year for the nuns to spin and for her to colour.

At first, experimenting, she had dyed the coarse spun wool in shades she saw around her; the lichen greens, golds, rusts. The variety of natural colours from roots and berries were endless. It had been three years before she discovered that by adding minimal amounts of synthetic dyes she could produce dramatic shades with all the subtlety of the originals, but with added depth. Soon after the spring shearing, she'd be able to start thinking about dyeing her wool again; she couldn't wait. Maybe this time, she'd be able to get the clear scarlet she wanted, the colour of the Estée Lauder nail varnish she'd worn the day she entered.

She lifted her free hand and inspected the nails critically in the fading light. Terrible. And nail varnish today would actually make her hands look worse, drawing attention to them.

Perhaps that was why she had always avoided red in her dyes until recently. It was a sexy colour, it had that image, and she had loved it before she entered. It had been one of the things she had missed most when she went into the habit. It had cost her to give it up but she hadn't minded; it was a price she was prepared to pay, it was part of her sacrifice. She had wanted to wear the habit, to be a sign of God in the world.

She must go in a minute, it was nearly dark and she had no torch. On the hill to her right she saw a movement, the white scuts of a pair of rabbits, and the sight of them brought to mind Sister Dominic. Lis. The only person here who called her Anna.

She folded her arms beneath her chin and leant on the top bar of the gate, thinking about Lis, and the things they had said in the cooking office. The whole thing had got out of hand, but how? She hadn't sought it out, this difficult relationship, but then neither had she run from it.

Sister Dominic had arrived four years ago, after Anna had been inside for nearly nine, at a moment when she was at her lowest ebb. She had turned inward on herself, and even the smallest things seemed to conspire against her.

She'd felt dried up and useless, locked in a cycle of prayer and work which should have been deeply satisfying, but gave her no sense of renewal, no hope. The long littleness of every succeeding day sapped energy and vitality, so that she could hardly get out of bed in the mornings.

In all her time there, she had formed no close ties. Through the years when outside young women in their twenties fell in love, married, cared for children, she had gone on alone. It was the path she had freely chosen and she did not think of it as hardship: everyone was alone. And she had God. But her body and her heart had been deprived.

She was amazed by the way days were suddenly transformed, that the presence of another person in the same building could make such a difference. She hummed under her breath as she worked in the garden, moved with a new confidence. She no longer felt neglected and unimportant, because she mattered to Lis.

It had not occurred to either to them that their gentle friendship would be apparent to others until Sister Godric said quietly to Anna one day when she found the younger woman picking herbs, 'When you go in twos, the devil makes a third.'

Anna straightened up, her basket on her arm.

'I beg your pardon, Sister?' she answered carefully. The old nun shook her head.

'You understand, Sister Gabriel. I can scarcely see these days, but even I have noticed.'

'It's a friendship, Sister Godric.' She was hurt. 'That's all it is. I feel nothing but affection for Sister Dominic, and I know she'd say the same.'

Sister Godric remained silent.

'You do believe me?'

'I believe you, Sister. To live in chastity doesn't mean to live without a heart.'

She picked a sprig of rosemary and rolled it between her fingers. 'We all have emotions, and to a great extent here we repress and smother them, because they don't fit in with our ideas of ourselves, or what we want to be. We should be "like mirrors, shining lamps, glowing torches, brilliant stars" – isn't that it? I've been in this house a long time, and when I first entered they were so strict. We had to learn it off by heart.' She quoted from the *Manual for Novices on the Cultivation of Chastity.* '"Repress and fly from as a mortal plague, even though spiritual in their origin, particular friendships and familiar conversations arising from an attractive appearance, pleasing manner or an agreeable disposition."'

Particular friendships. That was the first time anyone had said that to Anna. Pf's, they called them in the convent. From the French *amitiés particulières*. Friendships between the same sex. Something to be avoided, abhorred. But no one could think that of her and Lis. It was actually painful to have to say, 'It's not . . . a sensual relationship. It's not possessive at all, not exclusive. It won't hurt the community. And I'm a better person because of her.' That was true, surely. She felt immense tenderness for Lis, but they never so much as touched. Just that one time, when Lis had put both hands round Anna's face, framed in the wimple, and whispered, 'Your lovely medieval face'. Silently she had put away Lis's hands but she'd wanted to cry: it was recompense for all the years when she had no idea what she looked like.

The old lady by her side folded her hands into the wide sleeves of her habit and said slowly, 'I can only tell what I know: a deep human love may lead one away from religious life.'

Anna had listened but had not believed her. It had taken her a long time to discover that Sister Godric was right. Loving Lis had not made her more content with her life, but less. And Lis had not been satisfied with the little they had. *I need you to love me. I need you to trust me.* Anna understood. Lis was the younger by seven years, not yet used to monastic ways. Impulsive, demonstrative, she was forcing herself to curb her natural instincts, to conform to a pattern alien to her nature. She needed Anna as a focus for her affections, she could not do without personal support.

At first Anna had been in similar need, had drawn strength from being available when Lis wanted to walk beside her, to chat at recreation. But gradually she began to see that she was standing in the way. As long as Lis was turning to her, the younger woman was not facing up to the life here. She was a swimmer who refused to let go her lifebelt.

And Anna found she could not concentrate her mind on her God. Perhaps she was losing her vocation? It was a terrifying thought, for she had nothing else. She realised that whatever was happening to her had begun years ago. Briefly, her love for Lis made her happy enough to be able to continue, but at the same time it had given her a glimpse of possibilities she had never experienced.

She might have been wrong when she chose the veil at that ceremony of tacit profession the evening before she made her vows for life. They had placed two tables in the chapel. On one the ring, the cowl and mitre, and the little silver crown of a virgin. On the other, neatly folded, the clothes she had worn to enter five years before. She had been asked to decide between the two, to lay her hand on one table or the other.

She had no doubts then. She had nothing but doubts now.

8

'I shouldn't phone you, Anna, but I'll go mad if I don't talk to someone. I'm so frightened of everything, I can't manage by myself . . .' The distant words were obliterated by sobs.

Anna shook her head and whispered, 'I can't make out what she's saying.'

She had been summoned to the prioress's office to answer Lynn's call while Mother Emmanuel busied herself with bills. Head bent over her papers the prioress said resignedly, 'Try to calm her.'

Anna interrupted Lynn's hysterical voice, attempting to sound authoritative.

'Stop crying. Tell me quietly what's happened.' She heard Lynn draw breath. 'That's better. Now then.'

'The doctor says I'm to rest more. But there's no one to help with the children. I'd ask Jean, only her little girl's got chicken-pox. Anna, could you come back here? Please?' She was weeping again.

'Is there no one else?' All too well, she knew the answer.

'Who can I ask?' Lynn wailed, her normally soft, controlled voice cracked with emotion. 'Peggy'd do it, but you know her husband's been an invalid for years. All my friends are too busy themselves. Dr Barnes says if I don't rest, he can't be responsible for the consequences.'

Anna frowned. 'What are you saying?'

'I think he means . . . I might lose . . .' Lynn couldn't finish.

Anna caught her breath and shut her lips hard on the

protestations of sympathy: that would only make the poor girl worse. She needed practical help, not words.

'Don't upset yourself. I'll call you back later.' She glanced at the prioress's bent head. 'When I've had a chance to talk to Reverend Mother. Are the boys all right? Give them my love. And try to take things easy.' She waited for a reply. 'Are you there, Lynn?' She could hear Lynn crying again and then a crash followed by a wail from James. 'Lynn?' Her sister-in-law's harsh tones came to her faintly.

'. . . little *brat*, get away from me, you're driving me mad!' Anna heard a sharp smack and another howl from the child.

'Lynn, don't,' and this time she got an answer, got Lynn screaming down the phone so that even Mother Emmanuel looked up.

'. . . am I to do, there isn't a minute to . . . Go up to your bedroom and don't come out . . .' Lynn was sobbing again. 'I can't, Anna, I can't cope, I can't. I wish I was *dead*.'

'Now calm down.' Anna's voice was reason itself. 'There's no need to shout at Jamie, that won't help things at . . .' She recoiled as Lynn slammed down her receiver.

Anna slowly put the mouthpiece back on its hook. The convent telephone was an ancient stand and trumpet affair the nuns found in the stable when they took over the house and had persuaded a reluctant telephone exchange to install. Reception was marred by crackles, but that, Mother Emmanuel declared, was a bonus since they used it rarely and it would discourage callers.

'She's in a terrible state.'

'So I gathered,' the prioress commented.

'There seems to be no one who can help her.' Anna waited. 'The baby's due in a few weeks. Mother, you did say this was a special case. Could I go to her again?'

'Back to Bradford?' Mother Emmanuel frowned. 'I really do not see, Sister, how that can be permitted. We are enclosed nuns, we can't go running out every time someone's in trouble.'

Accustomed to absolute obedience, it was an effort to plead

her case. 'I'm not asking for myself, but for Lynn. She's so alone, Mother. You heard her on the phone: I'm afraid she might do something silly. Surely I could be permitted. In the circumstances.'

Mother Emmanuel took off her glasses and with two fingers massaged the bridge of her nose.

'I didn't go to Simon's funeral,' Anna added.

'My own mother died alone soon after I entered. I wasn't allowed home, either.' Mother Emmanuel sighed. 'That wasn't Holy God.'

Anna said nothing. When – years ago – the prioress told her in a rare moment of confidence that she would have liked to be a stone-mason, Anna had dismissed it as unlikely. It was only now she saw the truth of it in the broad, spatulate fingers, that said this was a practical woman more interested in action than in thought. The superior's existence, though, was the absolute opposite: in forty-five years she had stepped outside enclosure perhaps a dozen times, on convent business.

Maybe that explained what she often read in Mother Emmanuel's face: resignation, as though life had never taken her to the point she'd wanted. She frowned and fixed her gaze above Anna's head on the black and white photograph of an old Irish gravestone, slightly askew against blurred hills. 'I suppose,' she said doubtfully, 'it's possible to extend your leave of absence. But the Bishop won't like it. Not a bit.'

Anna made one last attempt. 'Lynn was screaming at Jamie. He's only four, Mother, a dear little boy. She'd never do that if she was in a normal state.' She paused. 'And the doctor's afraid she might lose the baby if she doesn't rest.'

Mother Emmanuel blinked. 'You didn't tell me that.' She put the bills back in their box. 'Lynn has no relatives at all, did you say? Not a sister or an aunt.'

'There's none for her.'

'Except you.' Mother Emmanuel replaced her glasses and shut the file-box with a snap. 'All right, Sister. I'll let you know what I decide.'

*

It was Anna's turn to do the washing up after supper the following evening. Wrapped in a long oilcloth apron, she ran hot water into the teak bowl. Sister Dominic dried cups and plates and put away. For ten minutes they worked in companionable silence, while Sister Rosalie busied herself setting out cereal in the clean bowls for the morning. When she went up to join the others in the community room, Anna said in a low voice, 'I've something to tell you.'

Sister Dominic took a bundle of spoons and wiped them carefully, waiting. Anna glanced at her, at the crescents of eyelashes shining under the glare of the bare light bulb, the white band, the glowing skin.

'Tomorrow I'm going back to Bradford. Mother Emmanuel arranged it, so I can help Lynn.' She turned on the cold tap and rinsed a dish.

'For how long?' Drying forks, now.

'I'm getting a formal permission this time, Mother Emmanuel says, from the Bishop. She's asked for a month. That's why I'm telling you.'

Getting no reply, she turned to Lis, who was rubbing cutlery so it gleamed, concentrating fiercely. She moved to the table and laid them down with exaggerated precision in a neat row. Then she said, 'Tomorrow?'

'Eight o'clock train.'

Lis came back to the sink and picked up an oval serving dish. Anna changed the water and started on the pans. Her sleeves were pinned back, her bare arms in the soapy water. She had almost finished, just two to go, when Lis said, 'Here,' dropping the clean, dried pan back into the bowl. Anna glanced up in surprise, hands still in the water. Lis took a step closer and kissed her on the mouth, so hard Anna could feel the shape of her teeth, the little rough ridge from the cold, taste the gingerbread they'd had for pudding: it was like being kissed by a passionate child. Only Lis was no child. Anna moved her head and Lis stepped back, eyes darker than usual, face drained of colour. She lifted her arm and slowly wiped her open lips with her sleeve, still watching Anna. Then she turned and strode from the kitchen.

She was walking down the platform at Bradford's Interchange station when someone took the case from her hand.

'I'll carry that for you, Sister.' A denim shoulder, curly bright brown hair, warm decisive voice.

'Good heavens.' She released the case. 'It's you.' She collected herself. 'Thank you very much.' They smiled uncertainly at one another. Peter Hallam fell into step beside her, moving towards the barrier.

'Are you going somewhere?'

'Me? No, I came to meet you. Mrs Simon told me you'd be on this train.'

'That was kind.' Even without looking, she could tell he was blushing. She didn't know which of them was more shy. He stood back to allow her past the ticket collector first, then handed in his platform ticket.

'The car's outside.'

When she saw the trim white Volkswagen parked between the Escorts and Astras she had to smile: it was so clearly the only vehicle there that could have belonged to him. He saw her expression and said solemnly, 'You see one of these, you know a vegetarian's driving it. Other cars are terrifying fast carnivores, but we tootle gently along, overtaking nothing, stopping for pedestrians and hooting at pretty girls.'

'And eating sweets.' The ashtray was crammed with wrappers, more were lodged in the cubbyhole.

He followed her look and admitted ruefully, 'M&Ms – my secret vice.'

She wondered what they were as he put the car into reverse and it hiccuped out of line. He made no attempt at conversation on the way to Lynn's, driving with total concentration.

They were turning into Kingswalk before he said, 'Is it all right for me to talk to you? I mean . . .' He gestured with his left hand toward her habit.

'Of course you can. Was there something in particular?'

He glanced in the rear-view mirror and guided the Volkswagen in beside the kerb. 'Maybe we should talk here. I don't want to worry your sister-in-law.' He turned to her, leaning back against his door, and she tried not to notice the long lashes over his hazel eyes. He tapped his front teeth with a thumbnail while he thought. They were good teeth, square and even. Abruptly, she transferred her attention to opening her window. From the house opposite she could hear a cello haltingly played.

'It's about Stan Beattie. He's my boss, I shouldn't be saying this to you. But I know as he's up to something, and it means no good. Am I to tell you?' He sounded anxious. 'I'd not bother you with it, but I can't tell Mrs Summers.'

Anna remembered Peggy's warnings when she visited the mill. 'Is it about Beattie pretending things are worse than they are?'

'Oh, you're onto that, are you? That's just scare-mongering: Peggy told me what he'd said. He'd no call to frighten you both, but things are bad and no mistake.' He unpeeled a packet of mints and offered it. She shook her head. He put one into his mouth. 'No, this is something worse or I'd not be here gossiping. Well, I've a mate works over Lands' place – d'you know them?' She nodded. It was a mill producing similar yarns to their own, run by two brothers. 'Seems Beattie was in there a week ago, and not for the first time neither. Mike's a bloke likes to know what's going on, and he took one of the invoice clerks out for a drink.' He grinned. 'It wasn't a hardship, she's a beaut. She's a chatterbox an' all, told him Beattie was offering to bring them in new business in exchange for a share of the profits.' He paused. 'You see what I'm saying?'

Anna frowned. 'He'd take Summers' orders and give them to Lands to fulfil?'

He nodded.

'He can't do that!' she exlaimed furiously. 'That's unheard of – it must be a criminal offence.'

'Stan Beattie's no fool. You'd have to prove it, wouldn't

you? And he'd not be obvious about it. He'd most likely go to the firms who're regular customers, tell them Summers are in problems, but he can guarantee quick delivery if they go to Lands. That way, we would never see the orders. Mind,' he added hastily, 'I'm not saying he's going to do that. Maybe he's just seeing how the land lies, how people'd react. But it doesn't bode well.'

Anna was horrified. 'I can't believe it. I just can't. Stan Beattie's worked for us for years. My father gave him a job, trained him. Trusted him.' She looked at Peter Hallam's sympathetic face. 'How could he do such a thing? Or even think about it?' Another thought occurred to her and she added, furious, 'And to make things much worse for Lynn at a time like this – he's a, he's a . . .'

The young man nodded soberly and fidgeted with the indicator lever, flicking it on and off. 'I'm not making excuses for him, but there is another way of looking at it. You say he's been with Summers for years, and now it looks maybe as if the mill mightn't make it. Well, he'd lose his job.'

The cello was playing *Robin Adair*. She said quietly, 'If the worst happened, so would you, and you're not going round handing out bits of someone else's business.'

'But don't you see, Beattie's fifty and more. I'm twenty-seven. I'd get another job . . .' He snapped his fingers '. . . like that. Beattie might get taken on by Lands, or someone like them, if he's done them a favour.' He shrugged. 'Or they might think if he'd scheme against one employer, he'd do it to them given half a chance. Either way, he's a frightened man. And fear makes people do strange things.'

'So it seems.' She stared out at a woman passing the car with a child holding either hand. It seemed quite natural to ask him, 'What can we do, then?'

'Peggy's the one to talk to, I'd say. I've told her none of this, but I don't imagine she'll be surprised. The main thing is to make sure Beattie can't go on doing as he pleases and no one to say him nay. Someone from the family should be around a bit more, if you don't mind my saying so.'

'Mrs Simon's baby is due in a few weeks. We can't expect her to do it.' Anna thought of Lynn's outburst when they left the mill together. 'And she says she won't go in anyway, it's too painful. I can see that. And there's nobody else.'

'Isn't there?' asked Peter Hallam innocently.

Lynn's face was pale and her cheek creased from the cushion, her hair straggling and over-long. She was like a forlorn child, Anna thought, until you saw the heavy pregnancy. The rest of her body seemed emaciated, her eyes huge, as if everything was drawn into her laden belly. She lay on the leather sofa in the lavish room, apparently oblivious to the mess, warming her hands on a mug of tea.

Toys were everywhere, comics, a paintbox upside down on the cream carpet. Anna picked it up and found the stains beneath.

'It's only water-colour,' Lynn said indifferently. 'It'll come off, I expect.' She shivered, though she was covered by a blanket. 'Are you warm enough?'

Anna touched the thick skirt of her habit. 'I'm used to worse than this.'

'I just put the heating on when it gets dark now. And I go to bed at eight to save electricity anyway.' She shut her eyes. 'Thank God you're here. Thank God you've come. You must stay this time, you've got to stay. Please. Anna, please.'

'I can stay a while. Don't think about that just now.'

Lynn opened her eyes. 'I do nothing but think. I sit here and think about what happened, and Simon, and what I'm to do. Thinking's all that's left.' Her voice was bitter. 'I had a man to see about selling this stuff' - she gestured round at the furniture. 'Three hundred, he offered, for the lot. I told him it's leather – just one chair cost three times that – but he said there wasn't the market for it and he had to make his cut. Things're so bad, I thought should I sell, but three hundred wouldn't cover one bill. The Jag's gone, though. I'm using the old runabout from the mill.'

Anna asked carefully, 'Have you been there?'

'No. And I'm not bloody well going, either. The horrible place can burn down for all I care: I wish it would.'

'You should think very hard before you refuse, Lynn. You need that income, it's all you've got. You're not going to be working for a bit after the baby's born. And even when you do, it could only be part time.'

Lynn tipped her head back so she was looking at the ceiling. Tears trickled out of the corners of her eyes and ran into her hair, but she made no sound. Anna went on, doing her best to be encouraging speaking of the need to keep active, to take an interest, to take control of her life. 'Maybe we should see about getting a mother's help, or whatever they're called. If you had someone here now, before the baby arrives, it would give you freedom sooner.'

Lynn said flatly, 'I had a mother's help, she went when we started to have real money problems. We've had several, that's how I managed to keep working with the other two. I'll tell you about mother's helps, shall I? They're nice enough girls, even if they're in the bathroom most of the day. They like kids, but not that much: they take them to the park and stick them in the sandpit and then half a dozen of them gather in a group to giggle and talk about boys and do each other's hair. Jamie fell and cut his head open and another mother cleaned him up and comforted him, and spent ten minutes looking for whoever was with him.' She wiped her eyes with a crumpled tissue. 'One we had, I'd check each morning she'd taken the pill, I was so worried about what she got up to. Another was actually in bed with her boyfriend when we got home late one night, and Jamie was playing in the hall: she'd never noticed.' She turned her head to look at Anna. 'How could I go out to work and leave a tiny baby with someone like that? And a proper nanny is out of the question, I couldn't ever earn enough.' Her voice faded away into exhaustion.

After a pause, Anna offered, 'You mustn't let yourself be defeated. You have to be positive, there's always a way. You speak as if you were alone but you're not, none of us is. We are all watched over.'

'Am I?'

Anna missed the sarcasm. As she missed the little warning signals, the rigidity of Lynn's body, the tight line of her jaw. 'Of course. You mustn't give way to despair, remember that no one is tried beyond their strength and – '

'Shut up!' Lynn erupted. Her voice had changed completely, it was wild and sharp and she was sitting up and struggling to her feet, pushing the blanket aside, spilling her tea. 'Shut up, shut up, shut up!' She was yelling now, her face contorted, spitting out the words. 'Don't give me that damn nunnish nonsense, don't tell me about inner strength and being watched over! It's all very well for you, what's ever happened to ruin *your* life? I've been abandoned and I can't cope. I've *got* no inner strength . . .' She pressed both hands against her jutting stomach '. . . I've just got a baby in here and I can't think beyond having it by myself, facing that alone, for God's sake. For God's *sake!*'

Shocked, Anna could find no response. She hadn't heard anyone scream at her since her mother, thirteen years before. In the convent no one raised their voice in anger. You learned to control your emotions, to bite back retorts that rose to your lips. It was easier than it sounded: most rows were between people who lived too closely, shared too much. They sprang from family life, from intimate relationships. Anna had given up these things, and in doing so had evaded those stresses at least. There were others: more than twenty women living in community, of widely differing ages and temperaments, sharing a common life, could not be expected to do so day in, day out without some tensions and troubles. Overcoming them was part of life, though, and in more than a decade she had never had to face up to anything like this. Unable to summon any retort, she stared stupidly at Lynn. This seemed to enrage her sister-in-law more than any words could have done.

'Don't just peer at me,' she shouted, 'As if I was some kind of madwoman, don't you dare sit there all calm and dignified in those stupid bloody clothes out of the *Sound of Music*, who do you think you are to tell me what to do? What do you know about being tied down, not able to get out because there's no one to take care of the kids?'

She paused, more for breath than because she had finished, and Anna took the opportunity to say, 'I'm tied too. In a different way perhaps, but I'm less free even than you.'

'Don't talk crap,' Lynn said wearily.

'And I meant to say,' Anna went on, 'you shouldn't hit Jamie, you know.'

'You miserable cow, you don't think I meant to hit him?' Lynn's contempt was like a lash. 'I adore him, the boys are the only thing keeping me sane. But he drives me mad, always clinging to me, asking when Daddy's coming home, trying to do things and making them even worse. I couldn't help it, everything just got too much.' She thrust her hands through her hair to clutch the back of her head, fingers white with tension. 'What the hell can you know about kids or families or any other damn thing?'

Anna heard herself say primly, 'I don't have to be in your position to appreciate your problems.' She knew before the sentence was out how awful it sounded, just like that wretched health visitor.

'You haven't understood a word I've said.' Even Lynn's lips were pale now. 'You just don't know what I'm talking about.' She drew a shuddering breath and said slowly, 'I hate you. You don't know anything, you haven't done anything. You've no one in the world to worry about, you haven't got anyone to look after, you're free as air . . .'

Anna had been getting to her feet to walk out of the room, to get away somewhere quiet. She should never have come back here.

'That's right, run away. You're good at that, you self-centred bitch,' Lynn jeered.

Anna could feel herself sweating under the tight headband, losing control. Her own voice was too loud.

'You don't know what you're saying. I'm the last person you can call self-centred. Nothing I do is for myself, nothing. I've given up everything for the sake of others.'

Lynn turned and grabbed the end of Anna's black veil, giving it a yank so she had to grab to hold it in place.

'You've given up everything! Don't give me that! You've not given up security, or three meals a day, or warm clothes. Anxiety, that's all you've given up, worry, responsibility. You gave up caring for others when you walked out on your family at eighteen. You never gave a damn what happened here after you'd gone. Your mother *really* started drinking then, but you didn't even know about it.' Her voice dropped. 'And it was *your* fault. Your father blamed her for you going and she couldn't live with it so . . .'

Anna put her hands over her ears, but Lynn still had hold of her veil. The two women struggled, Lynn shouting., 'And you left Simon to hold things together for them, to go into a mill he hated because there was no one else. And *you've* given up everything. You never thought of what other people have to give up.'

'It's not my fault if people mess up their lives.' Anna was hoarse. 'And it's not true about my mother.'

'Isn't it? You can't face up to it, you can't face that you were responsible for making someone unhappy. She was a very respectable alcoholic, you'll be glad to know.' Lynn's tone was dangerous now, seeking to hurt. 'Not much in public, just a sherry before dinner. But my God, what she knocked back in the kitchen. Your father used to phone Simon some nights, he couldn't get her upstairs.'

'*Let go.*' Anna heard herself yelling, 'Let me *go.*' She pulled harder and Lynn suddenly released her grip. Off balance, Anna fell against a low glass table and the heavy folds of her habit sent a lighted lamp crashing to the floor. She struggled to get up from hands and knees, impeded by her cumbersome clothes. Lynn watched, the anger gone out of her, breathing heavily. Jamie, who had been playing with his train set in the hall, appeared in the doorway, face screwed up in concern.

'You're shouting,' he said accusingly. 'Snoopy hates it when you shout and break things.'

'Sorry darling. Everything's fine now, see?'

Anna picked up the lamp and replaced it on the table, listening with amazement to Lynn's matter-of-fact tone after her outburst. Reassured, the child nodded and went back to his solitary game.

Lynn held out a hand to Anna, who took it gratefully. When she was back on her feet, the two women avoided each other's eyes whilst Anna tugged her scapular straight and Lynn smoothed her hair, quiet again.

'I'm sorry, Anna, I really am. I don't know what made me say all that.'

Anna pulled her belt straight. 'A lot of it was true. Unfortunately.' She couldn't bring herself to look directly at her sister-in-law, focused on her hands. 'I apologise for trying to tell you how to run your life. You're right: I don't understand anything.' She swallowed. 'There was one thing you didn't say, though. You pointed out that I had no one to worry about or look after. The other side of that is, there's no one to give a damn about me.' She straightened her veil and looked directly at Lynn. 'I'd just come to realise this myself. It hits very hard, when you're my age and discover that you have no one *for yourself*. Not a husand or a lover or a child. They say that when a nun dies, it's like breaking a pane of glass: you put in another. I *feel* like a pane of glass, Lynn. Colourless, Unmarked. The same as all the others.' She shivered. 'It *is* cold in here.'

'You mean you're not happy in your convent?' Lynn was puzzled. 'You always looked so tranquil, when we visited, so – I don't know, so self-contained. We thought you were absolutely contented there.'

'I was.' Anna crossed her arms over her chest. 'The place hasn't changed; the meaning of it hasn't changed. But I have. And when you said those things – well, they were too near the truth for comfort.'

'I shouldn't have said that, about your mother.'

'It wasn't anything new,' Anna frowned at the memory. 'When I was nine and ten, Mum would meet me from school and the other girls would snigger because she talked too loudly and her lipstick was always smeared. Someone told me my mother drank but I never repeated it at home. After that I'd watch her, and often she had that awful sweet smell on her breath.' She held the rosary at her waist, letting the beads slip through her fingers. 'She never neglected Simon or me. We always had clean clothes and she was a marvellous cook. She used it to take the edge off things, I suppose. Looking back, she and my father were totally unsuited, and she had no life outside.'

'When I knew her, she was much worse. As if she could only communicate when she was released by drink.'

'You don't really think it was my fault?' She so desperately wanted it not to be that the words escaped, childish and silly. Lynn leant forward for emphasis, laying her hand on Anna's arm.

'I wanted to hurt you. I'm sure losing you to the life you chose was part of it – she couldn't understand it, she never saw you, there was no possibility of a wedding, or grandchildren – but honestly Anna, if it hadn't been that, then it would have been something else. Alcoholism is an illness after all, she'd had it for years. Anything could have been the trigger. She might have been the same if you were still living here.'

Anna nodded, grateful for the reassurance, even if she couldn't quite bring herself to believe it. Jamie had wandered back into the room and was lying across his mother's knees, humming. Anna watched Lynn absently pulling down his jumper, doing up the strap of his dungarees.

'Just the same, perhaps she did need me, and I walked away like you said. And in the end, I've failed. During the last few months I used to lie in bed sometimes and think I wouldn't be able to get up because what difference would it make to anyone? I don't matter as an individual. No one needs me.'

From his comfortable resting place the child looked up at her. Beneath his square-cut fringe it was Simon's face in miniature, Simon's melancholy brown eyes. But there was nothing melancholy about Jamie. He removed a thoughtful thumb from his mouth and said seriously, 'We need you, Auntie Anna.'

Lynn rubbed a hand over his head.

'And how,' she added fervently.

That week a pattern was established. Anna would take Bax to school and drop Jamie at his playgroup, leaving Lynn to get up slowly and tidy the house, before meeting the little boy at twelve. Anna would stay at the mill until after three, collecting Bax on her way home. She usually took them both for a walk before cooking supper and putting them to bed. For her, it was busy but pleasant. For Lynn, her presence relieved a terrible anxiety.

The worst part for Anna was the mill. Driving there each day was interesting: the people on the streets, the advertisements on hoardings, the sense of being back in the world. But turning into Nightingale Street, parking the car, going through the narrow passageway to the side-door of Summers & Son, she was conscious of her heart's apprehensive thudding. Her nervousness was allayed by Peggy's welcome, returned each time she was faced with something new. She tried to keep to the office but occasionally it was essential that she go upstairs. She would mount them slowly to keep the moment at bay, pause outside the old-fashioned door at the top with its square of dimpled glass, listening to the thump and thunder of machinery, the loud music, the shouted conversations. She dreaded the blast of warm air mingling wool and cheap talc and hot metal: it always halted her for a moment, reduced her to ten again, dried the inside of her mouth. Then Rene or Sylv would wave and shout a greeting and she'd smile and answer and check the progress of an order before she could escape, pulling the sliding door behind her with a gasp of relief.

Her greatest fear had been that she would not know what to do when she was there, and be worse than useless. But she had underestimated how closely her childhood had been welded to Nightingale Mill. She had absorbed information in those years and never realised how much she knew. She could still read an order book and type invoices, fill in order forms and check out stock as she had during those long weekend hours with her father. He had always hoped she would go into the mill as well as Simon. Summers & Son & Daughter. He'd encouraged her interest, had taken her with him on viewing days to inspect the fleeces for auction at the old Wool Exchange in the centre of the city.

On the Friday of Anna's first week, Peggy came into the cramped clerk's office, plonked a cup of tea on her desk and announced firmly, 'You and me and Stan Beattie'd best talk this morning.'

Anna bit into her biscuit and agreed without enthusiasm.

Peggy laughed, 'Keen as mustard, you are. But problems don't just go away, unfortunately, and we've a couple of whoppers.' She glanced at her watch. 'Five minutes?'

The door of what the black lettering on the crinkly glass called 'Director's Office' stood open. Stan Beattie was sitting at his own desk, but Anna noticed that he had now started using Simon's as well. Opened letters lay on it, a newspaper folded at a photograph of a girl whose ballooning bare breasts she wished she hadn't seen. Catching her glance, Peggy made a cross sound and reached out from where she was sitting opposite Stan Beattie to turn the paper over.

'Sorry, love.'

Stan Beattie remarked, without glancing up from the figures he was scribbling, 'I expect Miss Summers knows the facts of life by now, Peggy.'

Anna took the third chair and folded her hands inside her sleeves. Nasty little man. The top of his head gleamed with the stuff he used on his thinning hair as he bent over his page, underlining something heavily.

'I told Peggy I thought Mrs Simon should hear this.'

I'll bet you did. Anna kept that to herself. The words she chose were smooth.

'She's not to be involved at the moment as I'm sure you can appreciate. I hope I can speak for her.'

'Mebbe.' He didn't sound convinced. 'I've been going

through the month's figures and if anything they're worse than I expected. We had six thou from Mrs Simon after she sold the Jaguar but most of that had to go on raw materials and wages.' He rubbed the loose skin under his chin. 'I'd have expected that car to fetch a lot more.'

Anna kept silent. The Jaguar sold for twenty-one thousand pounds. Lynn had used ten thousand to pay household debts and the bills Anna had found that night in the roll-top desk. She had already written out a cheque to give the remaining five thousand to the mill but Anna had stopped her, arguing that properly invested it would provide at least a small weekly amount of security. If Beattie were not to be trusted, Lynn could lose anything she put in. And she had nothing else – no insurance policies, no savings. If the mill were to fail, there would be nothing to salvage. The new machinery was not paid for, the old was worthless. Lynn had tried to insist but Anna had been adamant: it relieved some of her anxiety to know the family had at least that security.

'What's the shortfall?' Peggy asked.

'If Alexanders pay us for the last order we'll only be out a thousand. If they don't . . .' He shrugged. 'We can't go to the bank.'

'The day Alexanders pay on time, pigs'll fly,' Peggy said grimly. 'They're so big, they reckon they can call the tune.'

'Surely,' Anna asked, 'You could insist for once that they do?'

Stan Beattie stood up and came round to the front of his desk where he perched, looking down at her, leg swinging, thigh bulging under the shiny material of his trousers. He deliberately invaded her space, crowding her, so she wanted to move her chair back. She made herself keep still, trying to ignore the smell of sweetish cologne masking sweat.

'Oh yes, indeed.' He mocked her. 'Naturally. I just tell them we insist and Bob's my uncle. Have you any idea,' he asked, leaning toward her, 'any idea at all of the number of firms who supply Alexanders with yarn? They only take the best, they have outlets all over the country, they export to

France and Germany. We need them, believe me, more than they need us.'

'I still don't see why we can't send a reminder.'

'Because that's not the way you do business.' He drummed his fingers on the desk, 'I can't go cap in hand to a firm that size, and that's all there is to it. And that's not our biggest problem.' He reached behind him for his untidy figures. 'We're paying an arm and a leg for the new fancy-spinner Mr Simon bought. Thousand quid a month and it stands idle half the time. It's criminal. The way things are, we could send it back.'

'We can't afford the cost of the raw materials,' Peggy turned to Anna. 'We were operating on a knife edge. Mr Simon had big plans for expanding, but he hadn't got anything under way . . .' she let the sentence slip. But Anna could complete it for herself. And now Simon was dead, their credit had tumbled. The sensible thing might be to close the mill, sell up, salvage what she could for Lynn.

As if he had heard, Beattie knocked that thought down with his next words.

'We're going from bad to worse. If we stop trading, we're immediately liable for all our debts. The plant wouldn't fetch two ha'pence. The fancy-spinner'd be repossessed. The good-will and customers'd be worth something, but I doubt the lot'd do more than pay a third of what we owe.' He examined the gold signet ring on his little finger with satisfaction, buffed it on his shirt sleeve. Simon's phone rang. Peggy answered, spoke briefly and hurried to the door. 'Back in a sec. Latimers have mislaid an order.'

Stan Beattie continued to sit on the edge of his desk, drumming his fingers. Immersed in her thoughts – could they get help from someone other than the bank – she didn't notice at first what he was saying. His tone alerted her. Beattie's voice was quite loud but occasionally, as now, it dropped to the confidential note of a market trader offering an illegal bargain.

'First thing, we must lay off some of the girls for a few weeks, nothing permanent, just till trade looks up.'

Under her wide concealing sleeves, Anna's fingers locked together as she made the huge effort to state her own opinion.

'My father always . . .' She swallowed. 'He said, never get rid of your workforce, however bad things are. They can't sit around waiting for you to whistle, and you'll not see them again.'

'Your father's daughter, all right.' He evidently did not intend this as a compliment. 'Well, I've no more suggestions to offer. There's no easy answers here.' He got off the desk, accidentally brushing her knee with his own. 'Oops, sorry. Nothing personal.'

Anna resisted the impulse to rub her knee violently where he had touched it. She heard him say, the market trader again, 'Must be strange, Miss Anna, living the way you do, lot of women all shut up together. I'd like to be a fly on the wall when you all get talking.'

'We speak very little.' Anna was on her feet, trying to keep the contempt out of her voice. Whatever she thought of the wretched man, Lỳnn needed him. For a moment too long he stood in her way. One of his front teeth was grey when he smiled.

'You'd best have a copy of this.' He handed over the accounts Peggy had prepared. 'Let me know if you find a solution.'

Anna worked on in her stuffy cubicle when the others went out for lunch. Peggy had asked her repeatedly to join them but she always refused. The local Cat & Kettle was obviously impossible for her, and though she would have loved to try the Indian restaurant in Orchard Street, she had not eaten in public for so long, it was too much to contemplate. Instead, she had a cheese and pickle sandwich and a mug of instant coffee while she jotted figures on a pad, going over and over the items on the account sheets.

It was no hardship. From childhood she had always liked being alone in the offices with the muffled clatter from the workroom above which would not cease until five thirty. It was almost an annoyance when just before one thirty someone went into Peggy's room and plugged in the kettle. There was the clink of a stirring spoon and after a while Stan Beattie's voice. She was vaguely aware he was making business calls, she caught remarks about staple length, fleece weight, 64's quality being more suitable.

Going over it afterwards, she couldn't have said what seized her attention: a phrase, perhaps, or the way his voice dropped to the confidential tone she so distrusted.

'. . . rough here at the moment, all very dicey.' He listened, then said, 'I'd not like to see you waiting on an order we couldn't in all honesty guarantee.' A pause. 'No, I wouldn't. No, of course not.'

There was silence, and Anna put down the apple she'd been eating: her mouth had suddenly gone so dry she thought she would choke. What in heaven's name was Beattie talking about?'

'Yes,' she heard, 'yes, I'm saying just that. Well, you know how things've been here for a long time. It's all been downhill and now . . .'

There was no window in her cubicle, the light was on, but the room seemed suddenly dark. She huddled low in her chair, not wanting to hear any more, unable to stop. He was turning away orders, telling a customer they were unable to fulfil them.

'It's against my interests but in yours. Just say I'm taking the long view.' A grunting laugh. 'Right, squire. No problem.' Another pause. 'You do that. Cheer-oh.'

She wasn't mistaken. The words – and the tone – had been explicit enough. What other meaning could that call have had? She sat staring at nothing. He was dialling again, talking to someone else. So far as she could tell, nothing untoward was said. Only, how did the conversations go when he sat in other people's offices?

How could he, how dare he? Was he trying to ruin Nightingale Mill? She would scarcely have believed it but for Hal's story about the approach to Lands. It was impossible to understand what Beattie's motives could be – he would be out of a job, everyone would. Shock gradually gave way to anger. She dropped the remains of her fruit into a plastic bag, screwed it up with a vicious twist and chucked it in the bin. Pity she couldn't dispose of Beattie as easily. She got to her feet, determined to go in and confront him.

She reached the door and stopped. Confront him with what? Commonsense said she couldn't accuse him of planning to harm the mill on the basis of a few overheard sentences. Nor of offering to take their orders to Lands – that was little more than suspicion. Beattie would deny everything, claim she'd misunderstood.

That was what she told herself, In reality, such an action was anyway beyond her. All the convent training told her not to interfere, to follow her own path with honesty and conviction and leave others be.

She banged a desk drawer hard so Beattie would know someone was about, then went to the washroom and splashed her face with cold water. There was no sign of him when she returned to her desk.

It was useless to try to work, her concentration was broken. She was boiling with anger she hadn't felt in years, that she would never have felt on her own account. The pressure of the serré-tête on the crown of her head was unbearable. She pulled at the confining head-dress, trying unsuccessfully to ease it.

The wretched man wanted to ruin Summers. He didn't care that Lynn and the boys were dependent on the mill – and therefore on him. The only logical thing to do was sack him.

As soon as she came to this thought, she rejected it. Who then would go out to get the orders they needed to survive? She remembered how her father cherished his buyers, traded on his long-standing relationships with them. It was bad enough without Simon, but without Beattie's expertise and contacts, it would be hopeless.

Hopeless. But if Beattie was turning away orders, what point in keeping him? She must find a way to tell him she knew what he was up to. And she'd check the order book, make sure they were not dwindling away. What had Peggy said, about business slackening off after Simon died? They couldn't lay everything at Beattie's door.

Anna stared down at the pages of figures which made no sense now. She pushed the heavy ledgers aside and leaned her elbows on the desk, cupping her chin in her hands. Sister Godric had always said she wasn't a natural accountant. She found herself thinking about the woman who had taught her bookkeeping, the depositrix of the order. Sister Godric's eyes were failing and she needed help to make out the figures which jumped even with the aid of a magnifying glass. But she required no assistance to work them out, doing everything mentally at top speed. You weren't supposed to chat about yourself, not to discuss your background, but Anna learned that Sister Godric had been a financial director of the John Lewis Partnership until, in her late forties, she had decided to become a nun.

'Maybe,' she had once remarked to Anna – for they had permission to talk when they worked on accounts – 'maybe I was sent to sort out the appalling muddle my predecessor got us into.' It seemed extraordinary to Anna that enclosed nuns were not regarded as charities for the purposes of income tax. The contemplatives with their struggling cottage industries laboured under the same massive burden of corporation tax as giant companies. 'In this modern age,' Sister Godric had observed, 'saying prayers is not considered a charitable act.'

Anna thought of the elderly nun with affection: her quick mind and quirky eccentricities; the way she insisted on sitting in the dark when she was alone. 'Why should I keep lights on, my dear, when I can scarcely see? I'd sooner save the money. Never take what you don't need.'

She pulled the heavy sheaf of the current accounts across the desk and ran a pencil down the list of outgoings. Under 'Plant' she stopped at the huge monthly figure they now paid out for the new Swiss fancy-spinner Simon acquired at the beginning of the year. What on earth had possessed him to buy that machine? She knew the answer, of course: it must have looked like the future to him, with its infinite capacity for producing complex yarns. She thought with distaste of the fancy finishes they turned out now, the floating ends that must prickle the wearer, the lurex mixes, the slubs. She found them brash and fussy: hard to believe they were what people wanted. She supposed Simon had known what he was doing, had based his decision on market research of some kind.

Her taste was for natural fibres, the simplicity only money and taste could buy. The yarns she preferred would be more expensive, certainly. The finest wools, soft dyes. But timeless, classic. And distinctive. Anyone buying or wearing them anywhere in the world would know they were Yorkshire-made.

Anna stared down at the white sheets of accounts and saw behind her eyes swathes of colour and texture. Nightingale Mill had always produced fine yarns, back in the old days before fashion changed so fast: she remembered the heavy wood and metal machinery that had stood up in the workroom in her grandfather's day, and her father's. Simon had replaced much of it with ugly modern equipment, putting them into debt for novelty's sake. But what they'd done once, they could surely do again.

She rubbed the crown of her head with the unconscious gesture of irritation that had become a habit over the last months. And the idea that had been growing somewhere at the back of her mind dropped like Newton's apple. *Never take what you don't need*.

She sipped her coffee: it had gone cold. She considered making some more, but instead went in search of Peter Hallam.

She found him in the enclosed yard sitting cross-legged on the vast wood table where the packers worked, in a patch of sunshine from a skylight. He was bundled into an anorak and reading a paperback about dolphins with such absorption he didn't hear her till she spoke his name. When he looked up, she liked the way he managed to convey good feeling without actually smiling – something to do with his expressive eyes. They were an astonishing colour in the sun, green flecked with brown and gold . . . she caught herself. Stop that. And anyway, he was years younger than her, twenty-seven, he'd said. He waited till she reached him, then held out a neatly packed plastic box.

'Fancy a buttie? Beansprouts.'

'That's kind of you. But I've eaten.' She inspected the box. 'Yours look nicer, though.'

'Maybe another time.' He sounded as if he meant it. He closed the book and placed it neatly on top of his canvas bag. He gave her his absolute attention, she felt it as surely as if he'd switched on a lamp, and for a second it made her falter, like a horse before a daunting jump. Or an uncertain woman before a desirable man. 'Is there something I can do for you?'

'Hope so.' She pulled herself together. 'D'you know what happened to the old flyer-spinner my brother replaced?'

9

The cellars were probably older than the mill itself. Dimly lit and low, they stretched back into darkness. Anna was grateful for the heavy folds of her habit and thrust her hands into her sleeves against the stony chill. Her father would never let them come down here as youngsters, after Simon had sneaked in once and gashed his leg on an old wicker skip. Being here even now made her feel anxious.

'It's a long time since anyone was down. Most of the bulbs've gone.' Hal pressed another switch. 'I'll get some new ones later.' He dug in the pockets of his anorak, bringing out peanuts in their shells, a Swiss army knife. She noticed two badges on his sweater. One read SAVE THE WHALE, the other HANDS OFF OUR CHANNEL.

'You wear your social conscience on your sleeve.' She regretted the words immediately; they were too personal, implied criticism. Convent training made light conversation almost impossibly difficult for her: she didn't know how to be casual.

To her relief he didn't seem to mind, but replied seriously, 'If you care about things, you should speak out. Apathy kills as effectively as aggression, you think about it.' He finally produced a torch. 'I'll get you some Greenpeace badges if you like,' he offered. 'They'd brighten up that grey thing you wear. If you don't mind my saying so,' he added hastily.

'Greenpeace?'

'Oh, yeah, I forgot. Tell you sometime.' He was poking around against a side wall, shining the thin beam under lumpy tarpaulins. He gave a grunt of triumph. 'Found it.' She helped him pull back the coverings from the frame of the flyer-spinner. It was tilted at a precarious angle against the wall, too high to stand upright in the low space, its twenty-foot length cumbersome and top heavy. Hal rubbed his hand across the worn wood affectionately.

'Hall & Shell, Keighley, 1926,' he read off the tarnished brass plate screwed onto it. 'Lovely.'

Anna was working her way along the doffer frame, which for sixty years had twisted the raw yarn and spun it on two banks of bobbins, narrow at the bottom, wider ones at the top.

'Where are the bobbins?' It came out as a wail. She knew they would be irreplaceable. Hal frowned.

'Thought we left 'em on . . . half a mo.' He rooted round again under the tarpaulins and uncovered three waist-high skips. He held up a stubby wood bobbin bound with dull metal. 'The big ones are here as well.'

'There should be a hundred and sixty.'

He laughed. 'Right. How'd you know that?'

'I used to count them when I was little. I'd spend hours watching them. I liked the noise.' She ran a finger along the dark wood, inspected it, 'It's dusty even under the covers. Has anything rusted, can you see?'

'Nothing drastic. Needs a bit of work. But nothing's split or cracked. You'd get another century out of this baby.' He looked puzzled. 'But it doesn't matter, does it? Unless you're planning to give it to the Industrial Museum down Moorside. And I think they've got one of these.'

'Hal.' She had not used his nickname before and it made her self-conscious. 'We could get this back upstairs, back in the workroom, couldn't we?'

He stared at her.

'There's no room, not with that new thing Mr Simon brought in.' He wrinkled his face in distaste. 'Fancy-spinning isn't my bag. Don't like the yarns they produce, too elaborate and dressy, with all those slubs and knots and extra bits hanging off 'em. Must have cost a packet, too.'

'Seventy thousand pounds.'

He whistled. 'Strewth.' He caught her expression. 'Sorry. But what a price. I knew they were expensive, but I'd no idea it was in that range. We've never even used it to capacity, it's a crime at that price.' He peered at her in the poor light. 'What's all this about, anyway? Why do you want the flyer-spinner back upstairs?'

'Just tell me first about this . . .' she gestured towards the frame. 'What it does best.'

'Well, it's slower in production than the fancy-spinner upstairs. We used to deal in small amounts – it takes a hundred and fifty kilos to cover this frame, the big new one take five hundred. We're producing almost entirely artificial materials now, not quality stuff. You can see that for yourself.'

Anna nodded, thinking of the banks of brightly coloured fibres waiting to go on the reeler, the harsh colours, the thin texture.

'I hate it, the colours are awful. I like the crisp feel of wool.'

'Well, it's market forces, isn't it? And that's where the demand is.'

She sighed. 'I suppose.' She rubbed a bobbin between her palms. The polished wood warmed, left a faint film of wool grease on her skin. She sniffed the milky smell with pleasure.

'If we got rid of the fancy-spinner – I don't know, maybe it's possible – could we revert to producing real yarns again?'

'Sure.' He patted the wood. 'This old thing's really better for producing hand-knitting wool.'

'I mean, would the other machinery do it?'

'The new twister wouldn't work, but we've got the old one down here too, somewhere. The Italian one copes with the fancy-spinning – you know, twists the threads in the opposite direction to which it's being spun so it holds tight. You don't need such an elaborate one for straightforward yarns.' He paused. 'But you'd have to find new markets. Alexanders are only interested in selling cheap yarns. If we go back to producing good quality wools, they're going to cost more. I don't know as people are willing to pay, these days.'

'I've thought about that.' Anna hesitated. Years of enforced silence, of learning to stifle comment, not to put herself forward, not to have opinions, made it hard now to express herself. As if sensing unease, Hal turned away and started to rub dust from the flyer-spinner. It was to his back she said, cautiously, 'I – that is, we – produce knitting wools at the convent.' He rubbed more slowly as he listened. 'We've a small flock of Beulah Speckled-face, and we started spinning the wool. Then I found we could achieve marvellous colours using natural dyes – and people were mad about them.' Her voice lifted with enthusiasm and Hal turn to watch her. 'We sold them to a shop in Welshpool and after a couple of months the demand was so great we just couldn't supply enough. They put the price up but still it sold. So people *do* want good quality wools.'

'Sounds like.' He nodded at her. 'That's impressive. And you reckon you could find buyers for that kind of product yourself?'

'I'd need help. But I know where to find that. And I think once we've got going, demand will grow the way it did in Welshpool.'

'Ha! shook his head. 'I'm still miles behind you. We've got all the new equipment, the mill's geared up to synthetics. We can't just go back.'

Still holding the bobbin like a talisman, Anna moved towards the steps. She turned at the bottom and gave him a wide smile.

'Do what?' Stan Beattie croaked and cleared his throat loudly to give himself time to think. 'You must be joking.'

Out of sight inside her wide sleeves, Anna held her thumbs. It was a struggle to keep her voice innocent.

'But you suggested it, Mr Beattie. You said, the way things were, we could send that fancy-spinner back. I thought about it, and you're right. We don't need it. Let's send it back and bring the old one out of the cellar. There's nothing wrong with it. And we'd save a great deal of money.'

He sniffed, suspicious. 'Who told you? Oh, aye, that young – '

'I asked,' she interrupted hastily, 'I asked Peter Hallam. It was my idea.' She didn't want to make trouble for the overlooker.

Beattie made an obvious effort. 'Look, Miss Anna, no offence but you don't know what you're talking about. We can't produce the fancy yarns Alexanders want on the old flyer-spinner and that's all there is to it.'

'But Alexanders are taking the bulk of our production and making us wait for payment.' She paused. Don't argue, just state facts. 'We'll go under if we go on trading this way.'

'We have to produce what the customers want. The old machine won't do all this.' He picked up sample balls from his desk and tossed them over to her. One had silvery loops feathering off the yarn at intervals, the other was multi-coloured and sparkled with metallic threads. Anna handled them with no pleasure.

'If this is what our customers like, maybe we'll have to find new customers. I've got ideas about that, too. But the main thing is to get that debt off our backs.'

He gave a theatrical sigh. 'You're living in a fool's paradise. The suppliers'll not take it back. Or if they do they'll give us a pittance.'

'I telephoned the textile agents, Batsons, yesterday. They'll send someone round to assess its condition. It's hardly been used, as you said.' She smiled, made her voice deliberately cajoling. Like she did with the children, she thought to herself. 'Let's see what they say. Things couldn't be much worse.'

Beattie took a swallow of the coffee she had brought into the office. 'It's muddled thinking. If we get a big order, we'll not be able to fulfil it.'

She was ready for that. 'Half a dozen of those looms upstairs – the ones my father put in – do top grade work. I remember when thing were busy, he used to put the mill on double time, work through the night.'

He snorted. 'We can't do that now, have you any idea what our wages bill would be?'

Peggy had come in and stood listening. 'I've worked it out, Stan. We could do an order the size of the last one for Alexanders in two weeks, and if we didn't have the debt for the fancy-spinner we're still better off.'

Beattie got to his feet, giving his chair an irritated push. 'An order for what, I'd like to know? We'll have no capacity to produce the fancy yarns. And our orders for traditional ones have fallen right off.'

Anna forced herself to look him straight in the eye though her stomach churned with nervousness. 'But that's due to something other than market forces. Isn't it, Mr Beattie?' There was a subtle change in his truculent expression, his face darkened perceptibly. 'And that reminds me,' she added, her tone spiked with meaning, 'we must try to keep our phone bill down this quarter. Especially if things are as bad as you say.'

He was very still as he absorbed the implication of her words. She was dropping the glittering balls of wool from hand to hand to hide the fact they were shaking, and he watched as if mesmerised. Peggy, sensing but not understanding the tension in the room, looked from one to the other.

When Anna was sure he understood he had been overheard in Peggy's office, she flipped the fancy yarns back on his desk with a dismissive gesture. 'But we've all the Aran upstairs waiting to be spun for the Scandinavian order. That'll take near two weeks. It'll give us time to think.' she added diplomatically, 'Perhaps you'll see Batsons with me.'

Beattie swung his lowered head from one woman to the other. Anna felt a flash of near-sympathy: he looked like a bullock cornered in a farmyard.

'I'm too busy. Do what you like, ruin the business your father built up here, makes no odds to me. I know what I think: you've lost your effin' marbles.' He pulled his mackintosh off the coatstand and burst through the door, letting it bang behind him. Anna turned to Peggy with an expression of comical dismay and let out a long sigh of relief.

'I've never done anything remotely like that before.'

'A giant step for womankind.' Peggy gave two slow claps.

'A giant step for me, at any rate.' She drew a deep breath. 'Would you call Batsons for me?' She was apologetic. 'I still feel strange using the phone.'

'No need.' Peggy acknowledged Anna's look of surprise. 'I already fixed for them to come this afternoon. I knew you were set on it.'

'But what if Beattie had said no?'

Peggy picked up a folder from his desk, dropped the copy of the *Star* which lay beneath into the waste-bin with fastidious fingers.

'No chance. Poor bloke doesn't know what hit him.'

When Anna finished the invoices at four o'clock she looked at the telephone on her desk. It was ridiculous that she still used it only when someone else dialled: she'd spoken to Reverend Mother last night, and Lynn had got the number for her, as if she were incapable. She dialled the Heaton number to tell Lynn she would be late.

Peggy left early on Fridays and the offices were empty as she went through to the mill. The cellars were colder than she'd remembered, the flashlight she had bought from Simon's garage casting sharp shadows on the lumpy walls, making a monstrous horned shape of her head-dress. She pulled the tarpaulins off the old gill-box and the wicker baskets of bobbins. She checked carefully, not wanting to find too late they were warped or missing.

She'd brought a soft cloth with her and she started to rub the wood of the flyer-spinner, worn sleek by years of use. It was more than just a piece of industrial machinery. Her grandfather had bought it when her father was ten-years-old, and he had watched as an awe-struck child, just as she had done: singing clatter, streeling threads. In a few days, it would be hauled up the outside of the mill, back into the workroom where it belonged.

In her grandfather's day, and her father's, it had spun high-quality wool from Clun Forest sheep; lustre yarns from the Bluefaced Leicester, the Derbyshire Gritstone. By the time she was fifteen, under her father's tuition, she had been able to identify many of the fleeces by their look and feel: she'd always been far more interested that her brother. Looking back it was difficult for her to decide whether her interest had stemmed just from her desire to please her father, or from some deeper pleasure in an ancient craft. But as she grew older she went less often to the mill, unwilling to have her friends learn of this eccentric enthusiasm.

She had forgotten how much she liked the whole process of spinning yarn, from scouring the fleece to free it of grease and dirt, extracting seeds and burrs, through the carding to produce thin ropes of wool, and finally the spinning process to draw it out and twist it into yarn. Only when the convent had been presented with half a dozen mountain sheep had she started to apply what she knew. She had carried out all the processes herself, had even helped with the shearing of the thick, high-quality fleece. She had dyed with anything she found – chysanthemums, daffodils, walnuts, berries and lichens, producing subtle and unusual colours.

Ann stopped her polishing and stood lost in thought. Her wool had been a huge success. Clover Connection had wanted more than she could produce. Maybe other people would be as enthusiastic. But the problem with organic colour, as she well knew, was dyeing large quantities and getting the colour match exact each time: she'd found shades varied noticeably.

A professional dyer would know what she did not – how to stabilise colours, which ingredients to add.

She shivered and noticed how silent it was in the same moment: how long had she been down here? Leaving the looms uncovered she turned off her torch and hurried up the steps. When she emerged into the inner packers' yard it was pitch dark and she thought there'd been a power cut. But the stillness told her the building was deserted. It must be very late. She slid back the wooden door to the offices. Darkness here too, and her torch showed seven thirty-five on the wooden clock her grandfather had installed, with the Summers' name engraved on the face.

Everyone must have thought she went home early. That would teach her to say what she was doing. It was one thing not to speak in the convent, another altogether in the world. She was an idiot. The realisation hit her that she was probably locked in and there was no nightwatchman. The corridors suddenly looked very high in the thin beams of the torch, empty offices gaping black on either side. Nightingale Mill was isolated. And closed up until Monday. Sweat prickled under her tight headband.

She pulled herself together. The telephone: anyone else would have thought of it straight away. She was in the doorway of Peggy's office, shining her torch to find the light switch, when she saw the row of hooks hung with labelled keys. Front offices, safe . . . Relieved, she picked out the side-door key and turned to go.

Behind her, where Peggy's desk stood in shadow, something moved. Anna hardly breathed. Imagination, she scolded herself, but she couldn't look round. There was a rapid scrabbling, a sharp crash and this time she whirled, holding the torch in front of her. And seeing the overturned milk bottle, the lean black cat jumping down, purring with enthusiasm at the sight of company. It pressed against her leg and she bent to fondle the round skull under warm fur, feeling the reassuring rumble through her fingertips.

She left it there. It supplemented its diet with mice, roaming from office to mill through a cat-flap that had served generations before it. Humming to herself, without bothering about the lights, she went to the side door, was actually inserting the key in the lock when she heard a groan of pain.

This time, there was no mistake. Her fingers went to the rosary at her waist. Holy Mary, Mother of God . . . there it was again. A man's voice. Someone was hurt, had broken in and injured himself.

Anna held the key in the lock, turned it carefully, lifted the latch. She would fetch the police. Before she had the door open the voice spoke, indistinctly as if to himself, and she recognised it as Stan Beattie. He must have been taken ill, a heart attack . . . Without giving herself time to think, not pausing to switch on a light, using her torch, she hurried towards his office.

It was separate from the others, and that must be why she hadn't noticed the light earlier. Years of training made her silent, she didn't call out to him, her footsteps were soundless in soft leather sandals. She opened the door, prepared to see him lying on the floor, clutching a broken limb, needing help.

A desk lamp on a flexible stem had been bent so there was only a circular stain of light on Simon's desk. Beyond its glow, in semi-darkness, Stan Beattie slumped on a low armchair in a corner, used for visitors' coats and briefcases. Head thrown back on the brown leatherette, he was pleading in a monotone, his words thick and blurred, speaking nonsense.

'Oh yes, oh yes, take it, take it all, you love it you little slut . . .'

Dear God, what was happening to him? She could make nothing of the shapes and sounds in front of her. Standing in the doorway as if turned to stone, one hand still on the handle, Anna realised that she was looking at two people, not one. A woman with dark hair knelt between the clamp of Beattie's thighs. Above a tight skirt she was naked, her pale breasts hanging loose. The soles of her high-heeled shoes were towards Anna, small white price tags still stuck to the insteps. The woman's head was in Beattie's lap, his hand holding her down, pressing her face into his crotch. The other hand was at the woman's left breast, pulling at her nipple. In the same instant Anna saw this she realised his trousers were undone, under-pants pushed away so that the woman's long hair brushed his bare flesh.

Anna must have gasped because Beattie opened his eyes. He had surely seen her, he looked straight at her, but without recognition. He stared wildly, his face tense, the muscles of his jaws clenched in a grimace.

'*Now*,' he grunted. 'Now now *now*.'

The room was boiling hot and smelled of cigarettes and Beattie's over-sweet cologne. And something else, something unfamiliar, musky, that caught in her throat. She stumbled back, one hand shielding her eyes. Too late to block out the sight of dishevelled clothing, unbuckled belt, puckered white skin and straggles of pubic hair.

Anna was in the corridor, at the side-door, the key stiff, wrenching open the door, leaving it wide, holding up her cumbersome habit as she ran through the passageway, hitting her arm against the wall in her haste, slipping on the cobbles in the yard, fumbling in her wide underskirt for the pocket, the car-key, jabbing it at the lock, missing because she couldn't see, breath locked tight in her chest. Somehow she got the door open and struggled into the driving seat, blast her long skirt, stabbing with the key again for the ignition, the engine cold. Where was the choke? Releasing the handbrake, using gears all wrong. The car jerked down the street, jerked the way Stan Beattie had in spasm back there, body tensing, muscles twitching.

Almost at the bottom of Nightingale Street, outside what used to be an off-licence but was now Khan Food Stores, Prop. A. A. Shan, a dark-skinned man waved at her, yelling something and pointing. She'd turned into Berry Street before it dawned on her that she hadn't switched on her lights. She pulled in beside the boarded up fish and chip shop, turned off the engine and opened her door just in time. She retched violently, body heaving, throat hurting, stomach contracting. She hadn't eaten for hours and brought up nothing but a slither of mucus, bitter taste of iron.

She felt better then, wiped her lips on one of the Babywipes Lynn kept in the car for the boys and pulled the door shut. Then she held onto the steering wheel and rested her head on the back of her hands.

She should never have left the convent. The old nuns were right: the world was dangerous, unknowable, full of hazard. She had shut it out when she entered – it was madness now to think she could deal with it. Ignorance, not innocence, had protected her so far. She started to murmur a prayer but the words dried and crumbled away. She couldn't use prayer at a time like this, it wasn't an amulet to guard against evil.

She remembered the rules of the order, commanding that the eyes should be for the most part cast down, care being taken lest they wander from side to side. Men should not be looked at indiscreetly. Men were dangerous.

The nuns used to joke about that, for apart from occasional visits from relatives, men were about as common in the convent as polar bears. The taciturn priest who came up to the convent from the village church daily for Mass and to hear Confession had once or twice entered the visitors' parlour. Old Mr Dunbabbin talked to his plants in preference to people. The British Telecom engineer called in to Reverend Mother's telephone was the only stranger who'd passed beyond the enclosure doors. They never even needed a plumber: Sister Peter tackled blocked drains and replaced downpipes with the best of them.

Two young Pakistani women pattered past the car, their flimsy silks incongruous under bulky anoraks, stiletto heels emerging from clinging trousers. They turned to stare, gazelle eyes emphasised by kohl. Anna heard the click of silver bracelets as they pulled their saris round their faces and realised that in her cap and veil, she looked at first glance like one of them.

She couldn't sit here any longer. She checked her lights this time, glanced in her rear mirror and drove slowly home.

In bed that night she couldn't sleep. If she shut her eyes she saw it all again, the whole sordid sweaty scene. How could he, in Simon's office, how could that woman, whoever she was, do such things? Repulsive. She recalled the woman's bare breast, the dark pointed nipple. No, pathetic. In the end she switched on Jamie's bedside light and lay staring into the bright interior with its innocent animals.

They'd been like animals. No, worse. The sheep mounting each other were only behaving naturally, while Stan Beattie and that unknown woman had been engaged in an obscene act. She would never be able to speak to him again.

She scolded herself. You'll have to act on Monday exactly as you did before. We are all sinners. God alone can judge.

She pressed the backs of her hands over her eyes so fiercely she saw patterns of red and yellow on her closed lids. If only she hadn't seen them. What you don't know won't hurt you. But she did know.

That was what custody of the eyes was all about. In the old days, in her order, it had been a minor breach of the rule to raise the eyes unnecessarily even for a moment in the choir or refectory, to avoid distracting the thoughts from God.

It was hard to keep custody of the eyes in Bradford. During the weeks in Lynn's house, Anna had avoided watching television. She'd never liked it much anyway and she had little free time, so it wasn't difficult to leave the room quietly when it was turned on. Occasionally, like the time she'd seen the African famine on the news, she had been drawn to watch: she was bound to take that grief into herself. But more often she caught glimpses of overdressed women, plump chatshow hosts, nervous couples grasping each other's hands as they gazed at freezers, sets of glasses, lawnmowers. She didn't like the bursts of artificial laughter, the endless ads the children chanted, the blasts of music. Careful as she was, she'd still seen people embracing half-naked, sometimes in bed, had learned that such situations could apparently occur in any programme. They were as likely on a comedy show in the early evening as on a thriller, apparently as acceptable as shots of eating or smoking.

Perhaps she was more sensitive now, made vulnerable by unfamiliarity, but she couldn't recall such blatancy when she was in the world. There'd been plenty to shock. All the fuss about Brando in *Last Tango in Paris*, she'd had to promise her parents she wouldn't see it. And the gyrations of pop stars had been explicit even to her, the grinding hips and coital moans. There'd even been a record banned by the BBC they'd played in the lunch hour at school, a dozen of them crowded round the old pick-up gramophone kept in the gym. She could smell the odour of adolescent bodies, rope and plimsolls, clearly recall her own bewildered response to Jane Birkin breathily exhaling. 'MMMmmmmmmm, je t'aime . . . je t'aime . . .' When Mr McColl demanded to know where they'd all been, they'd been able to say truthfully, 'Doing our French.'

Those things had all been in their compartments, out of the way. They didn't intrude, force themselves on you. A dirty little thrill at lunchtime was one thing. She had come back to find that everywhere, at every turning, she was confronted by an emphasis on the crudely physical. She couldn't shut out the images that thrust themselves at her as she drove each day through the city. A woman's leg in sheer black nylon, a man's hand caressing her thigh, fiteen-foot high on a hoarding. A huge photograph of a youth naked except for a pair of briefs patterned in stars and stripes taking up the entire window: it had been a week before she recognised a promotion for jeans.

Anna had a headache. She'd been having them for years, the result of constant pressure where the serré-tête pressed hard on the crown. She even dreamt she was begging permission to remove the cap and veil but was always refused: she would wake with a lump in her throat and the familiar ache.

She rubbed a hand across the top of her head, digging her fingers hard into the skin, moving the scalp. She'd neglected to put on her bonnet last night. No, she'd chosen not to wear it. Her hand slowed. Freedom of choice. She'd surrendered that right thirteen years ago. For all that time she had submitted. To timetables, regulations, the Rule, the mother prioress.

Anna felt like a traveller in a strange country. In the convent she had known what each day, each hour, would bring. Her life was planned and pre-ordained. This time, this task. Eight times a day, chapel for prayer. Three times a day, the refectory. Even meals were the same on the same day of each week: nut rissoles on Wednesdays, cheese dreams on Thursdays, baked fish on Fridays. You ate, like it or not, hungry or not.

So she never had to think. It was the same in the encapsulated space of her cell, where she knew the length of reach needed to perform the smallest task. At night, once Great Silence had descended on the house, they were not allowed to use electric light, undressing and washing, cleaning their teeth, in the dark.

She opened her eyes and looked round the bright little room. A row of button-eyed creatures sat on a low shelf above the bed: elephants and pandas, a grubby Snoopy leaning against a mouse in velvet trousers. A set of highly-coloured prints showed more elephants sitting in bath-tubs scrubbing themselves with loofahs held in their trunks, doing press-ups in jogging suits with large E's on the chest. Her head-dress, perched on top of a pine cupboard, veil falling almost to the ground, looked like something from another world.

Anna had thought for a long time it was the sameness of the convent days she hated. When she had allowed herself to acknowledge it, her antipathy to the over-regulated existence increased a thousand-fold. She had pined for freedom from rules, from the rigid timetable.

She reached out to switch off the lamp. Soft darkness dulled the pain at the crown of her head, and she felt the muscles of her neck and jaw slacken in relief. How could she have failed to anticipate that freedom would itself bring problems? Like a newly released prisoner she had been high on it, filled with wild elation. The scene she witnessed this evening had brought an unexpected fear, and despite herself she began to yearn for what she had thought she hated.

The captive longing for her bonds.

10

Cross hog extra fine. Scotch locks, Lincoln and lustre. Welsh steel. Shafty and pick tegs. Swaledale daggings.

Anna flipped through the catalogue of British Wool Sale No 43 and tried to control her nervousness. The wool warehouse at Oak Mills in Clayton, fifteen minutes from the city centre, was high and bare as an aircraft hangar. Bales of wool were piled against the walls on every side. In the centre hundreds of untreated fleeces were strewn in roped-off pens, graded into types and each lot numbered. The air was freezing in here, the oily animal smell of sheep strong enough to taste.

It was late Tuesday afternoon, the last opportunity to examine the lots before the formal auction started in the adjoining saleroom early in the morning. Even with Hal beside her – Peggy had suggested he accompany her – she was intimidated by the scale of what she had to do here.

'Eh up!' An overalled driver guided a forklift truck into position beside them, scooped up a bale of wool wrapped in black stamped sacking and drove off. Glancing down, Anna found her dark grey skirt was already covered with floating filaments of wool. Hal followed her eyes.

'That'll be worse before we're done. Let's go over and have a closer look.' As they approached the fleeces he added, 'Never seen so much wool in one place.' He stroked a hand over one. 'Welsh Rad,' he read off the description and added, 'nice for tweeds.'

She was amused. 'I didn't know you were an expert. I thought machinery was your line.'

'I'm not,' he said hastily, 'not at all. When I was a kid, a sheep was something that produced our Sunday lunch complete with mint sauce and roast potatoes.'

'What did your father do?' Back in the convent, personal questions weren't permitted and it was an effort to ask. But she genuinely wanted to know, and he evidently didn't mind.

'Bus driver for thirty years and the rest. He's an inspector now but he says it's not the same. And Mum worked in a school canteen. I was a real little Yorkshire tyke, my horizon stopped at the chip shop and Woolworths.' He pulled his ear reflectively and she registered it as an oddly appealing, unconscious gesture of a young boy.

Anna smiled at him. 'Unlikely start for a conservationist and friend of the earth.'

'Not really.' She liked the way he treated even flippant remarks carefully. 'I was twelve-years-old when I saw my first kestrel: it was nesting in Leeds Town Hall, It floated round the dome like a creature from another world and I was so excited . . .' He hesitated, as if wondering whether to trust her with a secret 'I nearly threw up. After that, I used to go a shilling busride every Sunday, even when it was pissing down, out to where there's just bracken and crags and heather and becks.' His voice was quick with enthusiasm, he was oblivious to everything but the vision he was describing to her. 'I found the same wind blowing crushed Coke cans along our street howled round rocks up on Ilkley Moor. And the streams full of trout flowing through the Dales were the source of the mucky river I saw on my way to school, covered in soap scum from cleaning wool.' He stopped short. 'Get me. David Bellamy, eat your heart out. We'd best get started.'

Anna fished in the deep front pocket of her habit for a pen and folded the catalogue open. 'I used to come to viewing days with Dad. He'd never take me to the auctions though. In those days, they were held in the old Wool Exchange. Let's hope I haven't forgotten everything he taught me.'

'It's like riding a bicycle.' She caught his grin. 'Once you can do it, you always know how.'

'Wish I had your confidence.' She bent and picked up a strand of fleece, pulled so that the fibres separated. She looked at the lustre, the colour. Sight and touch, her father used to say, sight and touch. She rubbed the fibres between her fingers, felt the roughness of straw or grass in the long hairs: if the animals had been housed during the winter and feedracks placed too high, vegetable matter dropped into the fleece.

She moved on to the Devon Longwool, and beside her Hal said, 'That's discoloured.'

'You get a pink tinge from the soils in some places. Berwickshire, I think, Devon, Brecon . . .' she turned to look at him. 'You're teasing me.' Ridiculously, she knew she was blushing under the tight headband. Damn. But Hal's voice was serious.

'I'd not do that to you. Not when you're trying so hard.'

The look she gave him was full of gratitude. 'Sorry. I'm probably over-sensitive. I'm finding this more difficult than I'd imagined.'

'It must be really hard for you, not being used to this kind of thing.' He rubbed the toe of his sneaker against the edge of a woolbale. 'I probably shouldn't be saying this, but it's a pretty expensive business, buying at auction. Stan Beattie reckons you should be sticking with the artificial fibres and the wool that came in as outside orders. That would be the way to keep costs down.'

'It'd hold us up for months. There's not another auction for eight weeks. In that time, we can have what we buy tomorrow finished and sold. It's cost us – but I'm hoping we'll make a real profit if we get it right. More important, it should set the mill on a new road.'

'And,' he finished for her, 'Stan Beattie doesn't particularly want that.'

She flashed him a quick glance, but she knew she could rely on his discretion. 'You said it.' She turned back to the fleece. 'It'd do if we intend to use strong shades.'

'You sound a bit doubtful.'

'I want deep blues and reds – you know, like cardinals'

robes.' She hesitated, uncertain what his reaction would be. 'I don't want to use chemical colours.'

He was puzzled. 'What other kinds are there?'

'Natural dyes. From berries and lichens and things. I've made beautiful yarn at the convent.' Her voice lifted with enthusiasm. 'Elderberry leaves boiled with copper sulphate as a mordant for soft greens. Blackberries with tin and vinegar for purply-pinks. I grew woad for the blues, fantastic shades. Red's more difficult, I'll have to buy cochineal beetles . . .'

'Hold on, hold on.' Hal was shaking his head. 'You have to, like, crush and strain the plants, before you can use them?'

'Sure. I used a pestle and mortar, but for larger amounts . . .' She faltered. 'Well, I can always get hold of some simple machinery.'

'Probably,' he agreed. 'But you'll need tons of fruit and flowers or whatever. I don't know how much wool you produced, but with all respect, it wasn't commercial quantities.' When she nodded reluctantly he added, 'And anyway, who gives a cuss if you've gone to that kind of trouble to get a colour? The woman who buys your wool just wants to match up her skirt, she won't pay out good money for your hand-picked blackberries.'

Anna was furious. 'Of course she will! People want quality, something different. You're making judgements before you've even seen what can be done and how on earth can I achieve anything if even you won't consider what I'm trying to –'

'OK, OK.' It was only when he tried to hush her, holding his hands palm out in a placating gesture, that she realised how loudly she was speaking. 'Don't get so mad, I'm not beating up your gran.'

Anna remembered where she was before she remembered who she was, and lowered her voice. 'I tell you, demand for my wool . . .' she stopped, amended that, 'for our wool in Welshpool was so great we couldn't supply enough. And that was expensive. They paid for the unusual colours, because they knew the finished garment they knitted would be unique.' She struggled to convince him. 'Hal, I know I can do it.' She glowed up at him. 'Up on the moors, that's where we'll find the berries and mosses we need.' She saw the moors as a magic place, remembering them from years before, rich with promise.

Hal said, hesitant, 'Honestly, I think you're being over-optimistic.'

She seized on his uncertainty. 'No, it'll be great. If you'll come with me, we'll take sacks and collect what we need. Maybe we'll take a couple of trips, but that's no problem. You will, won't you?' She appealed to him, her face alive with eagerness. Hal smiled back, unable to resist.

'Sure. Whatever you say. But you'd better buy the wool first.' He checked the number of the lot Anna had fingered. 'What'll this go for?'

She blew out a long breath of exasperation at her own ignorance. 'No idea.'

'I thought Stan Beattie was going to come with you.' He said it simply, without guile.

'He's developed a bad cold this morning.' The pause was explicit. 'I said he must be sure to get better by tomorrow. I think he's probably embarrassed to be seen with me.'

'More fool him.' There was no rancour in his voice. Anna glanced round at the half-empty building, the small groups of men deep in discussion over the fleeces, conscious that eyes slid away as she did so. She turned back to Hal.

'We're attracting more attention than I care for. I daren't think what it'll be like at the auction tomorrow. I'm beginning to feel as if I'm in fancy dress.'

He opened his coat. 'You and me both.' She could have hugged him. It was an ancient black cashmere, the sort of garment her grandfather used to wear, with wide lapels edged in velvet and a classic stylishness. She and Lynn had spent a lot of time lately going through quality fashion magazines for ideas, and she recognised that Hal would not look out of place in any European city. Beneath the coat he had baggy black trousers and a voluminous white T-shirt proclaiming NICARA-GUA MUST SURVIVE in heavy black letters. 'I reckon we make a

perfect pair. And you let tomorrow take care of itself. Now
. . .' He led the way across to the next aisle. 'What d'you
reckon to Devon lamb No 3?'

'Lot 409 then, gentlemen. Fine Radnor lamb, twenty-four
bales.'

The auctioneer's voice was crisp with authority. He domi-
nated the room from his raised dais, tanned and lean in well-
cut worsted. 'Do I have fourteen? Twelve? Ten? Seven is bid,
eight I can take.' He paused. 'To Sutcliffe & Street then.' The
gavel came down and a solid man two rows from the front shot
his cuffs with evident satisfaction. The auctioneer drank from
a glass of water and one of the two men seated beside him
made a note.

'Lot 410. Two bales. At two pence, two and a half, three
pence, three and a half . . .' He glanced down at the rows of
men seated before him in the long, modern room. Anna
secretly thought they were like overgrown schoolboys at their
slanted wooden desks. On the walls hung photographs of the
Yorkshire Dales, a huge wool appliqué picture of hills and
fields full of sheep. There were shouts from all over the room:
'Four!' 'Five!'

'I'm going to sell this one at a hundred ninety-five pence,
I'm selling to Waterhouse . . . Lot 412 now, Mule lamb, three
bales. fifty is bid, one, two, three, four, five – one hundred
fifty-five I'm selling at, one hundred fifty-five.'

Anna was in the same row as Stan Beattie, though she'd left
two chairs empty before she sat down. They had studiously
avoided being alone together since the night last week when
she had seen him in Simon's office with that woman. Neither
had referred to it but they would not forget. It festered between
them, poisoning their already difficult and edgy relationship.
Her disquiet and his enmity were clear as balloon captions
above characters in a cartoon strip.

This morning, Beattie had kept her waiting outside the
auction room, arriving late and red-faced from the efffort of
hurrying up the stairs. Seeing her patiently standing in the

foyer, trying to ignore the other buyers' curious glances at her habit, he'd given her a belligerent glare: her apparent passivity brought out the bully in him. He had cut short her attempts to point out in the catalogue the marked lots she wanted him to buy and swaggered before her into the auction room.

That had made it even harder for her, walking in alone. She knew she looked composed, her hands slipped in her sleeves, back straight. But a tiny nerve ticked frantically in her temple at the way heads turned and voices dropped as the buyers became conscious of her presence. She felt the by now familiar blend of irritation and amusement as the auctioneer actually stopped talking to his colleague on the dais and watched her approach: hadn't any of these people seen a nun before?

Now Anna leant across the two chairs between them and murmured, 'I'd like the next one, will you bid.'

Stan Beattie shifted and she caught the chemical smell of cheap cologne. 'That'll go too high for us. I've told you, we can't go ahead with this.' He was whispering, tense with annoyance. 'You don't know what you're asking. You shouldn't be here at all by rights. It's like I said, there's no women come to auction. You're showing me up.'

Anna said nothing. They'd been through all this, she and Peggy arguing that there was no restriction on women, simply that none were buyers. Beattie, morose and reluctant, had been reduced to making transparent excuses not to travel out here to Clayton with her.

'Lot 413, Devon and Cornwall Longwool, five bales.' The auctioneer looked round the room. 'Have I two pence? Two and a half, three pence, three and a half, four pence . . .'

'Will you bid?' Anna wanted to shout, but she hissed softly into the space between them, 'Will you please *bid*.' For answer, Beattie got up and moved into the row across the aisle, seating himself beside a man in tweeds and starting a muttered conversation. Left alone, Anna crossed one hand over the over to stop them shaking: anger and anxiety were hard for her to deal with. She forced herself to watch carefully, to see how bids were made. Gestures were almost undetectable: a nod, a finger laid against the side of a nose. The bidding was so rapid she had already lost track: she was confused by the verbal shorthand of the auction room, the way the bidding advanced by such apparently small amounts on an already established base price.

'Nine pence I'm bid,' the auctioneer rattled on. 'I'm going to sell at a hundred fifty nine then, all gone to Bussey Hewitt.' The gavel came down, and a young man in a hacking jacket moved to the back of the room to collect a claims form for his purchase. The next lot was another Anna had marked in her sale catalogue. It was a small one, but high quality. She wanted it. The next auction was weeks away, and the same wool would cost far more if she had to buy it already cleaned. 'Now then, Lot 415, North Leicester Blue Face, we've three bales. Two. Two and a half. Three. Three and a half! Four.' The auctioneer's voice rang staccato. 'Four pence I've got. And a half anywhere? A half is bid now.'

Before she let herself think Anna moved a hand, nodded. The auctioneer caught her eye and waited, nonplussed. He murmured something to the man beside him and both stared at her as she said, hoarse from embarrassment, 'I'm bidding for Summers. I'm Anna Summers. Please take my bid.'

The auctioneer, clearly startled, said, 'I'm afraid that's not possible. I can only take bids from accredited buyers in this saleroom . . .' Heads turned, there was a low buzz of good-natured interest. Someone shouted from the back of the room, 'Give lass a chance!' and the auctioneer frowned and spoke to his colleague. The second man leant over his desk.

'Are you bidding today, Mr Beattie?'

Anna held her breath, willing Beattie to co-operate. His face devoid of expression, he met her eyes across the aisle. She thought everyone in that room must be conscious of his antagonism – to her, it appeared open as an unsheathed blade. The moment drew itself out until finally she heard him say, 'Miss Summers is bidding, sir.' He cleared his throat ostentatiously. 'A bad cold, losing my voice. Sorry I didn't discuss it with you first.'

'Very well,' said the auctioneer. 'I'll accept Miss Summers on this occasion.'

'Thank you.' She said it as much to Stan Beattie as to him.

'Five pence then,' the auctioneer rattled on as if he'd never been interrupted. 'Do I have five and a half?' Anna nodded again. 'Six. Six and a half.' He lifted a forefinger, 'It's against you. Seven pence is bid at the back, have I got seven and a half?' Anna looked across at Stan Beattie for guidance but got only his stony profile. There was no time to think. She lifted her head again. 'Seven and a half I hear.' He paused. She heard the ringing voice announce, 'I'm selling to Summers then, I'm going to sell this one at a hundred seventy-five pence, all gone to Summers . . .'

Anna was conscious of faces turning inquisitively to her and concentrated on jotting the figures on a pad. She listened carefully as the next dozen lots were cleared, bid again and secured another five bales of wool. She kept her eyes lowered demurely, fighting the unexpected sense of elation. She was almost sorry when the auctioneer brought the auction to a close.

'That's all done. Thank you, gentlemen. And lady,' he added drily, raising his voice so she could hear him above the noise as chairs were pushed back and conversation burst out around her. The three men at the auctioneer's table waited to collect in the completed claim forms from successful purchasers.

Anna moved to the tray for her forms, found Stan Beattie on the other side of it. She said quietly, 'I appreciate your doing that. I was afraid you weren't going to.'

He shrugged and the sneer was in his voice. 'You want to make a noose to hang yourself with, why should I stand in your way.'

Drat the man, why did he have to be so surly? She made her tone light. 'Spin, Mr Beattie. I'm going to spin my noose. I'm sorry if I stepped out of line by bidding, but I didn't see any alternative.'

He was opening his mouth to reply when she felt a heavy hand on her shoulder.

'Well now Anna. Or do I call you Sister Something?'

She recognised that rich Yorkshire dialect before she looked round: it would take more than the passage of thirteen years to alter its owner. 'Mr Street. Walter. How wonderful to see you.' She didn't have to feign delight: she had known him since she was tiny. Her father's oldest friend, he had been unofficial godfather to both Simon and Anna. The fat brown bear he'd given on her fifth birthday had lived on her bed until she left home. 'How are you keeping?'

'Not so good as you, judging by your performance back there.' The hand squeezed her upper arm. 'Eh, but you're Ted's girl and no mistake. He was an obstinate bugger too, wouldn't take no for an answer. What say, Beattie, she stole your thunder all right.'

Beattie muttered something unintelligible and headed for the stairs. Walter Street watched him go with an expression as bland as his seamed face would permit. She observed with old affection the portly stomach in the loud checked waistcoat, then short legs finishing in incongruously neat feet in shiny leather. He still reminded her of Mr Toad.

He swivelled round for a better view of her. 'I'm a bit 'urt, you know that?' Sharp words were belied by the benign look on his face. 'One minute I'm told you're 'ere in Bradford, and when I telephone you've gone off again. But you gave us all a surprise turning up like this.'

'Walter, I'm sorry. You can imagine what it's been like, with Lynn and the mill . . .' She was genuinely repentant: Walter Street was the one person in the city she should have made an effort to see. Apart from his connection with her family, he knew more about yarn-spinning than any man alive. But all that was less important than his connection with her old self: he made her feel like the Summers girl again.

'Don't be daft, 'course I understand.' He brushed aside her apology and his mouth set tight with recalled annoyance as he gestured with his head towards the stairs down which Beattie had departed. 'It's not my place to comment, girlie, but that's no way for your man to behave.' She glanced round nervously: Walter Street's idea of a discreet undertone was not hers.

'I'll manage, Walter. I got what I wanted in there, despite his lack of co-operation.'

'You did an' all.' The old man took the forms firmly out of her hand.

'Now, you'll permit me to 'elp you fill these in. And then you'll give me the very great pleasure of buying you a cup of coffee.'

They sat companionably in the brightly lit shop of the British Wool Centre, at the pine tables set beyond the display of blankets and slippers, soap made from fleece lanolin, racks of sweaters and skirts, toy lambs and posters of well-groomed sheep. Walter Street ordered coffee and Danish pastries, loosened his belt beforehand to accommodate them and sat back to consider Anna.

Smiling, she returned his gaze, seeing a figure that was a calculated caricature of a Victorian mill-owner. Walter Street had cultivated mutton-chop whiskers when his hair deserted him, slipping towards the back of his head like an eiderdown in the night. He wore a gold chain slung across his waistcoat, and though she knew there was a gold hunter in the fob pocket, she'd never seen him consult it. His manner could on occasion be bluff and blustery as a ham actor playing a Yorkshireman. But there was nothing of caricature in his features. The determinedly carved nose and jaw, the shrewd alert eyes in their pouches of weather-worn skin, the generous mouth, added up to a face of humour and integrity.

Walter Street and her father had been lifelong friends. Even their grandfathers had known each other: the young Street born into a tiny house provided by the Summers family to house workers in the shadow of their mill. By the time Anna's grandfather had built Nightingale Mill, Walter Street's father had achieved one of his own. Now, thought Anna wryly, Summers were on the brink of bankruptcy while Sutcliffe &

Street had become enormous, with a vast modern mill set in landscaped grounds out at Keighley. Peggy said he had some of the largest and most up-to-date machinery in Bradford and three sons working with him, though he must be well over seventy. He offered her a cigarette from a leather case, shook his head over her refusal.

'Expect you to give up everything, do they?'

She started to bristle defensively. 'It's not like that at all . . .' when she caught the gleam in his eye. You didn't fool Walter Street. 'More or less,' she admitted. 'I mean, I wouldn't want to smoke anyway, but the question simply doesn't arise.'

'Like the outfit,' he observed. 'Women look good in long skirts. But if the life is as medieval as your clothes, then I'd say you've an 'ard row to hoe.' He lit his own cigarette. ''Appy, are you?' He asked with such bluntness she was taken aback and said 'No' before she'd realised. The waitress put down their coffee and pastries and exchanged banter with Walter, clearly a regular customer.

When she'd gone, he stirred in a lot of brown sugar and remarked, concentrating on the coffee, 'I was right sorry to hear about your brother. He didn't come to me. Wish he had, I'd not have sent him away empty-handed. Between us we could mebbe have straightened things out a bit. If he'd only asked me.' He went on stirring, unnecessarily now. 'I feel badly about the whole business.' She could see he was grieved.

'Poor Simon. You know Lynn's expecting a baby soon?'

''Eard that was why you came home. Though I'm damned if I can see you bringing the mill through.' She took no offence from his blunt comments: Walter Street was one of the old breed of Yorkshiremen. He's all backbone, her father used to say. You can lean on him but you'll not bend him. He went on now, reflectively, 'That Beattie would bear watching on the evidence of his behaviour this morning.' He gave her a searching look from beneath unruly brows black as ever. As a child she used to think he dyed them, since what remained of his hair was almost white. 'I was surprised back there when you bought 'igh-quality wool. Understood Summers had moved over to artificial fibres.'

'I'm planning to drop them.'

A large wedge of Danish pastry was suspended in midair. 'Are you, by 'eck.' Amazement exaggerated the Bradford in his voice.

'I think Simon made a mistake and I'm going to try and put it right, go back to classic yarns, find new markets.'

The Danish pastry disappeared from view and the old man chewed reflectively. 'Fighting words,' he observed at last. 'And if you'll permit an old man to make an observation, that's not something you can do from behind convent walls.' He put the last piece of pastry into his mouth and chewed with relish.

Anna tugged her veil straight. 'I know it.'

'You said a minute ago you weren't 'appy. and now I look at you properly, you are a mite peaky. So the life doesn't suit after all.'

'I loved it at first, Walter. But I've been there a long time. Thirteen years.'

He waited a few moments before prompting her. 'And?'

She swirled the coffee around in her cup, playing for time. Strong near-black coffee, the greatest luxury she'd found in the world. She could say to this outspoken old man what no one knew apart from Mother Emmanuel back in the convent. Walter Street, like all Yorkshiremen, disliked excessive emotion, but he was staunchly loyal to his friends.

'I've more or less decided to give it up. I think maybe it's already given *me* up.'

He registered no more surprise than if she had announced she was about to leave her job.

'No sense wasting any more time then. If you're in the wrong place, you'll 'ave to get yourself out. Do they let you go once they've got their 'ands on you?'

'You make it sound as if I was in the clutches of an ogre.' She giggled despite herself. 'Of course they do. Leaving has become more common in religious life, just as divorce has in the world.'

'Why's that then?'

She shrugged. 'The feeling of being bound for life by a vow has lessened for us too. And people's expectations are different, they demand more for themselves. That's true in religious life just as it is in society.'

He snorted. 'You're talking like a bloody sociologist, Anna. Don't understand what you're on about. The 'ell with religious life and society, what about *you*. Are you coming out of your convent for real, or are you 'ere on some sort of parole?'

Anna finished her coffee. 'I'm officially here for a month to help Lynn. I hope to be back regularly to see her – there's no one else. I'll be able to keep an eye on the mill.'

He grunted. 'It'll need more than an eye, take it from me. Buying expensive wool is no 'obby. You'll find you 'ave to take it seriously.'

'I do, Walter, honestly. I probably will leave, but it all takes time.' She added anxiously, 'Please don't mention it to anyone yet. I still haven't really made up my mind.'

He reached across the table and patted her hand. 'Don't be daft, I'm no gossip. But you can't find it easy going around looking like the Flying Nun.'

She laughed. 'You're all compliments, Walter. These are the only clothes I have. They don't change the person I am.'

'What's the point of 'em, then?'

'I'm supposed to be a sign of God in the world.'

'And frighten the lads off at the same time, no doubt.' His gaze became more quizzical than ever. 'What are those vows you 'ave to make? To give up money and possessions . . .'

'Poverty, Chastity, Obedience.'

'Oh aye.' He put a wealth of meaning into the laconic comment and she remembered he was no churchgoer. He drained his coffee cup. 'Right then, let's get down to business. You can't afford costly mistakes and I can mebbe stop you making a few. You tell me what you want to achieve with that old-fashioned mill of yours and I'll give you best advice I can.' He frowned at his thoughts. 'But don't waste my time. What you want to do won't be achieved overnight – you've learned enough about yarnspinning from your father to know that. I can take it then you'll be 'ere to carry out these fine plans you're making.'

It wasn't asked as a question and she made no reply. She had no doubts that she would manage, with the help of Hal and Peggy. She was high on the adrenalin of her achievement at the auction and anything seemed possible.

Anna convinced herself that Reverend Mother and the bishop would never be able to refuse her a week's leave of absence here, a fortnight there. She'd surely be allowed to return regularly to Simon's family and the mill: Lynn's pregnancy and helplessness would be the justification.

She deliberately refused to acknowledge how rigid were the rules and regulations under which she lived in the convent. Here, in the warm, brightly-lit room, in the world she had foresworn, that life was distant and unreal. As if someone else had lived it.

Walter Street brought a leather notepad and a heavy black fountain pen from his breast pocket. 'One other thing you'll 'ave to come to terms with, girlie. 'Alf a lifetime of poverty, chastity and obedience is no ticket to success in commercial matters. You'd best remember that.'

11

There was no reason why that particular letter should look ominous: thick creamy paper with heavily embossed dark blue letterhead. Maynard Gideon (1870), White Lion Court, Cornhill, London EC2. It lay on top of the pile Peggy had left on her desk, the folds still holding so she could only see the salutation. Dear Mr Summers . . .

'I thought you ought to see this.' Peggy's face was creased in agitation. 'Mr Simon kept the whole matter very quiet. I was the only one who knew about it. I don't think you'll want Stan Beattie to see it.'

Anna picked it up, read the three paragraphs and had to go back over them twice before they made sense. Still holding the letter, she sat down heavily and stared at the immaculate black characters, the navy slash of signature.

'Oh, my Lord.'

'I never thought to hear you swear,' Peggy observed.

'That's not swearing. It's pleading.' She dropped the letter back onto her desk. 'Well. Do we fight or do we run?'

'Run where?' asked Peggy. 'To the bankruptcy court?'

'We may not have any option.' She picked up the letter again. 'Where is it . . . "It is a matter of grave concern that your last two payments are now overdue by nine and two weeks respectively. We must ask you to rectify this immediately or we shall be forced to take steps to withdraw your loan facility . . ."' She turned to Peggy. 'It says we owe them three thousand pounds – what *is* this? Why didn't you tell me before?'

Peggy fiddled with the necklace she wore under her sensible Crimplene suit jacket, fidgeting with the pink stones as if they were worry beads.

'I don't know. I should have. It just slipped my mind, love, I can't think how. Mr Simon wouldn't let me enter it into the books as a loan, he was convinced he could pay it back straight away and no one would be any the wiser. So it doesn't appear anywhere on the accounts – that's why I forgot.'

Anna said softly. 'That's illegal, not entering it. That's cooking the books.'

Peggy nodded miserably. 'I said that. I warned him the Inland Revenue would trace it through Maynard Gideon, but he wouldn't have it. I never could argue with your brother.'

'Who *are* Maynard Gideon anyway? I never heard of them.'

'A private bank. Your brother was put in touch with them by a business acquaintance when things got bad and they were marvellous, made him a loan immediately.'

Anna asked, dreading the answer, 'Lent how much?'

'Two hundred and fifty thousand.'

'They must have had security for that amount.' Her voice was thin with despair.

'The deeds of his house . . .'

She groaned her apprehension.

'. . . and the freehold of the mill,' Peggy finished flatly.

Anna rubbed her cheeks hard with both hands in a gesture of utter exasperation. 'I didn't think things could get any worse. So on top of everything else, we have to find another . . .' she glanced down at the letter '. . . fifteen hundred a month. And if we don't we stand to lose the mill and Lynn could be homeless.' She found she was fingering her rosary like Peggy with her beads. The older woman watched her for a moment.

'I'd like to think your prayers would help but my bones tell me you and Lynn had best get yourselves together and go up to London to see these people.' She nodded at Anna's horrified expression. 'I know, love, but they're human beings even if

168

they *are* bankers. You think about it,' she added persuasively, 'while I make us a nice cup of tea.'

Anna drank it, wishing it was the magic panacea Peggy clearly believed. Though it would take more than magic to sort out this mess. Her stunned disbelief had turned to sullen resentment. Simon had risked ruining the mill, had amassed huge debts he could not pay. And no one had known. What he had done was criminal, she was horrified by his duplicity. And even as she thought this, his image came into her mind: the harassed unhappy man who had come to the convent parlour needing her help and received only distant polite phrases.

She had not seen her brother's desperation because of her own. The two of them had sat there, locked into themselves, unable to communicate. *Because they were the same*. The sudden comprehension made her head reel.

They were brother and sister in more than name, though she had not seen it before. Both of them had carried on while hating what they did, hiding from the truth, refusing to admit anything was wrong. Least of all, she thought bitterly, to themselves. Where other people might have drawn attention to their growing wretchedness, she and Simon had simmered silently and struggled on.

Simon had done so because of Lynn and the boys, and the weight of the world's expectations. And she had felt the same pressures and responded as he had done. In her case, the vows had been to God and the community and not an individual, but that was the only difference. And that explained the heart-burning rage she felt for him.

In the introspective life of the convent, no thought went unexamined, no desire unquestioned. She had prayed, as they all did, that God would reveal her to herself. She understood her own unhappiness, and supposed that now there was nothing from which she had escaped. Until this.

Simon had led a double-life. And so did she.

Hal's white Volkswagen chugged through Keighley at nine o'clock next morning, bore right at Silsden and twenty minutes later he said 'Bradley Moor' and put his foot down hard so the vehicle bounced and jolted on the winding road between dry-stone walls. Beside him Anna sat silent, awed by the wide expanse of brooding moorland around them. She had forgotten the colours of heather and bracken, the high fells, limestone screes and scars.

It had been drizzling until a few minutes ago and sun filtered through slate-grey clouds, glittered off the grass and softened the outlines of this fierce country. Distant crags haloed in mist drifted in a fairy-tale haze. There wasn't another vehicle in sight here, nothing but soaring peaks and walls of uncoursed stone winding up to the endless horizon. Far off toy sheep bunched like burrs on a steep slope and a man trailed by a black and white dog disappeared over a ridge.

After another twenty minutes Hal drove off the road onto a sheep-track and stopped. They got out and leant against the car, saying nothing, just watching giant shadows sweep across a sea of pale grass, feeling the wind sing in their veins. At last Anna spoke.

'I didn't remember it was like this.'

Hal put on a heavy local accent.

'Tha's seen nuthin' yet. Wait'll we go ovver t'top.'

Anna moved away from the car and holding her heavy skirts struggled up a hillock so she could see back the way they had come. Far below them in the distance – she hadn't realised they had climbed so high – huddled an untidy nest of slender mill chimneys. She almost tripped going down again and remarked, half to herself, 'I'm definitely wearing the wrong clothes for fruit-picking.'

'Real walkers have dubbined boots. We should have brought some for you.'

'They also have enormous legs. Don't bother.'

Hal opened the boot and brought out the small sacks he had brought to carry the berries, tossed them over his shoulder and handed her a pair of gardening gloves. He led the way across to where the stone wall separating them from the open land had partially crumbled. They clambered through and started off towards a clump of bushes. Anna examined one carefully and stripped off a few berries. Hal watched her, then moved on to do the same. After ten minutes he called across, 'There's hardly anything on this one. Maybe we should go on a bit.'

Bent over a bush, she admitted, 'It's the same here. Birds probably had most of them, but we're picking very late anyway.'

It was like that wherever they went. In half an hour they had collected only a dozen handfuls of wizened blackberries, a scant assortment of green and yellow varieties neither of them had seen before, a few leaves. Anna straightened up with a groan.

'This is useless. Let's walk over to those rocks and see if we can find any lichens.'

Hal frowned. 'I'm not too keen. You know lichens are protected, don't you, like wild flowers. We're supposed to conserve them.'

Anna stopped. 'Oh, no!'

'I thought you'd know that.'

'How could I? In Wales, I just scraped the walls of the outbuildings. Everything was so wet and green, it was easy. And they made the most wonderful dyes – greeny golden colours. I was going to do the same with the wool I got on Wednesday, when it comes from the top-makers. Couldn't we just look, see if there is any?' She could hear herself deliberately wheedling.

'Well . . . I guess.'

They trudged across to the rocky outcrop. Close to, the stones were murderous, jagged and smooth without a foothold. Hal regarded them doubtfully.

'Doesn't look too promising.'

Anna moved to the foot of the nearest rocks and scraped with the garden trowel she took from her sack. She held out a tiny ball of moss on the palm of her hand.

'This isn't what I need at all.' She was cornered. Fruit and lichens would have been a cheap way of dyeing their wool. Wool she'd never have bought if the Maynard Gideon debt had come to light a day earlier. 'It's not going to work, Hal. And I was so sure I could do it.'

'We'll sort something out.' Dropping his sack to the ground he sat down on one of the smaller rocks. He rooted in his pocket for two blocks of chocolate and held one out to her.

'Always eat in a crisis. Preserves the finger nails.'

She accepted gratefully and chose a rock herself. The bar was sticky and oversweet, a wicked indulgence – the first she'd tasted for years. She wiped her fingers on the spiky grass. He chewed solemnly, watching the sky, then touched her arm, pointed, and said softly, 'Kestrel.' She saw the incredible hovering flight, the lazy freedom of the slow wingbeats. As she watched the outlines of the bird blurred and she found to her horror she was crying.

She got hastily to her feet and walked away so Hal shouldn't see, following a sheep-track downhill. She hardly saw where she was going, locked into despair at her failure. She was a fool. Hal had warned her she couldn't hope to use natural dyes for her wool. But she had convinced herself that out here she would find all the raw materials. She hadn't let herself see the doubt in Hal's face while she raved on about what they'd find on the moors. He'd given way to her conviction in the end, entering into the idiotic escapade with a good grace. She knew that he'd never say – as she fully deserved – I told you so.

She walked on, gathering speed as the slope steepened. Soon she would be on her way back to the convent. She had planned to start brewing the natural dyes before she went. Then, on her next trip to Bradford – she intended to ask for another leave of absence in two weeks, to visit Lynn – she would have been able to work on the prepared wool. In a week it would all have been finished.

But would even that have saved the mill? The ominous letter from Maynard Gideon lay stuffed in a file in her drawer. That debt would gobble up anything they could make, and more.

She thought; I should pray for guidance, but no words came. Preoccupied, she was only vaguely aware that the grass was greener here than she had expected so late in the year, a vivid colour suggesting there was water near.

On the instant she thought this, she stepped ankle-deep into mud: she'd wandered off the sheep-track straight into a bog. She held up the hem of her dripping habit, tried to step back to safety and her right foot sank down into the soggy ground to her knee. She struggled to release her leg and yelled 'Hal! Hal!' but the wind ripped the cry from her lips. She leant back, pulling up her right foot and it came out of the clinging mud with a sucking sound. She took a wide step to get herself back onto firm ground but the long woollen habit, its hem weighted with water, dragged her down. She overbalanced and fell clumsily sideways, hurting her back and neck. Her headdress was soaked immediately, the veil pressing against her cheek, a clump of prickly grass piercing the fabric so she had to squeeze her eyes shut for protection.

'Hal!' As she shouted, she got mud in her mouth and spat in disgust. 'Hal!' Lord, what an idiot she was. He'd never hear her. She struggled frantically to free herself, but as she did so, her other leg was sinking deeper and deeper. The mud felt loathesome, freezing and oozing around her. She couldn't bear to think how deep it might be, what lay buried in it. Desperately she yelled again. 'Hal!'

'I'm here. Don't panic.' He was calling to her as he sprinted down the sheep-track. 'Don't move, you'll only go in deeper!'

He was right, she was only succeeding in forcing herself further into the bog. The dense material of her veil was so heavy with water it was pulling her head down: with a great effort she kept still, concentrating on keeping her face free of the green slime. It took longer than she could have believed before Hal reached her. He tore off his long black overcoat with such haste the buttons were ripped from the fabric. He spread it over the marshy ground between them.

'Hold onto the coat, I'll pull you over.' He was yelling, although he was so close to her. 'I daren't come and get you, we might both get caught.'

She grabbed hold of a sleeve with both hands. He pulled firmly and she was able to drag herself towards him.

'Slowly,' he urged. 'Easy as you can, you're doing fine.' He was on his knees, hauling her in as if landing a huge fish. She could see the muscles knotting in his hands and the tendons at the side of his neck and then he was reaching for her, his fingers digging hard into her arm, his other hand warm on hers, grasping so hard he hurt her, dragging her chest down over the hard ground. And then she was lying on dry grass, panting for breath, weak with relief.

'Here, let's get this darn thing off you.' He was trying to undo her head-dress, fumbling in the muddy folds for a fastening. She put up a filthy hand to the old-fashioned pin hidden at the back. Hal yanked at the veil so hard that the once-white headband came loose. Wearily, Anna sat up and took off the tight-fitting cap that enclosed her hair, beyond caring what she looked like or what he thought.

'Up you get.' His hands were under her armpits, lifting her. 'Let's go back to the car, you look all in. And it's freezing here.'

Anna nodded. She gathered up the soaking skirt of her habit and discovered her right sandal had gone, sucked off in the bog. She started to laugh weakly, because her chest hurt, but Hal was hurrying her along and didn't bother to ask what she had suddenly found to amuse her. It was only when she drew her breath in sharply from pain as she trod on a stone that he looked down and saw that under its coating of mud her foot was bare. He stopped and undid his own shoe, steadied her while he pushed it onto her foot. It was a bright blue trainer, far too big for her. She protested. 'It'll get it all muddy,' but he said 'Doesn't matter,' and put his arm round her waist. She pushed him away.

'I'm all right. I can manage,' and in the same instant realised she couldn't, she was quivering with strain. She forced herself to take a step and almost fell again. Hal watched her with an odd expression.

'I'm offering you help. I'm not trying to take advantage of

you. Will you accept that you need it, or will you just give me another kick in the teeth?'

Anna tried to smile but it wasn't a success.

'I'm sorry, Hal, I really didn't mean it the way you think. It's just – I'm not used . . .'

He nodded.

'That's OK then.' He took a step towards her. 'Let's go.' His arm felt solid and reassuring, she had to fight an absurd impulse to lean against him. It took almost fifteen minutes to get back and by then she was shaking all over from cold despite the pace Hal set. He half-pushed her into the car and routed around in the boot. 'There's a blanket somewhere. I went out to look at owls the other night and used it then – here.' He started to tuck it round her and stopped. 'This is ridiculous. The whole of your robe thing is soaking, we'll never get you warm. You'd best take it off.'

'I couldn't do that.' She wished she hadn't sounded quite so scandalised. He was giving her another of those strange looks, then he shrugged.

'You know best, Sister.' He never called her that. 'It'll be your funeral. We're at least ten miles from the nearest house, even if they have any clothes you could borrow, and the car heater doesn't work.'

She felt the front of her habit. The heavy wool was felted with mud and slime and she knew it would take days to dry properly. They all had just two habits, and when the heavier winter ones got their annual wash they chose the warmest weather so they could hang them out for several days if necessary. She was as cold as she could ever remember being but that wasn't as bad as the rank smell rising from her clothes.

'You're right,' she said. 'But it'll take me a few minutes.'

'Good. Give me a yell when you're done.' He stripped off his sweater. 'My coat's too wet to use.' He ignored her protestations. 'I'll be fine till we can get hold of something else for you.' He shut the door and walked off: as she struggled out of the habit in the restricted space, she could see him, back carefully turned to the car, jogging around to keep warm.

She yanked the sleeveless coat, the scapular, over her head, forgetting the scapular pins and ripping the material. Then the grey robe, impossible to deal with in the confined space, clinging to her arms and legs, a soggy felted mass: maybe a day on one of Lynn's radiators would render it wearable when she went back to Wales. The thick tweed underskirt was easier, but the long-sleeved double-wool bodice – she couldn't see how this had become so stained with mud – clung to her skin. She finally managed to wrest it off, pulled on the sweater and wrapped herself in the blanket. It was one of those crocheted things, lots of brightly coloured squares with patterned middles. Her vest and pants were dry, thanks to the thickness of the habit. She made sure the blanket was secured round her waist like a sarong before she tapped on the window.

Hal peered in at the mounds of discarded clothing with a comical expression.

'I was wondering what was taking so long. You could outfit an army in that lot. Here.' He was holding out the plastic Thermos cup filled with coffee. 'Only instant, but better than nothing.' He climbed in beside her. 'How d'you feel?'

'Like a snail without its shell.' She missed the heavy weight of the habit. She wrapped both hands round the cup for warmth. She'd been aware that they were work-scarred from her labours on the convent's small-holding, but they had never looked too bad beneath the flowing sleeves of her robe. Now, emerging from the blanket, they might have belonged to a navvy: dark patterns of grime ingrained the skin and outlined her nails, callouses from using the rake made little yellow cushions on her palms. She wanted to hide them – but that was vanity. What was the matter with her?

She gave a shudder and then couldn't stop shivering, slipping lower in her seat, wrapping her arms across her chest. Her head and neck felt oddly light, just like that day when they had cut off her hair. She jumped when Hal touched her hand.

'You're freezing.'

She evaded his eyes, and the concern in them.

'We'll have to do something or you'll catch your death.' He took the empty cup from her hand, put his arm round her shoulders and pulled her towards him. She stiffened instinctively and started to protest but he only said 'Don't be so silly,' and laid his right hand squarely on her back so she was brought close against him, feeling his warmth through the shirt. She couldn't bear to move away, she didn't want to. When he'd helped her walk back to the car she had resisted the urge to lean against him: now she gave in to it.

She couldn't remember the last time anyone had held her. Dad had given an occasional embrace long ago, but they weren't a demonstrative family, physically or emotionally. Her mother would give the occasional peck on the cheek, but the day Anna left for Wales she had refused even that. Simon had kissed her though, hugged her swiftly, and this odd young man was casual as her brother used to be.

She was clenched against him tight as a fist but he didn't seem to mind. He rubbed her back through the sweater with a quick up and down movement that warmed her all through. 'Better?' he inquired and she found herself saying 'Yes', as if it was the most natural thing in the world for her to be in a man's arms.

Her! Sister Gabriel. Who at eighteen had chosen to relinquish for ever the human satisfactions she had never known, alienating her family by preferring the love of Christ to that of any man. She had prided herself on being different from the other girls in college. She had not wanted the ordinary things: a husband, a child. Entering so young, all her energy had been channelled into her new life. So when, these last years, she had been enmeshed in uncertainty, her mind clogged by doubt, she had tried to accept her desperate unhappiness. As so many had before her.

Since medieval times, the melancholy sadness peculiar to nuns had its own name: accidia. Teresa of Avila had understood. A subtle disease, she had called it, a cruel death of sorrows. At what cost, Anna wondered, had such knowledge been acquired? She herself found it as much physical as mental: there were days when her whole body hurt. A couple of times, she'd come out in a rash over her face and arms for which the convent doctor, summoned in case it was contagious, could find no cause. And she – who had never been bothered by the slightest menstrual problem – began in her late twenties to suffer such pain each month that her period became something to be dreaded.

It had never occurred to her that the pain might be in her mind: she'd never heard the word 'psychosomatic'. It was pure chance that she came across a book in the convent library by a religious psychologist which identified her rashes as the likely result of frustrated aggression. There was a section on painful periods. A nun suffering these, she read, would most likely be in her early thirties. She may well be pushing her yearning for physical love and children back into her subconscious and will neither admit nor discuss them. But at the same time the pain is regular proof that she is able to bear a baby, so in a way it is welcomed.

Anna had read through that several times: there, on paper, all the thoughts she had never allowed herself to acknowledge. She had finally understood that her body – those awful cramps, reminding her of yet another lost opportunity, another child that might have been – was wiser than she.

And now, Anna thought grimly, her body wanted to respond to the feel of Hal's, to curl up close and shut out everything else. Instead, she sat up straight, extricated herself from him and heard her prim voice. 'I'm quite recovered now, thank you.'

'Great,' said Hal, and leaning across the gap between their seats, brought his face to a level with hers. Unused to such intimacy, she tried to move back but in the rounded seat there was nowhere to go. Gold flecks in his green eyes. Little golden feathers of his eyebrows. The broad smooth planes of his face so close to hers, the strong cheekbones, generous curved mouth. When he put his right hand on her cheek, it was shaking. She thought, he's cold without his coat. And then: no, he's scared.

When he kissed her it was so quick, so light, she couldn't believe what was happening. She tried to pull away but his lips followed hers, a blind seeking. Dry and slightly rough on her own, a hard pressure, suggestion of toothpaste and Maxwell House and something unfamiliar and disturbing, a man's smell, clean sweat from his efforts to save her, young skin and something lemony.

She moved her head back. The words were difficult.

'There are all sorts of . . . reasons why you shouldn't be doing this.'

He didn't seem disconcerted. 'And there are all sorts of reasons why I should.' The low note of tenderness in his voice made the tiny hairs prickle on her arms as if he'd stroked her skin. She should get away from him, out of this situation. Dear Lord, what am I doing? But somehow it felt as if it was happening to someone else. Someone else held her breath as his lips returned to hers. Someone else gave a little groaning sigh that seemed to galvanise Hal: in response, he leant further across the gap between the seats, one hand behind her neck. His mouth pressed harder so she gasped in protest and her lips parted. He was holding her properly now, dear heaven, not like before, not like a brother but with an urgent grasp that emptied her mind and tightened her breathing. She felt his warm hand heavy on her thigh, felt it as though the bright blanket were not there, as though he touched bare flesh.

Anna opened her eyes – she wasn't aware she'd closed them – on the sight of his intent face so close she could only see bits of it, the smooth skin of his eyelids, fan of curly lashes. He must have felt her gaze because he shifted his weight slightly. He cupped both hands carefully round her face as if it were something precious he feared to drop, and in his grasp she felt small and protected. With his lips he touched her forehead, her eyelids. His mouth was on her damp hair, he rubbed his cheek against hers. He was whispering, nuzzling the side of her neck. She caught broken meaningless phrases: 'You're so . . . you are the most . . .'

In the confined space her own breathing sounded loud and

irregular. She had been sitting with her hands loose in her lap. She raised them now to fend him off. She pressed her palms flat against his chest, straightened her arms to push him away. But despite herself, despite her long years of self-denial – or more likely, God help her, because of them – she couldn't help responding to him, to his ardour, to the pressure of his body warm against her. Somehow, her stiff arms had opened wide, and her hands had slid round further than she intended so she could feel the strong muscles in his back and she was holding him.

He was solid, a protective wall for her to lean against. It was utterly different to touching the bony boys from college so long ago. Her sexual experience had been confined to necking with Dave Clough after a dance and some heavy petting with Alan Gow. She hadn't reckoned the boys much. Clammy hands and thick tongues they tried to stick right down her throat and the conversational range of a haddock. But she could still remember her appalled thrill when Alan got his hand down the top of her bra and kneaded her breast: the windows of his mother's Triumph Herald had steamed up with their heat. With all that, she was pretty sure she was even now a lot more innocent that sixteen- and seventeen-year-olds today.

Those adolescent fumblings had been exciting – and unnerving. She'd been deeply disturbed by her own incomprehensible feelings. At school, they'd covered human intercourse in Biology and after the initial excitement of the not very explicit textbook illustrations, Miss Robson had made it seem no more interesting than osmosis. The girls talked about 'it' in giggly groups and read advice columns out of *Honey* to each other, but Anna contributed little and learned less. There was one girl, Marion Breakell, famous for starting her periods first in their class. She would murmur bashful excuses to the gym mistress who snorted derisively. 'Exercise, that's what you need.' Marion was 'fast': everyone knew she let older boys touch her body in places Anna didn't want to think about.

She let no hint of this drop at home and never raised the

subject. Her mother did so once, but so obliquely and with such embarrassment Anna had pretended she had a lot of homework in order to stop her. Janet Summers managed to make it plain that she considered all sexual activity to be 'acting like animals'. The phrase had conjured up unpleasant images Anna wished she could forget.

Looking back, she could see how events had channelled her into the convent: all those experiences had been negative ones. Nothing there to deflect her from religious life.

She had accepted her vow of chastity, like the other vows, freely. Those were the Church's terms. And it was more than a mere physical continence: she truly believed it was the enamel of the soul. They said the suffering it brought was valuable in itself. They called the pangs of celibacy the little crucifixion. So sexual fulfilment wasn't much to give up, in that context.

It took years to realise that, however dedicated you were, to surrender it for ever was a real loss. Even now, there was no recognition in the convent of the women's sexual drive, or the difficulties total suppression inevitably brought: Anna's order, like so many others, dealt with such problems by refusing to admit they existed.

But they did exist. On pale summer nights when the scent of stock and honeysuckle invaded her cell, she often lay sleepless hour after belled hour. Hard to keep her thoughts pure and not wonder what it would be like, to know the imperative weight of a man's body on hers.

A nameless ache would nag her, impossible to ignore. It was both painful and pleasurable, like probing a bad tooth. Not for any particular person – she'd scarcely seen a man since she entered – just an anonymous wanting. She would be taut and vibrating like a stringed instrument, strung so tightly she didn't know what to do with herself.

Then one night she'd woken from a dream and remembered. It was vivid and unambiguous – even she realised it was about sex. She'd been horrified: what's happening to me, am I losing my vocation? There was no one she dared ask. Anna had the dream many times: small things changed, the scenery varied. But what she felt was always the same.

In her dream, she was running in some wooded place she knew was forbidden, pursued by strange winged men. They all wore black, and their faces were all covered in scales. She was absolutely alone, and helpless. They spoke in quiet voices but a foreign language. She ran on between high dark hedges and the men grabbed her, three or four of them held her arms and legs and started tearing off her clothes. Not any clothes she recognised but frilly, sheer garments. Now she was really frightened, begging and whimpering as she never had in her life, praying to them to stop, to leave her alone. But they took no notice and there was a terrible excitement in that, in her naked pleading, knowing they could do anything they wanted with her. They lifted her and one forced her thighs apart and his wings made everything black and she loved and hated it, both at once.

Then it was quite different and she was lying in a man's arms on wet cold grass. He was whispering and still she couldn't understand the language. By his side a scimitar hung in a golden scabbard. He was naked and his hair was gold too. She looked down and between his legs were three golden balls like a pawnbroker's sign and they were studded with jewels. And in her dream, she recognised then that he was a prince, reached up and held him to her breasts and they floated together above the green hedges.

Anna always woke bitterly disappointed, she was so sure it had been real. Her hand would be deep down between her legs, and it almost seemed as though she'd been masturbating in her sleep. She felt sticky and awful and ashamed. That first time, though it was the middle of the night, she'd got up and washed herself all over.

But it wasn't shame she felt now, in Hal's arms. She tried to control what he was rousing in her, impulses so long repressed, so explicitly physical they terrified her. It was as if she had touched an old wound which had been searingly painful long ago and started it throbbing again. Oh dear God yes, that's how it was. Now I remember.

He was stroking her throat, running his fingertips delicately down into the long V of the sweater, down deep between her breasts. He cupped one in his hands and she felt with a quiver her nipple puckering the way it did in the cold when she washed in her cell . . . What was she doing?

Anna had been trained to examine with unflinching honesty her every thought and act. She did so now and discovered she didn't want Hal to see she was wearing a soft flannel vest she'd made herself.

Shocked – that such a thing should worry her when she was breaking her vows like this – she struggled to get loose, prising his arms from round her, pushing against his warm weight. 'No, don't . . . we mustn't . . . Hal . . .' His face was buried against her neck and he became very still. 'Hal!' This time he released her, pulled back to his own side of the car. Anna drew a deep breath and without thinking wiped the back of her hand across her mouth. She didn't see the expression of amused disbelief cross Hal's face as he caught the furtive, childish gesture.

They sat quiet, not looking at each other. Hal fiddled with the dashboard, turned the windscreen wipers on and off, flicked the indicator switch. Anna, too churned up to speak, watched his hands. They were good hands, long fingered and deft. As capable as the man himself. She thought how they'd felt holding her . . . No, stop that.

'Want a mint?'

'What?' The prosaic offer caught her off balance: she did not see how much he wanted to make her a gift. 'No. No thanks.' This was ridiculous. 'I want to go home.'

She heard the childish wobble in her voice and hoped he hadn't. But he gave her a sharp look and agreed at once, 'Right. Let's get moving.' Sounding extremely cheerful, he switched on the engine and set off the way they had come.

She huddled beside him in her blanket, trying to identify the conflicting emotions that engulfed her. There was sorrow, because even this brief episode probably meant she had broken a solemn vow, and pure pleasure at the ease, the simplicity of it; guilt that she must have unwittingly led him on. But she didn't feel the furious self-disgust she had expected. In its place was triumph: so, despite her shorn hair and flattened breasts, despite the years of abstinence and total restraint, she hadn't lost her femininity. She was still normal. Still a woman after all.

12

Each Friday morning after Terce, Sext and None the nuns stretched their arms wide in the shape of a crucifix while they recited the Miserere.

Domine miserere super peccatrice.

Handmade candles smoked the chapel with the musky scent of beeswax. Slivers of emerald and turquoise sunlight pierced the stained glass window Sister Peter had designed and made that endless winter when they'd been snowed in from November till Easter.

Domine miserere super peccatrice. God have mercy on my soul.

Arms aching from strain, Anna fixed her mind on the statue of the adoring Virgin and concentrated on the long psalm. It was all that remained in their order of more severe penances practised for centuries which had been abandoned only ten years before. And I deserve them, Anna thought, I deserve to feel on my shoulders the agony of the discipline, traditional thrashing-cord of the monastery. She dwelt with a shudder on the foot long whip, the six straps of thin waxed cord with knotted tails. I deserve the excrutiating pain of the metal ring with five chains suspended from it, each chain ending in a hook. I deserve to wear the long sleeveless tunic of horsehair, the ends left loose to irritate the skin with every movement.

The terrifying gadgetry of physical penance still remained to some degree, though it was no longer obligatory. In Anna's order individuals continued to inflict pain upon themselves, though not daily as they once did. The ascetic Cistercian Bernard of Clairvaux had urged it: 'The body of Christ is crushed, let us learn how to subdue our bodies . . . our bodies must be conformed to the likeness of Our Lord's wounded body.'

Anna had scourged herself during her early years in the convent. It stood in a corner of her cell in the black cover she had sewn for it, waiting for the specified hour. Anticipation had been the worst part. 'The first time I used it,' one of the older sisters had confided, 'I almost went off my head in the cell.' Anna had not slept that night.

Friday was the day for mortification of the body. Penance Friday. After grace the nuns would kneel in rows of four, bare their arms and take the discipline, chanting the 'miserere mei'. She was assured it disciplined thoughts, acts and words. She accepted that, and only much later did it seem strange, to be directed to love of God by punishment.

Other days – three times a week, sometimes – they would take the discipline before they went to bed. Alone in her cell she'd slip her robe from her shoulders, telling herself she only had to do it for six minutes. Trying not to look at the horrible thing, she would whip herself first on her back, then on her legs and buttocks as their foundress had decreed. Under her breath, she'd recite prayers: the scourge could make a saint of her by mortifying the spirit. Humiliation made sweet by love of God offended.

She had been told she could strike her thigh above the knee. 'But you must take great care,' the novice mistress had added, 'not to smite the inner side, which might be harmful.' Then she gave Anna a book, written by a Jesuit, showing how and where to take the discipline.

Flagellation had terrified her. She could not have imagined such shrill pain, even though they were strictly forbidden to draw blood. Afterwards her skin had burned and smarted under her heavy clothes. And the next time, the beating was on already tender skin.

But far worse was the way it aroused dark feelings she could not bring herself to acknowledge. She wasn't even sure what they were. She had been too young and inexperienced to know then that such self-torture, even though undertaken for religious reasons, could produce physical pleasure. Because it hadn't felt like pleasure. It had been hateful. (And in a horrible way, exciting. That was when those dreams had started.)

The mistress of novices had explained. They must wage war upon the natural desires and inclinations of the body, it was a method of disciplining imagination and memory. And only by subjection of the body to the spirit could the highest adventures in the spiritual life be achieved. And as Anna continued in the life, so the number of permitted strokes would increase.

Anna understood but it hadn't helped. Perhaps because all that time ago, she hadn't known just what she was meant to be subduing.

But lying against Hal, she'd known all right. And that sudden revelation about herself had brought her hurrying home to the convent, back to safety. Back to sanity.

So it was bewildering to acknowledge that even here, she could not escape. Wherever you looked in religious ritual or literature, there it was – bridal and marital imagery. *Sexual* imagery. Though the emphasis now was changed, though they were no longer encouraged to think of themselves as passive brides, the words were still written and Christ was still the Bridegroom. Some of the old prayers – devout mental ejaculations, they were called – were almost crude, brazen in their physical allusion. 'Live, breathe and pant for your celestial Spouse,' went one. And another, 'Let Him kiss me with the kisses of His Divine Mouth'.

Some were secretive as love poems like the Canticle of Canticles, once considered an allegory of Christ's love for the soul. 'Look at me with the eyes of your heart. I am not a bold lover, I will embrace my beloved only in a retired place.'

Anna stretched her arms wider, back muscles aching, bloodless fingers numb, for the remaining minutes of the psalm. She wanted to hurt her faithless body, that had so easily forgotten that she was a woman set apart. A consecrated virgin. A sign of God in the world. A bride of Christ.

Domine miserere super peccatrice.

Anna thought of all the women before her who had offered up their pain for the sins of the world. St Rose of Lima, sleeping on her bed of pointed stones, wearing a spiked iron band around her head, carrying a cross on shoulders already bleeding from the discipline. Little Thérèse joyously coughing away her life in the Carmelite convent at Lisieux.

The psalm had still not ended. Very slowly, she lowered her arms.

It was no use. The images which in the past had always inspired her just seemed ridiculous, no more moving or meaningful than the tawdry religious pictures sold outside shrines.

The tears in her eyes made the slivers of sunlight quiver and dance on the damask altar. Like a suspect at last confessing a crime, Anna admitted what she had denied for so long.

The passionate conviction that had taken her into religious life had died.

God have mercy on her soul.

Sister Godric listened without a single interruption and Anna found herself thinking how different things were in the convent from the haste and hustle outside. Consideration for others was all-important, absolute courtesy commonplace. Their rule expected that in conversation nuns would wait 'with perfect patience' until the speaker had finished: it was very restful.

The two women were sitting in the hermitage in a quiet walk near the hen-run, facing what in summer would be flowering cherry trees but were now thin grey branches outlined against a lowering sky. It was little more than a garden shed with a single small window, but the community had waited years until they could afford such a luxury and had laboriously covered the ugly asbestos roof with willow branches secured with wire. Once a month, each nun had a day of recollection, free to do no work, attend no prayers except Divine Office. Even their meals were taken in solitude. Anna could remember when she had appreciated such isolation. Then in her last few months it had become a penance in itself.

The hut contained nothing but a table, a cross with a piece of fresh pine behind it, a statuette of the Virgin and an ancient and inefficient stove, unlit despite the cold because there was no money for oil that week. The elderly depositrix, the accountant of the order, occupied the single basketwork chair. Anna sat on the wooden floor, arms linked round her knees.

'What do you think I should do?' she appealed when she'd finished. 'I seem to be defeated at every turn.' She rested her chin in her pulled-up knees. 'I realise I shouldn't bother you with this. Reverend Mother cuts me off every time I start to speak about it. But I must try to save the mill for Lynn and the children, it's all they have.'

'Of course.' Sister Godric's voice had an even, hypnotic quality. 'I'm sure Mother Emmanuel understands. But you can see she cannot allow worldly matters to intrude on our life here.' She reached out a hand as if to touch Anna on the shoulder then drew it back, though not before Anna noticed how thin it had become, blue veins emphatic against skin as creased and fine as tissue paper. 'I don't suppose I should be talking to you about them either.' She looked up and gave a quick urchin grin, eyes alert and humorous. 'But appearances to the contrary, I'm just an old warhorse and there's nothing like the sound of battle. But I'd need to see the mill's books before I could give any sensible advice.'

Anna said hesitantly, 'I've got them in my cell, I brought them back with me. If you don't feel I'm pressurising you.'

Sister Godric leaned back and tucked both hands into the sleeves of her habit for warmth.

'You'd best fetch them. No one will be near the cells at this hour. And I'll need a pad and pencil.'

She worked for thirty-five minutes before taking off he glasses and massaging the bridge of her nose where the gold rims pinched. Anna watched, grateful for her scrutiny. 'You never really told me about your life before you entered. I only know you were a financial director at John Lewis.'

Sister Godric shrugged.

'Titles sound impressive. I just got on and did the best I

could. I didn't plan a career, I never even wanted one particularly. I thought I'd marry and then there'd be babies.' She lifted her shoulders in an expressive gesture. 'Well. We lived in London and a friend of my mother's worked in their Oxford Street shop. I started as a salesgirl in haberdashery when I was seventeen and then later on, after the war, I took night-classes in accountancy. It was the times, I suppose: the war changed life for so many of us.'

Sister Godric had once said she had been engaged, but the man had died. Anna did not ask, and Sister Godric did not tell her, what had happened. Perhaps he'd been a soldier. During the first years of Anna's novitiate, when she always worked under the eye of one of the older nuns, she used to spend hours in the vegetable garden with Sister Godric, who would hum away beneath her breath as she stripped the peas. Anna had been amazed. Knowing so little of convent life before she entered, she expected nuns to have no thoughts which were not strictly religious. Sister Godric's repertoire was extensive and secular: Cole Porter and Coward, Bobby Darin and Dietrich. Anna thought of the heart-aching words of the one she heard most often among the beans and sprouts: 'Put on some speed, Oh how I need, someone to watch over me.'

Impulsively she asked, not caring that she ought not to inquire, 'But Sister Godric, haven't you ever felt lonely? Haven't you ever regretted being here? You were in the world, you were successful, you could have married, had a family.' The older woman was silent for so long Anna thought she must have dozed off. When she spoke, her voice communicated certainty.

'Everyone who has dedicated their life to celibacy suffers from loneliness: before God we are all alone. When we made that vow, we knew it was a means to an end, a way for more than one person to have a claim on our love.'

'I understood it wasn't just a matter of physical continence, that it must be in the soul first, and pass to the body.' As she spoke, she twisted her fingers together in unconscious anxiety and the old nun watched compassionately. 'Only I expected God would make it easier to bear.'

'When I entered, we were told we had to put to death our natural inclinations.' Sister Godric leant forwarda conspiratorially. 'Do you know, we weren't allowed to cross our legs: it was "unreligious".' She pulled a face. 'It's an attitude only slowly disappearing. I think women are realising it's not possible totally to repress their sexuality. Though Lord knows, some still try. They seem to regard their sex as something attached to the side of themselves but not used. Like a spare tank of petrol on a car.'

Despite herself, Anna smiled. 'I do sometimes feel I need to talk about things properly. Personal things.' She paused: candour cost, after years of euphemism. 'Sexual things, I suppose I mean. I was totally ignorant when I entered. It was the main reason my parents opposed it, and looking back they had a point. I knew it all in theory, but I'd had no experience of life at all.' She tugged at her white headband, trying to allay the headache she could feel building up beneath its constricting grip. 'I didn't realise, of course. I assumed that was how it should be. But lately I've wondered – maybe I entered partly because my parents were so violently opposed. As an act of rebellion.' The fingers were still moving nervously, Sister Godric noted. 'And then I think, if that was the case, surely I'd not have been able to continue here for so long.'

'If you enter for the wrong reasons, it's certainly possible to be a religious – but not possible to be a *happy* religious. To do that you have to make a success of your life. I don't mean professionally, but personally.' She added wryly, 'You can of course delude yourself that you are carrying the cross. Plenty do.' She shifted slightly on the hard chair. 'It's so cold out here I get rheumaticky. Still, it's a small price to pay for so much peace.' She settled herself more comfortably and considered Sister Gabriel. The girl had always been a favourite of hers, though of course she never revealed even a hint of this. One must be as pleasant, as civil to those one liked as to those one did not. But if she'd been blessed with a granddaughter, she might have carried herself like Sister Gabriel, possessed the same strong profile, the long, curling mouth. The girl was restless and nervy, you could see clear as daylight that she had been away from the convent: the outside world had put its mark on her. 'It seems to me,' she observed gently, 'that this discussion is more than just theoretical.'

Anna blinked and gave a sudden little shiver. 'A goose walked over my grave.'

'When you're my age, Sister,' the old nun retorted, 'I doubt you'll find that funny. And you haven't answered me.'

'I'm not sure I can. I don't think anything of any significance happened – or rather, it was only significant to me.' She got up and leant her elbows on the window-sill, looking out across the darkening garden. 'It's my birthday soon. Thirty-two. I may have lived half my life already. And yet I have this extraordinary feeling that I'm at the beginning of something.' She looked back over her shoulder at the hunched figure of the old woman in the half-light. 'I responded to someone – a young man – as if I wasn't me, Sister Gabriel, at all. I could have been seventeen again.'

'Oh dear.'

Anna laughed. 'Don't worry. Seventeen for me was fat and spots and never having the right clothes. No, I meant *inside* I was nervous and unsure of myself. I didn't know how to act, what to say. It was terrifying. And,' she added reluctantly, 'it was fantastic.'

'So you're experiencing your lost youth.'

'Too late for that. I burned those bridges thirteen years ago.'

'If you're still breathing,' Sister Godric observed, 'then it's not too late. Believe me.' She straightened one leg with a grimace. 'The old have wrinkles and bags and bulges so it's easier to believe their emotions are in the same pitiful condition.' Even in the bad light, Anna saw her wry smile. 'But we decay only on the outside. You just said it: inside we go right on being seventeen.'

Anna turned back to the window. 'I'm beginning to find such problems. It had never occurred to me how easy it was, keeping my vows here in the convent, with the walls to shut out the world. There isn't any alternative to them, they're ingrained in the life.' She breathed on the glass and rubbed it clear with the sleeve of her habit. 'But in the last few weeks outside, I've begun to find it harder than I thought.' Her voice was so low Sister Godric could scarcely hear. 'I talk to people in a way I never have before. I talk to them properly, I'm forming friendships. I don't mean with men,' she added hastily, 'but caring friendships.'

'But there is a man.' It wasn't a question.

'Yes. No. I don't know.' She paused miserably. 'He's younger than me, he's not really interested, but I'm so out of touch with how people behave, I'm not sure. We went out to Bradley Moor last week, I was looking for berries to dye the wool – and it all went wrong and I fell in a marsh and he had to rescue me. I was soaked, I had to take my habit off in his car – can you imagine me doing that?' She paused in her breathless recital and looked back over her shoulder at the old nun, her face alive with rueful amusement and a pain Sister Godric didn't understand until Anna added, 'And when I was back home, and the day was over and I was myself again, Sister Gabriel, I found I was thinking: Oh, dear Lord, I don't want to be the way I am, always by myself, not imporant to anyone. I couldn't bear . . .' there was desperation in her voice '. . . I couldn't bear to go up the stairs to my bed alone.'

Sister Godric read the message of Anna's taut back. 'You do realise,' she started carefully, 'that in many ways, these are the worst years for you. And not only you,' she added hastily, 'for all of us, the early thirties are hard. When you first entered, you had so much you wanted to achieve here, so many goals to reach, everything to learn. There wasn't any spare time to think. But now there is, and you're naturally conscious of the things you lack. The things you may soon be too old to experience.' She paused, then added quietly, 'That's what that unhappiness of yours was really all about, wasn't it?'

Anna winced at the memory. 'That book I read said it was difficult to come to terms with the fact that in a few years, it would be impossible to have babies.' She couldn't look at Sister Godric. 'It's not just difficult, it's dreadful. I want a baby. I know it's just my body, just a biological impulse – but it doesn't *feel* that way. Sometimes I think I'll die if I can't have one.' It sounded terrible when she'd said it, hysterical, but she had no words to explain the physical pain of her wanting. 'Just to hold,' she said, 'just to love.' She bent her head to hide the stupid tears. 'I've never spoken like this to anyone else. I'm sorry.'

'Nonsense.' The older woman's tone was full of sympathy. 'Don't you dare to be sorry. You should thank the good Lord he made you a whole woman with all your emotions.'

Anna couldn't reply: she'd heard it before. God did not want dried up human beings with nothing to offer Him. The more she could sacrifice, the greater the love. The theory had convinced her, years ago. It did not convince her now. The old nun watched the averted face and understood more than Anna thought.

'I went through the menopause just like everyone else and I know what it cost me to accept it: there's a very special pain for a celibate woman. Not only did I never experience married love and children, but now I never could.' She straightened up, put her hands firmly on her knees. 'It taught me one thing and I'll tell it you, though maybe I shouldn't. If you feel like this now, at your age, you'll suffer a very great deal when that time comes. You'll need a strong faith to get you through.' She waited. 'Can you find that faith, Sister Gabriel?'

'I feel like a traitor,' Anna said, almost without thinking, unaware that this was the first time she had admitted to anyone in the order that she was seriously considering leaving. 'If I do go, I'd be deserting so many friends.'

Sister Godric looked down to hide the startled expression in her eyes. She had known Anna was struggling. She had not known it had gone this far. She wanted to cry, don't go, don't leave, I need you here, the pleasure of looking at you, talking to you.

But what she actually said was quite different. 'Abandoning

religious life used to be seen as faithlessness, like infidelity in a marriage. You can look at going in two ways. You can torture yourself and believe you can't live religious life any longer because you're inadequate. Or you can admit that you need deep human relationships, which we cannot have here because we concentrate on the love of God.' Sister Godric paused and added carefully, 'You aimed for the highest, when you entered. You lived the life for thirteen years. It's no crime to admit you failed: the crime would be to stay for negative reasons.'

'You do understand, it's not a question of my turning my back on Christ. But I feel I've given up my freedom and I can't take that any more.'

'You don't have to justify yourself to me, Sister. It's only the past that's holding you here. Security, and maybe not wanting to hurt some of us.' She waited for Anna's reluctant agreement. 'Of course your leaving would bring us sadness, because someone dear has gone.' Her voice was deep with conviction. 'You have a chance to rethink a decision you thought you'd taken irrevocably years ago. Make sure you get it right this time.' She lifted her head and listened attentively. 'It must be almost time for Vespers.' The gold-rimmed glasses tapped twice for emphasis on the heavy accounts book. 'We'd better decide how you are to approach these London bankers.'

'This can't go on, Sister.' Mother Emmanuel patted the earth firmly down over three hyacinth bulbs for emphasis. 'The situation's becoming farcical.'

They were in the old stables potting up bulbs for Christmas. Anna kneaded the crumbly compost between her fingers and let it sprinkle over the narcissus she was putting in a woven basket. She didn't answer. In the dim light – they'd shut the top half of the door as well to keep out the cold – her superior's mouth was a study in stubborn determination. When she added, 'I cannot continue to allow you such freedom. It's most irregular,' Anna judged it politic to agree.

'I know, Mother. I hadn't planned to take so much time.

It's just that there's such a lot to do at the mill. And the house. So many problems I can't seem to solve.'

'They are not your problems, Sister. You've taken on far more than you should.'

'I can't let Lynn down.' Certainty was eroded by Mother Emmanuel's disapproving expression as the superior placed the finished earthenware bowl on a bench with exaggerated care. In a moment of startling awareness, Anna felt barely contained violence beneath the restrained gestures.

'Do you really need me to point out that you're letting the order down? Letting me down?' Mother Emmanuel's tone was as controlled as her movements and equally unnerving: she was angry. 'Our Lord needs you here, Sister Gabriel. Your sisters need you. You're one of our best workers.' She gestured towards the neat rows of pots and bowls which bore evidence to the two hours Anna had spent in the icy stable. 'I think you're in danger of forgetting where your loyalties should lie.'

Anna blinked. It was always the same. Mother Emmanuel could be marvellous if she felt you leant on her: the weaker women in the order brought out her protectiveness. But she had little time for arguments, scant patience with people who had minds of their own. Whenever Anna tried to talk to her as if she were a responsible adult, the prioress's intimidating eyes reduced her to the old – and outlawed – status of 'inferior'.

'Have you anything to say, Sister?'

'No, Mother.' She made an effort. 'Yes, Mother. I have to do one more thing for Lynn.' Mother Emmanuel waited. 'The baby's due any time now, she really can't manage any business meetings. It's vital that I see the bank on her behalf. She can't cope.'

Refusal was forming like ice over the stern features. 'And you can?' The cool question.

'I . . . the mill needs to secure a loan Simon negotiated. We're afraid they'll want to call it in.' She plunged her hands into the bag of compost. 'Please, Mother. I only need a few extra days and it would make all the difference for Lynn.'

'The bank, you say.' Like everyone who never has sufficient money, Mother Emmanuel was awed by banks.

'Yes, Mother.' No need to confuse the issue by adding the bank was in London. She caught herself up: a few weeks ago, she would not have dared hold back such information.

The pause was endless. Anna went on with her potting, though she was unable to remember afterwards what she'd planted.

'How terrible, to be alone for the birth of a child. Your sister-in-law must be a very unhappy woman.' With unexpected gentleness, Mother Emmanuel popped a couple of bulbs into their compost bed and covered them over. In her movements now, Anna sensed the generosity of spirit of which this doughty woman was sometimes capable.

'You may have a further week, then.' She hesitated; it was almost as if she'd heard Anna's thoughts. 'No. I'll have to ask a formal permission of the Bishop anyway: I'd best make that two weeks.' She started to fill another bowl. 'Telephone if there's any news of the baby. We will pray for you all.'

13

'Five sixes're thirty, five sevens're thirty-five, five eights're forty, five . . .'

Anna was sewing buttons on a blue check school shirt while she listened to Bax recite his tables.

'. . . five twelves're . . .'

The crash from the kitchen was followed by Lynn's yell. 'What are you doing? You stupid little . . .' Jamie's howl of fear was punctuated by a smack and turned to a wail of pain. Bax dropped his tables book as he leapt up and tore into the kitchen.

'Stop it Mum, that's not *fair*, you said he could help make custard, you said you wanted us to help you, you *said*!' Anna, following, saw his face flush with indignation as he put his arms protectively round his sobbing brother. At the smaller child's feet, a thick yellow puddle spread slowly from a broken bowl.

Anna dropped a tea-towel on top of it and said in a low voice, so the children couldn't hear, 'There's no call to hit the child.'

Lynn leant against the wall, tears streaming down her face. She looked an utter wreck. She was gasping and speechless and Anna recognised hysteria.

'Go on boys, go in the hall for a minute, it's all right.' She bundled the children out of the kitchen, walked over and stood in front of her sister-in-law. She knew she ought to slap Lynn's face – wasn't that the way to deal with it? – but she couldn't bring herself to such drastic action. Instead she held out her arms. Lynn stared for a moment as if she couldn't believe what she was seeing, then flung herself against Anna, sobbing wildly.

'Oh Anna, Anna, what'm I going to *do* it's all so awful and hopeless and I'm frightened I can't manage by myself I need Simon . . .' The words were lost in tears as Anna cradled her, sharing her sorrow. 'I just want Simon, want him back and I'll never . . .' Anna found she was rocking forwards and back, patting Lynn's shoulder, feeling the unaccustomed warmth of another person.

'There there, don't cry, don't.' The terrible, sweet smell of Lynn's grief hurt her. 'Don't cry, hush now, hush.' However she tried, the pregnant woman's pain was too great for her to comprehend. But she actually felt her heart squeezed by it, and she murmured, 'I'm here, I'll help you, you're not alone.'

It seemed a long time before Lynn's tears slowed and she released Anna. 'Oh,' she said, 'I wish you'd done this before.' She wiped her eyes with her fingers and sniffed. 'I needed someone to hold on to. That's the worst thing, having no one to hold.'

'Are you all right now? It can't be good for the baby, you getting upset like that.'

'The baby's fine. Going to be a footballer. Feel.' Without warning Lynn took Anna's hand and held it against herself. Anna resisted for a minute and then, under her palm, she felt the quick, convulsive tremor beneath the hard drum of Lynn's stomach. 'That's his foot,' said Lynn. 'By the feel of it, he's got boots on already.'

Anna took her hand away fast. 'It's fantastic,' she said dutifully, pleased at Lynn's recovery. But she couldn't see how Lynn knew it was a foot, she couldn't envisage the baby curled in there. And she didn't want to: it seemed somehow distasteful, a growth.

Lynn sighed and pushed the tea-towel with her foot. 'Hell, what a mess. It's my fault, I wasn't watching him, poor little devil. I didn't mean to.'

'I know.' Anna started to clean up. 'I think Bax was more upset though. He feels responsible for Jamie.'

'They're such little boys.' Lynn's voice was mournful and Anna said hastily, 'Let's go and get fish and chips tonight. It'll cheer us all up. I'm paying.'

After supper Anna sat with the boys while they shared their bath. When she wrapped Jamie in a warm towel and rubbed his hair dry he leaned his damp little body against her, sucking his thumb and crooning a song about a spider. She put him to bed and tucked him in. Usually Lynn said, 'Give Auntie Anna a kiss' and he would comply politely. This was the first time he'd done it spontaneously. Arms tight round her neck, his lips making a patch on her cheek that stayed damp for a long time.

Afterwards, while Lynn watched television and did some sewing, Anna went back to the bathroom. Breaking the pattern of weeks – she never used the lights when she was in here alone – she turned on the battery of bulbs, bright as an actress's dressing-room, round the mirror. On an impulse, she turned her back on it while she pulled off the scapular, kicked away her sandals, unbuckled her belt, let the habit drop to the floor.

She took off the heavy veil and undid the white band and the tight serré-tête which encased her hair. Then she turned slowly to confront her naked reflection for the first time.

Her image stared gravely back, unexpectedly arresting. She examined with curiosity this face Hal had kissed. Years of conditioning – no mirrors, denial of all personal vanity – had left her feeling unconnected to her appearance. So she could scrutinise herself with absolute candour as if she were a stranger. A stranger older, calmer, than the girl she still thought of as herself. A woman looked back at her: eyes the deep blue-grey of Welsh slate, curving lips disconcertingly sensual against pale skin. She pressed the back of her hand against them, as if to blot out the print of Hal's kiss.

She stared in mounting horror at her hair. Or what was left

of it. Ran a hand over her head, rough and warm as always. She hadn't realised it was such a nondescript brown, dull and lifeless, flattened to her scalp in some places, standing up wildly in others, chopped into jagged points over the years by nail scissors used blind. She pulled a bit forward to see if she could make a fringe but it sprang back.

She'd had so much hair once she could hardly braid it. It had been a heavy golden-brown plait until the day of her Clothing.

That had been another autumn morning. She had knelt before the Bishop dressed as a bride, veiled in gauze and carrying yellow flowers. And hoping that the collar of her brother's old rugger shirt, which she'd worn underneath for warmth, wouldn't pop up and spoil the effect.

The elderly man had turned to her, splendid in vestments the colours of stained glass.

'What do you ask?'

'The mercy of God and the grace of the holy habit.'

'Do you ask it with your whole heart?'

'Yes, my lord, I do.'

'God grant you perseverance, my daughter.'

The service had passed in a blur. The second time she knelt before him, the two matrons of honour had removed her bridal head-dress, stripped off her veil. That was when he'd taken a pair of silver scissors that looked too small for their task and cut off her plait. It was a sign of her flight from worldly pomp. Afterwards, they burned it to ash in the sacristy: a pledge of immolation.

'She shall receive a blessing from the Lord, and mercy from God the saviour.' They'd taken her into a small room off the nuns' choir. It had been dark in there and the door closed behind her.

There was the eerie feeling she was being watched. Quickly she had turned and the horror of it was scarcely lessened by the whispered warnings she'd had from the other novices.

A nun sat in the darkest corner. She wore the full habit: grey and black, silver crucifix at her waist. But beneath the white headband hollow sockets gaped, gleam of bones and teeth. On her lap dreadful fingers drooped.

The skeleton had come to England with the order a hundred years before and this was its role. In a moment unintentionally combining heavy symbolism and black comedy, Sister Death was supposed to move forward and embrace the new nun.

Anna couldn't help the little shriek, though she knew they were waiting outside. It was another relic of their medieval origins. Another sign – though of course she hadn't seen it then – of the cultural chasm which yawned between the practices of this ancient order and the modern young women who entered it. A chasm that had proved too wide, in the end, for her to leap.

The door had opened, the sisters had laughed. A schoolgirl joke with undertones she didn't want to think about. They helped her out of her wedding clothes and into a plain underslip, thick stockings, sandals. The next thing she knew, the prioress was running clippers quickly over her head and short locks lay on her shoulders and the ground: the shock, even though she had expected it, was profound.

They had dressed her in the habit. *Clothe my soul, O Lord, with the nuptial robe of chastity, that pure and undefiled I may wear it before Thy judgement seat*. Then the cincture and crown. *O my dear Lord Jesus Christ, who for my sake became obedient unto death, even unto the death of the cross, grant me the true spirit of religious obedience and prayer*. Then the band round her head. *Place Thyself, O lord, as a seal upon my forehead, that I may be of the number of those who followed the Lamb*.

They put on her the coif. *Create a clean heart in me, O my God, and renew a right spirit within my breast*. And the scapular. *O Jesus, meek and humble of heart, teach me to deny myself, to take up my cross daily and follow Thee*.

Anna had returned to the altar unrecognisable as the bride of minutes before. The Bishop had handed her the leather girdle for the matrons to buckle round her waist. *May the Lord gird you with justice and purity, so that you may be worthy to approach the divine bridal chamber.* Then the white veil. *O Immaculate Heart of Mary, obtain for me purity of body and soul.*

A lighted candle had been placed in her hand. 'Grant her grace to persevere,' the prelate intoned, 'so that with Thy protection and help she may accomplish the desire Thou has given her.'

Anna had knelt on the prie-dieu, the candle in its silver holder beside her, while the prelate spoke of the life she would lead; the pleasures of the senses she was giving up for ever, the hard work and obedience that faced her, the silence and loneliness that would be hers 'From now until death if all goes well.'

Afterwards, she had preceded him from the chapel, heading a procession through the convent grounds, across the gravelled drive to the door of the enclosure. She had knocked. 'Open to me the gates of justice.' And from inside, voices had answered. 'This is the gate of the Lord, the just shall enter.' The heavy panelled door had opened to reveal the prioress, the great crook of the order in her hand, the entire community behind her.

Anna had stepped onto the threshold and knelt. 'This is my last resting place for ever.'

The prelate had taken her hand and given her to the prioress. 'We hereby entrust to you our sister,' he had said, 'and pray that, under the guidance of the holy Rule and through obedience, she may deserve to obtain perfect union with God. May the peace of the Lord be always with you.'

And she had passed over the threshold into the enclosure. Behind her, the door had been closed and locked.

Anna brushed quick fingers across her eyes and sniffed. She'd been so young. In all the years since then she had never once seen her own reflection and she'd somehow supposed she still looked the same. Whereas the reality was awful, worse than she'd ever imagined.

The red indentation over her eyebrows where the white band had pressed for so many years was an angry scar. She stared at it for a long time, pressed with a cautious finger as if expecting it to hurt. She touched under her lower lashes where tiny lines slid intimation of how she would look in another ten years. She noted shadows of fatigue, but not how the faint blue beneath her eyes intensified their colour.

Then she considered her body. The light emphasised the pallor of her flesh against the darker hands and forearms, which had been exposed to sun and wind in the convent garden. Years of hard work and simple food had got rid of the rounded limbs of the seventeen-year-old girl she had seen the last time she looked in a glass. She put her hands on her hips and felt the sturdy knobs of her pelvic bones. She'd known she was slimmer but hadn't anticipated this leanness, the taut flesh of arms and legs. She was spare and fit as a greyhound. She pressed her breasts with her fingertips, gingerly, as if they weren't hers. They were no bigger than when she was a girl. Smaller, in fact, soft suggestions of breasts set far apart, nipples crinkled dark in the harsh light.

Her shoulders seemed too broad for her shorn head so it looked ridiculously small, out of proportion. Even the strong column of her neck looked odd. Maybe it would be better if she could grow her hair. She twisted round to see the back. Not so bad: it grew long on the nape of her neck where she hadn't cut it. In fact her rear view was a decided improvement, the long waist narrow and graceful.

She glanced at her other, darker hair, the curly bush at the base of her belly. The only unmistakably feminine bit of me, she thought wryly. She brushed a tentative hand over it, soft and electric, felt like a shock the answering anticipatory quiver between her legs.

The reminder of what she'd struggled so hard to obliterate brought her up short. She hadn't touched herself for a long time. The order's Rule advised: *Touch no one, and do not allow yourself to be touched by anyone without necessity or evident reason.* They were warned to watch the senses, the five guardians of the heart. The thin silver wedding band on her left hand meant she was a bride of Christ. Her novice mistress explained that though the expression was losing favour among some orders as the women argued against this masculine view of their role, these were in the active orders where the nuns had outside jobs. For enclosed like themselves, she had said, a married setting was very appropriate. 'You go through a courtship, an engagement, and then you're married and the love grows deeper as you go on.'

The words of her Solemn Profession had emphasised this. 'The King has greatly desired your beauty.' The Bishop had placed the ring on her finger. 'Keep perfect fidelity to your Bridegroom, that you may deserve to be admitted to the eternal marriage feast.'

'I am espoused to him,' she had replied, 'whom the angels serve; whose beauty sun and moon behold with wonder.'

It had seemed important then that she was a virgin. Untouched, unused, innocent. They assured her it was a consummation of love between God and the soul. Her virginity was valuable, a special gift. Virginity is of gold, they said, chastity of silver, marriage of brass. The root and flower of her virginity was a crucified life. A virgin was purity's immolation, the victim of chastity.

And she had accepted it all. Accepted that by her vow of chastity she had cleared the decks, cleared her soul for union with God. Accepted that it was pure grace, that it made her every act sacred.

And she had believed it all. It was only now, years later, that she saw it as piously motivated manipulation.

That was all a long time ago. As if it had happened to another person. The life had not changed. Only she had. For all those years she'd hidden her body beneath draperies, her spirit behind bars. She had neutralised herself and her emotions, taken a perverse pride in the denial of human needs and satisfactions.

Anna continued to stare at herself. Well, pride came before a fall. She was almost thirty-two years old. Maybe she should start to make another life for herself. Alone this time, without the strength and protection of a community.

It was a daunting prospect. She had no profession, no

training, no discernible talents. She did have a mill to run, an overdraft to service and her brother's family to support. And a bevy of London bankers to face.

That thought sent her closer to the mirror. She pulled her hair this way and that. On an impulse she filled the basin with hot water and washed it quickly using the children's shampoo, roughly towelled it dry. She opened the cupboard over the basin and poked around among Lynn's jars and tubes till she found a narrow silver canister. She read the instructions and squirted a mound of white mousse into her palm, worked it into her hair. She regarded the result dubiously and tried combing it. Not good. She found Lynn's bag of rollers and chose a couple of the smaller ones, winding her hair inexpertly round the bristles, biting her tongue with the effort. She tried larger ones on top but after a minute or two they all started to loosen and fall out.

She wrapped herself in a towel and perched on the step of the sunken bath staring at her pale and bony feet. They looked as neglected as the rest of her. Lynn wore scarlet varnish on her toe-nails. Lynn's legs didn't have faint dark hairs like her own, they were shaved smooth and silky. Lynn was like other women: even in her unhappiness she knew the rules.

She didn't know when she started crying but it was the first time she'd done so since the morning Mother Emmanuel had told her of Simon's death. As if Lynn's outburst had released her own sorrow, and once started she couldn't stop. It wasn't just her hair, it was for Lynn too, and Simon and everything she'd thought she'd found but had really lost, and the terrible mess of it all. She muffled her face in the bathtowel so no one would hear her gasping sobs. She rocked herself forward and back, finally giving way to her grief.

There was a scuffling outside the bathroom door. 'Auntie Anna, is that you in there?' Bax's voice cracked with concern. 'What's wrong?'

She sniffed, swallowed, wiped her face ineffectually with her towel. 'Nothing, Bax, I'm fine.'

'I heard you crying,' the boy insisted. 'I'm going to get

Mum.' He scurried away. Anna hauled herself upright, got into the terry-cloth robe Lynn had lent her, unlocked the door. When Lynn came in, she was washing her face. Lynn watched her bent back.

'What's up? Bax said . . .' As Anna raised her head from the basin, her sister-in-law stared in amazement. 'What on earth . . .?'

Anna put both hands over the rollers as if to hide them. 'Don't laugh.'

Lynn leaned against the door. 'I haven't felt like laughing for the last two months. But this . . .' She shook her head and her face curved into a huge grin. 'What have you been doing to yourself?'

Anna looked into the mirror again and hastily away. 'I was trying to set it or something,' she muttered, conscious of Bax listening outside. 'I didn't know it was such a mess.'

Lynn looked puzzled. 'But does it matter? No one can see it.'

'I'm going to London next week, I don't want to wear my habit. I want to look business-like. And no one wears hats, do they?'

'Oh, you poor girl.' Lynn was really laughing now, head back, eyes crinkling. 'I'm sorry,' she spluttered, 'I'm sorry. But I never saw anything so funny in my life. Ooh!' She held onto her waist. 'God, I'm getting a stitch.'

Her glee was impossible to resist. Anna started to smile. She caught sight of herself in the mirror: wild hair, absurd bright rollers at odd angles, and she was laughing too, staggering with mirth, holding on to the edge of the basin, unable to stop. But it was painful laughter, coming up from somewhere deep inside where she had never before dared venture. She was racked by it so that her ribs hurt and her jaws ached, out of all control.

It was Lynn, finally, who pulled herself together. Wiping her eyes with a tissue she gasped, 'You must go to a hairdresser.'

'I can't!' Anna laughed more at the idea. 'I don't know what

to ask for! I'd look such a fool!' This struck them both as
hilarious.

Lynn said, 'Here, let's have a go.' She pushed Anna down
onto a stool, pulled out the rollers and attempted to wind the
hair round them. 'It's all different lengths,' she conceded
reluctantly, 'I can't do anything. You'll have to get it properly
cut. I'll fix an appointment in the morning and I'll come with
you. If you can go to those bankers for me, this is the least I
can do for you.'

Anna started to protest, then stopped herself. For the first
time she felt at ease with Lynn. They'd come near that day
Lynn had lost her temper and screamed at her, but it hadn't
lasted. They had nothing in common but Simon, they were
from different worlds. She understood that Lynn was jealous
of her freedom but she couldn't explain her own envy – of her
sister-in-law's looks, her poise, her children. Her pregnancy.
She had to accept what Lynn wanted to do for her. Instead of
arguing she nodded.

'You're right. I'll leave it to you.'

Lynn was standing beside her, a roller in each hand. On an
impulse, she embraced Anna, holding her close. Anna resisted
for a moment, held back by the pattern of years. Something
must be happening to her: people were starting to touch her.
Then she hugged Lynn back warmly, the hard bulge of the
baby between them. 'Thanks, love.'

'Are you serious about going to London dressed . . .' Lynn
hesitated.

'. . . like a normal person,' Anna finished for her. 'I don't
know what I'm going to wear, though. Sister Godric said, if I
go in my habit, they'd not take me seriously and she's right. I
haven't thought about clothes yet,' she added in sudden alarm.
'D'you think I could maybe borrow something of yours?'

They spoke in whispers so that Jamie, thumb in mouth, slept
on oblivious as Anna tried on blazers and skirts, shirts and
coats. In the end they settled on a slim-fitting suit of deep blue
wool with a white silk shirt. The skirt was too big on the waist,

but a navy leather belt solved that. Because Anna was taller than Lynn the skirt was short on her, just skimming her knees, and she hissed, 'I can't, really,' but Lynn handed her an electric razor and a pair of sheer navy stockings and said, 'In for a penny, in for a pound.'

Anna took them with reluctance.

'And by the way,' Lynn went on inexorably, 'you'll have to get yourself some underwear. Nothing of mine will fit you, and those things of yours are too bulky. You need a bra under that shirt.' She watched the expression on Anna's face. 'And while you're at it, you need some decent shoes. With heels,' she added, 'that suit will look frumpy with flats.'

Anna nodded obediently, and next day on her way to work parked near Darley Street and walked down the hill through the shopping precinct. It was early, barely nine, and some of the stores were still closed. It was the first time she'd looked at clothes and related them to herself and she was taken aback by the brief skirts and minimal tops. Styles were extraordinary, she thought, tight matching leggings under straight skirts, or wide trousers like comic sailors with striped sweaters and heavy laced shoes. All the shops looked far too extreme for her.

At the bottom of Darley Street she found the only shop she remembered which seemed scarcely to have changed: the silk ties in Rackham's window tastefully draped over a riding crop, dinner dresses and pearls, expensive shoes. When she got inside, even the counters looked familiar, and the salesladies in Cosmetics, their faces immaculately overlaid with lipstick and eyeshadow even at this hour, could have been those she remembered from childhood visits. Her mother had always bought Cyclax, powder and creams in lilac pink boxes. She hurried past them, conscious of surreptitious glances at her habit, took the lift to the first floor and Ladies Lingerie. She stood for so long looking at the department that the elderly man who operated the lift asked her if this was the right floor. She smiled at him helplessly and moved forward, wishing fervently that she'd had the sense to wear Lynn's suit.

In front of her, in a perfumed pastel space, were creations of satin and swansdown, Lycra and lace. Shimmering silk slips hung next to oversized T-shirts printed with giant cartoon animals. Sheer camisoles jostled garments more suitable for Scarlett O'Hara than Bradford matrons: low-cut brassières all in one piece with boned corselets ending in a frill and long suspenders. Anna tore her gaze from these to find she was staring at briefs in flesh-coloured nylon which appeared to be totally transparent.

A couple of assistants glanced up from their desk and Anna felt their suspicious stares. Intimidated, she pushed through the tiers of knickers and frilly suspender belts to the far end of the department. Here were deep velvet wrappers and flowery padded housecoats bulky enough to keep out a winter's night at the North Pole. She glanced at a price-tag and blinked: surely not a hundred and forty-five pounds?

She picked out a pair of knickers decorous by the standards of the department but the height of frivolity for her and gazed at them doubtfully: they didn't look as if they'd keep out a determined draught. The pants she had on beneath her habit she had made herself, of soft flannel. And lucky to have them, as the older sisters pointed out. When many of those women entered religious life they hadn't worn pants at all, since they had not been part of the medieval wardrobe to which their order still adhered so strictly. Other sisters, she knew, had modernised sufficiently to purchase underwear in bulk from Marks & Spencer. She wondered if the St Michael brandname had clinched the choice.

With a sigh she went back to the circular stands of bras and read the descriptions on the packets. Wired, strapless, half-cup. Perfect control, added uplift, firm separation, hidden support: the promises could have been for marriage guidance rather than underwear.

There were photographs round the stands of underclad women exhibiting expanses of exuberant flesh encased in different styles. They weren't much help: although bosoms obviously came in more sizes and shapes than she would have believed, she couldn't see one who looked like her. She tried again with the labels. 34AA. 36C. 38B. And made a vain attempt to remember the size of her last bra. She had taken two into the convent with her. The day after her Clothing, when she'd moved from the short postulant's dress into the full habit, her washing was left as usual on her bed, but her underwear was never returned.

It was airless in the department and hushed music filtered through the racks. She glanced desperately over rails billowing with filmy things, many totally new to her. How could she have supposed a teddy was a cuddly toy? And when did women start wearing Merry Widows, all black satin and net and scarlet bows like costumes for a Viennese operetta?

Anna halted for a long time in front of a model on a stand displaying a full length nightdress and *peignoir* of satin the colour of a grey cloud, a flower embroidered on the bodice in tiny pearls. It was beautiful enough to be an evening dress: she gazed at it with awe. She had forgotten – if she had ever known – that such garments existed and that women wore them. Anyone would look lovely in it. She thought of her thick cotton nightdress with its long sleeves and round collar, the scratchy sheets in which she slept at the convent. This was another world. She put out a tentative hand to touch it – and drew back sharply, appalled by how roughened and work-stained it looked against the delicate fabric. Her eyes blurred with self-pity and she chided herself. You idiot, such things aren't for you. They're vanity and self-indulgence. Wicked extravagance.

But so pretty, a little voice in her head mourned. For other women, not for me. Never for me.

She turned from the blank-faced model, took a step back and her long veil caught on one of the many little hangers on the carousel behind. When she attempted to struggle free half a dozen tiny garments fell to the floor. She stopped to pick them up and crouched there, trying to sort out the tangle of broderie anglaise and ribbon, mortified by her clumsy incompetence. It was only when she saw dark marks on the pale fabrics that she realised she was crying. What was the matter with her? No one wept over bras and pants. She held the ridiculous flimsies crushed against her as she struggled to stifle her tears, her one thought to avoid attracting attention. As if – the little inner voice was ironic now – a sobbing nun among the knickers could go unnoticed.

'That's all right, Madam, I'll do it.' Trim black-stockinged legs stopped in front of her. Anna heard her own flustered apologies as the girl deftly sorted the hangers and replaced them. 'Now then, Madam, can I help you?' Her tone made it clear that Anna was expected to purchase something. She was very young, hair pinned neatly on top of her head, and if she found Anna's appearance odd, she didn't let it show. 'Are you looking for yourself or . . .' she paused delicately, 'for someone else?'

'That's right,' Anna agreed gratefully, blinking fast to clear her eyes. 'I'm buying a present for my sister-in-law. Only I don't know her measurements.' She gestured towards herself. 'She's about the same size as me, and she wants something very simple.' The girl nodded and eyed Anna's chest with professional disinterest.

'About a 34A, she'll want then.' Anna wondered how she could be so sure, given the bulk of the habit. The assistant moved round the carousel, took down three brassières. 'These are the plainest we do.' Anna pointed wordlessly to the middle one, handed over the knickers she was clutching and fished in her capacious central pocket for her purse. She'd had enough of shopping. Shoes could wait.

She borrowed a sweater and skirt from Lynn to go to the hairdresser, Stylist, Lynn corrected her. The shop ('salon' Lynn hissed) was large and white with black furniture and spotlights and washbasins along one side. No private curtained cubicles as she'd hoped, but a lot of black towels. Alan was a tough-looking man in his thirties wearing a baggy white shirt tucked into heavily-belted denims. His own dark hair was receding in front. Anna thought hopefully this would make him more sympathetic but it didn't. He pulled her short locks about ruthlessly.

'Terrible condition,' he said dispassionately. He fingered the ends. 'And you've been cutting it yourself.' It was an accusation.

Lynn interjected quickly, 'She's been . . . on a farm. In the middle of Wales. She never had time for haircuts.' She winked at Anna in the mirror and went off to buy fruit.

Alan grunted rudely and ran his comb through Anna's wet hair again. 'Head's a good shape,' he conceded. 'We'll even this out. Give you more body.' She tried not to watch as he attacked it with scissors and the expression of a man thinking about other things. Occasionally, clearly part of the job, he asked her a question impossible for her to answer. Where was she going on holiday this year? What shampoo did she normally use? When she told him home-made soap he stopped talking altogether.

It took two of them to dry her little bit of hair, with a bored fifteen-year-old assistant holding the dryer, and Alan pulling a stiff brush so hard through what was left she thought he'd loosened her scalp. Then he roughed it up with his fingers, hauling strands here and there into place before he fished out a mirror and silently showed her back and sides.

The reflection she saw could, as old Sister Edburga used to say, have been anybody. She was startled to discover the tough stylist had turned her into his sort of woman. He'd cropped her so short the hair at the front stood up thick and burnished as an animal's pelt. It was slightly longer on top, swept back to emphasise her well-shaped head, but exposing her neat ears. He'd given her tiny side-burns too, defining the high cheek-bones – she had somehow never noticed them before – and she could see in the glass that the back would have been almost masculine but for the skill with which he'd cut the sleek line where the hair tapered into the nape of her neck. She'd shaken her head, unable to accept the cool reflection as her own. 'That's . . . thank you,' had come out as a croak. The stylist had interpreted her wordless uncertainty as stunned delight and seemed pleased, managing a smile as Lynn paid what seemed to Anna an astronomic sum.

'Worth every penny,' she announced admiringly. 'So we'll eat spaghetti for a week.'

Then she drove to The Face Place and in answer to Anna's objections merely said, 'I've asked her to have a go at you. Don't argue. You've years of neglect to make up for.' Anna was draped in more towels, pink this time, and a girl with dauntingly perfect skin and *Denise* embroidered on her white overall plucked her eyebrows. ('I'm not taking out much, thick eyebrows are all the go at the moment, like Margaux Hemingway.') Anna wondered if she meant Ernest and kept quiet. She submitted to clarifying lotion and exfoliating cream, which sounded more suitable for forests, and then Denise made her up, showing how to shadow her eyes with smoky grey, choosing a clear lipstick. This time, Anna surveyed the result with guilty relief: she looked like other people. (*Better*, a triumphant little voice added, but she stifled it.) When she came out Lynn looked up from *Cosmopolitan*.

'My God,' she said. 'Cinderella isn't a fairy-story after all.'

14

Anna had no need of Lynn's borrowed alarm-clock to tell her it was almost five: she still kept convent hours. She lay for a moment savouring the warmth and softness of the duvet. More than two months since that bitter wakening in her cell – she glanced around at the bright colours of Jamie's room for reassurance. It was going to be a busy day and for once she allowed herself the luxury of saying her prayers in bed. Before she got up she heard Lynn going downstairs and when she'd bathed and dressed breakfast was waiting for her, although it was barely six.

Lynn was drinking a mug of tea leaning against the sink, her hair bunched on top of her head. She was pale and vulnerable, the skin round her eyes puffy from the tears she now allowed herself only at night, when she thought Anna could not hear, wrists painfully thin in the huge sleeves of Simon's striped bathrobe. She'd put on very little weight, making her pregnancy all the more pronounced. Her cheeks were hollow, Anna thought with pity, and she tried to sound more confident than she felt while she checked her papers, although she'd put everything ready the night before when she booked the mini-cab. As she left the house, she saw Lynn looking at the briefcase. Simon's of course. She'd got it out especially for this meeting and though Anna had protested she'd agreed in the end: the expensive black leather had a businesslike authority about it.

'You look great,' Lynn said at the door. 'Good luck.'

'I'll phone if it's all right. See you tonight. Take care.'

Peter Hallam had offered to drive her to the station but she had refused. After the disastrous trip to Bradley Moor she hadn't been to the mill in the two days before she returned to Wales. She'd told herself it was because her habit was soaking, but in truth she was too apprehensive. She'd been a fool – and told him so, on the drive back from the moor, saying how sorry she was for all the trouble she'd given him. He'd replied that she owed him no apologies.

She'd been working in her office for the last three days but Hal had been catching up on overtime and had only just returned. So they'd scarcely spoken. There had been other people around, and of course neither had referred to that embrace. It had meant nothing to him, she had concluded, it was just the sort of thing he'd have done with any woman in that situation. She resolved to put it out of her mind.

The shuttle to Leeds was a few minutes late and it was a rush to cross platforms to the already-packed London train. Conscious of Mother Emmanuel's injunction for travel ('Try to sit next to a nice woman, Sister Gabriel'), she dutifully attempted to do so. Even at this hour she had to search for a seat and found very few women. She passed a couple of carefully dressed executive types studying bulky documents, a third already dictating quietly into a machine. There were several young girls who might be secretaries going back to London after a weekend with Mum, and one twenty-year-old self-consciously taking off her navy coat to reveal a white shirt with epaulettes stamped HMP. There were no seats free near any of them except the prison officer and she was in a Smoking compartment. Anna had to settle for a window seat at the far end of the fourth carriage she tried.

She busied herself tucking her ticket away and then noticed someone had left a copy of the *Independent* tucked down the side of her seat. She'd considered buying a paper at the kiosk beside the escalator at Bradford but couldn't bring herself to spend the money on what still seemed to her a frivolity. At the convent, they took only *Osservatore Romano*, the official Vatican paper, and the *Tablet*. And Lynn, economising, bought just an occasional evening paper.

Anna pulled out the paper. It was the previous day's but the headlines seemed no less alarming for that: she hadn't realised so many countries were in chaos. Chile, Argentina, Lebanon. She read about Sikh shootings in India and blacks murdered in South African jails. The women's pages carried an article about a woman raped by her father when she was a child. Anna realised she was anxiously rubbing the slight mark that remained over her eyebrows and made herself stop or she'd smear the foundation Lynn had given her to conceal it.

A girl in a tailored blouse and a tie spoke at her shoulder, 'Would you like anything? Tea, coffee?' and gestured towards a loaded trolley.

Anna bought tea in a polystyrene cup which possibly accounted for the taste. Drinking it, she found herself watching the man sitting opposite. She usually made a conscious effort not to observe people around her. Custody of the eyes was an important part of convent practice. *An unchaste eye is partner to an unchaste heart.* One must look straight ahead, towards God. That was why some orders adopted blinkered head-dresses with exaggerated frills round the face, so the wearer's attention was not distracted. Anna dropped her eyes, but not before she'd seen the man's interested gaze on her knees. Embarrassed and affronted, she pulled her skirt down as far as she could, feeling a flush spreading over her neck. Damn, damn. She knew he was still watching, seeing her as just a pair of nice legs, giving her the sort of attention she didn't want, had not experienced for years.

No one looked at a nun like that. The occasional man she encountered in Wales – the gardener, the elderly priest who did not particularly care for nuns, but performed services for them because they were in his diocese – saw her not as an individual but as a stylised figure, part of a group. There had been no threats, she was absolutely safe. Even Stan Beattie's coarse jokes and deliberate stares had not fazed her. He was familiar, he knew who she was. What she had seen that night in Simon's office had not been meant for her eyes, and though it had been repellent, it had never threatened her.

She hadn't thought until now, when she was without it, that the habit had been a kind of costume. An identity she assumed each morning. She used to love all the details of it, like the cord at her waist with three knots for the three vows. Even now, when she was considering leaving the order, the habit was not one of her reasons. She was so accustomed to it that it had taken a curious event to make her realise that it no longer fitted her.

It had been in Bradford. She'd taken the boys to their nearby playground one afternoon while Lynn rested. It was cold and they had the place to themselves except for a young couple wrapped together on a bench oblivious to everything. Anna had noticed them with a little pang for their absorption and forgotten them. Jamie had fallen and cried loudly and the couple had become aware of them. Seeing Anna in her grey cloak and head-dress they had sprung apart and sat shamefaced and giggling. Anna had been horrified by their response. No matter what her private thoughts had been, they had seen only the message of her clothes: that she was against such expressions of life, of vitality and sexuality. Until then, she had thought of the habit as positive, a sign of God in the world. But perhaps it was a negative thing, making her into a cardboard image instead of a woman.

Well, she was being seen as a woman now and she wasn't particularly enjoying the experience. She'd asked for it, of course. The make-up she was wearing was little enough by normal standards but the flicker of mascara, the trace of lipstick, made her feel painted. And she was uncomfortably aware of the seat fabric against the skin of her legs: they felt ridiculously naked and long, she couldn't think what to do with them. She considered crossing them until she remembered Sister Godric and chastity. Nonsense, of course, but all the same it was a worldly thing to do. She pressed her knees together and wished she wasn't wearing a suspender belt, the little knobbly buttons dug into her thighs. The sheer stockings and unaccustomed heels – even though Lynn had sighed over them and said she'd meant *really* high – made her feel exposed and vulnerable, like a small creature that had been skinned. Anna shut her eyes. The carriage was stuffy and she was conscious of unfamiliar smells under the odour of British Rail coffee: deodorant and after-shave.

She was playing a game in the dark. She was beginning to realise that she was in many ways still a raw teenager. She might look sophisticated – the mirror that morning had shown that – but she was ignorant of even the simplest rules of behaviour between the sexes. She didn't know the moral standards of the day. How did other women cope with unwanted attentions like this? Would they be pleased, or annoyed? Maybe they were indifferent.

She didn't even know what to make of Hal's behaviour on Bradley Moor. She didn't think he'd ever try to repeat it. And if he did – she veered away from thinking about this – how would she react? She was still a nun, whatever her future plans, still bound by her vows. And by her faith. She did not think she could live the life any longer, but it had given her absolute conviction in her belief. Even so, she had to admit that Hal had moved and touched her. Impossible to deny that she had lain awake for hours at night since then.

Anna had been trained for so long to repress any thought of sex, to cast it out of her mind, that she could not now disentangle the knot of her emotions. On the one hand, Stan Beattie and that unknown woman doing those unspeakable things in the mill office had been deeply disturbing, had confirmed what she'd always supposed: sex was sordid and furtive, somehow dirty.

But that kiss in broad daylight out on the moor – it was hard for her to think that stemmed from lust also. It had been tender and sweet with a childlike simplicity. And it had excited her – she gave a quick little sigh at the thought – in ways she hardly dared admit. Her body had responded to his as if it wasn't bound to celibacy: it had wanted to hold him close, to act in ways she would not be able to control. There had been a dampness between her thighs and her breasts had ached to feel his hands on them . . .

Stop it. Stop it. Anna opened her eyes and sat up straight. God forgive me for such thoughts.

The man opposite smiled again and looked as though he was about to start a conversation.

She remembered a copy of the *Wool Record* Peggy had slipped into Simon's case and flipped through it more for something to hide behind than out of interest. She read most of one article before she realised the implications, went back over it with mounting excitement. 'Japan,' she read, 'heads the queue to sample new season's collections from the many Scottish mills now deeply involved in the silk trade. Strong Japanese interest was reported in silk/worsted blends. These suitings provide the executive in warmer climates with clothes which are light in weight and colour . . .' She skipped a paragraph. 'Mills now spin their own silk and wool blend yarns. The speciality for the coming season was a multi-fibre blend teaming wool with silk and linen.'

Pinch yourself in case you're dreaming, her grandmother used to say. She glanced away from the page, out of the grimy window. When she looked again the same words were still there. 'The Japanese, who have always been steady buyers of mohair . . . current feel for a silky handle and lighter weights . . . demand still growing . . . favourite combination is wool, silk and linen selling particularly well into Europe . . .'

This was what she'd been looking for. Why hadn't she seen it for herself? She and Lynn had already thought of dyeing pure silk yarn in toning colours which could be knitted in with their wools to make decorative patterns. But they hadn't taken it far enough. These Scottish mills were weavers, producing fabric for suitings and jacketings. What they did could be adapted for yarnspinning: now she'd had the idea it seemed incredible no one was doing so already. So far as she was aware, the only yarns which even approximated to what she had in mind were on a very small scale, at top prices, for the specialist market of couture fashion and art tapestries.

Nightingale Mill could produce not just her beautiful wool on its own but mixed with these speciality luxury fibres, silk and linen and mohair, light and lustrous, wonderful for knitting. And they could do it for the market Anna knew she could reach, the women in small towns like Welshpool, who knitted for pleasure.

She read the article carefully a third time then started making notes on the pad Simon had kept in his briefcase.

The bank occupied part of a large old building. Even the marble floors and uniformed commissionaire at the entrance failed to prepare her for the opulence of the offices within.

Two floors had been opened up to make a vast light space. From somewhere high up water cascaded through dense greenery to a blue pebbled pool. Curving iron staircases led to the floor above where she could see glass-walled offices. Although there was evidently great activity as people answered phones, typed or watched computer screens, she heard only water and very faint Spanish guitar music.

Except for the discreet lettering *Maynard Gideon* on the glossy brochure lying on the glass coffee table, this could have been part of a film-set. So could the man who now came towards her. He wore brown-tinted glasses and a slightly baggy suit even she recognised as being designed with international flair.

'Miss Summers, good to meet you. George Tyler. We talked on the phone.' He held out a hand. She hesitated for a fraction of a second. Two important points to remember, Sister Godric had said. 'First, make sure you look them in the eye. None of this downcast business. I know what we do here, but they'll think you a bashful idiot. And don't refuse to shake hands, whatever the rule says. A firm handshake, mind.'

Anna took his hand with a good grip. 'Good morning, Mr Tyler.' He held onto her for a moment longer than she had expected and she experienced a moment of worry. Maybe she'd held too tight, communicated something she hadn't meant. Not for the first time, she wished she knew the unspoken rules. 'Come and sit down.' He led the way towards the pool. Beside it, two pale leather couches stood at right angles as a conversation corner. In the angles, low tables carried Oriental lamps with shallow shades. The sofas were lower than she anticipated and she sat carefully, keeping her back straight. A uniformed maid brought a tray and poured coffee into large white cups. As she sipped, she looked around her. From the letter and address she had expected old-fashioned offices, heavy furniture, Dickensian authority.

She glanced across at George Tyler, who was placing a pocket dictaphone and a calculator beside his cup. She was thrown by this set-up: the interview was clearly going to take place informally.

'First of all, Miss Summers, can I say how sorry we were to hear about your brother? It must have been a great shock for you all.' She murmured something. He leant forward, switched on the small recorder. 'I understand you have a manager. A Mr Beattie? I'd hoped you would both be here today.'

Anna thought of Beattie, his increasingly truculent manner over the last weeks. To have told him of this massive debt would have presented him with a weapon. The less he knew, the better.

'We're very busy at the moment, he really couldn't spare a day. In fact, to fulfil present orders we're going to start working night shifts from next week.' She didn't feel it necessary to add this was because they were using the older, slower machines.

'That would be for . . .?'

'Courtaulds. We're doing a rush order of small lots for their shadecards.' She couldn't read his reaction behind those smokey glasses. She put down her coffee and reached for her briefcase. Sister Godric had shown her how to detail her plans and projections and Peggy had prepared them, setting them out clearly on separate pages. She'd gone to enormous trouble, getting a friend to type them on her word processor and running off extra copies. Then she'd taken them into town and had them bound in white folders with black spines. Anna had thought at the time this was unnecessary. She would have typed them on the old Olivetti and stapled them together. Not because she considered the papers unimportant, but that was the way things were done at the convent. It would have been considered false pride to present one's own work in such a fashion. Now, taking the professional-looking folders from Simon's beautiful leather case, she was profoundly grateful for Peggy's meticulous presentation.

While George Tyler was going through the folder, two men came over. They were introduced: one was clearly Tyler's boss. He spoke to Anna for a moment: he was sorry about their difficulties, hoped the situation could be satisfactorily resolved . . . A pocket phone bleeped and he excused himself. The second man stayed, poured coffee and sat in the far corner of the sofa opposite Anna.

Tyler made a couple of notes on a pad, then started to ask questions swiftly. What is your background for running a mill, your experience? Summers were now due to pay two instalments, when would this money be forthcoming? The bank needed assurances they would not default again, was she in a position to provide them? He laid the folder on the coffee table. There was a figure here he didn't understand – why had the mill returned a newly-purchased fancy-spinner? The loan had been negotiated for the purpose of acquiring new equipment.

The second man – she remembered his name on the letterhead, Daniel Stern – picked up her folder and leafed through it while he listened to her explain how she had spent the last two months familiarising herself with the mill and getting up to date. Tyler wanted to know what she had been doing until then and Anna thought of Lynn's answer to the hairdresser.

'I was farming in Wales,' she said. Well, it was true. 'I supplied local retailers with wool dyed to order and the demand was so great I couldn't keep up with it.' She leant forward, more animated now, sure of her ground, wanting him to understand. 'Summers is a small operation, I think probably the last vertical mill left in Bradford – '

'Vertical, Mrs Summers?' The quick query came from the second man, Daniel Stern. She'd forgotten about him. She turned slightly to see him.

'Miss,' she corrected him. 'A vertical mill is one which can carry out every process the wool goes through. Most are done by specialists these days, because the amounts are so huge. No one company takes the product literally from sheep to shop. But we do. We buy in the wool at auction and then it's cleaned and scoured for us. We even do some dyeing ourselves, so it goes through every stage at the mill.'

'But of course you don't market the end product.'

'No. It's delivered on huge reels and wholesalers package it in eight-ounce balls or whatever with their own name on it.' As she spoke, she considered Daniel Stern. He seemed far more conventional than Tyler, in a faultlessly-cut three piece suit and white shirt, silver links glinting in his cuffs. He was so immaculate that a silly joke came into her mind from years ago, one she used to make when her brother was dressed up for a dance: What time have you got to be back in the window? She felt her mouth widening into a smile and glanced down to hide it, then remembered Sister Godric's injunction and directed it at him instead. She didn't know, but it gave her an air of shining confidence which was almost entirely without foundation: she was gambling now, trying to sell her hopes.

'You'll see from the projections that we're moving into new areas, or rather,' she corrected herself, 'we hope to, if we can continue the financial arrangement with you. Up to now Nightingale Mill has produced conventional pure wool yarns, but I think we have to change that if we're to survive.'

George Tyler shifted his weight.

'With respect, Miss Summers, I sat here months ago and listened to your brother tell me he wanted to start producing – exotic yarns, I think he called them – hence his need for capital to purchase Swiss machinery. Which I see . . .' he held up her folder '. . . has been returned. Did it not prove satisfactory?'

His tone held a trace of sarcasm. 'Or did your brother misinterpret market trends?'

Anna kept still. For once, she blessed convent training. Never answer back. Never argue. Accept criticism. Use it. She consciously made herself relax. Anger would harm her, not George Tyler or Maynard Gideon.

'I'm sure my brother knew what he was doing when he bought the fancy-spinner,' she said quietly. 'He certainly made no mistake as to market direction. Go into any wool shop and the shelves are stacked with elaborate yarns with knots or sparkly finishes. You can even buy some that look like floating feathers, and they all sell. So yes, I believe Simon was right.' She paused.

After a moment Tyler said, 'But I understood Summers needed the fancy-spinner to produce all those yarns. So why didn't you keep it? If they're so popular.'

'The obvious answer is that it was costing us a great deal to repay and I think we can make that money work for us better in other ways.' She leaned forward. 'I can only use my own judgement. Simon was more adventurous than I am. He liked the new, he was excited by change. I'm very different, much more conventional. I prefer the past, traditional values.' Do I ever, she added to herself. Maybe she should have worn the habit after all.

'Perhaps you could elucidate,' Daniel Stern said. He sounded as if he was laughing at her, but his expression was serious. 'You mentioned possible new areas earlier, I think.'

Anna put a hand on her folder, saw his eyes follow and remembered the state of her hands. Oh, well.

'Yes. We're forming a new company to sell direct to the retailers. In the past, as you know, we've always supplied wholesale. I'd like to change that. Our original idea . . .' she gestured to the folder '. . . as you'll see, was to dye silk yarns to match and tone with our high-grade wool.' She didn't give herself time to worry, just plunged in with the ideas she'd juggled on the train. 'But now we're hoping to take that further. We'll actually mix natural fibres with our high-grade wool to produce at least three new yarns – silk for one, also linen and mohair.' She spoke faster, more fluently, absorbed in what she was saying. 'We may have old equipment, but it's effective and it produces good yarns. Our flyer-spinner can easily cope with what I've got in mind. Look.' She reached in the briefcase and brought out a sheaf of fashion magazines she'd bought at Euston. 'All these are designer clothes – and all use the mixtures I'm interested in. Their suppliers are probably Italian, judging by the colours. But any woman who can knit would want to buy similar yarns, and yet I only know of one or two specialist firms producing them here, and very expensively.'

'Just a minute,' Tyler objected, 'aren't you risking burning your fingers? I imagine if there was a demand, someone would have come along to fulfil it already. Summers are in no position to risk investing in an area they don't know. What if no one wants to buy?'

'There's a market,' Anna said with conviction. 'In Wales, I produced wool on a very small scale for a local shop. In just over a year, demand grew until it was greater than I could meet.'

'You didn't expand?' This was Stern, quietly. She thought fast.

'The wool was a sideline, and it wasn't my decision. The point I'm making is that I knew what people wanted, I got it right. That was five or six years ago, when the hand-knitting market really took off. And I'm certain I've got it right again.' She handed him the *Wool Record* opened at the article she'd read on the train. 'I intend to find fresh markets. You see from this that Japan is heavily into these fibres and they've always liked English wool. My brother wasn't really interested in exporting his yarns, I don't know why. But I intend to. I'm writing to the trade department at the Japanese embassy and I'll send samples. Then we'll see.'

'That sounds enterprising.' She thought Stern was laughing at her again, but no sign.

'But obviously still in the planning stages.' George Tyler

came in. 'You'll have quite a job to bring that off successfully. In the meantime, can you convince us that you have a product which will really interest people?'

Anna breathed slowly, to keep herself calm. Only she need ever know she was literally making this up as she went along. 'Our new yarns will all be four-ply so they're easy to knit up together. But the main thing is colour. They'll be dyed to match exactly in the most wonderful shades you can imagine. We'll also have a lot of creams and white, for summer wear. And where possible we'll use natural dyes, augmented with chemicals so they're constant.' She turned to Stern. 'Women like the idea of natural things, it fits with the mood of the times. You've only to look at the cosmetic firms specialising in cleansers and shampoos made from fruit and flowers.'

'Where will you get your silk?' he wanted to know.

She sent out a quick prayer of gratitude to Walter Street for the expertise he had shared so generously over their cup of coffee. 'Some Chinese. It's expensive but the standard's fantastic. For the mixture I'll use first quality Japanese. Handspun – another selling point for us. But it's very expensive: that's one of the reasons for sending back the fancy-spinner.'

'Supplies are going to be restricted.' She flashed him a look of surprise. She had read this in the *Wool Record* but surely he hadn't. 'The unit price of mulberry silk goods increased by almost sixteen per cent last year. The availability of raw silk from China has always presented a problem. Even with people prepared to pay high prices, the raw material just trickled out. And the political situation there now can only make things worse.'

Anna was impressed. Don't be silly, she had to tell herself, he's a banker. He's got nothing else to do.

'Where d'you plan to get your mohair?'

'There's excellent yarn available in this country which we'll start with. If we expand as I hope, we'll need to go to Texas.'

George Tyler asked, 'Why not Iran?' and Anna said another silent thank you to Walter.

'It's cheaper from Iran, but not such good quality. We'll use

227

kid mohair, eighty per cent to twenty silk.' She added, trying not to sound tentative, 'One of the reasons I hoped you would be able to continue financing us is that I'd like to gamble on the market. Buy in bulk as soon as possible. Not ridiculous amounts, but enough to ensure we can peg prices until we've established ourselves in this area.' This had been Peggy's idea.

George Tyler got up. 'I won't be a moment.' She watched him run up one of the wrought-iron staircases. Stern fished in his pocket for a battered pack and extracted a tiny cigar. 'Trying to give up cigarettes,' he explained. 'Do you . . .?' She shook her head. She noticed he wore an unlikely watch. She would have expected something as expensive as the rest of his clothes clearly were, but it was a heavy, old-fashioned square on a dark leather strap. And his shoes were unlikely, too, highly polished, round-toed, with green schoolboy laces. He didn't use a lighter, either, but a box of matches. The only thing was, she noted with amusement, they were French matches.

Tyler came back with two sheets of paper, gave one to Daniel Stern. 'Your proposals seem sound,' Tyler said, and the other man nodded. Anna felt herself relax. 'However,' he went on, 'even with the security your brother provided, I think we need to satisfy ourselves on one or two points. In view of the change in management.'

Waiting for what was going to come next, she unconsciously felt at her side to find the rosary before she remembered. If he asked something financially complex, she would be stuck: she'd actually learned the figures in her folder.

'We'll send someone along to have a look at the mill, Miss Summers, if that suits you.'

'Of course.' No alternative, but the thought of an accountant going through the books, talking to Beattie, was unnerving. 'When will that be?'

'Sometime during the next week, I expect. We don't want to keep you waiting for our answer.' He leaned forward. 'More coffee, Miss Summers?'

Anna was thoroughly pleased with herself, thrilled by the

way her ideas had fallen into place, by the reality they had already assumed. The new yarns would be hard work, but she was used to that. And once she'd got them under way, Nightingale Mill would be on its feet again.

She was out of the building before she realised that she was due to return to the convent the day after tomorrow.

Daniel Stern observed the straight-backed figure in the violet suit walking past the office block construction further along Cornhill. She suddenly stopped dead as though a thought had struck her and he saw with amusement that she didn't stir for a good half-minute. When she moved on again, a workman leaned on his drill appraising her, pursing his lips into a whistle Stern could not hear. Nor, apparently, could Miss Summers. Most women, he thought, might not have acknowledged the salutation but it would have put a swing into their walk. Anna Summers seemed entirely unconscious of the attention. Unusual girl.

He went back to his desk. It had come from the *Evening Standard* offices when Fleet Street died, a slanting wooden stand to hold open newspapers. He thought best on his feet and when colleagues protested, claimed it was the only exercise he had time for these days: he must get back to the gym.

Going through his papers, he found himself thinking about the Summers business. Pity about the brother. When the bank heard he'd killed himself, the initial reaction had been to call in the debt. He'd opposed such drastic action after reading their letter, had argued they should see what plans the Summers family had. It wasn't his client and when he'd chanced to be there while Tyler was interviewing, only curiosity had kept him. Daniel Stern was a tidy man – too tidy, his wife claimed, too cut and dried. Too pressed and brushed, she added, sweeping piles of shirts and sweaters from their shelves, ties from their racks, shoes from their stands in a last unforgivable gesture as she departed.

His mind was ordered, too, that was why he'd got where he had so fast, the youngest-ever director of Maynard Gideon. He liked to be able to file people as neatly in his mind as he could facts and figures. And Anna Summers didn't seem to fit in any category.

He turned from the desk, taking off his jacket and rolling up his sleeves. He stretched his arms wide, pulling back his elbows sharply and breathing deeply. Then he returned to his papers but his thoughts remained with Anna Summers.

What was it about that woman that intrigued him? She was good-looking – well, so were plenty of others. But this one seemed unaware of the fact. She didn't smooth her hair around or cross her legs or make exaggerated use of those clear eyes. Nothing about her had invited, suggested, *offered*. Most women drew attention to themselves either blatantly or subtly: clothes cut to emphasise a good body, elaborate hairstyles, perfume . . . Anna Summers employed none of these wiles. Her expensive suit wasn't particularly well-fitted, her haircut made Annie Lennox seem girly, he hadn't caught even a rumour of scent.

He got restlessly to his feet, crossed to the wall of flickering gadgetry, the tiny television screens showing world stockmarkets, and flipped through the computer information. A figure of thirty per cent caught his eye and he wondered about her age. Hard to tell, with that discreet make-up she probably appeared younger than she was. Late twenties, maybe. But those very restrained gestures belonged to an older woman, someone who'd had to rein herself back, hold things in. And she looked at the person she was addressing with total absorption, as if no one else existed. Or as if she were lip-reading. Maybe she was deaf – that would explain her indifference to the workman's wolf-whistle. But it hadn't seemed like that, more of a careful courtesy.

Daniel Stern stubbed out his cigar half-smoked, congratulating himself. The glint of his wedding ring – absurd that he was still wearing it, with the divorce under way – reminded him that Anna Summers had worn one, too. She'd corrected him fast when he called her Mrs, so presumably it signified a long-term relationship. It was her only jewellery: not so much as a silver chain to relieve the severity of the tailored suit and white silk shirt.

He'd looked down at her hands when they were introduced, surprised by her hard grip. They were a paradox. She clearly cared about her appearance, but they were neglected. And capable. He'd felt callouses on her palm and the nails were short with traces of grime darkening their edges. There was blue ink or dye on the skin, and the marks of old scars. She'd said something about farming.

He leafed through the first reports marked for his attention. Two hundred bound pages of information he didn't want to know. On an impulse he crossed to the low marble table and pressed a button on the internal phone.

'George? Just had a thought about that Bradford business.'

15

It was freezing at Keighley. A wild wind straight from the moors billowed round the car, searching through every gap and vent, threatening to lift the old vehicle off the short exposed stretch of motorway.

Sutcliffe & Street (Yarnspinners & Dyers) had moved from Bradford years before to a purpose built mill five miles outside the city. Anna drove through the gates in some awe at the expanse of lawn, the low modern buildings set amongst trees. The only space in the executive parking bay was beside a navy Rolls: she held her breath manoeuvring the scarred old Ford. Her habit flapped round her legs as she walked to the foyer where two receptionists examined her and their long red fingernails with equal curiosity while she sat on the cream wool couch and flipped Italian fashion magazines.

Walter Street hurried out of a meeting. He ignored her habit and greeted her affectionately, pressing her against his solid pin-striped paunch. ('Only time an old codger like me gets cuddled, girlie.') For a moment she held herself stiffly, as if to protest. But she couldn't hurt his feelings. And the bluff hug was comfortable and comforting; Walter was in charge and nothing could go wrong.

He led her away, shouting a command for coffee over his shoulder. With a square hand on his office door he paused. 'You'll mebbe not be out this way again. Come take a look see.' He hurried her down a succession of corridors, along a covered passage linked to another building and pushed through double doors into a swamp of sound.

They were in a vast fluorescent, windowless hangar. Stretching down endless aisles, gleaming machines throbbed and thrummed their power. As far as she could see in each direction, mechanical parts jerked and stammered in crazy unison, electronic rollers wound ceaseless miles of bright fibre. Huge steel heads were lifted and lowering with ponderous dinosaur movements, automaton arms tirelessly reaching and returning, reaching and returning, great loops of coloured yarn stretched between them in a gigantic game of cat's cradle. Along the robot rows, their faces white and tight with effort under the brutal battering of noise, overalled men and women hurried in the damp heat to serve them, checking valves and gears, tension and temperature.

'What say?' Walter Street was surveying his domain with narrowed eyes. He tapped a passing worker on the shoulder, pointed to a stationary roving and the man nodded and hurried to correct it. Anna was at a loss for words, taken aback by the size of the plant, the undoubtedly astronomic cost of the advanced equipment, the efficiency, the cleanliness, the speed. It showed Nightingale Mill up as the Victorian relic it undoubtedly was. And she hated it all.

Politely she listened as he regaled her with facts about the new humidifiers they'd had fitted and the electronic devices which cut off power to different parts of the plant for monitored seconds throughout the day so they had no noticeable effect but saved thousands on electricity bills.

'We're not spinners any more girlie,' Walter bawled in her ear. 'We're yarn designers.' He guided her among rollers and wheels, winders and drawers, gillers and twisters so advanced she scarcely recognised them even when Walter named them for her. Proudly he pointed out the towering fancy-spinners dripping with elaborate threads like monstrous cobwebs. 'All designed by computer,' he roared enthusiastically, showing her how the yarn was locked and twisted to form hanging knots and loops, the gear wheel with special teeth to produce a slub every quarter of an inch. 'We use computers for dyein', too. What d'you reckon to the colours, eh?'

She was grateful the din drowned her neutral reply. The synthetic fibres were lurid pinks, greens and yellows with a harsh metallic tinge that set her teeth on edge: impossible to imagine anyone wearing a garment knitted from these artificial materials.

'Can't produce enough of 'em,' he yelled. 'Course, we do all the old wool yarns as well. But with these man-made fibres you're lookin' at the future.' Anna thought of her plans and hoped very much he was wrong. 'You're into them now yourselves, aren't you?'

'Not really,' she shouted, 'I got rid of Simon's new fancy-spinner.'

'Bloody 'ell.' He stopped short. 'Sorry, girlie, but that seems a damn fool thing to do.'

'You made me think of it when you said Nightingale Mill was old-fashioned.' She wished she didn't have to scream like this: she still found it extraordinarily difficult to raise her voice. 'I believe old-fashioned is a virtue. I ought to be able to capitalise on the fact that the mill hasn't changed in a hundred years. I want to make yarns that're simple and natural, with all the values of the past.' It sounded laughable in the face of such sophisticated technology. No wonder Walter looked puzzled.

'You're talkin' top quality wool, not synthetics, right?'

'Yes. But we're also going to use pure silk, like we discussed after the auction. And we've decided to add blended yarns – linen and silk. All dyed in the same colours so they can be co-ordinated for different effects in a single garment.' She stopped to get her breath. She'd been so sure Walter would appreciate what she was trying to do. But that was before she'd seen all this.

'You didn't say you planned to drop synthetics entirely. You'll lose your present outlets. That's risky.'

'We owed a fortune on that fancy-spinner and we were barely breaking even. That's why Simon . . .' She swallowed. 'It would have been stupid to go on like that.'

Walter Street nodded. 'In your place, I'd probably 'ave done the same.' He paused before a machine so complex Anna

234

couldn't even guess its function and pointed to the fibre it held. 'Summer kid mohair. If I were you, that'd be something to consider.'

'We're going to combine that with the wool.'

'Could do.' He added diffidently, as if he weren't giving advice, 'Mix mohair with silk, you've got something really classy.'

She said slowly, 'I didn't think of that.'

'Got your suppliers fixed up?' She shook her head. 'I'll give you a couple of addresses before you go.' He pushed through more double doors into the storerooms where the bruising din was muffled.

'I'd appreciate that.' It was a relief to talk in a normal voice. They were passing racks where great cones of finished yarns fluffy as giant candyfloss were stacked. Her admiration here didn't have to be forced: the sheer scale of the operation was exciting. Without thinking she slipped her hand through Walter's arm in a spontaneous gesture she had never made with anyone else. He accepted it easily. She said, grateful, 'It's good of you to spare me this time.'

'No it isn't,' he contradicted amiably. 'I've all the time in the world. Semi-retired, me, but won't admit it.'

'I can't imagine you growing geraniums.'

He wheezed his amusement. 'Nor can the wife. But I'm only 'ere now for seven hours a day.'

Anna felt a rush of affection for him. 'I like your definition of semi-retired.'

'Each to 'is own. You'll need new markets for these yarns of yours.'

'I've talked to quite a lot of our customers. Some are interested, but not enough. That's why I wanted to see you. Walter, Simon never went for foreign markets, we hardly exported at all. But I'm convinced the Americans would buy these yarns – they're lightweight, perfect for warm weather. And I know the Japanese love English wool. But I don't know how to begin to reach potential customers on the scale we need.' She added ruefully, 'I convinced the bank I'd got it all sewn up, but really I'm right out of my depth.'

They were back at Walter's office and his secretary poured coffee. Walter waited until Anna was seated before settling himself behind a blond wood desk empty but for a folder, a silver inkstand and two phones.

He placed both elbows on his desk, laced his fingers together, looking towards the glass doors and the terrace that ran the length of the offices. 'Don't suppose,' he said finally, 'that you've 'eard the Ministry of Trade is planning to bring a group of Japanese buyers round the textile industry in four weeks' time.' He watched for her reaction from beneath unruly stage eyebrows.

'I read something about a new trade agreement. That's what made me sure the luxury market was the one to go for.'

Walter swung his chair from side to side. 'Convent 'asn't addled your brains,' he observed. 'Anyway, the buyers visit Huddersfield first, take a look at worsted-spinners, then come to Bradford. Wonder if you can guess who's co-ordinating their timetable?'

Anna put her coffee cup unsteadily onto her saucer. 'I can, Walter, I can. Someone who only spends seven hours a day at his mill.'

He leant back in his chair. 'I'm working with the Ministry of Trade right now. They're 'ere for two days, and during that time they'll visit several mills, including Sutcliffe & Street.' He winked at her. 'Now, if we show 'em the best of the new, reckon they should see the best of the old, too. Don't know why it didn't occur to me before.' He paused. 'I'd need to be sure you've 'ad production of these new lines of yours well in 'and. They're experts, they'll know what they're lookin' at.'

Anna swallowed the last of her coffee. 'We've silk on order already, Lynn's made the first payment. We're ready to start.'

'Dyein' yourselves?' A look of alarm creased his face. 'You're not goin' for that 'ome-brewed stuff you mentioned.'

'No.' She almost told him about her disastrous trip to collect berries but thought better of it. 'No, I . . . got kind of bogged down over that.' He should only know. 'I'm sorting that out now.'

He pulled a black leather notebook with heavy gold corners from his breastpocket and turned the pages, huffing over dates. 'I'll need something to show the Ministry. As soon as you've got those yarns through, let me see 'em.'

'Of course, Walter.' She stood up. 'And thanks – it's a wonderful offer.'

'It'll be as wonderful as you make it,' he said, and she knew he was embarrassed. He cleared his throat. 'I take it you'll be stayin' in town this time – you'll need to be at the mill every hour you can. A project like this won't run itself in your absence.'

'I've written to say I have to stay in Bradford.' She refrained from adding that the reply from Reverend Mother had been rapid and unequivocal: return immediately.

'Before you go, there's something I'd best tell you.' The seriousness of his tone made her sit down again. He hesitated. 'I was about to phone you when you asked to come over. You've got to do something about the manager of yours. Said 'e was a bugger, didn't I?' He pronounced it 'booger'.

Her heart sank – what now?

'Came over to see me two days ago. Wanted a job with us, didn' 'e?' His voice was rich with scorn. 'Got a lot of contacts, has your Mr Beattie.'

'All our customers.' She could have cried. That horrible man, up to no good again. He barely spoke to her now: if he said good morning it came out as a snarl. 'What did you tell him?'

He made a derisive noise and his accent grew noticeably broader. 'Nowt. 'Eard 'im out. Thanked 'im kindly and good afternoon. Didn't say what I thought of that kind of behaviour. Didn't mention you were near enough my god-daughter.' He gave a thin smile. 'Didn't tell 'im much of anythin', come to think of it. But I'm telling *you*. Get rid of 'im soon as may be, before there's real trouble caused. 'E said nothing about these

237

new plans of yours, so I reckon you've kept 'em quiet, but I don't believe we're the first mill Mr Beattie's offered to.'

'You're right. I heard he tried Lands ages ago.' She blew out a deep breath. 'Peggy's been on at me to let him go, but I was so preoccupied . . .' She remembered Hal saying Beattie was frightened and added, 'It's awful to sack a man with a family. What if he can't get another job? He's not young.' Walter Street looked at her as if she were mad.

'So bloody what? 'E doesn't scruple to take bread from the mouths of women and children.' She got the feeling he wanted to shake her in exasperation. 'You can't go round like one of your saints, or whatsername, Mother Teresa. Trouble with you, you look for the best in everyone. Throw 'im out. I can't say clearer than that. I tell you, turn the other cheek with that one and you'll get a knife in your back.' Oblivious to his mixed metaphors, he got to his feet and came round the desk to her. 'You'll 'ave to change your attitudes if you're to pull the mill through.' He put a heavy hand on her shoulder. 'What was it you said your vows were, obedience and poverty? They're neither of 'em goin' to be any use to you or anyone else out in the real world.' He gave her shoulder a shake. 'Wake up to reality, girlie. And stop frettin'. Worry about your own. That's all any of us can do.'

'Good news first or the bad news first?'

Peggy looked up from her typewriter, the dictaphone earpiece still in place. She hadn't heard the words, but Anna's expression told her enough.

'Hold on a mo, love, this is the last one. That temp didn't turn up this morning and I promised Stan a couple of letters . . .' She typed on for a minute, then removed her earpiece, clicked off the machine without taking her eyes from Anna's face.

'No good?'

'Walter was marvellous. Better even than we'd hoped.' She told Peggy about the trade delegation.

'We can do it.'

238

'We can try,' Anna said fervently.

'OK, hit me with the bad news, I can take anything after that.'

'Stan Beattie went to Streets and asked for a job. He offered to take our customers with him.'

'How kind.' Peggy loaded the words with sarcasm. 'How very thoughtful of him, knowing the position here, and Mrs Simon's circumstances.' She yanked the letter out of the typewriter as if she wished it were Beattie's neck. 'He's a nasty piece of work, and no mistake. And Hal's got something to tell you, too.' She buzzed him on the crackling intercom.

When he came down, Anna listened with amusement to Peggy offering him a cup of tea, a biscuit. Motherly Peggy, who considered Hal far too thin, who thought his endless chocolate bars bad for his teeth, regularly brought him in home-made cakes or slices of pie. He refused politely and held out an order sheet.

'We made a delivery couple of days ago to Howletts. They rang as soon as they'd got it open to ask why they'd received Aran when they ordered Southdown.' Anna took the order from him. It was made out in Stan Beattie's neat hand, absolutely legible, checked off, initialled and dated. She showed Peggy.

'Stan knows Howletts wouldn't use Aran.' Peggy went to the ledger in which every order was logged in and out. 'We've been supplying them with fine quality wools for longer than even I can remember. They make lightweight underwear. What's Stan thinking of?' She ran her pen down the pages of incoming orders, thinking aloud. 'Did I write it in? I don't remember – no, here it is. Stan booked it.' She frowned in bewilderment. 'How on earth did he let the order go out?'

'I should have picked it up,' Hal volunteered. 'But I can't understand how it got all the way through to delivery without anyone spotting it.' He tugged the lobe of his ear in irritation. 'Crazy.'

Anna said slowly, 'We'll have to take the Aran back and

hold on to it till we get a buyer. And I'm pretty sure we haven't any Southdown ready, have we?'

'Nope. And they're in a flap, so they may have to go elsewhere. Best we could do is offer an alternative at a reduced figure.'

'Peggy, I could really use a cup of that tea.' Anna realised she hadn't yet taken off her cape.

While the older woman put on the kettle, she said wearily to Hal, 'Either way, we lose. Cash if we sell a different wool at a lower figure than we should. A customer if we don't and Howletts have to go elsewhere.'

'There is an alternative,' Peggy said over her shoulder. 'We've done it before.'

'Right,' said Hal. 'Like that time . . .'

'Yes,' Peggy interrupted with a meaningful look. 'We should buy in what Howletts need and sell to them at the quoted price. It'll cost us a bit, but we don't lose a customer or goodwill.'

'It's a brilliant idea,' Anna admitted. 'But when was the last time you had to do this?'

Peggy kept her head averted. 'When Mr Simon . . .'

'Oh. I see.' She pulled the telephone towards her. 'I'd better get on with it.'

'I'll do it,' Hal offered. 'It'll be less noticeable coming from me.' He took the empty desk and reached across for the phone book. 'We're cash buyers?'

'I suppose so.' She didn't have to check to know how little cash was available. Peggy had already told her they'd had a difficult month and this was just about the last straw. She burst out, 'This can't have been a mistake, can it? Stan Beattie *must* have known what he was doing.'

Hal, his ear to the phone, nodded.

Peggy handed her a mug of tea. 'It's possible to make a mistake on the original order. Anyone can be careless. But he should have picked it up later.'

'Deliberate, then?' She didn't need an answer.

When Hal had finished – he had to go to two mills for the

amounts they needed – she asked quietly, 'There've been other things, haven't there? This wasn't the first mistake you've found, but it's the first you've had to tell us about.'

He said reluctantly, 'Any of them could just have been slips. On their own. That's why I never said. Stuff we needed wasn't ordered – we ran out of packing paper, another time I had to ask over and over before he got replacement roller lapping and that held up the scouring. On other things he's over-stocked: did you know we've two full boxes of light bulbs? It'll be months before we get through those; it's tied up cash unnecessarily.' He stood up. 'I'm still not sure it was deliberate, more like lack of interest.'

Anna felt a headache tightening the crown of her head. She'd just remembered Stan Beattie on the phone the day she and Hal had found the old flyer-spinner. In the light of all this, that looked like more evidence. 'Lack of interest took him to Sutcliffe & Street two days ago.'

Hal whistled. 'So he's up to that again.'

'I'll have to let him go.'

'Seems like,' Hal was deliberately laconic. 'I've got to get back upstairs. See you.'

When he'd gone, she asked, 'Could he do Beattie's job?'

'*What* job?' Peggy demanded. 'You cover virtually all his office work and Hal's in charge upstairs. There's one thing, though.' She fished an envelope out of the stationary stand on her desk and fiddled with the dictaphone. 'First of all, you should make a point of going round our biggest customers locally and writing letters to the others to introduce yourself. You've kept too much in the background. You want to tell them your Simon's sister, and you've big plans, and you hope they'll continue to be happy with our service – you know the sort of thing. And then follow up with phone calls.' She screwed the envelope viciously into her typewriter. '*Then* you sack the bastard.'

'So whatever Beattie says, they'll know we're still very much in business,' Anna finished. 'I'd never have thought of that.'

'No, I don't believe you would. You'd have trusted to his better nature. Only thing is, I don't believe he has one.'

Two days later, Stan Beattie ambled in after a long lunch with 'a client', belched twice and settled down to polish off his post. He liked using the dictaphone because he could read the *Star* at the same time. It was an old-fashioned dark grey affair weighing a ton, with a single tape which recorded and was then re-used. Peggy had done a couple of letters for him and missed out a third: rather than dictate it again, he'd put the new stuff on after that. He spun the tape on, stopped it about where he thought the missing letter should be, switched to PLAY.

He sat up straighter as he heard the voices and pressed STOP. He jumped to his feet and slammed the office door so violently the walls shook. Then he turned on PLAY again.

Peggy's voice asked. 'No good?'

'Walter was marvellous,' Anna was harder to hear, she must have been standing in the doorway. 'Better even than we'd hoped.'

Stan Beattie listened all the way through to Peggy saying, 'There's one thing, though.' After that, all he got was his own voice: 'This one's to Hogbin's about that import order . . .'

He got up and walked over to the window. He stared through the smeared panes at the cobbled yard. He'd known they'd find out, of course, people talked. He'd just hoped that by the time they cottoned on, his feet would have been securely tucked under another table. Now he'd have to think again. Damn and blast.

He played the tape twice more. Then he rubbed it clean, taped his four letters and left the office. He needed a drink.

'So I hope you'll accept my apologies.' Stan Beattie and Anna were standing in her office and he met her eyes with an openness she found unnerving. 'I was well out of order. I'm more sorry than I can say. But I've been so worried lately I've not known which way to turn. I pulled out all the stops before your brother died,' he added virtuously. 'He went through a bad time, worse than you know. I did my best to carry things.' He shrugged. 'Didn't do no good. Then afterwards, what with all the stress and that . . .' he fished a bottle of pills from his pocket and flourished them in front of her. 'My doctor's prescribed these. My wife was so concerned she made me go and see him and now he reckons I'm heading for an ulcer.'

Anna struggled with herself. She wanted to believe him, to be convinced his behaviour was the result of circumstance rather than evil nature. But his actions had been appalling, dangerous. 'You could have ruined us.'

'I'd not have done that.' His very light blue eyes were set shallow in the puffy face. She wondered if his nature had decided and defined his untrustworthy looks. 'Oh, I know what you must have thought. I expect you heard I went to Lands and old Mr Street. But I'd not have taken Summers' customers with me.' His voice rang with honesty. 'I was just looking to find a job without all this strain and anxiety. You can't blame me for that, Miss Summers, not after what we've had here. I've a family, same as everyone, I owe it to them to do the best I can.' She thought: He can't say anything straight. And then he disarmed her by his sad confession. 'But I found that a man my age isn't as employable as I'd thought.' He stopped at last.

She said sharply, 'What about the wool for Howletts you got wrong? It cost us time and money, not to mention almost losing their goodwill. You must have known it was wrong.'

'Course I did,' he agreed, too easily. 'The minute Peggy showed me the book I said Stan, you've made a mistake there.' He shook his head dolefully. 'I don't know how that happened, cross my heart. I must have been very tired, it's been a bad week. I'm just grateful that young man spotted it. But he did, and no harm's done. Tell you what,' he offered, 'I'll meet the extra cost of buying in that Southdown, I'll put it in petty cash.'

'All right.' She agreed without enthusiasm.

'I hope you'll accept my apology. I realise now I need

243

Summers. More than you need me, perhaps.' He permitted himself a half-smile, let it die when she didn't join in. She moved back a little: in his earnestness, he'd come very near. She didn't believe him any more than she liked him, it was all too glib, too pat. And she knew she was going to have to accept his explanation.. After all, he had come to her with it of his own accord, before anyone had had a chance to say a word to him. People did behave stupidly – he'd volunteered that. And maybe she was too ready to criticise him. Perhaps he did mean it. She could not refuse a genuine apology. Everyone deserved a second chance.

'All right,' she repeated. 'But it's on the understanding that we know what you have done. If there's any more – '

'There won't be,' he broke in. 'I can promise you that, Miss Summers. From now on, I'm putting my back into my work.'

'Let's leave it at that, then.' She accepted his thanks unwillingly. She'd done the only thing she could, but still she was disturbed: she would never be able to trust him. And Walter Street would think she was mad.

When Stan Beattie had gone she forced herself to work on, checking through the price lists Peggy had got in for linen and mohair. At the small amounts they were purchasing initially, these would not be negotiable. At precisely five o'clock she made a telephone call. As she had expected, Mother Emmanuel answered immediately.

'You got my letter, Sister Gabriel? We're expecting you here tomorrow.'

'Mother, I must beg permission to stay a little longer.'

It was another difficult conversation: the prioress's displeasure made itself clear in taut phrases. Anna could not tell the absolute truth to her superior – commercial considerations would cut no ice there – but nor could she lie.

'The bank have given us the overdraft, but in return they want us to send them details of our trading. No one else is competent to . . .' She listened for a moment. 'No, I don't think he could. And Lynn's in no state to help, even if she understood the figures. She's very disturbed at the moment.'

That, at least, was true enough: Lynn was sunk in lethargy and could hardly find the energy to wash a cup.

'She's near her time now, isn't she? And what she's been through . . .' the sigh was audible down the phone '. . . very well.'

'I can't thank you enough, Mother.' Anna's gratitude was genuine, a rush of affection for this stern woman who responded to helplessness. She answered the fire of questions: How much longer did she want? *Two weeks?* Was she keeping time for prayer and recollection? She hoped Anna realised that if the Bishop disapproved, there was to be no argument.

Anna put the phone down at last and made preparations to go home. She was about to cover her typewriter when Hal knocked on the glass panel beside her desk.

'Could I have a word? If you're not busy?' He leant against the frame of the door and she noticed again how physically at ease he always appeared. There was nothing angular about him, nothing stiff: his body had a natural relaxed quality, an unthinking grace. There were things she wanted to say to him, but she couldn't remember any of them. Sudden shyness made her fumble and drop the cover, hide her confusion by taking a long time to retrieve it. She was too inexperienced to recognise that the same emotion made him more subdued than usual.

There was an awkward silence before he said, 'Look, I've been thinking. What you were saying about the way you wanted to dye the yarns. I know a guy I think might help.'

They heard the frenzied, catchy rhythm long before they got out of Hal's car at the community centre, a wild skirling unlike any Indian music Anna had ever heard. As they crossed the tarmac they could see, in the floor windows, moving figures silhouetted against the light. Hal led the way past the canteen and the noticeboards and the wood-roofed hall where two dozen shouting youths leapt and twisted for a basketball, satin vests and shorts bright against sweating brown skin.

'They're rockin' in the ol' town tonight.' He spoke in an

exaggerated Western accent as they climbed the stairs. The music was resounding now, the broken beat nervy, exciting.

'What are they doing?'

'I thought it was just a rehearsal – Tel plays drums. But it sounds as if . . .' They reached the first door and he finished comically, '. . . I've got it wrong again.'

The doorway of the long room was blocked by people squashed together trying to get in: it was evidently some kind of celebration. Anna and Hal stood back until the jam cleared and she could see the source of the sound. There must have been fifteen drums, heavily decorated on their flat bases like large egg cups. Some were double-headed, clasped under the arms of the musicians – cheerful, moustached young Indians. Behind them on a small platform another played the electronic keyboard standing up, his wavy hair glistening as he pranced on the spot, fingers flashing with artificial stones as they swept over the keys. Like the other players he was dressed in pale trousers and a long embroidered shirt.

Hal leaned close. 'These blokes play at all the Indian festivals, traditional Hindi and Gujerati music.'

Anna was so enthralled she stared like a child in a sweetshop, for once oblivious to the rule of decorous behaviour. The music was as showy as its makers, and the crowd sparkled too. Women wore tunics rich with gold and silver threads, and the younger ones, in trousers and western sweaters with loose hair, had shimmering chandelier earrings. Some people – men and women – were draped with chains of what looked like elaborate tinsel. Children, many of them quite small, were dressed as miniature adults in the trousers and tunic. Among the dark faces were a number of white ones clearly enjoying themselves: girls in micro-skirts and high-heels, two or three couples with young families. People were dancing in the middle of the crowd, moving with stately abandon, not touching.

After ten minutes the music stopped. Hal lifted a hand and waved, and one of the drummers stood up and pushed his way through to them. He was a slender Sikh, dressed like the others in silky embroidered shirt and matching trousers, head wrapped in a turban of rich blue. He regarded Anna solemnly, dark eyes taking her in from head-dress to sandalled feet. He inclined his head with grave formality.

'Thought we'd never spot you,' Hal greeted him. 'That's a great sound.' The Sikh looked pleased and the two men slapped palms in a way that showed they knew each other well. Hal introduced Terry Singh and added, 'Tel, meet my new boss.'

He had to yell to be heard. Anna felt herself flush and made a gesture of denial, but Hal was unperturbed. 'She's hoping you can do some work for us. Couldn't get you at the works.' He grinned. 'And now I see why.'

Terry Singh shouted. ''Ad a week off, didn't I. When I wasn't playin' I was shopping.' He turned to Anna. 'Diwali's one of our biggest religious occasions, the festival of Light. It's gone mad though: we used to just give sweets, now it's presents, cars, new kitchens. 'Ouses, even, if you've real money.' He jerked his head to indicate the dancing crowd behind him and the irony was gentle. 'Guess the idea of a Diwali disco owes something to British culture too. Bit later, we let off fireworks.'

'Like Bonfire Night.'

'*Better* than Bonfire Night.' He smiled for the first time, very white teeth uneven. 'Local councils're tryin' to turn it into what they call the Indian Christmas.' He shook his head in mock despair.

'Why would they want to do that?' Anna asked. 'I can't see the sense of it.'

'Multi-ethnic wins votes,' Hal explained. 'They hope. There're twenty thousand Sikhs in Bradford.' The music started up again, deeper in pitch. The tempo increased, the electronic keyboard throbbing. An arresting figure jogged onto the stage, a white-turbaned Sikh of about thirty. He was dressed in white trousers and shirt covered with silver studs. A wide chain belt corseting his considerable belly, the initials DR were displayed in sequins on his back. He started to sing and it was four or five bars before it dawned on Anna that she knew it, a Presley song. 'Blue, blue bayou . . .' and surely she hadn't caught the word 'poppadum'. The Indian's fleshy, sensual features were not unlike his idol's, but his mimicked movements were a parody and she turned back to Terry Singh.

'What can I do for you?' Singh yelled. For answer, Hal beckoned them outside into the relative calm of the corridor. They walked to the end and leaned on the open-plan staircase, looking down. Even above the sounds of the disco, they could hear the shouts and thuds from the basketball boys.

'We were wondering, could you fit in a job for us? Well, three to be exact, we've three different yarns need dyeing.' Hal offered Terry Singh a mint but the Indian smiled and waved it away. He took a cigarette from a pack patterned with Indian symbols. His slim fingers were heavily stained with nicotine and, Anna noticed, the fading marks of dyes like her own. He listened to Hal, nodded politely. Anna took over.

'I wanted to use berries and mosses. But of course it won't work, not in the amounts I need. I wondered, maybe it's possible to use some natural products, though, mixed with synthetic dyes.'

'Why d'you want to do that?' The light gleamed in his dark eyes. 'I can do anythin' with synthetics, anythin'.'

'It's for marketing, really. The *idea* of natural dyes is very appealing – it fits in with a lot of other things, with fashion, the wool and silk and linen mixtures we're spinning. I'm sure it'll be an advantage for selling ourselves abroad. And I love the shades, the depth of colour.'

Terry Singh's face was impassive as he drew heavily on his cigarette. 'Could be interestin'. It'd not be cheap. An' it'd take time. Fiddly job, mixin' dyes like that.'

Anna heard his non-commital answer with a little thud of disappointment. Then the Indian added, 'Just up my street, that.'

Hal clapped Singh on the back. 'You'll give it a go? We're really grateful, Tel. Can we come round to see you Monday first thing?'

'Sure. I'll be there.' A woman called and waved to him from the doorway of the disco and he grinned at the two of them, shrugged and made his way back to the noisy room. In the foyer below a group of slim dark teenagers fooled around a soft-drinks machine. Hal ran down and brought up two cans, and they sat on the top step and drank companionably.

'Had a brainwave while you were talking about marketing natural dyes. Have you thought about breed stories?'

'The only stories I've thought about lately are bedtime ones for Jamie.' Hal flashed her a quick look and she regretted her flippancy: he was so obviously serious about this. But he didn't seem to mind. 'Foreign buyers like them – Japanese particularly. You print a label and it goes on every ball of wool, describing the pedigree of the animal that produced it, whether it's Hampshire Down or Dartmoor or whatever.' He tipped his head back and finished off his drink. 'You tell them where it comes from, and the type of wool and what it's used for.'

Anna cradled her knees as she listened. 'And we could add something about Nightingale Mill.' Her face was vivid with excitement as he'd never seen her. A different woman was sitting beside him. 'After all, we've been producing fine yarns for a century. That's something to shout about.'

He said appreciatively, 'Great stuff. A special image, that's the thing to go for. We'll get something down on paper tomorrow. And now, let's join the party.'

She laughed at the very idea, not taking him seriously. 'I can't.'

'I don't see why not. You heard what Terry said. Diwali is a religious festival.'

'Hal, I can't go in there.' She saw his expression. 'I mean, it's not . . .'

'Are you saying . . .' he looked disbelieving, 'you can't go to a religious festival if it's not your religion?'

That stung. 'No! It's just that I . . .'

'Come on, don't be negative. How often in a lifetime will you have a chance like this?' She dithered: he was right, it all looked so alive in there, it was more than anyone could resist.

She thought of Saint Teresa of Avila, the great Teresa, who played the little Spanish pipes and drums, who urged her nuns to dance and make music in their time of recreation. Their order, like all the enclosed, encouraged the flashes of joy which illuminated their lives. She remembered how Lis and Sister Louis had danced for them all one snowy afternoon when it was too cold to go out, holding up their habits and doing steps they'd learnt at ballet class as children, pirouetting to a scratchy record of *Coppelia*.

Still uncertain, she followed Hal into the noisy room. He created a small space for them near the back wall and they stood watching the throng. After a couple of minutes Hal turned to her. 'Dance?' He took a couple of steps.

'I couldn't.'

'Yes you could. There's absolutely no touching.' He was looking at her with his head slightly on one side, teasing. 'C'mon. You can do it.'

'Well, I . . .' She took a tentative step, imitating him. She was ridiculously clumsy, with no idea what she was supposed to be doing: it had been years since she'd danced at college parties and then she'd never been much of a success, never among the silent clinging couples in darkened rooms.

But Hal moved easily to the strange, high-pitched music. That and the babble of excited voices made it impossible to talk and when she protested that she really couldn't, there wasn't room, he just smiled and went on dancing. Reluctantly she copied his movements, started to relax into the beat. All around them, men and women sparkled in their Diwali finery. Kohl-rimmed eyes gleamed, gold bands circled throats and arms, the mixture of musky perfumes, sweat and spices and some sweet orangey drink she didn't know was foreign and fascinating.

At first, she'd felt conspicuous in her habit, but the few people who glanced her way showed only casual interest. Much less, in fact, than she encountered regularly on the train to and from Wales. It finally dawned on her that everyone was far too busy enjoyng themselves to care that she was a nun, even if they were aware what that meant.

Exactly the same, she reflected, was probably true of Hal. The two of them had never discussed religion, which made her suspect he associated it only with Christmas and funerals. This worried her, for his own sake. But she now realised that it also freed her – he had no pre-conceived idea of how she was supposed to behave.

Gradually she lost her self-consciousness and her face softened into a smile. The room had filled even more so that she was pushed closer to Hal. Who opened his arms, and put them loosely round her shoulders.

She held herself ready to pull back as his body touched the length of hers, chest and thighs and knees. She didn't want to acknowledge the new and painful realisation of how beautiful he was. She was so long accustomed to the way women looked, to their soft bulk, their rounded shoulders. Hal was all straight lines: solid triangle of wide shoulders and narrow hips. Forearms firmly muscled under rolled white shirtsleeves. Strong throat and curling hair . . .

But not for her. Never for her. She drew in her breath sharply at that and the tension must have transmitted itself.

He said, his voice low, his lips almost touching her cheek, 'Look, it's no big deal. We're just dancing. We can stop if you want.' And he moved gently against her, slower now, his arms heavy on her shoulders.

She could not answer. She knew she should walk away but the minutes drifted by. She gave herself up to the slow delight of standing almost still in his embrace. On the platform beside the electronic keyboard a figure in an amber sari was singing, her voice shivering and sinuous as her wreathing body.

Anna closed her eyes against the lights so there was nothing but arms holding her and the rapid hypnotic drumbeats and the sweet wild wailing. She couldn't understand the words but their meaning was universal: the sound of a woman luring a man.

Anna wrenched away from him with such force that the

youth she bumped into turned in annoyance. 'Whatya doin' hey?'

'I'm so . . . I must just . . .' She squeezed and wriggled through the happy bobbing crowd, out of the door to the relative quiet of the corridor. Hal followed, frowning.

'All right, are you?' He was clearly puzzled and there was no way she could explain her panic. He hadn't forced her. No other girl would have objected to such sedate dancing.

But she wasn't any other girl. She was Sister Gabriel still, and she couldn't admit to the terrible tenderness for him that pulsed in her like a darker drumbeat.

'It was so hot in there.' She proffered the lame excuse.

'I guess.' She could see he knew there was more to it than that but mercifully, he didn't pursue it. He stood very still, hands in his pockets, those serene green and gold eyes. The lights put a sheen on his skin and lashes, his damp hair looked curlier than ever. He considered her, running a hand over his jaw, rubbing the gold stubble. She couldn't meet his eyes and dropped her own (habit, again) but then she was staring at the sturdy neck, the broad chest under the white cotton shirt.

'I must go home.' Hadn't she said that to him on Bradley Moor? He must think her a fool.

But he simply agreed. 'Sure. I'll take you.' She was embarrassed at the warm concern in his voice.

As Hal and Anna left, a group of small children were on the stage, enchanting little faces lit by candles in their hands, black hair caught up with tinsel bows and crowns. They were singing, to a tune Anna knew well, an unfamiliar version of *Sing Hosanna: Sing Diwali, sing Diwali, sing Diwali to the King, to the King* . . .

16

Terry Singh wiped his hands on a piece of cotton waste. In the dim light as he stood in the doorway, his dark turban melded with the colour of his skin, made his shy grin very white.

'Evenin'. 'Ope I 'aven't kept you waitin'.' A red sweater and denims made him younger, slighter than the glossy figure he'd cut at the Diwali disco.

Waiting for him, Anna had almost fallen asleep. She was sitting in a swivel chair which had a dingy cushion covering the broken spring. A grateful cat was kneading its claws on her knee, the air was thick with gas fire and the memory of Marmite sandwiches. She smiled a greeting to the dye-works manager.

'Hallo.' She held out the skein of vivid mohair she had found on the desk among the orders marked with biro and the brown circles of tea mugs. 'I was just admiring your samples.'

His face lit up.

'Innit great? We dyed that for Calvin Klein. We got the colours 'e wanted, luminous like, but they faded in sunlight. So we rang the States an' 'e said not to worry, the people who wear my clothes only go out at night.' Delighted by her interest, he showed off the narrow shelves which ran round three sides of the cramped room. Endless brown paper bags packed to the ceiling were scrawled with the colour of their contents. Marina, lovat, geranium, polar red, acid green, nylosan violet. She reached up and touched a packet labelled German olive, gave Terry Singh a questioning look.

'Army uniforms,' he said. And added drily, 'The Middle Eastern war was a godsend to the Bradford textile industry.'

Anna's first visit to the dye-works in Jasper Street four days earlier had been formal, with Terry Singh at his desk while she sat beside Hal on the upright visitors' chairs cleared of colour swatches and papers. They'd talked reactive dyes and pre-metallised, chrome dyes and sodium dichromate. She'd listened while they agreed dark chrome dyes were hard to handle. Then they'd got round to money. Peter Hallam had explained they were trying to cut corners and Terry Singh had listened, his eyes darting from Hal's face to Anna's, nodding politely. He'd thought for a bit. 'I could mebbe pick somethin' up abroad,' he'd suggested. 'Or from a redundant stock list.'

Terry Singh had promised that once he got hold of the dyes, and Summers had delivered the top, the raw wool, he would have it ready in three weeks. Being a small specialist dyers, he'd said with some pride, Pickles could handle her limited orders where big firms would refuse them. Anna had shown him the colours she'd painted with Bax's water-colours from school.

'Could you repeat these colours exactly if we work in small lots? Hal says you don't use a computer for mixing shades.'

He'd drawn himself up tall. 'A computer can give you a rough guide but it can't match accurately. The newest machines, they're somethin' else, work on radio frequency. But that's bulk stuff.' His mild expression had not changed, the scorn had shown in his voice. He was proud of his expertise.

'How did you get into this business?' The moment she spoke she regretted it: she should have realised he was a secretive man, he might feel her interest was intrusive. She was becoming increasingly aware that her convent years, spent always with the same few people, had made her inept with strangers.

There was an awkward pause before Terry Singh offered, 'Everyone's gone 'ome so it's quiet. Want to see what we're doin' with your order?'

Anna accepted with such enthusiasm his unwillingness

evaporated. She hadn't been shown round on that first visit to Jasper Street, though she'd wanted to. Now she followed the Indian into long dark corridors, up stone stairs with nothing but a wooden handrail against the drop.

'It's a Victorian building,' he explained, pushing through a crooked door. Only one of the panes remained, the dirt-encrusted glass etched with a flower pattern. The floors of the upper storeys sagged alarmingly beneath the weight of bulky equipment. A huge wooden slide was full of treated lengths of wool and great hooks set in the ceiling swung with folding hanks slowly drying. As they went, Singh described the different processes; she had carried most of them out herself but on so small a scale compared to this she hardly recognised them.

When they returned to the ground floor he led her to the back of the building. 'Watch out for rats.' She looked at him sharply but he clearly wasn't joking: following him over the water-slicked stone floor she held her habit up with both hands.

They stopped at the first of the dye-baths, a high-sided tub big enough to take an elephant. In the bad light she could just make out the steam pipes leading from the big central boiler, the propellor which ensured fabrics took colour evenly. Nearby a row of metal buckets held the bright dye powders, ready for morning. He pointed to them. 'Synthetic dyes, you need eight kilos of pure powdered colour for two hundred kilos of yarn.'

'How are these amounts measured out?' She laughed. 'I always used kitchen scales. You must have to be more scientific.'

He shrugged. 'Dunno about that. I do it meself: it's partly on weight, but you can't rely on that, the dye strength can vary from batch to batch. It's calculated guesswork. You get better the more you do it. I bin doin' it ten years, and in another twenty I'll be a better dyer than I am now.' He spoke without boasting: he was a good craftsman. He took her over to where hanks of an unrecognisable dark fibre were spread.

'Your silk is the most difficult to 'andle, it's very soft, then gets 'ard when it's wet.'

'Did you train here?' She hoped he would see she was genuinely interested.

'No way. The industry's stopped trainin' dyers, reckon they can do it all with their bloody computers. I was in a wool warehouse, then I moved to the laboratory and went on day release to Bradford Tech. I came 'ere when old Pickles was still comin' in every day. He was an old wool man from way back, ninety-three an' still workin'. It's 'ard, too, twelve hours a day.' Singh thumped the side of the tank with a balled fist. 'This stuff is nuthin' compared to what you can get now. But even a secondhand dye-bath you're talkin' a thousand quid an' there's no slack in this business for mod rnisation.' He waved an arm towards the dimly lit dye-works, adding in mock despair, 'We've got equipment goes back to the year dot.'

She said with feeling, 'Don't I know. Some of ours was put in when my grandfather was a little boy and we're still using it.' She thought for a moment. 'Mind you, I've produced knitting wool in Wales using a foot-operated wheel.'

'You never. Like the Sleepin' Beauty?'

'Just like.' She made a face. 'I'm not only a spinster, I can actually spin. We've a flock of Beulah Speckled-Face. I use organic dyes and sell to a local shop. They work beautifully on small amounts, and it didn't matter if colours weren't accurate.'

'Natural dyes are tricky.' He grinned. 'Doctors bury their mistakes. Dyers dye 'em black.' He thought for a moment and added, puzzled, 'But you're a nun, right? Nuns don't work.'

'Oh, we work all right. I drive a tractor, build walls, grow potatoes.' She held out her hands, palms down. 'I can prove it.'

He looked at them, back to her face. 'You're 'avin me on.'

'No. Honest. We have no money, we have to rely on charity and what we can provide for ourselves.'

'You beg? In the streets?'

'Not exactly. Some orders do: the Poor Clares go out to

collect alms. We're not permitted to do that, but people give us money, or maybe leave us something in their will. The farmer next to us gave the sheep when he retired. If you don't want much, somehow there's always enough.' The last bit sounded pious. Funny, she'd said and heard the phrase a thousand times and it had never struck her that way before.

He gave a rueful grunt. 'Not when you've four kids, it ain't.' He was suddenly talking easily, responding to her own confidences. 'I've three sons and a daughter. I was married at eighteen: my parents brought a bride over from Bombay. Sura's marvellous with the kids but . . .' He ran a thumbnail across his teeth.

'They sound like a wonderful family.' She hoped she wasn't going to be told more than she'd bargained for.

'Yeah, they're great. It's just that – Sura is home all day, I think she gets bored. The third one'll be at school in a few months, even the baby's nearly two an' she's started 'intin' about another already. But we can't afford it.'

'Maybe she should get a job.'

He shook his head. 'She don't speak very good English, even after ten years. An' I don' want 'er workin' in a factory. It'd be nice, though, to 'ave more bread, feel it's not all on my shoulders.' He sighed. 'I dunno. Sorry to go on about it.' He sounded surprised at himself. ''Ow'd we get onto all that? You don't 'ave any family worries.'

Anna thought of Lynn and the boys. They seemed somehow to have become very much her responsibility. She put out a hand to feel the wet silks waiting to go up to the drying rooms and said, more to reassure herself than him, 'I'm sure it'll all work out. As long as the family's together.'

It was a platitude, of course, her mind was back on her current worry. Lynn was so listless these days, drained of energy and interest: she scarcely seemed to listen even to the children's chatter. So Anna was unprepared for Terry Singh's response, the odd combination of envy and superiority in his tone.

'You're on your own. You've no one else to worry about.

You've no problems.' As he spoke his eyes flickered over her habit, her long veil. He didn't add: What do you know about it? but she heard the words as clearly as if he had. She looked directly at him: it was obvious he wasn't trying to be unpleasant, he was simply stating a fact. She had thought they were communicating with each other, and all the time he had not been talking to her at all, but to a cardboard image. It doesn't matter, she told herself, it's not his faith, how should he understand. She moved towards the door, stiff as an old woman. The day had gone on too long.

'Thanks for showing me round, Mr Singh. I must go, it's late.'

He's an intellient man, she thought as she struggled with the cold ignition. He even seems to like me. And yet he thinks I live without a heart.

'Eat your toast at least, there's a good girl.'

Lynn lay in bed with the cup of tea Anna had brought in untouched beside her.

'Don't,' she protested. 'It's all greasy, I couldn't.' Anna inspected the offending item.

'There's not even a trace of Flora on it,' she pointed out, 'only raspberry jam.' Lynn groaned and turned her head away.

'Jam,' she echoed in hollow disgust. 'Yuck.'

'Move up.' Anna sat on the edge of the bed and inspected her sister-in-law's pale face. 'You look like someone who needs a rest. I think I should arrange for Peggy to pick up Jamie and give him lunch. There's not a lot for her to do today at the mill. You stay in bed this morning, and have your hair done this afternoon. You'll be going into hospital any day now, you need to look tidy.'

'It doesn't matter.' Lynn gave a wan smile. 'I'm not being self-pitying, it's the way it is.' She put up a hand, dragged the hair back from her forehead. 'I know how I look. Terrible.' She tipped her head back and a single tear dripped down the side of her nose. She seemed utterly drained. 'I don't want to go to hospital for the baby.'

'If I said, it's not quite my scene, it'd be a massive understatement.'

'Yeah.' Even in her predicament Lynn could see the joke was on Anna. She fumbled for a tissue. 'It'd also demonstrate that your slang is seriously out of date.'

'I'll work on it.' It had had its effect, though: Lynn sounded more like herself. 'But surely everyone has babies in hospital, don't they?'

'I asked to have this one quietly at home with a midwife. Home deliveries can be arranged now, though hospitals don't like the trouble. But the gynaecologist said no, he'd prefer me there in case of problems. But I know there won't be any: I've had two straightforward deliveries.' She grimaced. 'It's the one thing I can do, for God's sake.'

'It's surely safer in hospital, though. You'll be better there.'

'No!' Agitated, Lynn pushed herself up in bed. 'It's awful, you've no idea. They stuff you into a paper nightie that's open at the back – it must be the most humiliating garment ever invented. They shave your pubic hair off for some prudish reason of their own and make you have an enema and they examine you constantly, as if you were nothing but a huge stomach, not a person at all – Christ. it's such an intrusion.' Her face was streaked with angry tears. 'And the delivery room is like an airport lounge, full of people you don't know who barge in without warning. And then afterwards, in the maternity ward it's impossible to sleep, people wander round all the time. But the worst thing, what I can't face, is being there all alone. What'll I do when the proud fathers turn up with flowers and parcels? Who'll come to see my baby?' She caught hold of Anna's arm. 'I know you will, but you must see how it's going to be.'

Anna had put her free arm round Lynn before she thought: A month ago I would not have done this, I would have tried to help with words. Now she did not even offer them, but simply held on. After a while, when she felt Lynn's breathing slow, she said, 'We should maybe book you a private room, that'd make it easier.'

'Too expensive.' Lynn wiped her eyes on the belt of Simon's towelling robe. 'I expect it'll be all right on the night.' She sniffed. 'I'll get my hair cut, though.'

Anna prepared Bax's lunch box ('Auntie Anna, you've forgotten the crisps again'), dropped him at school, took Jamie to playgroup. All the way to work she worried about her sister-in-law, and had to pull her thoughts back to the questions the day would bring as she turned into Nightingale Street. There was an order of scoured Aran that must be finished and sent out; one of the reelers had been off ill all week. Her desk was mounded with bills and Peggy had a headache.

At eleven, she tried to snatch a quiet moment. Her mind was a jangle of problems she couldn't solve. Maybe a prayer would help. She pushed aside her coffee cup and closed her eyes but nothing would come. She fingered the rosary at her waist. Hail Mary, Mother of God . . .

There was a tap on her open door. 'Got a minute, love? Problem upstairs.'

Anna sighed and counted to five, turned to Peggy with a calm face.

'Of course. Couldn't you find Stan Beattie.' It was more a statement than a question.

Peggy gave one of her famous snorts.

'He's out seeing customers, as usual.' The two women looked at each other without comment: the manager now spent much of his time away from the mill. 'You'll have to do something about him.'

'I know.' Anna went on. 'But not today.'

Upstairs, she made her way across the workroom, careless of the fine white dust over every surface which specked her dark habit as she passed.

'Quick, over here!' Hal was in the far corner where the reelers worked. A flurry of women parted to let her through. The reeler who had been off sick for several days, a wizened woman called Dawn, lay on the dusty boards, her face grey under the pink and yellow headscarf knotted at the front. She looked shrunken, no bigger than a child, and for an awful moment Anna thought she was dead. But the crumpled arm moved, a leg jerked, and Dawn mumbled.

'Said we should 'ave a nurse 'ere,' a woman in the crowd remarked loudly.

'Don't move her,' Anna ordered. 'Let me see.' She knelt beside Dawn, took her wrist between forefinger and thumb. The woman struggled to rise.

''Ere, let us up.'

Anna pressed her shoulder. 'Just a minute.' She glanced up. Hal interpreted her look, shooed the watching women back to their tasks.

'All right, girls, excitement's over.'

He and Anna helped Dawn up, their arms round her waist. She joked feebly, 'Watch out. Me money's in me corsets.' Hal found her a chair and Anna held the glass of water someone brought, and perched beside her on the edge of the wicker skip that held cones of reeled wool Dawn had finished that day. The reelers had the most highly skilled job in the mill operating the beaters, fourteen-foot long wooden bars. No place for someone who was sick.

'Keep your head down, Dawn, towards your knees. Looks as if you came back to work too soon.'

'Aye, I bin a bit previous. Sorry, Miss Anna.'

'You couldn't help it. We'll get Hal to drive you home. Is someone there to look after you?'

'I've good neighbours, thanks be.' Dawn sat up, some colour back in her face, but her lipsticked mouth with its painted cupid's bow was harsh against lined skin. After five minutes, Anna helped with her coat and Hal came over.

'I'll stay and make her a cup of tea, if that suits. Be back by twelve.'

'Fine. Thanks, Hal.'

Since she was up there anyway, she went across to talk to Rene and Sylv, ask if everything was all right. Above the clattering of the spindles Sylv greeted her.

'Mornin, lovey. Yer lookin' a bit peaky. Must be gaddin' about nights mekin' up for lost time.' She winked meaningfully. Anna would have taken aback a month ago: now she just smiled. But Rene sprang to her defence.

'Shurrup, you. Cheeky cow.' Her raucous tones must be audible to everyone. She gave Sylv a good-natured shove and both women burst into roars of laughter. Anna laughed with them. Her childish self-consciousness up here had finally evaporated: she was well aware of how much she owed to the hard work of the 'girls'. She was still laughing as she turned towards the sliding door that led back to the offices.

It was a dark corner, and the man who stood there was silhouetted against the single bulb at the top of the narrow stairs.

'If you're delivering top, the entrance is downstairs by the cardboard boxes, please.'

'Is that . . . I'm looking for Miss Summers.' A deep voice, the slight drawl of a Southerner. He wasn't delivering top, for sure. She still couldn't make out his features. He took a step forward. 'This *is* Miss Summers, isn't it?' Why did he sound so amazed? 'Daniel Stern. From Maynard Gideon. We met ten days ago.'

The women were still cackling behind her and his expression made her sharply aware of the figure she presented. His eyes took in her grey habit, the wide leather belt, the crucifix slung at her waist, her bare sandalled feet. She brushed ineffectually at the white dust she always collected on her woollen robes from the mill. Recalling Sister Godric, she held out her hand. 'Good-morning. You must forgive me, but I wasn't expecting . . .'

'I know. I apologise, I should have made an appointment.' He gripped her hand. 'But I found myself near Bradford and I thought . . . I'm on holiday, actually.' She saw now that he wore casual clothes: or rather, a City man's idea of casual clothes. Jacket of soft black leather, cashmere sweater. There was a silence until she pulled herself together.

'Let's go down to the office.' She passed him, led the way down the stairs. He followed her into Simon's room without speaking. For once, Beattie's absence was a positive relief.

She'd not set foot in here since she'd found him that night but it was unusually tidy: no newspapers.

'Thank you.' Daniel Stern put his hand on the back of the chair she indicated, but didn't sit down. 'I hope this isn't too inconvenient. You knew we wanted to come up and see the mill?'

'Yes. I just hadn't realised – it's good of you to take the trouble.' She was having to work hard to stop herself sounding defensive. Why didn't you ring first? And then, why you anyway, and not George Tyler? Since when do directors of banks do little jobs like this?

'Would you like coffee?' As she asked, she was conscious of his expression. She tugged her veil straight: she must look a sight.

'Are you actually . . .' For the second time he looked carefully from her head-dress, past the rosary at her waist to her feet. As though, she thought, he's wondering if it's fancy dress.

'Yes. I actually am.'

'My . . . God.' He sounded as if he was about to laugh. She raised her eyebrows and he shook his head. 'I don't meant to be rude but I honestly cannot believe this.' He spread his hands. 'You weren't like this in London. That *was* you? I mean, I don't know the first thing about nuns, but I sure as hell didn't think they wandered around City banks in silk shirts and high heels.'

She'd obviously made an impact: the knowledge caused her considerable pleasure which she tried to stifle.

'These clothes seemed inappropriate for a business meeting.' I sound so prissy. 'I was afraid . . .' she paused. Might as well be honest. 'I was afraid you wouldn't take me seriously over the mill if you thought – if you knew – I was a nun.'

'Damn right. Oh, I'm sorry, Miss Summers. Sister. Is that what I call you now?' She nodded. 'I'd love a cup of that coffee you were talking about. If that's possible.' He sat down. She lifted the phone, pressed twice for Peggy.

'Could you bring coffee for two? Mr Stern's here, from

Maynard Gideon.' She replaced the phone fast to stifle Peggy's exclamation. 'Then I expect you'd like to see over the mill.'

'I expect I would.' He unbuttoned his jacket, crossed his legs. Anna made polite conversation while she waited for Peggy, learned that Daniel Stern had always wanted to visit the Yorkshire Dales and had his nine-year-old son with him.

'So you really are on holiday?'

'Well, it's a weird time of year, but a few days off school won't hurt Sam at his age and it suited his mother.'

'Where is he now? At your hotel?'

He jerked his head. 'Out in the car. Reading *Beano*.'

'You must bring him in. Really. You can't leave a child outside alone.'

The boy was the image of his father: intent brown eyes, hair cut short at the sides, left long on top to balance the long face. The father's narrow Roman nose would be the son's when he was older, the slightly curling lips were his already. They shared even the same faintly anxious expression. Both worriers, she thought. Sam shook her hand and said 'Pleased to meet you' then sat beside his father and listened to their conversation. More composed, she felt, than any nine-year-old should be.

Peggy brought coffee in china cups, she hadn't known the mill possessed and biscuits on a plate with a doily – an unprecedented refinement. After the introductions she offered to show Sam her office but he said politely, 'No thank you. I'll stay with Dad.' Watching father and son, Anna noted how comfortable they were together: they clearly spent a lot of time in each other's company.

So she showed them both round Nightingale Mill. As they went across the packers' yard she remarked to Daniel Stern that the earlier stages wouldn't interest him. He stopped half way.

'Hold on there. You mean, we're not starting at the beginning?'

'Well. I'll tell you about it all but – '

'Look, Miss Summers. Sister. I know very little about the

yarn industry and I'm keen to find out. So please, let's do it properly.'

'It'll take some time,' she said doubtfully.

'I have some time.'

So she showed Daniel Stern every process right through, starting with opening and scouring the bales of raw wool she had bought at auction. Before they went into the big workroom she took Sam to wait in Peggy's office.

'My father never let us upstairs while work was going on,' she told him carefully, not to hurt his feelings. 'It can be dangerous. There's so many tempting places to poke your fingers.'

She became, as always, absorbed as she explained to his father the tasks of drawers and spinners, twisters and reelers. She caught the sidelong glances the girls shot at him, the way they smoothed their overalls as he and Anna approached. She looked at him again, seeing the intensity of his concentration, the lines of his mouth, the faintly tanned skin. He's an attractive man, she thought, and I was so busy thinking of the impression I was making, I never noticed. Maybe the convent is the right place for me after all.

'This is the gill-box.' She was shouting to be heard over the clatter of machinery. 'The front rollers travel faster than the back ones, drawing out the threads all the time.' As she spoke she saw Hal come through the door, jacket over his shoulder. He gave her a thumbs up: Dawn was obviously safely home. She beckoned him over.

'Thanks for doing that. Mr Stern, I'd like you to meet our overlooker, Peter Hallam. He's in charge up here. Hal, I met Mr Stern when I went to London recently.' The two men acknowledged each other. She thought Hal did so gracelessly but soon forgot about it, involved in her explanations of the mill.

As he left, Stern said, 'I must give Sam lunch. There's quite a lot I still want to know.' He took out car-keys, jiggled them while he thought. 'We're staying in Bradford overnight, at the Victoria. Could you be free this evening?'

265

'You mean, come to your hotel?' Damn, damn. That sounded half-witted, but it was so unexpected. 'I'm afraid that's impossible. That is, I could talk to you but I don't . . .' She stopped. I haven't set foot in an hotel for thirteen years.

Daniel Stern waited. Now it was his turn to raise his eyebrows.

'This isn't a date, Miss Summers. If that's what's worrying you.' His tone was sardonic. 'It's business. And this is the only time I have.'

'Yes, I see. All right, I could be there around seven thirty.'

'Good. I'll look forward to it.' He took the boy's hand. 'Say goodbye, Sam.'

As she stood watching him drive away Hal said behind her, 'That's one nosy gent. What'd he want?'

Even before she'd turned round, seen his face, she recognised rivalry in Hal's voice.

A mean December wind haunted the streets as she left Kingswalk and as usual the Ford required coaxing to start. She was glad she'd decided to wear the habit, it kept her warm as nothing else did. She'd looked doubtfully at Lynn's suit and decided against it. There was a car-park right outside the Victoria Hotel and she held up her long skirt and skipped across a couple of puddles on her way in. So it was embarrassing to find Daniel Stern waiting for her inside the revolving doors. He might have seen: the light out there was bad, but maybe not bad enough.

They sat in a corner of the lounge on tapestry chairs, a heavy brass lamp on the low table between them. Immense draped windows, vases of formal flowers – not much had changed since her day, though walls that were now fashionably stripped wood had been painted then. It had a solid, provincial feel to it, an atmosphere compounded of respectability and substantial dinners. On her right a group of men who must be local traders talked of shopping malls and building costs: uncompromising Yorkshire faces, blunt and vigorous, thick bodies to withstand harsh Yorkshire winters. The sensible fortyish woman sitting opposite looked as if she lived in a commuter village and kept dachshunds. Anna watched Daniel Stern summon a waiter and thought how out-of-place he seemed among them, how unpredictable. With his clever, cryptic, city face that belonged in boardrooms.

'What will you have to drink?'

'I'd . . .' Quick, girl, think. 'Tonic, please.'

'Just?' His voice was quiet, assured. Nice. He ordered it with ice and lemon; whisky and water for himself. Waiting, she could smell furniture wax, a faint promise of roast beef from the dining-room. She'd meant to make a sandwich before leaving home but had been in a rush. Daniel Stern inquired politely after her sister-in-law. Did she spend time at the mill? Anna thought of Lynn's slim shape bowed with the baby and shook her head. She'd urged her to come this evening to meet Stern, arguing that the mill was hers now, she should make the effort. 'He's a married man,' Anna had protested, 'he'll understand.' But Lynn was adamant: she couldn't face anyone in her present state.

'Is Sam with your wife?' Presumably she was here somewhere.

'Up in the room watching TV. The housekeeper's checking on him for me.' He ignored the second part of her question. 'Tell me more about the management side of the mill please. You have a manager, don't you?'

Dangerous ground. She wasn't about to tell him that she planned to dismiss Beattie. She concentrated on Hal, explaining the tasks of an overlooker, how he organised the workforce. They'd finished their drinks before she realised and when Stern said, 'You will have dinner with me?' she floundered.

'That's very kind of you but . . .' Up went those expressive eyebrows again. 'I have to get back.'

'You've only been here thirty minutes. And you'd be doing me a favour, I don't like to eat alone.' He laughed. 'Sam had his hours ago.'

Anna set down her glass. So he was obviously not travelling

with his wife. 'I can't eat with you, because . . .' she touched the skirt of her habit. You fool, she was thinking, you told yourself he was out of place here when all the time the only oddity in this room is you.

'When I was a kid,' he observed, 'we used to think nuns didn't have legs, just wheels under their skirts. I guess we were right. It'd certainly explain why you don't need meals like the rest of us.'

She flushed. 'There's no need to make fun of me: I can see you're not a Catholic. It's just that social occasions aren't . . . appropriate for a nun.'

She faltered on the last words. What kind of hypocrisy was she mouthing, when only a few days before she'd danced with Hal at an Indian disco? She'd been in a room with a hundred people, and still had the nerve to claim she did not attend social occasions. She touched the rosary at her waist and promised penance.

It was a relief when Daniel Stern nodded without question. 'Sorry, I stand corrected. But in case you're under a misapprehension, not only am I not Catholic, I'm not anything at all.'

'That's not possible.'

He stared at her, started to say 'Not for you, perhaps,' and then stopped, visibly changing his mind. As if, she thought, he'd decided not to argue with me. 'You're right, of course. I'm a Jew. To the extent that my parents were believers of a kind, and twenty-five fountain pens say I'm official.' He grinned at her puzzlement. 'When he's thirteen a Jewish boy reads a portion of the Law in synagogue. Haven't you heard the joke? Steven Spielberg's mother meets ET and says: I don't care where's he from, now he's here he's going to be Barmitzvah.' He watched her reaction. 'You haven't heard of ET either? Don't tell Sam, that's all, he thinks you're from the moon already.'

'You can't just disregard your faith.'

'I don't disregard it. I'm a Jew whether I practise my faith or not. It's what I am. It's how I look and what I do and the way I behave.' He was playing with the book of matches he'd picked off the table. He had one leg crossed, the ankle resting on his knee, and his foot jiggled with nervous energy. 'My wife's not Jewish, which caused problems with my parents. I couldn't make them understand it's something which just doesn't interest me. In fact . . .' he gave her an assessing sidelong glance, 'I sometimes think I strongly disapprove of religion. And don't take offence, but I consider fundamentalists of any creed to be absolutely terrifying.' He peered round the large room, mock-conspiratorial. 'If I can say things like that in Bradford.'

'Don't say them too loudly,' she suggested, 'and don't say them in Shearbridge Road. I hope you don't put members of religious orders into that category.'

'Depends. You aren't a missionary, by any chance?'

'By no chance.' She was beginning to enjoy this slightly aggressive banter.

'If you were, of course, you'd be fair game. As a heathen unbeliever I could with clear conscience boil and eat you. Although I'm a little uncertain about the procedure with your headgear. Maybe it could be a garnish.'

'Like those little ruffs on lamb chops?'

'Precisely. Still, since you insist you aren't a missionary and I take it that even if we continue our business discussion, you still refuse to enter the sacred portals over there . . .' he nodded towards the dining-room and paused for a moment. She was suddenly aware that she had eaten only fruit for lunch. Years of convent cooking had rendered her more or less indifferent to food but she longed suddenly for an old-fashioned English meal, beef and gravy and roast potatoes.

'So it'll have to be sandwiches out here,' Stern was saying. 'Smoked salmon and chicken, suit you? I'm an authority, having been through their entire repertoire earlier with Sam.'

After the sandwiches they had cheesecake at his insistence. She hardly noticed how many questions he asked, how much she talked, how excited she became about her plans for the mill. She'd been too late this year, she explained, but she and

Lynn planned to go to the two major European yarn trade fairs.

'Which are?'

'Expo Fil in Paris. Pitti Filatti in Florence.'

He stretched his legs and asked casually, 'Why don't you go in for cashmere? Surely that appeals to the top end of the market?'

'The *very* top. Although people actually seem to be attracted just because prices are so high.' She finished her cheesecake while she ran through what Walter Street had told her when she'd suggested the same thing. 'There are two arguments against our going in for cashmere. The first is the problem of pegging prices. The very big suppliers can invest in huge amounts and fix them for the next six months. You're looking to China and Iran mainly.'

'And the second argument?'

'It has to be specially treated, you get a very low percentage of strong hair.' She put down her plate. 'I'm not ruling it out. But it's beyond us at the moment.'

'You could ask us for a larger investment. I know George Tyler was impressed with what you told him, and you strike me as capable of doing anything you set your mind to. It wouldn't be hard to arrange. If we had security, of course,' he added.

She glanced at him over her last forkful of cheesecake, uncertain how to take this. Surely he realised she would not be here much of the time, capable or otherwise. Then she thought, he knows nothing of nuns or convents, nothing of the way she lived. She had not mentioned Wales, or that she was enclosed. Maybe he assumed she belonged to a local order, or that she lived with her family. She wanted to tell him the truth but even as the words formed in her mind, she foresaw the consequences: the loan withdrawn, payment of their debt demanded. So she chose her words carefully.

'If that's a suggestion, thank you, but no.' She put down her plate and leaned back. 'I'm not trying to build an empire – just save one mill. I'm doing my best to be realistic, and it's something I'm sure I can manage.' Her fingers had unconsciously found the rosary slung at her waist. 'The prospect of borrowing more and more money frightens me. My priority is to make classic, timeless products which people want – and will go on wanting. And we need to find new markets. If the yarns are the success I believe, it'll take us all our time to meet the demand.'

Daniel Stern fiddled with his battered cigar pack again, turning it over and over while he thought. 'I've been impressed today. Both with what I've seen and what I've heard. I'll confirm it officially when I get back to London. But I think you can stop worrying.'

She felt herself grinning like an idiot. 'That's wonderful. Really wonderful. I'm so glad.' She had to stop herself babbling out her relief. This was a business arrangement, she was going to make money for them. And she must tell Lynn. It was a relief when a clock somewhere struck ten. She hastily swallowed the last of her coffee. 'I must go. I promised Lynn I'd not be late: she gets nervous in the house with just the boys.'

He insisted on seeing her to her car. It was snowing now, sparse flakes filming the Ford and glossing the pavements, blowing haphazard in all directions. She thanked him, and he said she must come to London again soon and he would show her round his offices for a change. She slammed the car door and was immediately struck by two facts. The first was that he'd really asked no questions which a quick phone call would not have answered.

The second was that the car would not start.

17

He ignored her protests and drove her home. ('You'll wait hours for a cab tonight.') Before leaving the hotel, she went up with him to check that Sam was asleep and pick up a coat. The lamps were on, the television flickered in front of Sam's bed where he lay sideways, thumb lodged firmly in his mouth. Stern switched off the set and all but one of the lamps, phoned through to ask the housekeeper to keep checking the room and kissed the sleeping child, pulling up the blankets, tucking in the chubby leg that hung over the edge of the bed and settling the toy monster on the pillow. She was charmed by his practised air, his open adoration of the child. His wife was a lucky woman, she thought, sitting beside him in the plush silence of a metallic grey BMW.

Bradford glittered in his headlights. The buff stone of City Hall with its immodestly high campanile tower was silvered with sleet. On the edges of the wide square opposite, Pakistani taxi-drivers huddled against the cold in explosive conversation. He glanced at them, then across to her and she smiled but made no comment. The solid curve of Princes Way cut a swathe through the city, past the bright signs of the National Museum of Photography, Film and Television, the illuminated glasshouse of the Alhambra Theatre.

They didn't talk: she guided him in a low voice. 'Left at the lights. Take a right at the end of those shops.' Even the suburbs were transformed, trees and hedges edged in crystal as they swept past. Once he said, 'You'll have to tell me if it's clear your side – I can't see round your head-dress.' She'd leant back, embarrassment lending determination to a decision taken a couple of days before: it was time to abandon the habit when she was outside the convent.

The ground-floor lights were on as Stern turned into the drive: Lynn's bedroom was in darkness. Like a polite teenager, she invited him in for a coffee, and was taken aback when he accepted. In the living-room a mug of cold tea and the remains of a block of white chocolate showed Lynn had skipped another meal. In the kitchen she found the usual clutter; saucepans half-full of water, wooden spoons coated with sauce, the floor smeared with flour. Half a dozen foil containers were filled with savoury pies and quiches, another four contained fruit flans. She'd never known Lynn to cook so much at one time. It looked as though Bax had attempted to clean up and abandoned the idea. Two of the quiches had been burnt black: Lynn must have forgotten about them. Stifling a flash of annoyance at the mess, she started clearing up while the kettle boiled.

They had scarcely touched their coffee when they heard the sound. Anna's raised cup stayed in midair. 'What on earth . . . just a minute.' She was across the room, already starting up the stairs when it was repeated. The bathroom light was on, door ajar, towels on the floor. The exhalation came again, a harsh sigh. She raced up the half-flight to Lynn's room, dashed in without knocking.

The bed was empty, the room dark so that she thought at first no one was there, but a movement alerted her. In the light from the hall she made out the squatting figure in the corner, head thrown back. Her skin prickled – it looked like some large animal huddled with its back against the wall – and then Lynn said, 'Anna?' Her voice was slow, as if speech was an almost impossible effort.

Anna gasped, 'What are you *doing*?' As Lynn looked up, her face etched with pain-lines that were a presentiment of age, she knew. 'My God, the baby's started. It's early!'

'You don't say.' Lynn's voice cracked.

'But why are you down there? Let me help you get up.' She

was across the room, hands outstretched. But Lynn flung up an arm as if shielding herself from attack. For a moment Anna wanted to protest: I only want to help you. And then she realised that Lynn was protecting not herself, but her unborn child.

When the crouching woman tried to smile, it emerged as a grimace lending the lie to her muttered, 'I'm fine. Better down here.' Here words were expelled in breathless bursts, like someone gasping for air during an arduous race. 'Doesn't hurt. As much.'

'I'll get an ambulance.'

'No! Don't!' It was a plea. 'Anna, don't. Wait.'

Anna put a hand on Lynn's where it rested on her thigh: it was quivering. Lynn's muscles were twitching with strain. Tears of sympathy gathered behind her eyes. 'How do you feel now?'

'Not too bad. I've got through. The first stage.'

'Oh my God. How long have you been like this?' And I was cross about the state of the kitchen.

'Been in labour. About two hours since. You went out. Just got through. Transition.'

'I don't . . .' Anna had never felt so inadequate.

'Worst part. Awful. Better now. Not long to go.'

'We must get you to hospital.' Anna started to pull away but Lynn grasped her arm fiercely.

'If you send me to. Hospital so help me I'll. Jump out of the fucking window.' Her grip tightened. 'For God's sake let. Me have this. Baby at home.' In the half-light Anna could see her mouth curving into a smile. 'If you'd come. Back half an hour later baby. Would have been here.'

'I'm going to switch on this lamp so I can see you, OK?' Anna knelt on the floor to get closer to her, to explain. 'You've been told you'll be safer in hospital with proper equipment, painkillers, doctors. We can't take risks, and I'm responsible for you now.'

Lynn shook the arm she held with that fierce grip. '*I'm* responsible. For myself and. The baby and. Anyway it's too late.' She grunted with pain. 'If you call. Ambulance now I'll. Have poor little thing on. The way.' She licked dry lips. 'Please, please. Let me stay here. I can't face hospital. It'll be awful without. Simon. I'll be so. Lonely.' Her voice was hoarse. 'I can do it all myself. I can.' She giggled suddenly. 'I have world's. Fastest deliveries. No time for. Painkillers and anyway. They're horrible. Give me hangovers.'

Bewildered by the rapid change of mood Anna said, 'I must ring the hospital, I'll ask them if it's all right for you to stay here. I wouldn't be able to live with myself if something went wrong.'

'They'll say I've got to go in.' She sounded desolate. Anna crossed the room to the telephone extension. She picked it up, listened for the dialling tone. Nothing. She tried again, dialled the hospital number Lynn had stuck to the sides of both phones. Silence. 'The phone's dead.'

'I know. It's my fault. Sorry.' She didn't sound it.

In sudden comprehension Anna accused her. 'You didn't pay the bill.'

Lynn said nothing.

'Why didn't you tell me?' She blamed herself: she so rarely made – and never received – calls, she had noticed nothing amiss. Maybe it was a sign, though. Maybe she should do as Lynn wished. 'I'll have to go next door.' She spoke without much conviction.

'The Stafford's are. Away and. The other side's still empty.' She pressed both hands against her swelling stomach and shut her eyes. 'Bastard,' she muttered. 'Bastard bastard bastard. Leaving me to. Go through this alone. Bastard . . .' She was talking to Simon. But harsher than anger in her voice was grey bitterness.

'Don't worry. I'll do what you want.' She spoke before she thought, to silence her own guilt for her brother's behaviour, to assuage Lynn's sorrow, was rewarded by the expression in Lynn's eyes more eloquent than any words. 'Let's make you comfy, at least.' Lynn let herself be helped up, but refused to get into bed. Instead, she lowered herself clumsily onto her knees and lay across the mattress. Anna was horrified. 'You must get in.'

'Much better. Like this. Baby's coming. Down, isn't it. Oh God.' She buried her face in an outflung arm and when she raised it, Anna saw purplish teethmarks in the pale skin.

'Let me help get this off.' Lynn had obviously started to undress and found she could not continue: the wrapover maternity garment was unzipped, easy to remove. Underneath she still had on knickers, streaked with blood.

'Waters broke. Early on.' Lynn gestured. 'Used a towel.' It had been bunched between her thighs and soaked with clear, scentless fluid. She struggled out of her underwear and Anna, glimpsing damp distended flesh, had to repress a pang of apprehension. She'd never witnessed a human birth – nor ever thought to – but she'd delivered lambs in Wales, had worked with the local vet on emergencies. Presumably any experience was better than nothing. It didn't feel like it, though. For a year she'd held the post of infirmarian to the convent. She remembered writing this in a letter to Simon, joking that it was as well she'd only been asked for asprin so far. He'd sent her an *Encyclopaedia of Nursing* he'd found in a second-hand book shop. That had rapidly been confiscated: Reverend Mother felt it contained too much that was unnecessary for her to know. She'd been left with a single copy of Black's *Medical Dictionary*. It was a first edition, 1906, full of gruesome illustrations of gouty hands and gangrenous toes. She'd just had her twenty-seventh birthday, time was passing her by and discontent nibbled at the edges of her mind. In a few years, her body would be too old to bear a child: there would no longer be any question of choice. More than once she'd glanced in horrid fascination at the section on 'Labour or Parturition, the act of bringing forth young'. The dry medical terminology hadn't prepared her for what was happening in this Bradford bedroom.

'Nightie in drawer.' It was a command and Anna obeyed it, bringing the folded garment to the bed, helping Lynn off with the smock. The other woman's skin had a damp sheen from her efforts, she saw that Lynn was in a state of such sensitivity, she had actually to grit her teeth to endure being touched. Anna's throat was sore as she tried to imagine her pain. Lynn groaned again, a sound dredged up from deep inside. She muttered, chiding herself, 'Must be quiet. Don't want. Boys to hear.'

'I'll check they're asleep.' Anna went to Bax's room, opened the door. The room smelled of little boys' feet and sleep, both children were invisible but for tousled hair sticking out of the covers. She gently pulled back the duvets. In the glow of the nightlight their faces were pink and closed. 'God bless,' she murmured.

Shutting the door she heard Daniel Stern ask from the stairs, 'What's going on? Is everything all right up there?'

'It's Lynn. The baby's nearly here.' She was whispering.

'Shouldn't she be in hospital?'

'She's determined not to go. She wants to have the baby at home.'

'That doesn't sound unreasonable. Pregnancy isn't an illness.' Anna heard this with interest. 'Don't you need a midwife, though?'

She stared at him. 'I never thought. Just a minute.' In the bedroom, Lynn crouched over the bed. 'Lynn, d'you have a number for a midwife, then? She'd know what to do. I'll go to the call-box at the end of the road.'

'No problem,' Stern said. 'Phone from my car.'

Lynn spoke without lifting her head, voice muffled against her arm, ignoring Anna's question. 'It's going to be quick, it's. Nearly *here*.' The last word was loud with effort but her eyes were shining, her voice full of determination. Ann was petrified. She'd anticipated hours of exhorting Lynn to push – she must have read about that somewhere. But if she was right . . . Anna was beside her, telephones forgotten.

'Let's get you on the bed. I can't do anything down on the floor.' She started to pull at Lynn's shoulders, then Stern said, 'I'll do it,' and pushed Anna aside. He picked Lynn up bodily, laying her on the rumpled bed.

Anna said, 'A big towel. Cupboard in the hall,' and when he brought it, she spread it doubled beneath the labouring woman.

'It's cold in here. It should be warm for the baby. I'm going down to find an electric fire or something. Am I to phone for an ambulance?' He asked Lynn and she shook her head violently.

'No, please, no, there's. No need.' It was the nearest she'd come to shouting.

'I think she's right. If we do, by the time they get here we'll probably just ensure the baby's born on a stretcher in the middle of Heaton.' Anna stroked the hair back from Lynn's sweating forehead. 'Keep calm, we'll do it.' She was beginning to see that Lynn was coping with the birth as she had not been able to do with day-to-day living. Anna was the one who was frightened. Lynn understood her pain and so it was not unendurable. 'We'll manage beautifully,' Anna said, and meant it.

Daniel Stern looked from one to the other.

'OK,' he agreed, the laconic phrase contrasting oddly with his tense face. He turned at the door. 'D'you want me to boil water?'

'Old wives' tales.' Lynn's eyes were closed now. 'That's just to. Keep anxious fathers occupied.' Something clicked into Anna's mind from that old medical dictionary.

'We should boil a pair of scissors to sterilise them for cutting the cord. Bathroom cupboard, could you . . .'

He came back with an electric fire and a fan-heater, plugged both in. Anna had yanked off her head-dress and scapular, pushed up the sleeves of her habit. 'Stay here a minute, while I wash.' When she returned he was holding Lynn's hand while she groaned, talking to her in an even voice.

'Don't breathe so fast, there's a good girl. Slow down, keep it slow, gently, gently.' He took deliberate long breaths, made her copy him. 'How far apart are the contractions?' Anna couldn't believe what she was hearing: he wasn't a doctor as well, surely?

'You can always spot. Husbands who go to natural. Child-birth classes with their wives.'

Stern didn't appear to be at all disconcerted by Lynn's breathless, disjointed speech. 'Wait till I start singing through the noisy bits,' he threatened.

'Oh no!' Lynn screwed up her face in mock horror. Anna was astonished at the rapport between the two of them: she'd thought Daniel Stern would rush out of the room, but he seemed to want to stay. 'I think contractions are . . . about every minute or so. I'd like to sit up a bit,' she added. They mounded pillows behind her. She shifted, trying to get comfortable. 'It's my back. Aching so much.'

'I'll rub it for you,' said Stern. 'If you like. I rubbed my wife's when she had Sam: I'm good at it. Move round a bit. Here?' He was taking of his jacket as he spoke, and he started massaging Lynn's back steadily as she wailed aloud, rocking herself forward and back. Anna was acutely embarrassed by this new, uninhibited Lynn. She knew she could never surrender, never let go like that, lose herself. She was too self-conscious, she had for so long considered control a virtue, that the outward show of birth feelings alarmed her. What was worse – inexplicable, really – was that Lynn could behave like this in front of a *man*. And a stranger at that, however kind. Disapproval and prudery made Anna switch out the central light again, mask what was going on with merciful half-darkness.

Daniel Stern, however, clearly didn't mind what was going on at all. After a couple of minutes, Anna could see the straining muscles of Lynn's throat relaxing, though her breathing was still the loudest sound in the room. She busied herself fetching more towels, getting out the shawl and babyclothes from their box in the hall. In the lull she remarked, 'I know this is ridiculous, but you two haven't been introduced.'

'Bit bloody late. For etiquette.' Lynn turned her head and said feelingly to Daniel Stern. 'That's good. How many times . . . have you done it?'

'Just once. My wife decided maternity wasn't for her.

Marriage either, come to that.' It was extraordinary, Anna reflected: there could be no more unlikely participants in this most intimate situation than a nun and a London banker. But in the hot room, atmosphere charged with the thrill of the impending birth, it seemed quite natural that they should talk easily. Still massaging Lynn's back, Stern added, 'We're in the middle of the divorce, which ain't a nice place to be. I still can't quite believe it.'

Lynn opened her eyes. Her look at Anna was full of sharp humour: as easily as if she'd spoken, Anna read what she was thinking and felt herself going pink. *A man like this, available?* She turned her head so he wouldn't see, but he was absorbed in his task.

'Stop, please. Going to be sick.' Lynn's voice was faint, she held a towel to her face.

Stern brought another wrung out in cold water and Anna reached over and held it to Lynn's forehead, held up her hair and wiped round the back of her neck, her throat. 'Nice.' She took Anna's hand, pressed it against her swollen belly. '*Now!*' Under their laced fingers the strong muscles contracted, grew rigid so her belly was stretched tight as a drum and hard. At the peak of the contraction Lynn's face contorted so she looked almost savage, lips drawn back over her teeth. Gradually the muscles softened and she felt the shiver of the skin that followed it before Lynn sank back, released Anna's hand. 'See? Few more and. We're there.'

Anna stared at her sister-in-law, so buffeted by emotion she couldn't say anything. The pallid figure who for weeks now had been drifting listlessly round the house ('I don't feel like going out, I don't want to walk, I can't face cooking, the smells') had vanished. In her place was this flushed, earthy creature, her flesh glowing with heat, glistening with sweat, nightdress wrinkling round her drawn-up thighs. Even her movements had changed. She had been limp and flaccid, nothing but a passive container for the child. She was not suffering through this in a nightmare haze. She was charged with a fierce energy, alight with power and purpose.

For of course she had a purpose: to give life to her child. '*To give life*'. God himself could do no more than this woman at this moment: she was about to make the greatest gift, play her part in the primitive pattern of survival. Anna put the wet towel on her lap and prayed swiftly for Lynn. Help her, Dear Lord, be with her in her hour of need, bring her safely through this trial. Only it didn't look like a trial. Lynn was in the grip of an inner force more compelling than anything Anna had ever experienced or even thought possible.

Ruefully Anna acknowledged that yet again she had managed to delude herself. Seeing Lynn transformed made it so clear, so obvious, she could not credit her own stupidity. She'd *thought* about it, that had always been her trouble. But a baby wasn't about thinking, about mental activity. It was physical, completely and utterly. It was sexual. And Anna had never come to terms with sex. Which was one of the reasons religious life had appealed to her: she'd been able to shut away her fears, make a grand gesture and secure the promise of eternal life, all in one go. A bumper package deal. A bargain at the price. Only the price had turned out to be her youth.

'I think I'm in the way.' Daniel Stern was on his feet. 'I'll be downstairs if you want me.'

'What about Sam? Shouldn't you go back to him?'

He paused in the doorway.

'There's a baby-sitting service so someone's always around. And he never wakes: too exhausted from wearing me out.'

As he went downstairs Lynn gasped, 'Anna! Oh God, oh God, oh God, oh God . . .' There was nothing blasphemous in her words, they were a soft-chanted litany, endlessly repeated like a charm. 'Oh God, oh God . . .' She caught a fold of Anna's robe, kneading her fingers in the thick material like the dye-works' cat, clinging for comfort.

'I'd better see how things are coming along.' Anna waited a moment, then patted the curled fingers and unclasped them so she could move reluctantly to the bottom of the bed. She had to force herself to overcome her years of conditioning to deal intimately with another person. She peered nervously between

281

Lynn's parted legs, splayed in the massive effort to urge the baby out.

God knows what she had expected. As a child of twelve she had learned that to be female was to endure something each month called 'the curse'. It had been her first identification of female sexuality. So that when 'it' had arrived, a year or so later, it had been no surprise that menstruation proved to be uncomfortable and messy. And childbirth was the next link in the chain of that curse: pain and anguish and labour, blood and sweat. Anna was sick with fear implanted twenty years before.

But what she saw between Lynn's thighs stopped any thoughts about herself, her anxiety, her ability to handle the situation. She hated the sight of blood but there was only a trace to be seen. The tissues of Lynn's body were unfolding like a dark and fleshy flower round the hard bud that was the child's head. Matted tendrils of dark hair were clearly visible at the opening of the birth channel.

'Oh God, oh God, oh God, oh God . . .' Lynn was panting harshly again, caught in a trap edged with knives, pulled all ways by pain, eyes unfocused and wild.

'Look at me. *Lynn, look at me.*' She obeyed, regained control. Anna reached up a hand to hold her bare legs and watched as with the next contraction the secret opening enlarged almost imperceptibly to reveal more of its core that was the child's head. Within Lynn's body, another body was moving towards its destiny like a star in darkness. In the hot room, Anna was cold with awe. No religious ceremony she had ever witnessed could compare with this miracle.

'If you put your hand down, you'll be able to touch the baby,' she said. Lynn reached down, her face wet with sweat and tears, her fingers slipping, feeling the top of the skull. Then the next contraction claimed her and she grabbed her knees and held on tight, eyes squeezed shut, heedless of the sight she presented, nightdress falling back over the jutting belly, teeth showing in a grimace. Only now Anna felt nothing but compassion for this woman in extremity: all her prim old-maidish criticisms of thirty minutes before had evaporated. She was totally involved at last, tiredness banished by excitement.

'It hurts, it hurts, it hurts . . .' Lynn wasn't complaining, just chanting it quietly over and over.

'It's got to, love, it must. You're almost there, not long now.' Anna knew she had at all costs to be encouraging, to keep Lynn going. She remembered how the vet had gentled the lambs out of the ewes, how the animals had not pushed at all but still the little creatures had made their irrevocable way. 'Don't push, keep it easy, it's coming by itself, don't strain . . .' She was down at the bottom of the bed, utterly absorbed in the incredible journey that was being enacted before her eyes.

Above her, Lynn was obediently trying to breathe lightly, muttering, 'One two, one two.'

Just when she thought she should see to Lynn, Daniel Stern's low voice asked from the door. 'Look, can I come back in? There must be something I can do.'

A rush of relief. 'Could you help Lynn?' And then uncertainty. 'Are you sure you want to?' But he was already beside the bed.

'Of course I'm sure.' He looked seriously at Lynn. 'This room feels like the centre of the universe tonight. It's the only place to be. If it's OK with you.'

'Tell you. What. You stay and. I'll go. I've bloody well. Had enough. Changed. My mind.' Lynn looked exhausted, her chin sunk on her chest. She was knotted with distress, fierce furrows between her brows, mouth thin and tight. Daniel Stern sat on the bed behind her, slid his hands under her armpits and up to hold her shoulders, pressing his chest against her back to support her.

'Lean on me. I'm here. I'm with you. Let go.' His voice was resonant with concern. But Lynn leaned stiffly away from him as if he were an unwelcome intruder and Anna thought, I was wrong, I should have said no. And then she sighed and relaxed against him, her head falling back onto his shoulder. 'Breathe with me, I'll get you through.' Anna marvelled at the response Lynn – no, Lynn's state – was provoking in herself, in Daniel Stern; the love and concern that was wrapping her and the coming child. He spoke to Anna. 'She should have a drink.'

'I'll get some water.'

Lynn sipped gratefully, and Anna wiped her face and neck again. Lynn said faintly, 'My feet are so cold.' Anna chafed them for her, warming them between her hands, letting go only when the next contraction began to surge through Lynn so that she grasped her knees even more tightly. 'I can't can't can't can't . . .'

'You can, Lynn, you can. The contractions are much shorter now.' As this one ebbed, Anna stood up. She crossed the room and pulled back a curtain. It was snowing properly now, flakes flying haphazardly across the beam of streetlights. She pulled the curtains apart so Lynn could see, and the pale night light invaded the room. 'I do think we should have a doctor.' She didn't realise she'd spoken aloud until Lynn answered her.

'I'm not ill, dammit. I'd far rather have. You. If I can't. Have Simon.' The look she gave Anna was a mixture of desolation and such love that Anna's first instinct was to turn away embarrassed to fuss with towels, a shawl. She stopped herself. *This was what you wanted, wasn't it? To be needed. To be loved.* She could find no words but she put her arm round Lynn's shoulders and buried her face against the streaky blonde hair.

They stayed like that for a long time, the three of them bound together by Lynn's need. Then Daniel Stern moved his right hand from Lynn's shoulder and took Anna's, turned it and – incredibly – kissed the inside of her wrist. His lips so light on her skin she couldn't be sure it was happening. If she hadn't felt the nubbly roughening of stubble, she would not have believed it. He opened her folded fingers and looked at the palm, the callouses from gardening. She made a move to pull her hand away – and then left it. You fool, don't break this moment. Take it.

When the next contraction wrenched Lynn's body, Stern

released Anna and she moved back to the end of the bed to monitor what was happening. One hand was on Lynn's thigh, the other on the firm bulge of her belly. As it tightened Lynn was already pushing, instinctively holding up her legs beneath the knees so that her feet were raised, pressing the child out. As she did so, Anna could feel her trembling with strain as the stretched cuff of flesh seemed to slip back over the child's face and Lynn called out, a harsh wordless cry of agony and elation. Anna was just in time to receive the wet warm little head that spurted smoothly in a brief explosion of water and blood and life to lie in the hollow of her hands.

'Oh look. Look!' She couldn't keep her voice down, it cracked with excitement. She really had not anticipated this moment. Lynn's labour had seemed everything, the end result somehow secondary in the face of her huge struggle. So she was not prepared for the simplicity and the wonder of it, the astounding, astonishing reality of another person suddenly here in the room with them. A miracle. Surely, the only one. 'Look, oh look. Oh, Lynn!' Lynn leant forward to see, her normally pale face scarlet and ecstatic. The round skull was sticky with creamy vernix and Anna wiped the child's mouth and nose with moist cottonwool so it could draw its first breath. The women watched the eyes open, alert and pure, slowly blinking, *there*, while the rest of the body was still inside Lynn. They saw the jewel-blue gaze of innocence and awareness, of unimagineable wisdom they might never come so near again; that everyone once had, and lost.

In that natural pause Lynn drew a great, quivering breath and at her back, still supporting her weight, Daniel Stern said quietly, 'That's wonderful. You're wonderful,' and Lynn laughed.

On the next contraction she gave a last grunting sigh that spoke of pleasure as well as pain and the shoulders were through, Anna still holding the head and guiding out the body of a tiny girl into the heat and half-dark.

Anna had vaguely imagined activity. She had somehow presumed the violence of dangling the child upside down so it would breathe, smacking it sharply into existence, red-faced and squalling. But the newborn slipped easily into earthlife, lay silently and sweetly on Lynn's body, skin on skin, heart on heart. Calm after the turbulence of birth. There was no need now to do anything. No one spoke. Lynn stroked the baby's back, while the strong cord linking mother and child still pulsated, completing its cycle. The baby breathed softly, her limbs stretched in the warm air, she made small murmurous sounds.

Stunned by tenderness, Anna looked at them both through a blur of tears as Lynn held the child to her breast straight away, the crumpled face turning instinctively to her warmth, the new mouth searching for her nipple. As if they were reunited, Anna thought, watching the blue-tinged skin flush pink.

It had not been Lynn's experience only, this gentle birthgiving. I have learnt from it too, Anna thought. I know more about myself than I did an hour ago. I know more about my body. I know more about my mother. I know more about men and women, more about what I want from the rest of my life.

18

She lay in Jamie's bed flat on her back, arms crossed on her chest, hands to shoulders. All the nuns slept like that. It was said to be in case they died in the night, but Anna had always assumed a more pragmatic and less religious motive. It didn't turn you blind or drive you mad, anyway.

It didn't help you sleep, either. Despite soaking for half an hour in a hot bath she was so keyed up she could hear the fibres of her pillow grating when she moved. She switched on Jamie's lamp and turned on her side, charmed as always by the pottery animals in their magic castle, and then she was thinking about the birth again, the panic and exhilaration. She would check on Lynn every hour or so. What a night.

Once the baby had been safely delivered, Stern had hurried back to his son as soon as Anna had telephoned the doctor's emergency service on the car-phone. Dr Barnes had arrived twenty minutes later breathing fire and demanding to know why Lynn hadn't called the ambulance and got herself to hospital for the birth. As he examined mother and child he'd muttered darkly about risking the baby's health and her own, he'd never heard of such . . . He calmed down when he'd reassured himself all was well, and even complimented both Lynn and Anna. 'Couldn't have done better myself,' he'd said finally. 'I'll make sure the midwife's here first thing in the morning and we'll keep an eye on you.' At the front door, he'd told Anna to call him immediately if the child had any breathing difficulties. 'Not likely with a breastfed baby but you never know. By rights, she should go into hospital for a few hours but in this weather I'm reluctant. And I know it's the last thing she wants.' He'd smiled. 'I think we'll let her get away with it, after an effort like that.'

Anna yawned and stretched and was counting Beulah Speckled-face when the doorbell chimed. Downstairs, she peered through the spyhole and saw a blurred figure clutching a large bottle. She opened the door.

'D'you like snow-chilled champagne?' Stern asked.

'Don't know. I'd quite like to find out.' She unhooked the safety chain. 'Why on earth have you come back?'

'You're very direct up here in the north,' he grumbled, taking off his coat. 'What about "Hallos" and "Nice to see yous".'

'Hallo.' She giggled, ridiculously light-hearted. 'It really is nice to see you. Again. So soon already.' She took the bottle he thrust into her hand. 'Where on earth did you find champagne at this hour?'

'Proper boy scout, me. Swiss Army knife. Thing for taking other things out of horses' feet and laudatory libations no problem.' He pulled a despairing face. 'I couldn't settle, if you really want to know. Too much excitement. There's a fridge in my room so I was just getting myself a soothing tonic water when bingo, I came upon this. Not exactly vintage but it seemed like a hint. And when I got here the bedroom light was on . . . if Lynn's still awake we can wet the baby's head.'

'What a wonderful idea.' She led the way into the kitchen to get glasses and he surveyed the pies and quiches laid out on every surface. 'Nature's nesting instinct,' she explained. 'Apparently some women clean bookshelves and scrub floors. Lynn cooked enough for a month. D'you want something?'

'Seems like hours since we had our sandwiches.' He inspected the pastries. 'Could I have some of that?' He cut several slices. 'You're never going to let me eat alone?' They carried two trays loaded with glasses and plates up to the bedroom to find an equally sleepless Lynn rocking the wooden cot beside her bed.

She greeted their appearance with delight. 'A party! Let's wake the boys.'

Bax and Jamie bumbled in full of sleepy excitement to see their new sister. The baby was toasted several times, and Lynn named her Sara and cried a little and laughed even more, and Anna found herself doing the same. Emotion and champagne diluted with orange juice sent Jamie to sleep half an hour later curled up on his mother's feet and Anna put him back to bed. Bax lasted another thirty minutes, sitting protectively beside Lynn holding her hand until he started to nod. Anna turned out his light and whispered that he could have a day off school tomorrow if he couldn't wake up, they'd make it a special holiday. 'That's real doody,' he said, eyes already closed.

It was four thirty before Lynn slept. Putting the trays back in the kitchen, Daniel Stern asked, 'Would we like a cup of coffee? There's not really enough night left for sleeping, and I must be back before Sam wakes.'

Filling the kettle, she was conscious for the first time that she had only a scarlet shawl of Lynn's over her thick convent nightdress, she'd mercifully abandoned the bonnet after her haircut. That thought stopped her short: *mercifully*? she had an unwelcome mental image of Stern's wife – ex-wife – with floating hair round a still face, and though the features were indistinct she was wearing a drift of grey satin decorated with pearls . . . Anna stuck a teaspoon viciously into the coffee jar. You idiot, what are you thinking of?

'Now I see why your coffee's full of bits – you need to let the water boil.' Daniel Stern sounded amused. 'Don't they drink instant coffee where you come from?'

'Never. Tea once a day if we're lucky.'

'What d'you drink then? In cold weather, I mean.'

She shrugged. 'Hot water.'

''Strewth. No wonder you can't make coffee.' He took the spoon out of her hand. 'Here, I'll do it. You must be really tired.'

'I always wake around this time anyway. If I tried to sleep now I'd only feel worse.' She carried her cup into the lounge.

'I don't usually sit in here because of the mirrors. D'you mind if we just turn one lamp on?' Daniel Stern crossed to the music centre. After a minute, a muted saxophone whispered in the shadows.

'I don't understand about the mirrors.' He sat down opposite her. 'Tell me.'

Her back stiffened against the leather chair. But he didn't look as if he was prying. He took the pack of short cigars from his pocket, and his battered French matches, making no attempt to light up but keeping his eyes on them, turning them over, examining them, giving her privacy. And after the incredible intimacy of the last few hours, he didn't seem a stranger any more. She thought of his low voice to Lynn: *Lean on me. I'm here. I'm with you.*

Once she'd started to tell him about convent life – the formal prayers, the hard labour, the long silences while they listened for the voice of God – she found it surprisingly easy. Only afterwards did it occur to her that she had never spoken like this to anyone else. Not Peggy, not even Lynn. When she finished he nodded.

'It explains a lot of things about you.' She raised her eyebrows. 'You listen rather than talk.'

'That's "conversion of manners". We're taught the opposite way of thinking to that in the world. Poverty and self-effacement are part of it.'

'And you have an almost exaggerated courtesy towards people, you seem to discount yourself.'

Anna blinked. 'It's not something I ever thought about. I had this very basic idea when I went into the convent, when I committed my life to Christ. I understood that a certain kind of behaviour was expected and I conformed to that.' She had a sudden picture of herself lying prostrate on the refectory floor to show she was a sinner, and that anyone might trample on her: her fault had been to speak during the night silence. 'It wasn't always easy,' she finished. Talk about understatement.

Daniel Stern went on fiddling with the cigar pack, opening the flap and flicking it back and forth as he remarked thoughtfully. 'Tucked away like that it sounds, with all respect, as if you're trapped in the Middle Ages in your Welsh hills. Without radio or newspapers, how can you seriously claim to be in touch with the sufferings of anybody? Except yourselves.'

His tone convinced her he wasn't trying to be unpleasant and she answered honestly, 'It's *because* we're aware of the anguish in the world that we're enclosed. We can help by loving God and loving people *in* God. We try to have a more intense sympathy and closeness with everyone in prison, or in those terrible camps. We know that love is needed – and so we give love.'

He looked a bit stunned. 'I do hope it gets through to them,' he said drily. 'I'm afraid that without faith, it all sounds supremely optimistic. Wouldn't you do better actually working among those people, then? Someone has to dole out the rations in the refugee camps, or nurse the dying. It seems to me a pretty selfish life for a lady who claims to be living for others.'

Anna pulled Lynn's shawl round her shoulders with a defensive gesture. 'I suppose. A lot of people make the same criticisms, but they're not recognising that enclosed religious – men or women – give themselves to God to use the way He wants. The whole point is that they *don't* make their own decisions, they *don't* determine their own path. They make themselves absolutely available to God.' She glanced across. He was still jiggling with the cigar pack but watching her face; in his she found interested scepticism. 'I wanted to be just a vessel – a conduit – so God could send love down into the world through me.' She pressed her fingertips on her chest just below the collarbones in emphasis. 'I know *I'm* not important. But I thought I could be part of something that was.' He noted it as the first vehement gesture he had seen her make, the first intimation that she was not as controlled as she seemed.

'You realise you're using the past tense?' She looked away, as if she'd admitted too much. He added kindly, 'You were important to Lynn tonight.'

She brightened at that. 'I was, wasn't I?' She yawned and stretched luxuriously back against the leather chair. 'I never thought it'd be like that. It was a huge experience, I still can't quite realise I was part of it. And I would never have believed Lynn'd have such strength, mentally or physically.'

'She really was in charge: we just did as we were told. She's a remarkable woman. And she never lost her dignity. It was fantastic.'

'I've nothing to measure it against. I just know I feel a different person after being involved.' His eyebrows went up. 'No, I do,' she insisted. 'Like looking through a doorway and seeing a place you've never been or even imagined.' She wanted to say, Being in that room last night had changed me. I've felt what I never thought to feel. I can't return to what I was. Unused to analysing feelings, still less to discussing them, she had never ventured so far beyond the boundaries she'd set for her emotions. She fell silent, plaiting the fringes of the shawl – scarlet, a sexy colour, a colour she had given up for ever the day she handed a piece of acetone-soaked cottonwool by the novice mistress all those years ago, to wipe off her long glossy nails. Daniel Stern watched her busy fingers.

'Everyone should have a child. Or better still three, like Lynn. You ought to give it serious thought. It's not too late for you, after all.' His voice softened. 'Sam's the best thing in my life. He drives me mad with his awful jokes, he never stops asking questions. But when he's not with me, I find I'm saving things up to show him or tell him about.'

'Just because I'm capable of bearing a child doesn't mean I have to do so.' It was the first time she'd ever answered a man back so sharply, and she was honest enough to recognise that it was because he had been too perceptive. She was instantly repentant. 'I didn't mean to be rude.'

He didn't seem offended. 'You don't have to think about all that, though, in your convent.' A thought struck him. 'Will they continue letting you out like this, as if you were on parole?'

She laughed at his choice of words. 'Mother Superior really doesn't like it, but she can't say a flat no, not like a few years ago. I have a formal permission from the Bishop, and I must ask for it to be extended from week to week. But while I'm in Bradford, I'm allowed to live a normal life.' She amended that. 'I mean, I must make time for prayer. In the convent it's eight times a day but of course here that's not always possible. I don't ever watch TV. I've never seen a film. I don't read modern novels. Or newspapers. I don't –'

'Eat in restaurants,' he finished for her. 'I see. Just your average antiquated day to day existence. Still, you've a business to run. I imagine that'll keep you more than occupied. Though I'm bound to say I don't think Maynard Gideon would have been quite so willing to continue the loan if we'd had all the facts at that meeting.'

'I'm sorry about that – it was a deception, I admit. But if I'd told you about the convent, the bank would have had no choice, they'd have called in the loan. It's for Lynn, so what else could I do?'

He nodded. 'I can't condone it. But I do understand.' He stuffed the cigars and matches back in his pocket.

'I've never seen you smoke one of those things.'

He pulled a face. 'I try not to. I gave up cigarettes a year ago and I'm giving up these too. I just have them around for something to do when I'm thinking. Twenty years ago I'd have used worry beads.' He stood up and stretched. 'God, I'm tired.' He went over to the stereo and put the same music on again. With his back still turned he observed, 'You still wear your wedding ring.'

'You still wear yours.'

'Touché.' He laughed.

'Being a nun – it's a bit like marriage.' She was able to say this because she couldn't see his expression. 'A lot of religious imagery is the same, too. Though the brides of Christ stuff is out of favour now.' She rubbed her forehead. 'Even nuns can be feminists. Anyway. I fell in love, and I thought it was going to last for ever. So I got engaged – I was a novice under temporary vows for three years first – and then there was this wedding. Just like any other bride. White dress, flowers, veils, the words, the works. There was a party, even a wedding cake.

When I went to my cell that night, the sisters had put little bunches of flowers all over my bed.' She paused, and recited softly. 'And now with all my heart I follow You: I fear You and I seek to see Your face.'

He blew out his breath in a long whistle. 'That's incredible.' she turned to look at him with shining eyes and it took him a moment to realise they were full of tears.

'I made a promise, and I'm terribly afraid I'm going to break it.'

'You're contemplating divorce, then. You and me both.' He sat down opposite her on an uncomfortable modern stool of steel and canvas. She sniffed and nodded.

'It's not as if I'm particularly unusual. Leaving religious life is more common now, just as divorce is more common outside. Lots of orders have actually disappeared or joined up with others because they've lost so many people.' She brushed the back of her hand across her cheek to dry it. 'Sorry about that. I shouldn't have talked so much. And I suppose I shouldn't be sitting here with you like this, either.'

'You want me to go.'

'Yes.' No.

'All right.' Neither moved. He added, so low she could hardly catch the words, 'Do I hear what you're not saying?'

'I . . . don't know.' Yes. He dragged the stool across the floor so he was sitting closer, their knees touching, her hands locked nervously round the mug of coffee. He leaned forward to catch hold of the edges of her shawl on both sides, pulling her towards him. It was all very slow. Anna had plenty of time to draw back, get up, say something to make him stop. But she did none of these things. He transferred the shawl to his right hand and reached out with his left to touch her face. His fingers on her cheek, tracing the spray of lashes beneath her eye so she blinked. He cupped her chin in his palm and smoothed his thumb over her lips, and when she opened her mouth she breathed in the smell of his hand. She recalled the slow moment of peace in the middle of the birth, the three of them touching, holding on in the damp heat of the snow-lit room. And for the first time in the intervening hours, she allowed herself to remember the sensation of his mouth against the skin of her inner wrist. She whispered, 'I never thanked you for helping us last night.'

He let go the shawl and took the coffee cup out of her fingers, set it on the floor. He held her upper arm tightly, stared intently into her face. Even in the dim light he could make out the complicated mouth, the concisely cut upper lip that belonged to a prim little girl, the full lower lip of a sensuous woman. He looked into wide, wary eyes beneath the feathery strokes of dark brows. He was close enough to see the delicate black line etched round the edges of the luminous irises. She was feminine, almost fragile in his grasp – and then the abrupt shock of the brutally close-cropped head. In any other woman it would be a signal of defiance, a declaration of aggression. But Anna had accepted the loss of her hair as an act of submission. Pity for her pointless offering was a stone in his chest and with a groan he pressed his hand against the shorn pelt, felt warm electricity as it prickled against his palm.

Under his gaze Anna turned her head, too shy to look back at him. He noted the curve of the round neck rising from the row of pearly buttons on her nightdress, the heavy fabric shielding the shape of her body. She put a hand to her throat and he put his own on top of it, conscious of roughened skin, short nails, the ridge of a scar along the middle finger.

She was all contradictions and complexes, as difficult and prickly as anyone he'd ever met. Not in speech – she was almost over-polite, too careful not to argue or offend: the product of convent discipline. But the discipline couldn't control the emotions that swept subtle changes over those cool features, stretching the skin over her cheekbones, drooping pale lids like bars over the transparent eyes. There was something unpredictable in her that was only explained now he knew about her convent background, something about the unexpected ways in which she reacted to quite simple things, like the workman's whistle from the building site in Cornhill: she had so little personal vanity, she'd not even connected it with herself. He was fascinated by the freshness she brought to even the simplest acts: she'd pored over the list of sandwiches in the lounge of the Victoria Hotel as if she'd never seen a menu before. It wasn't greed, she'd eaten with an abstracted air, her mind clearly elsewhere. (He didn't recognise yet another legacy of her training). There was nothing jaded about her, nothing dulled by use or hardened by knowledge. She reminded him of adolescence: his hands were sweating like a sixteen-year-old's. So it was a sixteen-year-old who asked, 'Can I kiss you?'

She swallowed and wouldn't look at him. And then she shut her eyes and held up her face for him in a child's trusting gesture, waiting.

He put his mouth on hers. No more than that, their lips just meeting. Hers were pressed tightly together, slightly puckered, making the sticky lipsticked touch of other women lascivious by comparison. She drew a quick breath but didn't move away from him. He increased the pressure slightly so he could feel the shape of her teeth and cursed inwardly as she made a move to withdraw. Too much, too fast. He could have laughed at himself. At thirty-seven he'd lived with two women and was divorcing a third. There'd been good years, when the passion of the moment could be treated as just that, slaked without cautious probings about previous partners, nervous jokes about safe sex and paralysing post-coital anxiety. He'd thought that particular hassle was over for him. He should have worked harder at family life, as Judy had waspishly remarked during that frightful meeting at her solicitor's.

Daniel Stern sighed. Anna thought it was because of her: she'd done something wrong, failed to respond adequately. She opened her eyes but by now he'd closed his, and she was able to examine his face without embarrassment. She liked what she could see: thick brown hair silvering at the temples, slightly hollow cheeks. He was clearly tired now, but he always had the pallor of someone who spent too much time working under artificial light. She pulled away from him and when he murmured a protest, put her fingers against his mouth. A down-curved mouth: a more knowledgeable woman would have thought, self-indulgent. She leant her forehead against his face and he said, above her head, 'Butterfly kisses. Mmm.'

'What?' She spluttered with laughter, the release of tension.

'Your eyelashes. Don't stop.' He pulled her close again. 'More.'

Anna felt a surge of confidence. Whatever she was doing, he clearly liked it. Emboldened, she rubbed her cheek against his, relishing the texture of his warm skin against her own. He put a hand round the back of her head, pushing his fingers into her hair so he could feel the bones, stroking the exposed nape of her neck which made her seem so defenceless.

Daniel Stern was a man who liked looking after people. He was protective towards Sam and had, at the start of their marriage, been the same with his wife. People who needed help touched and moved him. He'd have fought dragons for Lynn last night if it would have helped ease her.

But the realisation that Anna was vulnerable did not spark the usual reaction. Just the opposite. Inside his head, her image in wedding white bent submissive to symbolic scissors. Stern was speared by a double passion – for the eighteen-year-old Anna who had made herself into a living sacrifice, and for the forbidden flesh of the woman he was holding. With sudden strength he pulled her towards him so that she was dislodged from the edge of her chair. He supported her as she dropped to her knees, falling with her so they collapsed together. He twisted so he was beneath her, breaking her fall, and put both arms round her tightly, all the time expecting she would struggle, pull away.

Only she did neither. She lay inert, closed in on herself. Disconcerted, he kissed her again, his mouth hard now, seeking an answer. Getting none, he rolled them both over so he was above her.

Anna took the unaccustomed weight of his body with a little sigh of acceptance. He was heavy and warm, his chest squashing her breasts, his head on her shoulder. She lay with her arms by her sides, remembering the times she had wondered what it must be like to lie under a man. Those brief, quickly suppressed imaginings had been erotic – not for a moment had she anticipated this bear hug. She felt she could fall asleep on the carpet, let herself believe she had no part in what was happening.

This wasn't like Hal's unpremeditated embrace, so disconcerting in daylight on Bradley Moor, after she'd made such a fool of herself falling into that damn bog. And she'd been unable to put it out of her mind. She'd known she should erase it, blot it out, beg forgiveness. But something in her protested. One kiss. Her single – pathetically brief – lapse. Heaven knew how many times she'd gone over it, examining the clamour it had started in her heart. And her body.

Now Daniel Stern's mouth and hands transmitted urgent messages to Anna. But more than a decade of denial padlocked Sister Gabriel's responses: she was unable to bring herself to do what her body demanded – put her arms around him, hold him the way a woman holds a man she desires. Instead, she retreated mentally.

She sloughed off responsibility for her actions. For years she had been subject to the strictest supervision, reduced by rules to the status of a child. In Bradford she'd had to change but it wasn't easy to be in control, of herself or of others. Much easier, now, if she had no choice, if what was happening to her was inevitable. As inevitable as the birth of Lynn's child, woven to the same pattern. She wanted to be part of it, now, as desperately as once she had feared it: love and sex and birth and life.

The man had one hand behind her head while the other caressed her, stroking her neck, her long back, the dip of her waist. His lips found the pulse at the base of her throat and he licked her skin so she shivered. He stopped for a moment, nudging her with his knees as he kicked off his shoes. His knee came back, pushing at her own, insinuating itself between her legs but before she'd decided what to do about that, he was tasting her mouth with his tongue. He slid his right hand down from her throat to follow the line of her shoulder, the flesh of her upper arm, her ribs. She relaxed against him, enjoying the unaccustomed caresses, not letting herself think. He ran the back of his hand gently under the slight swell of her breast, bent his head to smooth his cheek against the fabric. She made a sound to warn him but he took it for assent and fastened his mouth on the cotton covering her nipple as she gasped with surprise, sucking so it puckered pointed against the damp cloth. He did the same for the other breast, his fingers squeezing one nipple, his lips the other, until wicked pleasure stopped her breath. She pressed her face into his shoulder so she couldn't see and let go, slipping into the tide of sensation closing over her head.

Anna wanted to give herself to Daniel Stern without any guilt. To complete the act and still be innocent of it. If she didn't look at him, acknowledge what he was doing, if she neither spoke nor initiated any action, then it wouldn't be her fault, she couldn't be blamed. So she lay in his arms as if she'd been hypnotised.

Stern realised she was distancing herself from him and he was intelligent enough to have a good idea why. She didn't want him to stop – but nor could she bring herself to actively encourage him. His problem was that he found it disconcerting, making love to a partner in a trance: it wasn't his style. He had no interest in forcing himself on any woman, he liked them to court him, to openly invite him. (His wife had been the single exception and what a disaster that had been). This preference wasn't due to shyness or lack of sexual confidence but merely to indolence. His idea of the perfect woman was a sultry siren, not a shy violet. Anna's charm was that of the unusual, the inexplicable: mouth and movements speaking of promise, eyes that said beware. He was excited by what he didn't know of her, by the idea of sexuality locked away, ardour unawakened. If she turned out to be a block of ice, he wasn't interested. He traced the shell of her ear while he thought about this and his fingers encountered her chopped hair. If anyone had told him a week ago he'd by lying on a living room floor in Bradford with a nun . . .

A memory clicked into place, filed years ago and forgotten until now. A Berlin stripclub after some conference, where half a dozen girls had postured, indecent and arousing. Elaborate nuns' head-dresses over heavily painted faces, skimpy parodies of black and white habits, crucifixes bouncing against bare breasts. He'd not thought of that disturbing, dingy evening in ten years. The airless underground room, walls covered in dark fabric that blotted up all sound but the magnified groans and sighs from the tiny stage as the 'nuns' menaced a shrinking schoolgirl with nothing but sheer black stockings beneath a frill of skirt, forcing her to undo her suspenders and bend over a chair. Then they'd turned their attention to a young man trussed naked between two pillars, beating him with a many-thronged leather discipline. The metal tips had drawn blood, the youth had sobbed and twisted. Writhing flesh sleek with sweat, one girl smiling, straddling her torso, lowering herself slowly over his face . . .

His hand moved urgently up from Anna's knee, ruckling her nightdress as he pushed it up, the pressure of his fingers denting soft flesh. The change in his breathing penetrated the warm cocoon Anna was weaving round herself. Jerked back into awareness she opened her eyes. He let go her head and pulled himself up so he was half-crouched over her while she waited, puzzled, sensing the change in him but unable to identify what it was that made him grasp her so tightly.

He bent again and clamped his open mouth on the curve of her inner thigh. Burning with shock and embarrassment she tried to pull away. But his hand moved up and his mouth followed and he had his other arm tight as a vice under her knees. Her nightdress was caught up somewhere, his hand was planted between her thighs. He stroked the – she couldn't think *her* – curling body hair and twined his fingers in it and his face was down there and the blood fluttered in her veins.

'No!' It came out as a groan. She tried to haul herself to a sitting position, caught hold of his head to stop him, tugging at his hair. 'Don't!' He ignored her protests, following her movements, burying his face deeper between her legs. His tongue hot on her flesh and shame fiery on her skin. He had found the little hidden hood and the awful thing was, she had to fight the urge to open her legs wider for him, press herself against his face, circle her hips to a rhythm she somehow knew, intensify the wild quivers his mouth was stirring up inside her own, other mouth. He was lapping the very tip of her clitoris where she'd never allowed herself to touch however badly she'd wanted to. In her womb silk flags were waving convulsively, she was soft and opening and, dear God . . .

Anna wrenched away from him so violently some material tore with a jagged rip and he gasped 'What the hell are you . . .' A muscle pulled in her back, a sharp pain under her elbow when she turned, cold wetness as she scrambled free.

Splinters of the coffee cup sharp on the carpet. Her guilt spreading a dark stain on pale wool. Without thinking she fell to her knees, attempting to mop it up with the hem of her nightdress.

I confess to you dear Mother and to you dear Sisters . . .

Beside her, Daniel Stern lay silently propped on one elbow, a hand over his eyes. He raked his fingers down his face, dragging the skin roughly as if he wanted to obliterate the last few minutes. He reached in his pocket for the battered French cigars and attempted to strike a match. When the third one failed he grunted with annoyance and stuffed them back into his pocket. If she'd looked at him, his expression would have been unreadable.

'Until you came along,' he remarked in a toneless voice, getting to his feet and reaching for his jacket, 'I'd never met a professional virgin.'

19

'Behold, that which I longed for already I see, that which I hoped for already I hold; I am united in heaven to Him whom on earth I have loved with my whole heart.'

Anna lay prostrate on the ground before the altar, alone in near-darkness. Her arms were stretched wide in the shape of the crucifix, embracing cold stone. She'd been there so long her bare feet were freezing.

She had lain like this long years ago, at the ceremony of Final Profession. Stretched on the ground while her sisters put over her the black pall, covering of the dead, and placed a lighted candle at each corner. She felt again the numbing, suffocating blackness, the heavy weight of fabric squashing her breasts painfully against the earth.

They had sung the *Dies Irae* as if it had been her funeral, showing all who watched that she was dead to the world. Even above the singing, even beneath the embroidered pall, Anna had heard her mother's wordless cry of protest, heard her footsteps and the slam of the heavy door.

Her mother had not returned for the rest of the ceremony. In the moment of greatest poignancy Anna – Sister Gabriel for ever now – had stood with arms outstretched before the altar. She had sung three times, each on a higher note:

Uphold me, Lord, according to your promise, and I shall live; let my hope in You not be in vain.

Nor had her mother heard the words with which her daughter, now a professed nun, was blessed.

'When you enter the chamber of the Bridegroom, may you

carry a shining lamp in your hand and meet Him with joy. May he find in you nothing disgraceful, nothing sordid, nothing dishonourable, but a snow-white soul and a clear and shining body.'

The entire church had turned to her, and in that moment Anna had known utter certainty.

'Thy beauty now is all for the King's delight. He is thy Lord and God.'

All for the King's delight. Anna stretched her arms wider till her fingertips scraped on stone.

I'm a sinner. She punished herself by pressing her face so fiercely against the ground it hurt. I've made a mockery of those words by my thoughts and desires even more than my actions. I deserve to suffer the old penances, the pain from the small wooden cross studded with nails worn beneath my clothes and against my skin. I deserve the metal band with inward-facing spikes clamped round my thigh so the points press into my flesh when I move.

Sex is dirty, sordid. I've always known that. And still I failed utterly to subdue the body to the spirit. I tried to do as I was taught and emulate the angels. But angels don't have bodies.

Angels don't have bodies. But so help me, I do. She remembered the touch of Daniel Stern's mouth on her flesh and with an involuntary movement bit the back of her own hand. When she looked, it bore the faint purple teethmarks she'd seen on Lynn's skin the night of the birth. God forgive me.

She raised her head and above her the Virgin gazed adoring at her beautiful baby. O Mary, refuge of sinners, pray for me. But Anna saw Lynn's face. Her mind jumped and twisted, trying to reconcile the wonder of birth and what she had experienced afterwards with Daniel Stern.

They were totally different and yet she was groping towards the realisation that they sprang from the same source. Lynn had lost herself during the delivery, had allowed emotions and sensations to rule her body. And Anna knew that in another moment she would have done so too, with Stern: she'd felt herself start to go, sliding over a dark precipice. And she had wanted it. How she had wanted it.

The admission was a knife in her side. She shut her eyes, trying to force the prayer that should have filled her heart. But nothing came.

It was true, then, the terrifying conviction that had been eating into her day after day for so long.

She had lost her vocation. She could no longer accept the belief essential to any nun – that she was living the life she was meant to live, in the place she was meant to be. The fountain of her faith had dried. And it wasn't one of God's silences, it wasn't something that in time – in a few months, a year – would pass and leave her stronger, more resilient.

To her left, in the nuns' choir, she heard the soft slurp of sandalled feet and the sounds of Sister Thomas à Kempis settling herself behind the harp to practise. It was a concert-sized instrument which the nuns loved. Sister Thomas had hoped to become a professional harpist but when she decided to give herself and her talent to God, she brought the harp in with her.

One or two of the nuns had thought it was an indulgence but Mother Emmanuel had quoted Teresa of Avila, the great Teresa, who used to play the drum and little Spanish pipes: *We need all this, my daughters, to make life liveable.*

Clear notes cascaded through the choir and washed over Anna at the foot of the cross. She lay in the centre of the music and it rippled away from her as if she'd been flung into it like a pebble. She concentrated until she almost forgot to breathe. But even that pure sound did not do it for her any more, did not lift her out of herself, take her from confusion into calm.

Then she knew with absolute certainty that she couldn't go on. Sister Godric had seen it: the world had put its mark on her. And she ground her face into the stone with the pity of it, scraping soft skin, welcoming raw pain.

She could not look inward any more, endlessly searching for that deep quiet place where God and the soul meet. She could not bear any longer to lock herself away and turn her heart to the sorrows of the world beyond the convent's walled acres.

She wanted to be part of that world herself.

Anna's first task next morning was to clean the refectory tables. Enveloped in a huge sacking apron, hands wrinkling red in hot soapy water, she worked methodically along the rows with her scrubbing brush. Each table took ten minutes to do properly, wiping down the legs and underneath with a damp cloth, finishing off with a dry towel. When they were completely dry, they would be polished with more of the beeswax from the convent hives. Anna wondered how many women like her had scrubbed as she was scrubbing. Thousands, probably. *A nun is like a pane of glass. When one breaks, you put in another.*

As she worked, her hands made wide circles on the smooth old wood, and her thoughts circled too, back to the convent in Huddersfield when she was fifteen, and Sister Morag, who had told her of the fear and desire that had brought so many women into religious life.

In her case, it had been fear of letting go. Since adolescence she had been afraid of the power of her own sexuality, terrified of not being in control. And so she had avoided involvement with anyone, had never allowed herself to be in a situation where that natural force might have taken her over.

The prospect of lifelong chastity had been a relief. A professional virgin, Stern had called her. He'd wanted to hurt, but maybe there was something in what he'd said. Perhaps, after all, she'd used the church's demand for chastity as an excuse to run from the complexities of human love.

She dropped the scrubbing brush into the bucket and started to wipe the table over with a cloth, careful to get up all the suds. She'd felt deep envy for Lynn that night – envy of her power, her exhilaration, the pure pagan pleasure on her face in the final moments. She had been utterly fulfilled, as Anna never had. Completed. Part of life, not looking on.

She picked up bucket and cloths, moved to the next table,

started to scrub furiously at the worn wood, finding relief in physical activity. Physical, like the birth. Physical, like ecstasy. She forced herself to admit, like orgasm. Maybe fear of one was fear of the other. It seemed to her she had always been tense, always drawing back. The very idea of the fusion of man and woman – and the results of that fusion – had scared her.

She would soon be free to go back to the world without ties and lies and subterfuge. But she saw now that if she couldn't overcome this fear of her own sexuality, she'd be as locked away from ordinary human experience as she was here inside the enclosure. And she didn't want that anymore, whatever the cost.

She knew that for certain: sometime, sooner or later, it would cost her. Look how Lynn had suffered and would continue to do so. In sharing her life with Simon she had laid herself open to unhappiness. Despite that, Anna knew she'd change places in a minute if only she could. She rubbed the table more slowly, stopped. Remembered the warm weight of the baby's tiny new body. *If only*. They said they were the saddest words in any language. If only she had the chance to hold in her arms the child of her own body, her own loving.

Unhappiness wouldn't kill her. Religious life had given her two things: a rock certainty in the existence of God, and the ability to live with few material comforts. Convent discipline had shown the possibilities within herself. Emotional austerity had forged out of the timorous eighteen-year-old a woman of thirty-one who could – what was it Sister Godric used to say? – who could be free and sitting on a halfpenny because of the experience. She had learned what she could endure.

Sister Dominic peeped round the door, two fingers to her lips. Anna stopped work and wiped the back of her hand over her damp forehead. 'Benedicite.'

'Dominus,' responded Lis, and came into the refectory, her arms as always full of washing from the garden to be ironed. 'Mother Emmanuel will see you in her office after scriptures.'

'Thank you.'

'I know what it's about.' Anna nodded. Extraordinary how

in an almost silent community like theirs, information spread with viral speed. 'You're really going then.' Lis was clearly upset, to be breaking silence. They would have to kneel in the middle of refectory, their napkins bound around their mouths as sign of the fault for which they atoned. They would wait until Reverend Mother rang her bell, when they could unbind their mouths and kiss the floor.

'It's really only making official what I've been feeling for months now,' Anna whispered cautiously. The younger woman looked doleful.

'I haven't been back here much lately,' Anna tried, consolingly.

'But at least you came back,' Lis sniffed.

Anna picked up the bucket and moved on to the next table, working up a vigorous lather to give herself time to think. Lis watched and her eyes reminded Anna of the chinchilla rabbit again, soft and grey and easily hurt.

'I'll help.' The younger woman dumped her pile of laundry on a bench.

'You don't have to.'

'I want to.' She picked up the cloth, wrung it out, and started wiping the table. Glancing across, Anna saw that she was wiping her own tears off the wood.

'Lis, don't cry,' she whispered urgently. 'It's nothing to cry about. It's *my* loss, not yours.'

'How can you say that?' She rounded on Anna sharply, hissing the words so no one should hear. 'You'll go off and start a new life and leave me here alone and it's your loss? You're either mad or cruel.'

'No.' Anna threw her scrubbing brush into the water. 'I'm neither. I've been here years longer than you. I've tried so hard, I've struggled, I've – '

'Don't go. For God's sake, don't go.' Lis sat down sideways on one of the long benches and buried her face in her arms, heedless of her habit on the wet table.

'I'd stay if I could, you know that. I don't *want* to leave.' Anna looked round the long refectory, at the whitewashed walls, the spray of dried flowers on the window-sill. 'I'll be leaving my home. My family.' She put a hand to Lis. For a minute she hesitated, then laid it on the shoulder that shuddered under her touch. 'I'm the one who'll be alone, Lis, I'll be the outsider.'

Lis turned quickly and grabbed her soapy hand. 'Don't make me sorry for you. I'm sorry for *me*.' She looked up. Even crying, even with her nose red and her eyes pink, she was appealing. 'You won't be alone for long. You'll have a life outside, and you'll have more and more. And I . . .' she was making herself angry now, 'I'll have less and less. I don't want to see it that way, but I can't help it.' She pressed Anna's hand against her wet eyes and dragged her words. 'I can't live without you.'

Anna stood as if she'd been turned to stone, her hand blindfolding the younger woman, transfixed by the depth of Lis's desolation. She had not sought this love, had not nurtured it. But it had grown anyway, had sprouted somehow in the dry soil of convent life. It was winding its tendrils round her, holding her here, pinning her down . . .

She pulled away with a sharp movement but Lis was fast too, grabbing Anna's hand in both her own, pressing it to her mouth now, frantically kissing the back, the soapy palm.

'No!' Anna wrenched her hand free. Lis reacted by lurching forward, falling to her knees. 'Get up!' said Anna sharply but Lis wouldn't. She wrapped her arms round Anna's thighs, holding her in a grip she couldn't break, so she was afraid she'd be pulled over.

'Don't go, don't go, don't go and leave me here . . .' Lis chanted in a muffled monotone, face pressed into Anna's habit. 'Don't, oh please don't . . .' She was like Jamie when he'd hurt himself, and Anna had watched him burrow his head against Lynn's side for consolation. 'Please don't . . .' The whimper was pathetic as a puppy and her head was hard against Anna's waist.

Anna gave a shudder of distaste, repelled by the crouching figure, the desperate clutching arms, the constrictions of this unwanted love. With a ferocious clarity she knew she could not stay here, and Lis became all the things that conspired to keep her: love and guilt, fear and promises made not to be broken.

She bent, put her hands on the younger woman's shoulders and thrust her violently away. The sound of her revulsion was an ugly grunt of disgust. Lis let herself collapse to the ground and lay uncomfortably twisted, face in the crook of her arm.

Anna took a step back, and another, leant against the door, hands behind her back, trying to still her harsh breathing. She was bewildered by the ferocity of her reactions. When Lis had arrived at the convent four years before, it had been like turning on a light. Her gaiety, her chatter, her interest in everything had warmed Anna when she had been cold and unhappy. She had leaned towards this bright creature with an affection no one had stirred for so long. Impossible to believe this was the same girl. Impossible to convince herself it was not her fault.

Still Lis didn't move. 'I can't live without you.' She whispered into her arm and her cheek was red, marked by the heavy belt buckle. Anna stared at the weal and for a moment she wavered, tempted by old affection and the habit of loving Lis to console, commiserate, to say what the younger woman wanted so desperately to hear.

No. That would be another lie. She didn't want this. She was leaving. In half an hour, she would ask Mother Emmanuel for dispensation from her vows, and in a few weeks she would be free.

She let out a long breath. So she could spare pity for Lis, who loved her. And if they'd misunderstood each other – if she had supposed she was offering one sort of love, and Lis had inferred another – that was the people they were.

'I can't live without you.'

Anna tugged at Lis's shoulders and her voice was tired. 'Yes you can. Get up. Get up *now*.' The authority got through and after a moment Lis hauled herself wearily into a sitting position. She reached for one of the clean towels from the pile she'd brought and wiped her eyes.

'Sorry.'

'I'm the one who's sorry. I'm the one who's failed. Not you.' Anna held out her hand and pulled Lis to her feet. She held on for a minute longer than necessary, looking down at the younger woman's hand, smoother than her own but showing the same telltale signs, the scars and marks from heavy work. And Anna understood for the first time what drew her so to Lis: she could have been herself, at twenty-four, grown out of the adolescent fervour that had taken her into religious life, uneasily aware of all she was missing, searching for something which maybe wasn't there for her. 'Go on,' she said gently. 'Go and do your ironing. You'll be all right.' Still without looking at her, Lis nodded, picked up her pile of laundry and went quietly away.

When she'd gone, Anna's careful calm evaporated. She plunged her hands into the grey soapy water and started on the last table, scrubbing savagely till she was breathless, furious with Lis and herself. When had their innocent friendship turned into this? Without her being aware of any difference, it had slipped from something she valued to something shameful, to be hidden and denied. Sister Peter had been right that day in the cellar, she should have been more wary. She hated herself for hurting another person, for making misery when she'd thought she was bringing happiness.

Her hand slowed and stopped, and she wiped her forehead with the back of her arm in its rolled up sleeve. The girl would get over it, she was young, just the way she herself had been in the first years here. More outgoing, perhaps, more full of laughter – though that had not been very noticeable lately. But she too seemed unable to survive happily without a personal relationship to give meaning to her days.

She sighed. How obsessed the old founders had been, with all their strictures against particular friendship. In those days monasteries and convents took people who should never have been in religious life: younger sons without land or money, inconvenient daughters, misfits. That no longer applied, and nor should the old rules. It wasn't a question of sexual relief. In all her time at the convent, she'd never come across anything physical taking place among the women.

But people needed simple human affection. How extraordinary that the love of God was beyond words, it filled the huge spaces. And yet still it could not totally satisfy the cravings of the heart.

Half an hour later she added soda to the washing water and poured it down an outside drain to clean it. Waste nothing. In the stone-floored scullery she rinsed brush and cloths in the low sink with cold water only. Glancing round to make sure she was alone, she fished a small tube out of the capacious loose pocket beneath her scapular and creamed her hands carefully.

Mother Emmanuel had her door open as always while she worked. Anna watched for a moment before she knocked, seeing what she'd often noticed before: the two vertical creases like quotation marks that deepened between the prioress's eyes as she signed a cheque and dropped two more bills onto a second pile. The ones she couldn't pay this week, Anna thought. A juggling act she must constantly perform and which never even crossed my mind. Until I had to do it myself, at the mill, it meant nothing. Feeling the younger woman's eyes on her, the prioress looked up and squeezed her eyes shut to rest them.

'I really don't know how I'm to meet these,' she gestured towards the larger pile. 'I must take them to the chapel and show them to Our Lord, and remind Him of His promise.'

Anna nodded, sympathy without speech. What would Peggy think if she tried that at the mill? But as she knew very well, here it seemed to work. The money did turn up when it was needed, and in the strangest ways. Their only income came from the altar breads, the beeswax candles and the knitting wool. Though all three together scarcely made enough to keep up the old house, somehow they struggled through year after year with the aid of an unexpected gift, something left in a will. Divine providence, they called it.

Reverend Mother leant back in her chair but left Anna standing. 'You asked to see me, Sister Gabriel?'

It burst out in a rush, unrehearsed. 'I want . . . I must ask to be released from my vows.'

She hadn't realised how harsh the words would sound. She couldn't look up, and the silence made her go on. 'I can't live the life any longer, Mother. I've tried and tried, and now I know I made the wrong choice.'

When she risked a glance at the prioress, she saw the heavy frowning face of the New York security guard, watchful and suspicious. Mother Emmanuel's worst expectations had been confirmed.

'It is not we who choose, but He.'

There was no answer to that. 'I feel I've failed,' she offered weakly.

'We all face problems at one time or another,' the prioress retorted. 'We all find things exceptionally difficult. We have to learn to use difficulties in a constructive way. The test is whether we stay put. Whether we see it through.' Her tone was neutral, almost indifferent. The presage, with her, to anger she never vented.

Anna kept her eyes down, but she knew the prioress so well, she could see without looking. Stubby and shapeless, her body was obviously that of a woman who had never given it a moment's thought. Even when she was in her prime she could never have allowed it beauty and now the low bustline had merged with the wide waist and the shoulders were rounded, the feet splayed in leather sandals.

'I'm sure this is just a temptation,' she was saying now, conciliatory. 'I believe you have a vocation.' The broad artist's hands clasped each other, wide silver wedding band and the carved amethyst of her office gleaming rich against brown wrinkles. 'God has called you. To retract would be to repudiate an invitation.'

'Mother, I think . . .' she had to clear her throat before she could go on. 'I'm sure I made a mistake. A dreadful mistake.'

The remote voice said, 'That hardly seems sufficient reason for running away from what you have taken on. You cannot expect immediate and perfect fulfilment.'

'Thirteen years is a long time. And I'm further from feeling that, not nearer.'

Mother Emmanuel softened her tone. 'You've been through an emotional period and returning home has clearly disturbed you. Perhaps it was my fault, I may have been mistaken to let you go back repeatedly. You evidently need peace to regain the strength of your interior life. Go and think this through, Sister. You don't want to take a decision you will regret.'

Obedience was so entrenched in her, Anna automatically turned to the door. And stopped.

'I have to leave, Mother. I'm not happy here any more.'

The voice behind her sounded old suddenly, tired. 'Happiness? A dog asleep in the sun is happy. You have dedicated your life to God, not for reward in this life, but in the next. You may miss study today, Sister. Go to your cell and think quietly. Pray to know.'

Anna took a single obedient step towards the door. Only in exceptional circumstances did they ever go to their cells during the day, and then only when given permission.

Her cell was the one haven, the single place she could be absolutely alone and unobserved. But there had been a time when she'd not felt that. She'd started to experience terrible panic during Great Silence. In that confined space – ten paces from door to window, seven across – she would find herself in the grip of hideous apprehension, shapeless as a scream. Panic would close her throat and slick her palms with sweat. And there was no reason, no cause: she'd been convinced she was going mad.

Experience gradually proved it was claustrophobia: it only happened when the door of her cell was closed and endless night lay ahead. It took a long time before she was able to put it together with her growing disillusion in the life. After one particularly bad episode she asked Reverend Mother if she might be permitted to sleep in the Infirmary, a large room rarely needed.

'You may not,' the prioress had replied. There'd been no unkindness there, just practical commonsense and a complete lack of comprehension. 'I'm sorry about your difficulty, Sister. But that is your cross, and you must bear it.'

She had borne it, heaven knew how. Some nights had been worse than others. But she'd been lucky. It was then that her affection for Lis had started, and new confidence slowly cured the symptoms. But although she knew it was the system, the rigid rules of convent life that had dictated the response, still she didn't think she could ever forgive the prioress that stern and unyielding sentence. 'That is your cross, and you must bear it.'

Anna clasped her hands tightly in her voluminous sleeves. There would be no other answer for her in that small white room.

'Mother, what will make you realise I will not change my mind.' She turned back to the superior. 'This isn't a sudden impulse. I've been thinking about it for years.'

'I'm convinced your future lies with us.' The prioress leant forward, subjecting Anna to the full force of her indomitable spirit, that had energised a failing house and brought it round. 'You must deposit your personal judgement in His hands. God wants you here. And Sister Gabriel . . .' her tired eyes were alight with the strength of her conviction '. . . the community needs you. We need you in this house where God has work for you. You are dear to us. Our sister. We're a family, and what happens to one happens to everyone. You must not take this course.'

'Mother, I'm truly sorry.' The silence went on and on.

'Very well, then.' The prioress sat back. Dignity would not permit her to ask again. She recognised the sharp little spasm in her chest as resentment at Sister Gabriel's ingratitude. 'You will write to Rome today.' She heard herself, and she sounded aggrieved. 'You realise it could be settled in a matter of weeks.

Or it could take a long time – maybe months.' She tidied the papers on her desk with automatic movements.

'That long?' Anna was stunned.

'The papers have to be signed and processed, by the Holy See. In the old days there used to be visitations from the Bishop as well, but that doesn't often happen now. If Rome considers the reasons sound, a rescript will be granted.'

Anna had a sudden surge of alarm. It sounded so final, far worse than divorce. 'But when it comes, I'll still be a member of the church?'

'Of course. There's no official stigma attached. There are too many men and women leaving orders today for that.' The two women looked at each other and the prioress handed Anna a sheet of paper. 'Sit down, Sister Gabriel, we've a good many practical arrangements to make. You start your letter: Dear Holy Father . . .'

'I write this to the *Pope*?' Anna nearly dropped the paper.

'To who else? You say what you want, but something like . . .' the prioress shut her eyes in thought. 'After much prayer and very great heartbreak, I am certain that I will have to ask for a dispensation of my vow. I have been living outside for some time, I have had the advice of Father So-and-So. Then you state your reasons.' She sighed.

'I thought . . .' Surely she'd explained them.

The prioress took up her own pen. 'We'll call it incompatibility of temperament. Which it is, after all's said and done. And then there's the question of money. You can't just walk out of here like a vagrant. You must be provided for.' The hands that never made an unnecessary movement were trembling slightly, the only sign of emotion she could not suppress.

'Thank you, Mother.' Now it was happening, Anna felt shaky herself: and although the prioress smiled, her eyes were sad and deep grooves of disappointment bracketed her folded mouth.

20

Sister Godric passed her days in the recreation room, seated on an upright chair. Behind her, open wooden shutters let in wintry light to detail the creamy wall petalled with flaking paint. Her grey and white robes gave her a timeless look, a figure drawn in a Dutch interior. Her head was bent over her work, both feet rested on a stool. She had terrible trouble with them, misshapen and gouty through years in harsh leather sandals. She was supposed to rest, but didn't seem to know the meaning of the word. Heaps mushroomed beside her chair: accounts to be checked, letters to be answered, a box of bookmarks and a manuscript pen for adding short verses in her elegant script. When Anna brought in her cup of tea in deference to her years and frailty, she put the box aside.

'I've just reached ninety,' she announced with satisfaction. 'And I don't mean years. Enough to pay for a new pair of kitchen scissors. When you have a moment, would you take them down to the visitors' room?' Anna put the box on her knee, glancing at the top one. It had a bluebell in one corner and 'May your prayers ascend to God this happy day and draw upon you the blessings of heaven' in italic script beneath it. She smiled affectionately at Sister Godric. The old nun seemed hardly to have changed for all Anna's religious life. She must have been over seventy when the younger woman entered, but her enthusiasms were irresistible, and though the hands holding the pen were speckled by age, the fingers were deft as ever.

Mother Emmanuel had told Anna to stay with Sister Godric until Vespers. She held her own cup of hot water: they only had tea first thing in the morning. The two women sat in companionable silence until Sister Godric observed, 'It's official, then. You've asked for your dispensation.'

Everyone seemed to know, and she'd only made the request three hours before. 'I've seen Reverend Mother. Now it's happened, I'm full of doubt.'

'Uprooting your whole life is difficult, especially when you'd expected to stay here for ever.' Sister Godric sipped her tea reflectively. 'But it's not as difficult as staying for the wrong reasons. Misplaced loyalty, shame – who needs that?'

Anna rubbed her forehead. The pressure of the serré-tête had become increasingly intolerable. How had she borne all these years the tight band, the weight on the crown of her head? Her voice was very low. 'I'll miss you all. But I must say, it feels as if the habit doesn't fit me any more.'

'That comment would tell a psychoanalyst something, wouldn't you say?' She considered Anna, head on one side, sharp as a bird. 'You're telling me you've outgrown the life.'

She wanted to deny it, but perhaps it was true. And yet it wasn't all of the truth. These women had given themselves and their love to what they believed. They lived under the glance of God in an austerity few could match, confining the body in order to free the spirit. If she could no longer sustain the life, she still had admiration for it.

'If you want my opinion, which I doubt,' Sister Godric was saying, 'you've done the right thing. I'm sorry you're leaving but make no mistake, it's we who'll do the missing. It won't be the same here without you.'

'Reverend Mother told me I was only the second fully professed nun to leave this house since she can remember.'

'She'll have to get used to it.' Sister Godric winced as she moved her painful foot. 'You won't be the last and she knows it. Religious are walking out of their orders everywhere. Not that anyone's making it easy to do so,' she added. 'I think you'll find quite a lot of hostility from the others.' She met Anna's eyes with a small smile. 'Try to understand that it's hard for them. It's as if you were saying, this isn't good enough for me.' She noted the small movement of denial. 'It's just the same as people moving to a new job. Colleagues watch them with a mixture of envy and annoyance. Now,' she went on briskly, 'you've told us all about dear Lynn and the baby. But not a word of the mill.'

The old nun's calm expression masked sadness as Anna put down her cup and leant forward, eager to talk. For thirteen years she had done her best to nurture and encourage this young woman, had watched her grow from a tentative beginning to bloom in religious life.

Sister Godric had not entered the convent until she was almost fifty. Thirty years before, when a young subaltern died in the trenches of the first war, she had fought grief and bitterness and somehow survived. She'd achieved equanimity by concluding this was God's plan: denying her husband and children, He had offered her a place at His side.

So she had empathised with the young woman, and the difficulties she had gone through in the last few years. She had seen unhappiness blight tranquillity in other faces here, and known them overcome it and recover. But not Sister Gabriel. With her it had been pure biology: the time-clock ticking relentlessly away, bringing imperceptible changes to the body shaped by nature for loving men and bearing children . . . She gave herself a little shake. She was always doing that these days, going off into her own thoughts. She concentrated on the younger woman describing the interview with Maynard Gideon and Danièl Stern's visit to Nightingale Mill. 'Well,' she commented finally, 'he's said he'll back you. I'm sure everything will go through on the nod.'

Anna who had given a carefully edited version of events, blew out her breath in exasperation. 'I'm not. It's absolutely maddening but,' she turned her head in case she blushed. 'It's not just the mill. I have the feeling he's sort of deciding about me personally.' She answered Sister Godric's puzzled frown. 'The London bank had no idea I was a nun. I let them assume I was working at the mill all the time. But Daniel Stern turned up unexpectedly and saw me in the habit. I never meant to tell him about living here, and asking permission all the time, but somehow I did. I don't think he was very pleased,' she added sombrely. Sister Godric, whose marketing career had included personnel training and who had served her term as superior, missed nothing.

'When will you hear from your banker? Dear me, you sound like an heiress.'

'I wish.' Anna heard herself and stopped short. 'I mean . . . he's gone on to do some fishing. In the Lake District.' And probably with a flaming temper, she added silently.

'What about that manager of yours, the man you thought was trying to sabotage the mill? You got rid of him, I imagine.'

'No. He's still with us.' She explained the circumstances of Beattie's apology. 'So I couldn't yet fire him,' she finished. 'He'd had such a bad time, and he admitted what he'd done.' She caught Sister Godric's eye. 'You think I was wrong, don't you?'

'I think you may have been naïve,' Sister Godric said drily. 'I forget how little experience you've really had of the world. From all you said, he's not a man I'd want on my payroll.'

'He deserved another chance.'

'You mean, you couldn't bring yourself to do it.' The older woman pursed her lips. 'Well, what's done is done and you may be right. Though I'm bound to say in my experience, people rarely change.'

'That sounds cynical.'

'It is,' Sister Godric agreed. 'And you'll find a touch of cynicism an asset in business. Be cynical when you look at your Mr Beattie, all right? Now then, let's get back to basics. You say you're trying to get foreign buyers for your new lines. What stage have you reached?'

'If Maynard Gideon agree to continue the loan, I need to get a lot of samples and booklets ready fast. The problem is, they're complicated to put together because the colours and fibres are all different. And I don't want thousands of them, just a few hundred.' She put down her cup. 'They're going to be expensive to produce and I was wondering if the convent would do them for me? I'd pay, of course. D'you think Reverend Mother would agree?'

'No,' said Sister Godric, 'I don't. We're not permitted to accept work like that. Unless . . .' she put her head on one side again, calculating. 'Has Reverend Mother spoken to you about finances?'

'Only that I'd be given money when I left. I told her I didn't want any. It wouldn't be right – after all, I didn't bring anything in with me.' On Solemn Profession, each nun made a will giving everything away to make real the vow of poverty. A certain amount was made over to the order. It gave her a pang even now to remember how her parents had refused to continue her allowance in an attempt to make her change her mind. When she entered, they wrote to tell her they had changed their wills in Simon's favour.

'You're not to leave here destitute, that's the idea. You must have heard all the awful stories about nuns being given just five pounds and a single ticket to London? No one knew, a few years ago, how to set about dealing with the world again. But you'll take money for clothes and rent and so forth. And you're supposed to have enough to undertake some kind of training if you want.'

'All that doesn't apply to me, does it? I've somewhere to live, and a job.' She didn't add that until now, she had refused to allow Lynn to authorise her any payment for it.

Sister Godric traced an absent-minded pattern on her knee with her manuscript nib. 'I think you and I ought to have a word with Mother Emmanuel.'

The following day at four o'clock the recreation room was full. Anna saw them all in their accustomed places facing the window, work-baskets beside them holding handkerchiefs to hem, bedsocks to darn, embroidery. There was a low hum of conversation, a stifled giggle from the plump eighteen-year-old postulant who had just completed her first month with the order.

Only one nun was silent. Sister Dominic sat at the end of

the semi-circle of chairs, on the second row. Her head was studiously bent over her work. She was making lace on a small cushion, the dangle of clustered weights ornate and pretty. Anna could see it would be a marker for a prayerbook, white and frail as a skeleton leaf. She leant across to Lis and said, 'That's lovely,' but all she got was a cool stare and a formal little 'Thank you'.

Everyone was busy. If the devil made work for idle hands, he'd have no chance here. Conscious of deft fingers, flashing needles and scissors, it crossed her mind that here, hands and faces were all you ever knew of another's body: the habit covered everything else. That must be why she always looked at hands, even in the world.

Mother Emmanuel waited for silence. 'We have to take a community decision, since we would all be involved. Sister Gabriel has asked for our help. She would accept it rather than funds when she leaves us. It would benefit us because we have very little at the moment. And it's work she urgently needs.' The prioress looked round the circle of nuns. 'Sister Gabriel will explain it to you. The decision is yours.' She finished on a note of resignation, just as she'd sounded when she talked to Anna and Sister Godric. All the rancour had gone out of her.

At her nod, Anna started to tell them about the mill, and her plans for foreign trade, and the yarns Terry Singh was dyeing.

'The basic idea is that what people want is simplicity and style, not fancy knits. So women – and men too, lots of men knit now, the greys and creams are for them – can buy our yarns in mixtures of wool, mohair, linen and silk. They could have a garment in one material, and then a panel, or sleeves, or just a design, in another. They could choose a single colour but it will vary slightly depending on the mixture, so there'll be a subtle emphasis knitted into the pattern.'

'I thought,' she finished, 'that you might perhaps help me get the samples ready. I don't need money, I'm still living with Lynn, and I know how little the convent has. I desperately need this work done: I must have hundreds to distrubute. The first ones have to be ready when the Japanese trade delegates visit the mill.'

'What exactly do these samples look like?' Sister Thomas à Kempis spoke with interest. Anna passed round a handful she and Peggy had made up. They were nine inches by three, of good quality buff card folded to make a booklet. Stamped on the front were the words *Natural Spinning Company*. Inside, short lengths of the different yarns were fixed to an adhesive strip in colour sequence from white to deep red, each yarn named and numbered. The nuns exclaimed over texture and lustre and the names – one red was Cardinal, a deep violet was Incense and Candle a creamy white. She showed them the brief history of Nightingale Mill she had written at Hal's instigation, which was to be printed on matching card folded to the same size.

'You could have a picture of the mill on the front,' Sister Peter remarked. 'It'd be more memorable. What does it look like?'

'I never thought of that,' Anna said slowly. 'It's a Victorian industrial building. Three storeys high. Built of rough grey stone blocks, with rows of square windows and a dark slate roof.'

'Why is it called Nightingale Mill?' Sister Vincent wanted to know.

'It must have once been on the edge of a wood . . .' she laughed at the thought, 'a hundred years ago. It's nothing now but cobbled yards and narrow streets. There are half a dozen other mills nearby, but used for light industry now, engineering or car body shops. All the streets round about have country names – Berry Street, Farm Street, Orchard Yard. They're nothing like their names though, not romantic at all. A photograph would be very disillusioning.'

'Not a photograph.' Sister Peter was thoughtful. 'Though I'd need one. I could do a small line drawing of the building itself, with the wood behind – the way it might have looked when it was built. It would be easy for your printers to reproduce and I bet your Japanese buyers would love it.'

Anna took out a dozen sheets of paper. 'These are breed stories for the Japanese market too. They describe the sheep whose wool they're buying, and the part of the country they come from. They'll be printed on large labels for each pack of yarn.'

Sister Peter flipped through them. 'If you could get photographs of the sheep and the countryside they live in, I'll do you a tiny water-colour for each type. For the other side of the label.' Anna fished from her bag the British Wool Marketing Board book she and Hal had used for reference. Sister Peter pounced on it, exclaiming in delight over the Clun Forest and the Shropshire. She suddenly recollected herself and turned towards Mother Prioress. 'If I had your permission, Mother.'

The prioress waited for a slow moment before answering. Nothing showed in her face, but she felt defeated. For forty years, she'd wondered if she should have joined a missionary order and made her life in the territory of the unconverted. She believed she had the guts for it, the vigour and the vision. But this business with Sister Gabriel seemed to be her own failure and it had shaken her confidence.

She'd seen women try religious life and leave – no superior could say otherwise. Girls would come in for a few months, a year, and find the challenge of enclosure with its arduous work and long hours too demanding. That was what the novitiate was all about: a time of trial.

Only one of her finally professed nuns had ever departed, when her health deteriorated and their living conditions became too much for her. This case was different: Sister Gabriel was a valued member of their little community, an intelligent woman in her prime. If she had chosen to go, who else might follow?

Literally thousands had gone already, walking out of religious orders, enclosed and active, throughout the world. But although she knew it as a distant fact, the prioress had not felt it until now. It was a criticism, as though their way of life had been judged second-best. And if the loss of one sister back to the world was so painful, how could she have hoped to survive the buffeting of missionary life? Suddenly, the foolish dream of a lifetime had dissolved.

The prioress pulled herself together. Whatever the cause of Sister Gabriel's leaving, it had to be handled with due formality. If it meant encouraging her in her new life, so be it. 'Do you agree, my daughters?'

Sister Mark, who had not spoken at all, raised a hand for permission to speak. 'I'm not sure, Mother, that this is the correct thing to do. I know Sister Gabriel wants our help.' She stuttered in her nervousness. 'It's not . . . not our call, it can't be meant that we should do such work. It does no good in the world, it just makes money.'

'I concur.' Sister Vincent's predatory profile showed sharp against the flaking wall as she looked up from her needles. 'It's against the interior life to take this on. It will bring anxiety and trouble. We'll regret it.'

Anna caught Mother Emmanuel's expression: she looked as though she agreed. Sister Thomas à Becket shook her head, her face flushed with anxiety.

'I fear I must take the same view, though I'm most reluctant. But for us to be designing labels and so on – isn't that work for an advertising agency? Surely it's entering the market place. And we,' she added piously, 'have vowed to live on the mountain, the love and eye of our prayer fixed upon God, not on the news of the plain . . .'

Anna heard with amazement Lis mutter rudely behind her 'Sanctimonious . . .' but the words were lost in a fierce exclamation from across the room.

'Stuff and nonsense.' Sister Aelred was on her feet before Anne could even frame a reply, head-dress bouncing with the vigour of her argument. 'You're not talking sense, any of you. Making up these sample cards is *just* like all our work. It's repetitive and simple enough that once we're accustomed we can think our own thoughts as we do it.' She grinned across at Anna, the infectious smile of a hoydenish girl in an old lady's face, but she spoke to Mother Emmanuel. Standing, the diminutive wrinkled figure wasn't much taller than the seated women round her. 'Don't let our dear sisters speak for the rest of us, Mother. The young like the idea of doing something different just because they're young, bless 'em. And us older ones do too, because we've learnt that a tree will snap if it can't bend in a gale. But the middle-aged . . .' she nodded at Sister Mark, 'begging your pardons, Sisters . . . the middle-aged hate change and that's a fact. They see it as a threat, their every instinct is to preserve things the way they are. So they never go where they've never been.' She crossed her hands demurely and recited, 'Like a mighty tortoise moves the church of God. Sisters, we're treading where we've always trod.' She came over to Anna and picked up one of the sample cards. 'We could have a show of hands if you like, Mother. But we all know how it'll come out.'

'Sister Aelred, thank you,' Anna said it almost under her breath and the old nun gave her a wink. As she smiled in acknowledgment, Anna noticed Lis pick up her workbasket and move across to a chair placed alone beside the long window at the far end of the room.

Mother Emmanuel asked for any more comments and from round the circle of sewing women they came.

'We should help Sister Gabriel.'

'It's not for herself she's asking, but for her brother's young family. We couldn't refuse.' Sister Louis dropped her sewing in agitation. 'Looking after a young family is God's work too.' Her beautiful dark eyes luminous with feeling.

'I don't approve of her going.' This was Sister Thomas à Kempis. 'But that's no reason not to undertake this task.' Anna saw her fingers dart in agitation amongst the stockings she was darning.

Anna noticed that Lis attempted no contribution, apparently absorbed in her lacemaking. As if it made no difference to her, one way or the other. Sister Rosalie asked politely, 'What do you think, Mother? You've not said.'

The prioress laid down her darning egg. 'I too regret Sister Gabriel's leaving. But she has made her own decision. And now it is up to us to act with justice, charity and kindness.' At the nods and murmurs of assent she gestured towards the huge, baize-covered billiard table at the back of the room. 'If we set out cards and yarns we could all work over there. We'd have to drop some of our regular tasks. When do you need them, Sister?'

Anna thought aloud. 'In two weeks. The extern sisters could post the cards back to me – or better still, we'd collect them.'

She looked round at the semi-circle of women. At this moment she could appreciate what they had freely given her for so long: affection, companionship, patience, some happiness. Now she was no longer impelled to stay, she could see again how much the convent had been to her in the good years.

And in the bad years, what she had endured among these same sisters, how like a prison this place had seemed. She glanced briefly past them towards Lis, who had rescued her from a void. Whose hostile back and bent head would be a haunting reminder of her own failure here. As a nun and as a friend.

Anna turned away from Lis to the group of women, the prioress at their centre.

'Does that mean yes?' she asked.

She knew the moment she stepped inside her cell, even without seeing the unmade bed. She could smell the presence of someone else in her private place. She stared round, angry and puzzled. The cell was always tidy but now it was bleak. The bed had been stripped, showing the black and white ticking of the mattress to be stained and lumpy. Her few things – comb, nail scissors, the photographs of her parents and Simon's family she kept in her bedside drawer, were laid on top of the folded blankets.

Anna spun on her heel to find someone, to object, but Mother Emmanuel was already walking towards her down the long corridor. The superior stopped at the door.

'As you see, your cell has been cleared. Tonight you will sleep outside the enclosure: you may go there now. And tomorrow you wear the habit for the last time, to attend early morning prayers. Afterwards you will change into secular dress.' The eyes looking out of the prioress's sallow face were sour and accusatory as those of the guard at the Metropolitan Museum in New York years ago.

Anna was speechless. Her cell. Her home for thirteen years. Commonsense added, but what was there to clear after all? She had no possessions.

'The extern sisters have made up a bed in the guest house for you.' She had been in there once or twice. The outbuilding had been the old laundry when she joined the convent, part of the nuns' inner courtyard. They had bricked up the door and windows on the enclosure side, opened new ones looking on to the drive. It was self-contained, and visitors could stay there in retreat. But it was outside the convent itself.

'I can't come back into the convent?' she managed.

'Surely that was the idea.' A touch of malice at the edges of the thin smile.

'Mother, I've not said goodbye to anyone.' Not to Sister Peter. Not to Sister Thomas à Kempis. Or Sister Louis.

'I don't think that will be necessary. It's better so.' She hadn't said goodbye to Lis and the flat refusal was cruel.

'Mother, that's not fair.' The childish exclamation burst out. The prioress set her lips and her gaze was unavoidable.

'If you had stayed here, in the place where you should be, you would have spared us both these recriminations.' Heavily incised lines defined the drooping cheeks, little gathers seamed the flesh of her jaw. She had never appeared so intimidating.

Anna held out her hands in an appeasing gesture. 'I'm sorry, Mother, but I must just say goodbye. I *must*.' Too late, she saw Mother Emmanuel's eyes on her hands. Unmonastic behaviour. But she was devastated by the way this had happened. Now it was on her, brutal and swift as a slaughter. As if she'd committed some unspeakable crime.

But to Mother Emmanuel and the women who had been her sisters, she'd done just that. She had deserted them, and there would always be a huge rift between her and those who remained behind.

'You will be coming back to collect your samples. We'll see you then.' There was unexpected gentleness in Mother Emmanuel's voice. For a second, Anna glimpsed the gap between the superior as an institution and the superior as a woman.

The guest house was not quite so bare as their cells. The curtains were cream cotton with tiny flowers to match the bedspread, the stone floor carpeted with thin jute. There was a picture of St Winifred on one wall and a cross on the other. A cut glass vase stood on the small table, the sole ornament. When visitors seeking solace stayed here – souls, the nuns called them – this would be filled with flowers or leaves. It had not been filled for her.

The morning of her return to Bradford, the extern sisters left on her bed a green pinafore dress in which one of their community had arrived at the convent years before. Probably Sister Rosalie, judging from the size 16 and the flower print blouse. There was also a pink nylon slip, thick tan tights and a pair of black laced shoes too narrow for her. Hung on the peg behind the door she found a short duffle-coat with two toggles missing.

Anna came back from early Mass and ate breakfast off a tray. Then she removed the habit for the last time, looking at each item carefully before she hung it up. Dressed again, she was glad she couldn't see herself. She took her bag and walked down the drive to wait for her taxi by the lodge. She felt like a refugee.

She wanted to be invisible so badly she seemed to achieve it. No one so much as glanced at her on the trains that day. The station staff at Welshpool all knew her now and chatted easily, but this time no one acknowledged her. The ticket-collector at Bradford didn't smile, his eyes fixed on the queue behind her.

It was an unnerving experience. She had never been vain, but now for the first time she began to comprehend what it was to be physically unappealing. She thought she had the habit of self-effacement but this proved not to be true. She had become used to the interest of strangers, the quick turn of the head, the astonished eyes, occasionally the deference. 'Good-evening, Sister.' 'After you, Sister.'

Even Lynn answered the door at Kingwalk with a face briefly blank, momentarily failing to recognise her sister-in-law in the dispirited thirtyish woman who stood there. It was Jamie who shrilled cheerfully from the floor where he was busily pushing cars around, 'Hi Auntie Anna, did you bring me sweets again?'

Lynn continued to look at her, taking in the face drained of colour by the unfortunate green, the red indentation the head-dress had left on the forehead, the body normally slim and graceful in the habit and now merely shapeless. Then she held out both arms.

'You poor girl,' she said.

Lynn declared 'You need looking after,' and proceeded to do just that. She ran a bath while in Jamie's room Anna ripped off the horrible clothes. Beside the bath were soap and dusting powder. Both Lancôme, the ones Lynn hoarded, knowing she couldn't afford to replace them. She gave Anna a tray: a mug of tea, two chocolate biscuits and a tape recorder. 'Delius. I'm spoiling you today.'

Doubtful, Anna switched the machine on before she got into the water. As always, she left the room in darkness, and the yellow glow of streetlights filtered through the blind. The warmth and dim light worked on her tired body. But the music reached deeper. She'd never heard *The Mass of Life* before and it came to her wonderful as a promise.

Apart from music in chapel, there'd been scant leisure for it in the convent. If they listened at recreation it was to the same few records, a curious collection the order had been given over the years. Some Chopin, Gregorian Chant, Rawicz and Landauer. And *The Sound of Music* was a particular favourite with the nuns: the recollection made her smile for the first time all day.

So she was not accustomed to turning to music for pleasure

or inspiration. But lying in the bath after a day she would remember until she died, the music and voices wound their way into her heart and told her that perhaps she did not have to live upon the mountain to hear God's voice.

He would speak to her in other ways.

She dressed again in someone else's clothes. Only then did she switch on the light.

The person in front of the mirror surely wasn't her, with those slim thighs tightly outlined in Lynn's stonewashed denims. Earlier she had demurred: she couldn't wear trousers. But Lynn had pointed out, 'For heaven's sake, you went to London in a short skirt and sheer stockings. Denims are perfectly decent.'

'But they're so tight.'

'Of course – they're the modern woman's equivalent of corsets. And now you're a modern woman.'

The scarlet cashmere sweater was Simon's. She'd refused it at first as too luxurious for her but Lynn had been so upset ('I can't bring myself to wear it, and I can't bear to give it away – please!') that in the end she'd consented. It was huge on her so she looked almost like a schoolboy, but the wide neckline flattered her throat, the soft folds subtly disclosed the outline of her breasts.

She put on navy socks and Lynn's brown moccasins, finished towelling her hair and borrowed some of Lynn's mousse. Then she pulled it about a bit as the stylist had demonstrated.

She put on a little foundation to hide the red mark on her forehead, added a flicker of mascara, a gleam of lipstick. Very carefully, she applied a little grey shadow to her right eye. She considered the result carefully and wondered how long it would be before her reflection ceased to surprise.

With a violent gesture, she grabbed a tissue and rubbed it all off, wiped the back of her hand over her mouth to get rid of the lipstick.

She was like a child learning how to be an adult. The habit

had been a medieval chrysalis, protecting her from the twentieth century. It had given her a version of herself she could no longer accept: too passive, too patient, negative. And now she had to change. It wasn't just a question of appearing to be the same as everyone else. Everything had to alter: her attitudes, her mannerisms, her behaviour.

She must re-invent herself.

She ran down the stairs, something she hadn't done for years. It was the clothes, of course, the unaccustomed freedom of trousers after her dragging skirts.

Lynn had just finished chopping onions. 'Hallo, stranger.'

'Stranger is right. I don't even recognise myself.' The baby mewled and murmured restlessly in her Moses basket and Anna scooped her up without thinking. The top of Sara's head pulsed faintly under its downy cap of hair, smelling of warm vanilla. She hummed under her breath and patted the padded little back.

Lynn watched her over the frying onions and garlic. 'I've never seen you do that.'

Anna was startled. 'Pick up Sara, d'you mean?' She thought for a minute, and said ruefully, 'D'you know I think you're right? I was always afraid the head-dress would scratch her.'

'Liar.' There was no acrimony in Lynn's voice. 'You thought she'd be sick on your shoulder.' She added affectionately, 'And she would've.'

It must have been the smell of cooking, but Anna's mood had changed completely. 'Well, why not?' she asked gaily. 'It's all she can do, and she's very good at it.'

Bax was sitting at the table with a blank sheet of paper and an expression to match.

'I'm doing this project and I chose volcanoes. What d'you know about them?'

'Vesuvius. Hot. Streams of molten lava. Let's see – have you drawn one? Shall I have a go?'

She'd scarcely finished before Jamie, fearing he was being ignored, stuck a crayon into her free hand. 'Auntie Anna, you can do the clown's hat.' Anna complied, filling in red stripes. The baby burped gently and bumped its soft cheek against her shoulder. Anna finished the clown off in virulent yellow and surveyed the result with some pleasure.

'Which reminds me,' she said to no one in particular, 'I must go and see Terry Singh later.'

The dye-works manager wiped his face with a cloth he carried looped through his belt, leaving pale streaks on olive skin. Under the harsh light of bare bulbs, his eyes were sunken and he had a week's growth of beard. Anna knew he got to Jasper Street at a quarter to seven each morning and worked twelve hours on a good day.

There was a flash of astonishment as he saw what she was wearing, but he was too polite to comment. 'Can't gerrit right.' The Indian lilt in his voice, normally overlaid with broad Bradford vowels, was noticeable in his anxiety. 'Just 'ope this batch of powder'll be more true. I did warn you, this 'appens with some colours. They're just not as stable an' the shades vary. It's calculated guesswork.'

Anna peered into the huge dye-bath. Heated by hot pipes beneath, a witches' brew of greenish sludge heaved and bubbled. An elderly man with a filthy peaked cap and arms like oak trees muttered 'Mind out, Miss' as he stuck a wooden paddle in and brought it out loaded with a hank of sodden fibre. He and Singh stared at it without comment, then the man dunked it back.

'We're 'avin' one more go for you an' we're nearly done.' Singh fiddled with a valve at the base of the dye-bath like a cook adjusting the temperature of simmering soup. 'Green's always a sod to dye, 'cause it's reactive, if you don't boil it long enough you lose the colour as soon as you scour the wool.' He led the way back through the warren of workrooms all at different levels, up and down steps, past unlit corners, explaining how he'd got the new dye cheap. 'He wanted twenty-five quid a kilo but he knocked fifteen per cent off . . .' The machinery here was even more ancient than the collector's

332

items at Nightingale Mill: great vats and racks stained and etched with old dyes, rows of metal buckets filled with pure powdered colour measured ready for next day.

They reached the door where the single panel remained intact, delicate flowers traced on frosted glass, and he stopped at the sink to wash. 'Shall you 'ave a cup of coffee?' His telephone started ringing as he spoke.

'I'll make it.' She filled an electric kettle so old she inspected the plug nervously. Immaculate mugs hung on large hooks, spoons were kept in a plastic box, sugar in a screw-top jar: the only spick-and-span corner of the works. She took the mugs in to him and reeled from the heat. The one-bar fire must have been on for hours, the cramped office smelled of gas and cat. Terry Singh, holding the phone, reached across to shove the animal off the decrepit swivel-chair, but as soon as she seated herself it sprang back onto her lap. She stroked the marmalade fur absent-mindedly, trying not to listen, studying the lists of dyestuffs and twists of sample colours pinned to the walls. She could see how he fiddled incessantly with the papers in front of him. A worried man, and she wasn't making things any easier for him.

He put the phone down. 'Thanks, Anna.' He added her name carefully and she was quite unreasonably pleased: while she wore the habit, he'd studiously avoided calling her anything. He routed among the piles of papers and swatches of wool on his desk and handed her a large brown envelope. 'That's a twist of all the colours you wanted, in each yarn.' She spilled them out onto the table in front of her.

It was the first time she'd seen them like this, gleaming and lustrous, cool under her fingers. The pale shades, apricot and old rose, topaz and aquamarine, Chinese white and parchment. And the deep colours, glowing like Sister Peter's stained glass, for lacquer red and Persian blue, jade green and saffron, the amethyst that was proving so difficult to repeat in bulk. She turned them under the light: Terry Singh had brought the colour from the painted squares on the page she had given him. Anna looked up.

'Terry, they're wonderful. Better than I could have dreamed.'

He grinned with delight, suddenly boyish.

'Your colours work a treat.' He gathered the blues together. 'It's a good thing you can let me have that extra time. We've concentrated on the green, but now I can get – '

'Extra time? I didn't . . . What d'you mean?'

'Mr Beattie was round last week to see how we was gettin' on. Don't sweat on it, he said, Miss Summers changed her plans, the new yarns won't be started for a while yet.' He shifted nervously. 'That's right?'

She hadn't noticed how dark the little room was. Your own fault, she thought. Anyone with commonsense would have known Beattie was a liar through and through. He lied to you about the phone calls and going to Walter Street, he lied to save his job. He lied to Terry Singh for some other reason – out of spite? And anyone else would have seen it. Peggy told you. Hal warned you. Lynn disliked him. Even Sister Godric, up in Wales, mistrusted him. And then she thought – and it was more painful than anything else – how he must hate us.

'Terry, he was lying.' She sounded calm but panic slicked her palms and forehead. 'I don't know why, maybe he misheard something, but I don't think so. He's deliberately trying to sabotage us, there's no other explanation.' And this time, she promised herself, I won't listen to one.

The Indian listened quietly, 'So what d'you really need?'

'Last time we talked you reckoned we could have the yarns . . .' she riffled through the pocket diary she'd started carrying, the first she'd had since she was seventeen, 'in another ten days. I came down to ask . . . I must get my hands on small amounts of each colour. Really small,' she added hastily at the look that crossed his face. 'I need enough yarn to get five hundred sample shade cards made up fast, so I can start going for orders. I'm sorry,' she finished helplessly, 'I knew it would have been difficult before. But now – is there any way you can do it?'

He rubbed his hands slowly down the outside of his thighs.

'I'd not been pushin' it, when your man said there was no rush. I dunno.' He chewed his lip in thought. 'Even when your yarn's ready, you know it's all got to be gilled – combed out – that's what marries all the different shades. 'Ow'll you make 'em up that quick, even if I could deliver?'

'We've a couple of frames at the mill which haven't been used for years because they're so small. They'll take the silk and mohair. And I'm going to do the linen on a spinning wheel. Two solid days should give as much as we need.'

'You know your stuff.' No compliment could have pleased her more.

'I'm a spinster who can actually spin.'

'I remember. At your convent, you said.' He looked at her again, at the sweater and denims. 'What's this about, then? Changed your mind?'

'Sort of, yes.'

He finished his coffee in one gulp. 'So it's down to me.' He stared at the calendar over his desk, hissing through his teeth. 'Look, leave it with us, OK? I can't say for sure till I've checked it out, an' I thought I was ahead so I've not kept track. But when we do sample colours, we use quite large amounts. They're usually discarded, but if I can lay my 'ands on 'em . . . an' if the green's true, there's just a chance. I'm not promisin', mind.'

21

The dinosaur was padded pink with green spikes and a peaked cap proclaiming HI I'M BURT. It blocked their path, peering down at the tiny baby strapped in her canvas sling to Lynn's chest, then stepped politely aside.

'Beg pardon.' It had a pronounced Bradford accent. Anna blinked – some things still threw her. Jamie dragged at her hand. 'Can I go with him? Can I can I can I?'

'Later,' Lynn promised. It was Saturday and Anna had easily been persuaded to drive out to the superstore. Since the birth, she'd shouldered many of Lynn's tasks: housework, school runs. And then worked long hours at the mill, struggling to get the new yarns processed. The prospect of a morning's shopping and a cafeteria lunch had appealed. Not long ago, she reflected as they drove, it would have appalled her.

'We'll need two trolleys.' Lynn started to pick up Jamie and Anna caught her arm.

'Let me.' She scooped up the child and set him in the wire seat in front, giving him a quick hug as she did so, his responsive arms tight round her neck. 'You really must be careful. Dr Barnes said you mustn't do too much for a month or so.'

Lynn protested. 'This is the first time I've really been out since Sara was born. We've been living out of the freezer for three weeks!' A blast of iced air and sugared music wafted them past birthday cards, jogging suits, slippers and underwear through to plastic colanders and kettles.

'I've never seen anything like this.' Anna, who had shopped rarely and then only locally, was not prepared for this blatant availability, the screaming signs offering, promising, beseeching, REDUCED! GUARANTEED! BEST BARGAIN! NEW LOWER PRICE! FREE OFFER! GIVE-AWAY!

'It's a total shopping experience for which one has to be emotionally and financially at the peak of condition.' Lynn led them unerringly through the maze of stands and racks, almost her own slim self again, decisive and quick moving, the way Anna remembered from years before.

It was hard to think this was just a store. The arched windows of tinted glass, baskets of artificial flowers suspended round pretentious pillars, the tiled tower outside set with a futuristic clock, all reminded her of something. Only when an unseen choir started singing a musical comedy version of the *Ave Maria* did she realise what it was. At precisely that moment Lynn turned to her.

'Prepare to take part in an arcane ritual performed in celebration of family life.' She gestured towards the shelves under the 'Biscuits' sign. 'Look and wonder.' Anna stared at Rich Tea, Ginger, Lincoln Creams, Fig Rolls, Date, Digestive, Walnut Wafer, Shortcake, Bourbon, Sponge Finger, Kit-Kat, Breakaway, Trio, Taxi, Wagon Wheels, Club, Novo. So that's what Novo was. She picked up the pack and thought longingly of convent biscuits baked for feastdays, delicious shortbread rolled flat, dusted with sugar and topped with a bit of glacé cherry.

'Harry Barry Garry biscuits.' James tried to climb out of his wire seat in Anna's trolley to get them. Lynn pointed to packets of what Anna and Simon used to call squashed fly biscuits. 'I told him these were Garibaldi, now he mixes them up with kids at playgroup. Right, yoghourt.' By the time they'd been going for fifteen minutes and half-filled their trolleys, Anna's head was spinning with additives, colourings and ethylmethylcellulose. On a frozen cake she read. E.472 and her mind's eye saw a balance sheet.

'We still haven't heard from the bank and it's been three weeks. Daniel Stern is having a long fishing trip.'

'Thanks. I nearly forgot.' And Lynn dropped fish-fingers into her trolley. 'You said you were going to phone them again.'

'Did it. Useless. He hasn't contacted them, they've no idea where he is. And time's getting short.' Dangerously short. A timebomb ticking beneath them. Bills mounting up which must be met if they were to continue trading. Bills she dare not pay without confirmation Maynard Gideon would continue their loan. They'd reached the vegetables. Exotic imports – kiwi, passion fruit, star fruit, ladies' fingers, papayas – held her gaze. She couldn't remember having seen them before. How did you cook chillis? Zucchini? Cauliflowers and carrots were scrubbed, leeks and parsnips pristine.

'You're really worried, aren't you?' Lynn patted the squirming baby, made soothing noises. 'I can't think why. He said yes. He's not going to change his mind.' She flashed a look, suddenly shrewd. 'Unless there's something you haven't told me.' She paused. 'I'm right.'

'Let's just say you're right, but there's less to tell than you think. Which is why I'm worrying.'

'Pity.' Little Sara was asleep again, her cheek pressed against Lynn's sweater. 'Good men are hard to find.'

'I'm not sure I want to find one, thanks all the same.' Anxiety made her sharp but Lynn took her literally. She turned from the shelf, her hand on a bag of carrots.

'Oh for God's *sake*. Don't be bloody silly, just because Stern hasn't phoned.'

'I'm not looking for a date.' Anna's voice was shrill with annoyance: she made herself take a deep breath. 'I need to know about the loan. How can I be expected to run a business if I'm not kept informed? Do we want bananas?'

'Hold on a sec.' Lynn tucked the fruit on top of a frozen chicken. 'I think you're confusing things. He was marvellous when he was here. In a day or two, you'll hear about the loan. But it sounds as if you've mixed business and pleasure. If you want red roses and the Taj Mahal by moonlight you may have to wait a little longer.' Lynn watched Anna's expression change. She added gently, 'You've never been in love, have you? I forgot that you're not the same age as me. Emotionally you're about eighteen. I honestly don't know whether to envy you or pity you.' She bent suddenly to kiss the fluffy crown of the baby's head. 'It's incredible how fast a man can happen to you – one minute you've never seen him, an hour later you feel you've always known him. But for both of you to feel that at the same time – that's the difficult bit.' She pulled a plastic bag from a roll and chose some leeks. 'Love is a matter of timing as much as anything else.' Anna could hear the strain in her voice. 'And it may never happen for me again. But I'd like to think it will for you. You've been alone a long time. And you surely haven't come out of religious life in order to go on like that.'

Anna fingered a pack of mushrooms. Like lettuces and cucumbers they were uniform in size and shape, encased in plastic bubbles. Tomatoes, too; those she grew at the convent were irregular, rough-skinned, sweet. Odd that a few weeks ago she'd been the one giving advice, the one with all the answers. How little she'd known, to be so confident.,

'I might not be able to love anyone the way you mean. I'm so used to being solitary.' Funny, she hadn't known that was true until the words were out. She expected Lynn to dismiss her remark, but instead she considered it.

'When you first came out, you were – I'm sorry if it sounds unkind – but so stern. So harsh with yourself and with other people. But you've changed, that must have been' – she smiled briefly – 'force of habit. Only whatever happens, don't settle for too little. Lots of women do, for lots of reasons.'

'Such as?'

'Fear. Loneliness. Gratitude. Because time's passing them by.'

Anna said fervently. 'All right. I promise the only thing I'll settle for right now is that phone call.' Her greatest fear burst out, the worry she hadn't meant to share with Lynn. 'We'll

339

need to go on double-shift when we start on the new yarns, or we'll have nothing to show Walter's trade people. Hal and I talked to the girls, they're all willing to do it. And Hal's offered to drive anyone who works nights.' She touched a red apple and felt the coating of wax. Lynn filled a bag with satsumas, waiting for the rest of it. 'And double time means double pay. When we've found the second instalment for the silk and mohair there'll be just enough to meet one week's wages bill.' She moved her trolley to avoid a middle-aged couple wrangling over the avocados, halted for Lynn to catch her up. Grapes lay in bunches so perfectly shaped no vine could have borne them. There were no scents here, no odours or fragrances. Everything was primly processed, sprayed with artificial dew, so sterile they couldn't possibly do you any good, as if they'd never seen the rich earth. She picked up a pineapple, saw the price and put it back. Lynn retrieved it.

'We have to eat. Vitamins are important in winter.'

'Mum, I'm hungry.' Jamie peered hopefully from his perch. 'Can I have a banana?'

Anna chose one off the priced bunch in her trolley and peeled it halfway for him. 'Don't drop it.'

'Have you written that letter to Beattie yet?'

'We've given him a month's pay in lieu of notice. I've got it at home for you to sign.'

'We should have done it weeks ago,' Lynn's anger made her unfeeling. Anna thought: She can't care about his family when the man had threatened her own. 'He tried his damnedest to screw things up, why did we go on paying him wages?'

'Because I believe everyone's entitled to a second chance.' Anna sighed. 'And I still do. I can't understand why he behaved like that. He's been with Summers most of his working life. I suppose that's the trouble, really. He thinks by rights it should be his. And in a way, you can understand him.'

'Like hell.' Lynn gave her trolley a vindictive push, as if it was Stan Beattie. 'You're too soft. You always look for the good in people.' The baby burped and wriggled against her, and as she looked down, her expression changed completely. 'But thank goodness that's all over. We can make a new start. I'm going to use the money from the Jaguar to make the second payment so you can take delivery of the rest of your raw material.' Her tone was so even, Anna thought she'd misheard.

'It'd use up every penny you've got,' she protested. 'I don't want to take the risk. It's only a few thousand, but it means security for you and the children.'

'It'll be safe enough.' Lynn was unconcerned. 'Those yarns'll be the best thing we've ever produced. It's only until Maynard Gideon guarantee the loan. I know they will, whatever you say. Hold on a sec, I forgot something.' She dashed across to the freezer cabinets, coming back with tubs of frozen orange juice which she dropped into the trolley. 'I always remember those on the way home. And another thing: if I can find someone to look after Sara, I'll come to the mill. There must be something I could do.' Anna listened to her, hugging a bag of potatoes to her breast as if they'd been roses.

'Are you sure? You said you'd never go back to Nightingale Street.'

'I did, didn't I?' Lynn put a hand to Anna's cheek in a gesture that meant, I owe you. I trust you. Anna could not answer. Then Lynn took the potatoes from her, put them in the trolley and headed for Checkout. 'Come on. Time to offer up the sacrifice of the credit card.' From his seat at the front of Anna's trolley, Jamie beamed with excitement.

'Don't forget the monster, Mum.'

The Drunken Duck was a gentrified country pub where they'd fallen over backwards not to replace a thing, including the plumbing. Stuffed trout in glass boxes decorated the walls of the bar, uneven wooden floors creaked and blackened beams poked out of the ceiling like old bones, making even Stan Beattie's five foot six frame feel too tall. Not his sort of place.

Only chance had brought him here, the accident of taking a phone call in an empty office. He'd gone to the mill offices late when he was sure the place would be deserted. A secretary from those fancy bankers Maynard Gideon had left a message for Miss Summers. Daniel Stern was at Crummock Water on Lorton 5189. She'd get him there for another week.

Only it had been Stan Beattie who got him. He drove the whole way to the Lake District without noticing a thing, oblivious to peaks and fells and steep cobbled lanes.

He was the manager, he should have been told the mill had extra finance from London. They'd kept it from him, like the plans for the new yarns. He'd only learned about that when the first deliveries of silk arrived and it was too late to put his point of view. When he'd protested about the costs, the Summers woman said her sister-in-law had bought it in. He should have seen it then: there was no way Nightingale Mill could find that sort of money. How they must have laughed at him. Even his overlooker knew, and he did not.

Stan Beattie didn't consider what he intended to say to this Stern bloke till he was in the car and then anger and self-justification and fear came together. He'd a mortgage like everyone else, and anything over his kids seemed to need, even at their age. It shouldn't feel like a betrayal to take care of Number One. It did, though.

Stan Beatttie wasn't given to self-examination, priding himself he acted on instinct. He told his wife where he was going and during the row that followed she'd told him it wasn't instinct but self-interest. Nasty old fool, she'd called him. Amongst other things.

That had hurt. He was trying to look after her, that was his responsibility and the rest could go hang.

It was that nun's fault. Ignorant bloody woman thought she could drag Nightingale Mill kicking and screaming into the twentieth century, capture foreign markets and God knew what. He was too old a dog to learn new tricks. And a vertical mill was a hopeless proposition in these specialised days: the few he remembered had disappeared years before. Silly bitch couldn't see they'd be lucky just to jog on as they were. If it was up to him, he'd do it by tightening his belt and sacking some of the older hands upstairs, cutting overheads to the bone. It'd see him through to his pension any road.

But he wasn't going to be given that opportunity, not if he read the signs right. Resentment made his driving reckless and he ground the gears mercilessly: it was a company car.

If the new yarns were successful, and the mill concentrated on exports, he'd be out on his ear anyway. His contacts and customers would no longer be needed. He'd attempted to sabotage the new yarns, and supposed that at some point his visit to the dyers would become known – though not, with luck, until it was too late to get the stuff ready in time.

That wouldn't hold them up for long, though now they had backers and more money to call on. The only way to wreck them would be to ensure Maynard Gideon understood just how shaky Nightingale Mill really was.

He found Daniel Stern having tea with his kid in front of an open log fire, the pair of them easily identifiable as Londoners in new cords and Fairisle sweaters. Straight out of a Wool Marketing Board brochure, he commented dourly to himself. City bankers looked like actors these days. He caught a flash of irritation as Stern looked up and revised his opinion: a clever face.

'I don't believe I . . .'

He introduced himself. 'I run Nightingale Mill. For Miss Summers.'

'You're here on her behalf?' Stern hid neither his puzzlement nor his annoyance at being tracked down late in the afternoon.

'No, no. But there are problems.' Stan Beattie decided to ignore the chilly reception. He took a spindle-back chair without being asked and added, voice dropping confidentially, 'I wouldn't want your outfit to burn their fingers.'

That got Stern's attention all right. He put a hand on the shoulder of the small boy beside him. 'Spacegame?'

'You're the boss, Boss.' The boy stuffed the last of his tea-cake into his mouth and took the proferred handful of silver. The kiss he deposited on his father's cheek left a buttery smear. Stern wiped it off and watched him go into the next room. 'The hotel's single concession to the twentieth century. Sam's spent hours on their one machine.'

'Ah. Kids.' Stan Beattie did his best to establish the threadbare bond of parenthood. 'I've a girl at college. Boy's a bit of a tearaway. They'll be off our hands one day, I expect.' He gave a short laugh but Stern just looked at him and waited. Better not waste any more time. He crossed his legs and cleared his throat. 'I've been in the trade a long time. I don't want to see Nightingale Mill go under.'

'No one wants to see that, Mr . . . Beattie.' There was more than a hint of resignation. 'You'd probably like some tea.'

'I'd prefer a drink, if you don't mind. I've quite a thirst after that drive.' He hesitated – they'd Jennings on handpump – and finally chose whisky as he wasn't paying, waited as Daniel Stern ordered two from a trim girl in black and white.

Beattie started carefully, feeling his way into his story. He explained how long he'd been with Summers, how much of the business was in his hands. 'Well, you can imagine, I've tried to do all I can, but Miss Summers has her own ideas. I can't stand by and watch her come in knowing nothing about yarnspinning and less about what makes commercial sense, and not try to protect her best interests.' He was quite proud of the last touch. Stern nodded.

Encouraged, Beattie launched into the way she was trying to forecast fashion trends, misreading the signs in the market place. 'I don't want to rubbish the lady,' he finished with such sincerity Stern's eyebrows went up, 'but she's over-reaching herself with these new yarns. Our customers know what they want from us, and if we can't provide it they'll go elsewhere.'

'You sound very sure of that, Mr Beattie.' It was slipped in so quietly he accepted it as praise.

'More than thirty years I've worked those wholesalers, they'll all tell you. They know and trust me. I'm the one takes the orders and delivers the goods as far as they're concerned.' He watched Stern take a pack of small cigars from his pocket, a scruffy card of matches. He'd've expected a gold Dunhill lighter like Mr Simon's at least. 'If we turn over to luxury yarns they'll not be interested.'

'I understood Miss Summers plans to expand abroad. She's convinced that's where the future lies for good quality yarns.'

Beattie allowed himself a dismissive shrug. 'Nightingale Mill's never been into exporting. And this isn't the time to expand. It'll bring a whole range of different problems she's not prepared for. Currency fluctuations, for starters. Well, you know that better than most.' He tasted the malt. 'I've tried to explain you can't set up new markets overnight. If she has her head, I guarantee we'll not keep our present customers and they'll not find new ones.' Stern shifted at that. Careful. It had sounded a bit too much like a threat. He softened it with, 'Miss Summers is going for luxury fibres, top of the market stuff. If she doesn't break through with the exports like she thinks, they'll scarcely sell here in the present economic climate: that's why Mr Simon went into synthetics in the first place.' He sighed heavily. 'We'll likely be forced to close and you'll have lost your money.'

Stern nodded slowly. 'Thoughful of you to take the trouble to come and tell me all this.' Beattie gave him a quick glance: was that sarcasm? Stern barely touched his drink, just kept the glass in front of him. Good malt, too. Instead he got out a notebook and old-fashioned fountain pen with a heavy gold nib and clip, jotted something down, frowning. 'What do you want me to do?' Just like that, abrupt. It almost threw Beattie.

'That's not for me to say. I just wanted to be certain in my own mind that you had all the facts.' He hesitated for a second. 'And to tell you I'm – available. Should you need me.' That was as far as he dared go, but it had been enough. Stern gave him a cool look. For a minute there Beattie thought he'd screwed up.

'You'd run the mill better than Miss Summers, is that it?'

It was an effort to keep his voice from shaking. Go for it. 'That's what I had in mind, yes.'

Daniel Stern picked up his cigars and matches. 'I'm not empowered to make decision like that without putting the facts before my board. I'll be back in London in another week or so.'

Beattie could hardly believe it. He wanted to ask about money, but of course that would never do.

'I'm sure you appreciate I can't say anything more until the idea is approved in principle,' Stern went on. 'But I would stress that I'd prefer you to keep away from the mill until you hear from me. That way, anything that happens can clearly be laid at the door of the present management. If you follow me.' Suddenly impatient, he was on his feet. 'Use any excuse you like. Pretend to be ill, anything, but absolutely no further involvement.' Stan Beattie discovered it was impossible to read from that poker face what kind of result he could expect. As he went, he noticed Stern's glass was still untouched.

He did not, of course, know that after he left, Stern had pushed it away as if it had a bad taste and ordered another. Though it came from the same bottle, that tasted fine.

'Nadar needs a hand on the doffer-frame. If I take over can you finish this?' Hal was shouting, but it was hard to catch his words over the tumult of machinery at full speed. Anna took the clipboard from him. His T-shirt today showed a palm tree and DON'T BUNGLE THE JUNGLE.

'I'll get Lynn to do it. There's still some mohair to shift.'

'Leave it to me. I don't like you doing that heavy stuff.'

'I'm used to it,' she yelled back. René passed her on the way back to her machine, mug of tea in one hand.

'We don't want equality in 'ere, luv. Let your toy-boy do it.' She cackled with laughter and started coughing. Anna raked her fingers through her hair in a gesture of aggravation but 'You shouldn't smoke so much, Rene' was the only comment she allowed herself. The mill was airless, the smell of lanolin overpowering. She was tired, but it was more than that: she'd been working at full stretch for a week now. Her excitement over running the machinery on double-shift, the elation she'd felt at its new-found vigour, had evaporated into exhaustion. And Hal had been there many nights as well, sleeping for a couple of hours on a campbed in case he was needed.

She put the clipboard down and went back to opening the bales of mohair just arrived from the dyers to be spun. She slit the protective sacking with a knife, sliced the broad bands of plastic webbing. She began to fill wicker skips ready to shift and Lynn said loudly at her shoulder, 'I'll help.'

'You'll do no such thing. Here,' she thrust the clipboard into Lynn's hands. 'You might mark off completed lots, they're all numbered.' She pulled at a loaded skip but it wouldn't budge. She was waring a bulky skirt she'd found at a local Oxfam shop and an old sweater of Lynn's, both so grubby already it didn't matter what she did. She pushed the skip with hip and thigh, straining with the long muscles of her back, feeling it start to move.

She didn't see Hal coming up behind her until he caught her arm. 'What the hell're you doing?' His yell alerted two young Pakistani women working on the ten huge spindles at the nearby draw box: Anna could feel them listening.

'You can see what.' It sounded more aggressive than she intended because she was shouting to be heard. She went on pushing the skip, assuming he would release her but instead his grip tightened so it hurt. He'd never have touched her in the habit.

'I said, that's too much for you.' She straightened up, jerking her arm sharply so his hand fell away.

'For heaven's sake,' she yelled over the steady thumping of the wooden beaters, 'I'm used to it.' Turning away from his strained face, she bent to the skip again. His arms went round her waist from behind and he lifted her off her feet and carried her the few yards to the overlooker's tiny cubicle, slamming the door with a kick. He set her down and spoke to her back.

'Before you say anything, I apologise.' he still had to raise his voice over the sounds from outside. 'But that's no job for a woman. You wouldn't let Mrs Simon do it. You could really hurt yourself.'

Anger settled tight folds round her chest. She stood stiff and silent by the window. No paint was left on the warped wood. She wanted to shout and scream, to protest her strength, protect her dignity, her new-found independence. But thirteen years of passive obedience stifled the words in her throat.

And then through the grimy glass she saw, where the Aire ran below and beside the mill, a solitary swan. It floated light as a child's toy on water the colour of cold iron. Grey was reflected in its dingy feathers but it was a swan for all that, oblivious to the industrial ooze. It changed her mood as if it had been a burst of song. When she turned to face Hal, she was able to admit, 'I should have listened to you: that skip *was* too much. Sorry.'

His clenched hands relaxed and she realised the effort it had cost him to defy her.

'I know you're in a bit of a panic. Those Ministry people'll be round . . .' He hadn't shaved this morning, he must have been here all night, and the little hairs glinted gold.

'In three days.' She groaned. 'Don't talk about it.'

A single step brought him beside her. He noticed the swan too. 'Reminds me of you. Calm and unruffled on the surface. Paddling away like hell underneath.'

She was rueful. 'Not calm any more. Never was, really. Just the clothes made you think so.'

He examined the idea. 'You might have something there. Come to think of it, I haven't seen you in all those grey droopy things for days. Does that mean you've come out of the convent for good, then?'

She wasn't about to embark on an explanation so she just said, 'Yes.'

'Great. Doing anything Thursday night?'

22

'Thought we'd eat at my place. If that's OK?'

'Veggie?' she found she could tease him.

He answered seriously, 'It's good for you. Very wholesome.'

They were driving through drab streets punctuated by bomb-sites the size of football pitches. The grey shabbiness of the landscape was lit up by the bright shock of women's saris in burnt orange and magenta. Hal braked. 'I have to get something.'

They were outside what had once been featureless small shops she must have passed on the bus as a child. They were transformed into exotic greengroceries, sweet centres full of brightly-coloured delicacies. One sold slippers with curled-over toes, another enormous cooking-vats. A music store was crammed wall and ceiling with oriental instruments – patterned drums like the ones Terry Singh played, curved mandolins, slender pipes.

Saleem's Supermarket squeezed between a halal butcher and the Omar Khayyam Club. Anna had never been in an Indian bazaar and this more than compensated for what she'd missed. Its cramped and crowded aisles were a tribute to the new culture of the city, a revelation of spices. Orange blossom water and mango juice, frozen kulfi and kataifi pastry; saravago drumsticks and callaloo, tinned lotus roots and cluster beans; bottles of jallab syrup from Lebanon and nan, the flat Indian bread Hal chose from among more varieties than she'd ever seen.

Hal lived closer to the city centre, in Great Horton Road, in what had once been a row of tiny terraced houses, above The Peking Chinese restaurant; red lanterns and suggestion of soy sauce. Next door an Indian newsagent waved from behind his crowded counter as Hal took a *Telegraph and Argus*. The bookmakers on the other side was locking up: a burly wedge of a man offered "Ow do,' and looked at Anna with interest. 'Sally, isn't it?'

'Not by a million miles. 'Night George.' Hal unlocked the street door. 'I've been here years,' he explained, leading the way up unlit stairs, 'since I did textiles at Community College.'

Behind him in the dark she said, 'Sally's your girlfriend.' Why on earth had she said that?

'Past tense. Nice girl, we went out on and off for about eighteen months. She's in Leeds now, designing ties.'

'You must miss her.' She could almost hear him grin.

'Nope. It wasn't serious for either of us.' He went in first to switch on the lights, illuminating a small white room. She looked round as he drew the curtains, noting the low sofa covered in hessian, bright patterned Indian rugs on white painted floorboards. He had no ornaments of any kind, his lamps were classic white Anglepoise. An enormous navy velvet floor cushion and a circular café table of white painted wrought-iron with matching chairs were the only other furniture. The single picture took up a large space on one wall, a canvas in irregular horizontal stripes: palest green at the bottom deepening to midnight blue. He saw her interest. 'I don't know what it is – it changes depending on the light.'

'Sea, surely.'

'Maybe. It makes me think of a heat haze in a desert. Or rainforest. It's called "Atmospheric", which could mean just about anything.' He took her jacket. 'You look terrific.'

'A rag, a bone and a hank of hair,' she recited, but she was glad he'd noticed. She was wearing more clothes borrowed from Lynn. A flowing skirt in Liberty printed wool, a white silky blouse tucked into a wide belt. It was a romantic outfit, soft. She felt the way she had at a cousin's wedding when she was sixteen, feminine and pretty. Unbelievably, she'd not worn anything like it since.

She had longed to be in the habit, had thought it dignified and beautiful. But the voluminous garments had said something else, and it was only when she was outside convent walls that she heard it. Dark robes declared her different, apart. They cut her off from the touch of others.

She was accustomed to wearing the same garments for every task. For cooking, gardening, Eucharist, recreation. At the end of the day, all she could do was wash her face and put on a new linen band. It was only now, when she was able to change into something fresh, that she saw such freedom was an emotional safety valve for any woman.

Hal tugged up a venetian blind and went through into a kitchen she hadn't noticed. 'Make yourself comfy while I get things started. Put on some music.' She'd barely sat down when the phone rang and his tone told her before he did that it wasn't good news. 'Trouble at t'mill,' he said in broad parody adding, in his normal voice, 'Gill-box needs attention. I've been having problems with it for weeks. It would give out now.'

'Couldn't it wait? You must be starving?'

'It'll hold everyone up. No, I'll have to go. You needn't, though, there's nothing you can do. Stay here, have a rest. I'll be back in an hour.'

It was pleasant to be alone in the student simplicity of his home. She looked at his tapes. The top one was Dr Hook, a name she vaguely remembered from BC. Before convent. Her own irreverence was a surprise. She slipped it into the machine and wandered along the bookcase as it played. (Books on modern art – three on Hockney – travel, a whole section on pre-historic Britain. No fiction.) The music changed: above the heavy beat a used, sexy voice grated out the lyric.

'At the age of thirty-seven, she realised she'd never
Ride through Paris in a sports car with the warm wind
in her hair.'

She listened till she couldn't stand any more and switched it off. The words were trite, poignant – and a bit too near the bone. In six years, she would be thirty-seven. Maybe she'd be full of regret for all the things she hadn't done. Sins of omission. She contemplated phoning Lynn to stop the thoughts. And that brought other sadnesses – Lynn's loneliness, the fatherless boys, the baby girl Simon would never see.

The only answer was the one thing that never failed her: activity. It didn't matter what it was – driving the tractor, milking goats, scrubbing floors. She went into the cramped kitchen with its clean dark green and white cupboards and surfaces. On the worktop lay a bowl of eggs, fresh spinach, a packet of whole-grain rice. An apple pie in a tin-foil case stood on a plate beside Bath Olivers and in the fridge – full of greens, she might have known – two big triangles of good cheese were wrapped in film. It seemed perfectly natural to rinse her hands, soak the spinach in salt water, start to prepare the meal.

Hal got back two hours later, running up the stairs with a bottle of white wine. 'Damn thing took forever. I sent the girls home and closed up, we only lost an hour.' He sniffed. 'Something smells good.' He put the bottle on the table, which she'd laid ready. 'This is very nice. Very nice indeed. I'll just go and wash.'

When they had drunk a glass of wine, she lit the candle she'd stuck in an orange, brought bowls of rice and salad, slid the omelettes onto their plates. He was telling her about the town's industrial museum and started to eat without noticing. Then he glanced at the piece of omelette on his fork, ate a morsel and put the rest back on the plate. He pushed the rice about and left that, too.

'Aren't you hungry?' She put down her own knife and fork.

'Starving. But it tastes . . .' he paused delicately, 'different.'

Anna looked across at his plate. 'I'm the world's worst cook,' she admitted. 'When it was my turn in Wales, everyone used to say it was an extra penance. Mine tastes awful too,' she added cheerfully.

He took this in. 'What did you do to the omelettes?'

Anna laughed and picked up her fork.

'They've been in the oven for an hour, waiting: that makes them leathery. I always overcook them anyway, I never gauge when the butter's hot enough. And I'm sorry about the rice — the burnt taste is because it stuck to the bottom of the pan. But I've cleaned that.' She took another mouthful. 'It's not too bad.'

'It's terrible.' He leant back. 'Anna, I really can't eat it. Look, I'm the one that's sorry — I was longer than I said, it's all my fault. It was lovely of you to do it.' He got up. 'Don't eat anymore.' He was pulling on his jacket. 'I'll be back in a sec. Stick a couple of plates in the oven to warm,' he added over his shoulder.

When Hal returned ten minutes later she hadn't moved and congealing food remained on the table. He hurried into the kitchen with the newspaper parcel and brought back two plates loaded with fish and chips. It smelt wonderful. He'd draped a clean tea-towel over his arm and held out a bottle of brown sauce. 'Mademoiselle. Ze French accent is not authentic. Ze cod fish is.'

She pushed back her chair. 'I don't want any, thanks. I must get home, if you don't mind. It's late.' Her tone deliberately graceless.

'I do.'

She wasn't prepared for that. 'What?'

'I do mind,' he sounded patient, as if he were talking to a child. 'I object. I disagree. I protest. I mislike. I prefer not. It's an ex-parrot.' Anna met his eyes. He wasn't laughing, but he had that amused look. 'I've said I'm sorry, I really am. I appreciate what you did. But I only eat one real meal a day and I want to enjoy it. Now sit down and have another glass of wine and let's eat before it goes cold.'

She was stubborn. Always had been. When she had to speak her faults in Chapter, that had been a safe bet. She remained on her feet. Hal shrugged and sat down at the table. 'You'll have to excuse me, then, if I start without you.'

Anna took her jacket from the peg inside the door and put it on. She meant to go quietly, to contain her indignation, but found herself saying instead: 'I'm surprised at you. All that talk about wasting resources, and you throw away a perfectly good meal.' There was no reason for him to refuse her cooking, they ate it at the convent. She was right, so why did she sound so shrill?

Hal swallowed and kept his tone reasonable. 'But it wasn't perfectly good, Anna, it tasted like . . . It was terrible. I've worked a twelve-hour day with only a packed lunch and that was' – he glanced at his watch – 'nearly nine hours ago.' She had a sudden image of him sitting cross-legged at the mill eating beansprout butties in his anorak, and thrust it away. 'So if I've wasted a couple of eggs, it's not the end of the world. Please come and sit down, do.' He wasn't quite so calm now and something in her she didn't like spiked her words.

'Four eggs, actually. And everything else – food other people would be glad of.'

'You'll be telling me next about starving children in Africa.'

'I will, yes.' Reminded, she saw the haunted televised faces of Ethiopians in their brown tents. That hadn't stopped her raiding the supermarket shelves, greedy as the next person, filling her trolley with expensive goods she didn't need. Sins of commission.

'You're right to care about them. But haven't you seen what's on your own doorstep?' There was a harsh exasperation in his voice she hadn't heard before. 'You haven't been down Brierley estate, have you, when they're handing out free butter and tins of stewing steak to old age pensioners. Bradford's got poverty, low pay, hunger. It's got the highest infant mortality rate in Britain. Your job used to be praying for the world, didn't it – well, you could make a start outside this door.'

Anna stared at him, stricken. 'I didn't know . . . I never saw any of that.' And she hadn't seen it. Deep tiredness made the corner of her left eye twitch frantically. She'd never be able to cope with the world, there were too many problems, so many people needing help, so many desperate needs unmet.

She must have spoken aloud because Hal got up and came

round the table. 'Come on, you've been doing too much, that's all, it's getting on top of you. No one can worry about everything. Not even you. It's all right.' Two unaccustomed glasses of wine made her head spin, the blurred candle-flame flickered at the edge of her vision.

'It's *not* all right!' Perhaps she'd shouted because Hal looked as shocked as if she'd struck him. 'It's a terrible mess, it's all gone wrong. I can't do it after all, I can't do any of it. Simon couldn't cope and neither can I.' Once started, she couldn't stop. It was as if her years of self-control and careful decorum were a wall in which a crack had finally opened. The flood of worry welled out, all the stress she'd tamped down during her months back in the world. 'I'm too tired to go on and there isn't enough money anyway and there never will be. We'll have to sell the mill and . . .' her voice sank to a whisper, 'I'll go back to Wales and it'll all be over.'

He was arguing now, how she couldn't give up because of all the people who depended on her for their living. Some of the millgirls had been with Summers for ever. Peggy was too old to get another place. What about Lynn and the boys, the new baby?

And then she did strike him. She hit out at his neck, his chest, hoping to hurt, intending to inflict pain. '*I hate you. I hate you.*' Her arms swung wildly. She pummelled at him not with open palms, the way a woman hits, but with balled fists like a man, fierce and intent. Hal didn't attempt to defend himself. He just stood there and let her batter at him, only turning his head to protect his face. If he'd reacted differently she knew she would have become really violent. It was terrifying to acknowledge that in herself. In Sister Gabriel. Who had never in her life lifted a hand to anyone.

'But I love you.' He offered it to her helplessly. 'I love you.' He caught hold of her wrists, holding them together against his chest. 'I love you. Can you hear me? I love you. Anna.'

No. *No.* She didn't want love and the burdens it carried, she couldn't handle it. And anyway it wasn't meant for her, it would be taken back, leaving her empty and alone. She understood that she was the woman in the song, destined for disappointment. '*Don't. Get away.*' She struggled to free herself. 'Get your hands *off* me.' Locked together, they stood face to face: she could feel his quick breath. She tried to pull apart, twisting round to break his grasp, her shoulder against his body. She bent and straightened suddenly, giving him a violent shove. Caught off balance, his hold on her loosened and she whirled and pulled away to escape him, running into the dark bedroom, slamming the door in his face, leaning her back against it, panting out her fury.

Then she saw the bed.

It was just an ordinary bed: a single divan with a white cotton spread as simple as everything else in the room. But it blazed with light and colour. For a moment she thought she was hallucinating. She shut her eyes. When she opened them again it was just the same. Covered with balloons of every possible shade. Scarlet and orange, yellow and blue and green and purple, blown taut to bursting point, swaying gently on their strings in the draught of the slammed door. They were anchored down with streams of tiny lights, Christmas tree lights, each one set in a plastic flower. They criss-crossed the bed, dozens of them, winking and gleaming, pinpoints of silver reflected in the satin skins of the balloons.

Anna had been standing with her arms locked defensively, holding her elbows. Now she let them fall to her side. Her breathing slowed. After a couple of minutes the door handle turned and she moved aside. Hal came in.

She must be drunk, but not so drunk she couldn't see misery in his green-gold eyes, white tightness round his mouth: she'd really upset him, it was like hitting a little boy.

'I hate you.' It came out weak this time, without conviction.

'No you don't.' His quiet voice, flat with tiredness now, matched her own. 'Maybe you don't love me yet but you don't hate me.'

'No.' She drew a long, shuddering breath, agreeing with him. 'No.'

He looked over his shoulder. 'You saw it.'

'I could hardly help it.' She sniffed. 'D'you always sleep in a fairground?'

He took her absolutely seriously. 'I did it for you. I thought you'd like it.' She watched his face carefully.

'Why should I?'

Disconcerted he glanced down. 'It's not the way you think. I mean . . .' Her hands were hanging limp now, fingers curled. He caught hold of one and with the back wiped his cheek. She felt wet warmth on her skin and it took her a minute to work out that it was tears. Hal was crying. She stood very still, staring at him. Men don't cry. Do they?

'I wanted to make it special for you. Special *like* you. Only I was going to ask you to marry me, first.'

They were so close she could see moisture glistening on his lashes and her heart moved in her chest. 'First?'

'You know. Before.'

'Before what?' But for once – for once in all her life – she knew the answer. And knowing, she didn't wait for him to make the first move but put both hands to his face, felt the soft gold stubble. With her knuckles she smudged gently beneath his eyes. 'You're crying.' Her voice hushed with amazement.

'I let it go wrong. Sorry.' He looked so young, so utterly forlorn. 'I just don't know how it happened.'

'I bit your head off. It wasn't your fault.'

'I should have eaten your dinner.'

'It was horrible.'

'Right. I should have eaten your horrible dinner.' In his turn, he smoothed her temples where the thin skin was dark with exhaustion. 'You were crying too. Between the two of us, we've cried a lot.' He looked at his wet fingertips. Then, watching her, he licked them, tasting her tears. The intimate gesture made her gasp.

When he held her and rested his face against hers, she experienced only a soaring elation. No guilt, no fear. This felt right as nothing had ever felt right before.

She opened her arms to him. There were hard muscles

357

across his back, along his shoulders. He felt straight and tough, broader than he looked. The curves and hollows of her own body folded into his. He moved his hand up from her back to stroke her hair, running his fingers down to the vulnerable nape. 'I've been wanting to do that for weeks. It feels just like I thought.'

The physical agitation his touch started left her silent.

'It's like warm fur,' he went on. 'Your fur.' He buried his face in it and she felt his breathing become irregular, louder, as if he'd been hurt. In response hers changed too, catching ragged in her throat. He opened up longings in her.

I want you. I want you. Not like this, standing here. I want to lie down naked with you. Your lips against my skin.

Still holding onto her, he slipped to his knees. Tugging the edge of her blouse out of the waistband he smoothed his cheek against the soft flesh under her ribs, moved lower. Anna closed her eyes. Your lips on my skin. She folded her arms about him and hugged him close, cradling him. His voice reverberated against her. 'I can hear your heart beating through your navel.' She felt him kiss it, his tongue in the deep dimple. 'I knew it'd be hard to find your heart but this is ridiculous.'

'It's just like everyone else's.'

'*Nothing* about you is like anyone else. You're a one-off.'

She absorbed this in silence. For thirteen years she had struggled for self-effacement. She had allowed herself to be moulded by the rule into the pattern of her order. She had given up her opinions and her tastes. She had forced herself to stifle her individuality and she knew she had succeeded: she had become indistinguishable from her sisters. She was unexceptional, unmarked. She was like a pane of glass.

It had all been in the cause of community, and so it was an achievement. Of a sort. But she had grown to despise herself for it: here in the world she felt colourless, without interest to others. It had made her diffident, uncertain of herself. And now Hal was telling her that she was somehow special. It was impossible to be distrustful of him, he shone with honesty. She swallowed. 'That's the nicest thing you could have said.'

He got up. He was less than half a head taller. 'Nicer than, will you marry me?'

'You didn't mean that, though.' she forced lightness into her tone, to protect herself. (She couldn't allow the admission, from disappointment: that presumed too much.) He took hold of her upper arm, a tight grip. She got the distinct impression he could have shaken her.

'I don't say things I don't mean, you know that.'

There were all sorts of things she wanted to say, protests she wanted to make. I'm too old for you. You're too young. This is ridiculous. But she did not speak. She had never seen him so serious.

'You just don't want to face up to feelings. Mine or your own.' He loosened his hold and looked into her eyes: wary, blue-grey irises etched in black. 'When I'm out with field glasses waiting for foxes or deer, eyes like yours watch me from the long grass.' He followed the line of her eyebrow with a finger. 'And these are like wings.' He tugged her arm. 'Let's go to bed.' She tensed. He whispered, 'Come on, come to bed.' Desire thickened his words. She had never heard that note in a man's voice before. 'Come to bed, Anna. I've made you such a beautiful bed. Better than a bed of roses, it is. Look.' He took her shoulders to turn her round and despite her apprehension she laughed in delight. What a ridiculous, childish, gorgeous thing to do.

He gave her a little shove so she overbalanced, allowing herself to fall. He fell with her, both of them sinking down amongst the bright satin balloons and the glitter of fairylights. Tiny points gleamed in their eyes and the silky skins squeaked as they wriggled a space for themselves. One burst loudly. He pulled a balloon from under her head and it drifted to the ground. Anna shifted a strand of lights pressing into her back. She fingered them cautiously, expecting they would be hot, but they glinted with the cool intensity of fireflies. Their fragile prettiness, their absurdity, filled her with sudden gaiety. 'Hope we're not going to be electrocuted.'

'It's not in the script. This is, though.'

'A very corny line.'

'I'm a very corny man. You did say corny?' His breath warm on her face. His mouth opening on hers.

I want you. I want you. Don't talk any more, stop making jokes. I just want to feel you against me. I need that, I need it. Don't leave me empty, longing for something I can't imagine.

Hal pushed the jacket off her shoulders and she loosed her hold on him and slipped her arms from the sleeves so it dropped to the floor. He started to unbutton her blouse. With the fabric gathered in his hands, he paused.

'You're sure?'

'I'm sure.' She'd never been so sure of anything.

'You don't have to do this if you don't want. It won't change the way I feel about you.' For answer she wrenched the garment over her head. Still without speaking, she leaned forward to open his check work shirt. Beneath it he wore a string vest. 'The pattern imprinted on my chest is today's special.' The realisation that he was trying to mask his own nervousness was reasuring and she pulled the edge of the shirt free of his jeans. He said, 'Hold on. My turn.' The fairylights lit his frown of concentration. Underneath she had on the soft bra she'd bought in Rackhams. As he reached behind to undo the hooks, she thought with a pang of absurd regret about the grey satin nightdress.

With great care he eased the straps from her shoulders, traced round the slight outline of her breasts with careful fingers, scarcely touching. She didn't breathe, holding in the impulse to run before it was too late. Because if she ran now, she might never find this courage again.

At the age of thirty-seven, she realised she'd never . . .

He ran his hand up her leg beneath her skirt and she did not try to stop him. He went very still when he encountered the soft naked flesh of her thigh. She'd forgotten she was wearing stockings and suspenders and there was a flash of panic: He'll think I put them on deliberately. And then she thought: Perhaps I did? She raised herself from the bed to help him as he pulled her skirt off and dropped it on the floor.

She wanted to squeeze her eyes closed then because he was staring at her body. Only she couldn't not watch him and it was like being stroked, to be looked at with those green-gold eyes. Then he started kissing in the bend of her elbow, the curve of her shoulder. 'It's your turn now.'

She dropped her hands to his wide leather belt, tugged at the heavy buckle, fumbled with his buttons. (Why buttons?' she asked. He whispered, 'You buy 501s for their buttons.') And all the time he caressed her, gave little kisses. Here, in bed, he moved differently. He was slower, calmer than the Hal she knew. He exuded a warm sensuality that was impossible to resist. She had always been conscious of his glances, the quick interest he showed her. And the small courtesies – the opened doors, the dropped spools retrieved – he granted all the girls at the mill. She was all the more aware of such gestures, accustomed only to the society of women, who did not do such things for each other.

Lying beside him on the amazing, glowing bed, she gave up on the buttons and ran her hands over his chest fuzzed with dark gold hair, watching his face to learn if she was doing the right thing. His eyelashes curled up, shiny with health. With tender, avid little kisses she touched his closed eyelids. Even they were smooth and glossy. His youth hurt her. She knew from Lynn's mirror thirty-one years had flicked spider lines from the edges of her eyes, run tiny creases beside her mouth.

In her imaginings, when she'd wondered how this moment would be – if it would be – she had always been passive, waiting. That was how she thought of herself, as the recipient. The vessel. Her self-image was so ingrained it astonished her to find she was doing this, making these most explicit, non-verbal demands. It was against all her instincts, surely, all her training.

She stopped kissing him and he opened his eyes. 'I want you.' Dear God, had she really said that? He had to get up to take his trousers off, his remaining clothes. She tried not to look and then she did and almost in darkness his sex was smaller and sweeter than she'd expected. Than she'd feared.

Velvety shaft, vulnerable weighted pouch. Hal looked down at himself, resting limp against the sinewed thigh. 'He's been wanting you too long. We'll have to give him time to get used to the idea.'

She couldn't stifle the laugh of amazement. 'You make him sound as if he doesn't belong to you.'

'Well, he doesn't. But I am permitted to speak for him, and I understand a little decorous fondling would be very acceptable.'

Cautiously, she put out a hand. Hal took it, guided it between his legs. It felt incredibly smooth and under her touch it stiffened. 'Run your fingers along him,' he whispered. 'There's a little ridge down there.' She did as he asked. She had to force herself, it seemed so personal. But she couldn't think of what she was doing as wicked: it had a kind of funny innocence. And it gave her an extraordinary sense of power, when he hardened and grew sleek under her touch, like stroking an unknown and dangerous animal.

'And now,' Hal murmured, 'it's my go.' He whispered that her breasts were like stars. 'Stay still. Don't move.' He pulled at two of the strands of fairylights and carefully draped them round her breasts, the silver flowers against her skin. He hooked two fingers into the elastic of her briefs and she put her hand on his to stop him. 'You do it, then.' She raised her hips to push them off, kicked them away. He popped the suspender buttons open and peeled off her stockings.

'I rather like this,' he said, 'but we'll take it off anyway,' and he unhooked the satin suspender belt.

'Beautiful,' he said, and his voice sounded furry when he wove another silver flower through her soft fleece. He rested one hand on the slight mound of her stomach, cupped the other over her breast. Leaning over her, he opened his lips as if he'd take her all into his mouth.

I want you. I want you. You'll be like a dark animal pushing through a forest. Feel my leaves parting, opening for you.

Even then it wasn't easy to let herself go. She couldn't help saying no; her voice, her stiff body, her arms and legs that would not twine round him – they were all saying no. Only a secret shimmer of her hidden flesh said yes and yes and yes.

When she felt his penis butting its way into her, it was difficult. He was in a hurry now and clumsy and she, inept. He muttered, 'It's all right, it's all right, just open your legs for me, let me in,' but it wasn't. Perhaps because she had the absurd anxiety that another balloon would burst.

And then, finally, she understood what she should do, how to accept him, move against him. Hal's eyebrows knotted with absorption, he whispered to her the whole time, his eyes on her face. As he rose and fell above her, it was like lying beneath the surge of the sea; inexorable, an agonising pleasure.

Later, long minutes after his body had its climax that seemed to her like sobbing, she kissed his shoulder. Trace of salt. He was still inside her. Tenderly he wiped the sweat from her face, settled her thigh more comfortably over his hip. She felt very soft and wet. 'Are you all right?' A whisper, only. 'Was that all right?'

'Yes.' She ran her fingers along his arm that lay protectively across her breasts. 'Yes.'

'It'll be better for you next time. I promise.' She felt his lips against her forehead as he whispered, 'It's going to be wonderful for us.' She turned her head towards him. Already she trusted him to be right about her.

When he put his mouth on hers, when their lips met and sealed, they healed a wound Anna had borne for years. For an endless, untold moment they were alone. Nothing else existed. When they moved apart, both knew something had been given, something received. For a long time they lay quiet. Fairylights sparkled softly, changing the bed into a raft in the dark room.

He seemed to have drifted into sleep and she lay very still so as not to disturb him. There was no possibility of her doing the same. Her face was in the hollow of his shoulder, his arm protective across her body. When she was a small girl, Christmas Eve had been like this: strangely exciting, impossible to believe it was really happening. Hal stirred and spoke. 'I'm starving.'

She blinked at him. 'You're right, you *are* romantic.'

'Certainly I'm romantic.' He propped himself on an elbow to look at her. 'You make me romantic. But you've lost your flowers.'

'Metaphorically speaking.'

'And we need to get under the covers. Can't you see the headlines? "Ex-nun freezes to death in employee's bed".'

'You're not an employee. You're a co-worker.'

'That's what the *Guardian* will say. The *Mirror* will definitely call me an employee. Or possibly a mill-hand. I mean it, though, I am hungry, look.' He nuzzled her shoulder, nipping the flesh. 'It's now been . . .' he glanced at his wrist, 'ten hours since I ate. I'll waste away, you wouldn't want that.'

Anna agreed she wouldn't, and that held things up a few more minutes.

'You'd better phone Lynn soon,' he said after a while, uncharacteristically tentative. 'You could say you'll not be back tonight.'

'That sounds . . . what will she think of me?'

'She'll think you're of an age to run your own life.' His voice brusque, as if she'd offended him. 'You owe apologies to no one.'

She touched his chest with her fingertips. 'I know. It's just the way I've lived. I'm used to accounting for every minute.'

'Not now. And not here.' He sat up. 'We should have something to eat. I could wreak havoc on a plate of fish and chips.'

'They'll be all cold and greasy. No way.'

'They won't. They're in the oven, nice and warm. I put them in when you locked yourself in here to have your paddy.'

She turned her head and watched what he was doing. 'What's that?'

He looked at her quizzically as he knotted the end of the narrow transparent sheath he'd just peeled off himself. She blushed at her stupidity. 'I didn't think.'

'Fortunately, I did. I knew you wouldn't.' He put his hand on the little fold at her waist, rubbing the skin with his thumb. 'But just for the record, and in case you're having any doubts about the honour of my intentions, I want babies with you.' He bent to plant a kiss where he'd been touching. 'Please.'

She went very quiet, unable to give him the assurance he so clearly wanted. She had gone beyond any limit she could have imagined. The prospect of further commitment frightened her. She'd made the wrong choice once, and she could not afford to fail again. But he didn't seem to expect an answer, just went whistling into the bathroom.

She tidied the bed, putting balloons on the floor and winding the fairylights round the large plant in front of the window. Then she got back in to contemplate the sight of a naked man bringing in a loaded tray, a bottle of wine tucked under his arm.

'You just need a rose in your teeth.'

'Don't quibble, woman.' He climbed in beside her. 'Are you sitting comfortably in my bed, my darling?' He mimicked the precise tones of a radio programme she remembered from childhood. 'Then we'll begin.'

They fed each other fish and chips. He'd switched on the tape recorder in the living room as he passed, and Dr Hook were singing again, the breathy, charged voices: *At the age of thirty-seven, she knew she'd found forever . . .*

He slept with his hand on the curve of her hip, as if afraid she might escape him in the night. She lay with her body touching the length of his, too overcome, too happy, too much on her guard to sleep. She had not envisaged this steady masculine warmth.

In the glow from the fairylights she watched his face. She had never really allowed herself to examine it properly: her training and her uncertainty made that impossible. So it was as if she'd never really seen the way his thick light brown hair grew back from his wide forehead. His jaw was wide too, balanced by the strong throat, and his mouth pouted very slightly in sleep. It looked almost cherubic, but the rest of his face dispelled the idea: the broad cheek-bones, the line of an old scar that quizzically lifted one well-marked eyebrow.

How beautiful he was. She had fought that discovery, had never allowed herself to freely acknowledge before just how powerfully he attracted her. But before, it had not mattered. He'd just been Hal.

For thirteen convent years she had fed her mind and denied her body. Like a trained seal, it had been obedient because it knew no different. Normal urges had stirred it, when nature had rebelled at the sterile rule the vows imposed. But however strong the desire, it had been impersonal: the ache was for something never known, the longing for someone never seen.

The indoctrination had been so thorough that even when she was among people in the world, she experienced everything at one remove. She had always been a watcher, always apart. It had been that way with Daniel Stern, the night of the birth. She had wanted something to happen then, but could not bring herself to be responsible for it.

Even when Hal kissed her on the moor, even when they danced at the Diwali disco and she had noticed the shape of his body, his narrow waist – still she had felt remote. His youth and his strength were not for her.

All that had changed. Her logical mind said, ridiculous. You're no different, just because you've been penetrated. Only, it wasn't a question of logic but of the heart. The old fairytales were wise. The prince climbed the tower, or cut through brambles. He defeated the witch or slew the dragon. And made the princess free.

She shifted slightly, to be closer to the warm body beside her. She was intensely conscious of the different textures of a man, at once innocent and erotic: soft pubic tangle, curly chest hair. He murmured something in his sleep and moved too, and she propped herself on one elbow.

Almost against her will, she slid a tentative hand down his side, over his small buttock, let it rest on his thigh that was long and shapely. She bent over him. Downy against her lips.

He murmured her name: she had not know he was awake. Instinctively she pulled away but he put a hand on the back of her head, whispering 'No, stay. My little love, stay.'

She had not thought it was in her gift to please so much. She took his penis, damp and soft, into her mouth and he smelled of pollen and of herself. Thrilled and appalled at her own temerity, she played him like a flute and felt him stir and harden. He groaned softly, 'Don't stop, don't stop,' and the mix of her emotions was almost beyond bearing: the excitement and the fear. The fear and desire.

He disengaged her then, pushed her back on the bed. He touched her body as if he'd never seen a woman before. He kissed the slight fold of flesh at her waist, the little plumes in her armpits, her nipples. He wove a litany of love around her name and stroked between her thighs. She protested but he seemed not to hear, suddenly urgent, determined and demanding.

This time, her body accepted his easily, and the feel of him was nothing she could ever have imagined. He filled her and held her, he drove and guided her. And when she gasped and writhed in a shuddering shivering spiral he became, for endless moments, the pivot on which she turned.

Afterwards, he hugged her to him. They lay facing each other, laced together. *Look at me with the eyes of your heart.* She wanted to stay awake. But sleep broke over her head in a warm wave.

23

The mill cat stalked sedately past dark offices towards its box under the packer's table. Tail erect with pride, it dangled from its mouth the shadow flat corpse of a mouse. It stopped at the door with 'Managing Director' on stippled glass, the light on Stan Beattie's desk reflecting in its yellow eyes.

Beattie crumpled the letter he had just read for the second time and threw it at the cat. It fell short, and the animal continued to watch Beattie impassively. He went back to pulling from drawers the accumulated rubbish of years: a tin of cough pastilles and an empty bottle of linctus, worn pencils, endless wool samples, a teaspoon, a broken stapler. With a grunt of impatience he swept the top of the desk clear with one movement of his arm, knocking the wire paper-basket with all its contents into the bin. The cat retreated, abandoned the mouse in the middle of the hall and proceeded to wash its face.

Stan Beattie sat down heavily, elbows on the desk, and with his fingertips pushed up the skin of his cheeks into ridges below his eyes. It was proving harder than he'd have believed to sever himself from Nightingale Mill. He'd been twenty when old Frank Summers took him on, trained him and trusted him: Stan Beattie knew the business better than Mr Simon ever had.

Poor bloke, what a waste. Still, he'd gone and not cared about the people he left trying to hold things together.

Beattie chucked a pile of magazines into the waste-bin without so much as glancing at the fleshy smiling beauties on the covers and a sheaf of papers went in on top. He pulled open the last drawer, extracted the remains of the bottle of Scotch a customer had given him Christmastime, poured a good two measures into a teacup and slumped back in his chair.

So that was that. Summers had sacked him. After all this time. And then, to add insult to injury, a letter from Stern. He'd opened it slowly, relishing the thick linen-weave paper, the embossed letterhead, savouring his anticipation of its contents. And learned with mounting disbelief that Maynard Gideon regretted they had nothing to offer him at the present time.

No consultancy, no golden handshake. Fucking nothing. He should've known that sheeny banker would drop him in the shit. Stern had never intended to do anything, it had been a convenient way of muzzling him, making sure he didn't interfere with Anna Summers' wild plans. Come to think of it, Stern was probably responsible for getting him fired into the bargain.

Not that it mattered now, Nightingale Mill might lurch on for another couple of years and after that, who cared. He knew one thing – that idiot woman'd not succeed with her fancy ideas. She didn't know whether she was on her arse or her elbow. He lit a cigarette and flicked the match into the bin, put his feet on the desk and crossed his ankles: a confident pose but his hands were sweating.

The cat was back, sitting in the doorway watching him, eyes glowing with reflected light like blasted headlamps. He watched it morosely. The two of them had the place to themselves. He'd parked among the cars outside one of the bodywork shops and waited till he saw Hal and the Summers girl drive off after six. He'd been in here when Hal came back – some problem with one of the machines, as usual – and had just turned out the office light till the overlooker was in the workroom. He'd done the same when the girls clattered out at nine, sitting in darkness listening for the last time to the place being closed down for the night.

He'd nothing more to say to any of them. Thirty years wiped

out without so much as a thank you. What did you expect? his wife had wanted to know. A gold watch, after the way you behaved?

The cat twitched its ears and turned its head to look at the waste-bin. That was when Beattie smelled burning paper.

He didn't move. The bin was cheap woven cane and its loss no cause for concern. He sat there, angry and bitter, nursing his third teacup of whisky and his grievances. He never knew what made him rout among the papers on his desk for the Maynard Gideon letter and twist it viciously before aiming it at the bin. This time he saw a dangerous little flame leap as the magazines caught alight. And a sinister thought started to smoulder in his fuzzy and resentful brain.

Beattie got up clumsily and retrieved the crumpled letter he'd thrown at the cat, added it to the bin. The words curled as the formal dismissal from thirty years of work crisped and darkened. Mrs Summers had signed it, but he knew well enough who was responsible for those careful phrases.

The cat walked ahead of him with silent dignity as Beattie carried the bin past the offices. He set it down to unlock the sliding door leading to the covered packers' yard. He used no lights – he knew this place better than his own home – and only stopped when he reached the room where the great cones of finished wool were stacked on shelves and floor before wrapping and delivery.

For a moment he glanced round the room, noted the low ceiling. They were directly under the main workroom, with its floor and walls of ancient wood.

Holding it at arms' length – it was giving off quite a heat – Stan Beattie upended the waste-bin so blazing paper fell among the cardboard cones standing on the floor. He kicked one over, exposing the tip to the heat and waited long enough to see the pale card darken and smoke and finally glow red. With his foot he nudged a couple more cones right against the embers. He pottered round the room, gathering up smaller skeins of wool, building a bonfire. Against the wall he found a wicker skip full of unused cones and with a bit of effort upended the whole thing over the by now considerable blaze.

For a minute he considered finding some petrol or meths but commonsense stopped him: if he did that, there was no way this could be called an accidental fire. Taking the cane basket with its blackened interior, he went off to find a window overlooking the river below so he could chuck the bin into the Aire. He had to go right along to the men's lavatories, but the narrow window was so stiff he was forced to use the heel of his shoe to knock it open. Closed throughout the winter, it stuck halfway and the basket wouldn't fit through the narrow space. He picked a sodden paper towel off the floor and put it inside, left it under the washbasin.

He must have spent longer than he realised in the washroom, because in the passage he could hear the fire's ominous rushing, taste oily fumes at the back of his throat. He'd left the door of the storage room open – the more air the better – and the leaping light of the fire was bright on dingy walls. Peering in, it looked as if the whole floor was alight. He hadn't anticipated the brittle old boards would go up like that. It was immensely, wickedly, satisfying, a proper little furnace in there so he had to press against the far wall as he passed the door, away from the heat. Emboldened by alcohol, he took his time ambling back towards the packers' yard, testing his nerve.

The cat streaked past him going the wrong way, stupid bloody animal, dashing towards the stairs that led to the workroom where there would be no escape. He yelled something but he could see it was in a panic.

Like a fool, he stood there staring after it. The rest of the floorboards were blazing now, right across the passage, there was no way it could survive. But for some reason he took a couple of steps towards the heat, wavering. Burning wool smelt disgusting, like singeing human hair, and the air billowed with hot foul smoke.

The heat and fumes, the speed at which it had all happened, were unbelievable. He'd better get out, there was real danger now. He started back to the offices.

Christ! What was that? He whirled at the sound of a crash. Something had fallen in, and now the flames were higher than his head. He could feel them sucking in oxygen and he was memserised by the raw energy, the destructive power, the blistering heat of the vengeance he was wreaking.

And then he saw it. In the middle of the fiercest part of the blaze, in that airless furnace, a figure rose up. A towering, menacing shape, cloaked and hooded, faceless and vindictive. It was right in the heart of the fire, where no human being could be. Alone in the deserted mill, he stood trapped by horror and watched its cloak billow and lift in the wind of the flames. Over the fierce crackling, he could hear its fearful cries: it was screaming at him, he caught his own name!

Stan Beattie stared aghast, one arm up against the heat, mouth open in terror. His whisky-blurred brain recognised retribution. He couldn't move, he couldn't breathe, he couldn't see. His eyes were liquefying, streaming down his cheeks, his legs quivering, there was no strength in him.

It was moving towards him through the sweltering pyre he had made. He heard his name again. Gasping for air, choking on his own fear, he gave a hoarse cry of protest, wrenched himself out of his panic and made a frantic blind dash. Away from the hideous hooded figure. Into the fire.

That was when the wall fell on him.

The convent bell was ringing in her dream and she knew she would not answer it.

'Wake up! Anna, you must wake up!'

It was part of her dream and then it was real, and Hal's loud voice shocked her awake.

She was warm and naked in his bed. His agitation made no sense, nor did the way he was struggling into his clothes. She blinked at him in the lamp light. 'The matter?'

'Everything.' He knelt down by the side of the bed. She heard him saying 'Get dressed, Anna, we've got to get over to the mill. There's been a fire,' but all she really noticed was that his face and chest were wet. Hal rubbed his face hard with the towel round his shoulders, started to say something else and changed his mind. 'Get your clothes on.' He got up and routed through a drawer, dropped a sweater onto the bed. 'You wear this, it'll be cold.' He opened the bedroom door and then came back and leant over her. 'What a wakening for you. Sorry.' He kissed her mouth lightly. 'Come on now, move.'

She was up and in the bathroom, wishing she had time for a shower, running water in the basin instead, before it dawned on her. Dear Lord, the mill! She called, 'Hal – the yarn! Is that all right?'

'Don't know. It was the police on the phone, they didn't say much.' The next time he spoke, he was outside the bathroom door. 'One thing. I told them not to contact Lynn. She couldn't get there with those kids, no point in telling her till we know what's what.' She opened the door a fraction, she needed the reassurance of seeing him. 'And don't let's worry till we know what we're worrying about,' he added.

She stood in the mill yard on cobbles soaked by fire hoses. The building was in darkness but there was plenty of light from the headlights of the three fire-engines and the police car with their spinning lamps, the powerful beams of firemen's torches. A policeman was leaning into his vehicle, speaking into a receiver. She listened to the distorted voices of the radiophones, the repeated requests and commands.

'When can we go in?' she asked the fireman who stood beside her dripping black sweat.

'They'll not let you yet, but that's in case you injure yourself in the dark. Fire's all done but you've no electricity. Still, it could've been a lot worse.' He took off his hard yellow hat and inspected the inside, wiped his face with a forearm before replacing it. 'Lots of combustible material in these old buildings, even without the wool. Most of 'em go up like tinderboxes. This one would've, without that call.'

'Call?'

He looked down at her, the whites of his eyes gleaming in his dirty face. 'Yeah. You've that old girl to thank your mill's still standin'.' He gestured with his head to the ambulance which stood, blue light whirling, behind the police car. She felt Hal's hand on her arm: he had a second policeman with him.

'Anna, Peggy's in the ambulance. She's all right,' he added hastily, before she could remonstrate, 'just shocked. She'll tell you what happened. She was working late and says she fell asleep. When she woke, the place was going up in flames.'

'*Peggy?* You're sure she's not hurt?' All other questions could wait.

'She's fine. A lucky woman.'

As they hurried over to the ambulance the policeman said, 'They told you about your works manager?'

'Your colleague said he'd been taken away immediately. It sounds quite bad.'

'He was in a terrible state. Nasty burns on face and body – the ambulancemen reckoned he'd need skin grafts. And probably a broken leg. Looks as if a wall collapsed on him, and he burnt his hands getting himself free. He apparently managed to crawl through to that enclosed yard and the fire-chief says that saved him, stone floor an' all.'

She was bewildered. 'I can't imagine what he was doing there anyway, and certainly not at that hour.'

'No more can we.' The policeman sounded grim. 'He was in too much pain to talk – and too drunk. We'll not find out anything now till daylight. And mebbe not then – depends on the state of the place.'

We can talk to Peggy for a minute,' Hal volunteered. 'But we've got to take it easy.'

She was lying wrapped in blankets on a stretcher. Her face was smeared with tears and dirt, and circles of rouge stood out bright as blemishes. She coughed as Anna took her cold hand.

'Thank Heaven you're all right. I couldn't believe it when they said you were here. I'll come to the hospital with you.'

'Thanks love. That'd be grand.' Peggy managed a smile. 'I've myself to blame, staying on late without telling anyone. I'd have yelled blue murder if anyone else did that.'

'Why did you, Peggy?' Anna's voice shook: she'd just seen that Peggy's forehead was red and raw-looking, her front hair frizzled by the fire. And her eyebrows had almost gone. The older woman shut her eyes in exhaustion.

'Wanted to give you a surprise,' she whispered. 'You said you couldn't wait to see those yarns from Pickles all done up with the new labels . . .'

'Peggy, you didn't!'

'Thought it'd only take a couple of hours.' She patted Anna's hand. Her pearly blue eyelids had smudged. 'Not your fault, love, I'm a fool. I was working in that little cubbyhole near the storage room, it's got an electric fire.' Anna nodded. She used it herself for labelling the yarns, and the cellophane was kept there. 'I dozed off in the warm and when I woke there was smoke and a terrible smell and that awful crackling bonfire noise and I realised . . .' She shuddered. Anna squeezed her shoulder and she winced. 'That hurts!' She was quiet for a minute. 'I tried to open the door but the handle wouldn't budge and there's no window: I was trapped. I shouted . . .' her voice trembled, 'then I realised everyone'd gone.' There were tears in her eyes, mascara clogged her lashes. 'You saved me.'

'What d'you mean?'

'That long mantle thing with a hood you used to wear – it was on a peg, you must've left it. I wrapped myself in that and just sort of ran at the door.' She touched her shoulder. 'It just gave way and I was almost in the fire, I couldn't stop myself. I couldn't see, there was so much smoke, so I pulled your hood over my face and guessed which was the right way to go.' She added ruefully. 'Ruined those new shoes, didn't I.'

Anna sent up a quick prayer of thanks: if she'd guessed wrong she'd not have survived.

'The mill would have been lost, all the yarn burnt, if you'd not been there. We'll keep you in shoes for the rest of your life, Peggy.'

But Peggy hadn't finished. 'That's when I saw Stan.' Her whisper was hoarse and strained. 'I saw him there, the other side of the fire, staring at me like I was a ghost. "Stan," I screams "help me." But he didn't move, just gawped with his eyes popping out. Never tried to reach me, nothing.' She coughed again and Anna put an arm behind her back to raise and ease her. 'It's the smoke. Thought I was going to choke in there.'

The ambulanceman peered in. 'We're moving off in a minute, Miss.'

'Yes, of course, just a second.' She looked down at Peggy. 'Go on.'

'Like I said, he just stared – and then he ran the wrong way, right into the fire. I was shouting to him to go back, but he just went on like a madman and then something collapsed on top of him. Poor Stan.' Peggy shut her eyes in exhaustion and a tear ran down the side of her nose.

Hal said softly, 'You saved him though, Peggy.'

'Not really. He'd reached the packers' yard himself, I just pulled the metal door across, and that gave me time to telephone.' This time the coughing was a paroxysm and the ambulanceman jumped up the steps to her. Anna touched Hal's arm lightly.

'I'll ride to the hospital. And I'll be here early tomorrow.' There were other things she wanted to say, but she put it all into two words. 'Be careful.'

'OK.' He gripped her knee for a moment and even in the ambulance light his eyes were green and gold and full of meaning as he answered her silently. All he said was, 'I'll take care of it all. See you in the morning.'

Almost all the beautiful yarns Anna had devised were untouched. Lynn joined Anna and Hal to assess the damage and that was the first thing they checked. Some bales of mohair had been burnt or too charred to be of use. A couple of the silk and wool cones were blackened by smoke and some, otherwise unmarked, had been soaked beyond saving by the firehoses. But the bulk of those lost were the synthetics Anna hated, far more inflammable than the natural fibres and stored where the flames reached them easily.

They gazed round the wreck of the room, the piles of rubble where the old wall had collapsed, the yawning gaps where floorboards had gone. There was filthy water everywhere, and the bonfire smell. They picked their way along the corridor where walls and floor were blackened and charred and up the stairs, only the lower ones damaged here. The workroom was unusable. The fire hadn't destroyed anything, but smoke had fingered its way through the joists and gaps of the old floor, filming every surface with black grease and bringing the reek of an uncleaned chimney.

The three of them sat silently in Peggy's office with mugs of tea.

'Feels funny in here without her.' Lynn stirred in sugar. 'She's resting at home for a few days. Under duress,' she added. 'She insists she can come back the minute we need her. I've had flowers sent round.'

It was Anna who asked 'Do we know how Stan is?'

'I've not enquired,' Lynn answered tartly. She caught Anna's eye. 'I can't help it,' she said defensively. 'We know it was all his fault. I'll never forgive him for nearly killing Peggy. I can't be as charitable as you.'

'He's as well as can be expected, the hospital said.' Hal spoke without emotion. 'He's a pretty sick man. And he's in a lot of pain.'

'He'll recover?' Anna had to ask.

'It'll take a long time. That chap was right about skin grafts. It'll be months before he's anything like healed.'

No one spoke. Whatever Stan Beattie had done, the price he was paying was unimaginable.

'Did you tell Daniel Stern about the fire yet?'

'I've left messages. They keep asking if someone else can deal with it.'

'I thought he said something about using his car-phone, the night Sara was born. Or did I dream it?'

Anna frowned. 'I'm an idiot, I never thought. But they

377

didn't give me a number for him. Should I ask for it?' She looked at them doubtfully. 'We don't want to chase him too hard, it'll make all this sound worse than it is: I think we're better keeping it low-key.' She rubbed her thumbs against her fingers and Lynn noted the first impatient gesture she'd seen Anna make.

'I'd ring,' she volunteered.

'Oh, all right.' Anna didn't need much convincing. She dialled the London number she now had by heart. The switchboard put her through to Stern's office and a crisp woman's voice answered.

'Didn't you get the message I left for you, Miss Summers – the Lorton number?'

'No, I'm afraid I didn't. Will he still be there?'

'He left last night, I believe. But I'm sure he'd prefer to contact you himself.'

'Right, thank you.' She put the phone down and pulled a face. 'We don't seem to be getting very far. And Walter's trade people will be here in four days.' They looked at each other. Four days to patch up, clean up, get things humming again.

'D'you think we can do it?' Lynn finally put it into words. Before anyone could answer, she pointed to the open door. 'Look!' The mill cat stood there. Bedraggled fur made it look thin, the white chest and paws it cleaned so obsessively were matted and dirty. It stared at them and gave a harsh mew. Lynn poured milk into a saucer and they watched the animal settle down in front of it.

Hal bent and scratched it behind the ears. 'If the moggy can survive that lot, we can.'

After Lynn had left to collect the children, Anna went back to helping Hal and the salvage men. They worked steadily for most of the day.

'That's about it.' Bert Cowley chucked the last of the burned floorboards in the open truck and wiped his hands on what looked to Anna uncomfortably like a moleskin waistcoat. 'Can't do no more till your builder's seen it.'

'Right,' Hal said. 'And the insurance people have to take another look too. I'll call you when we're ready.'

When they'd driven away, Anna gave a groan. 'I'm too tired to think. And I must have a bath.'

'Let's stop. We'll have to take it a day at a time.'

They walked back towards Anna's old car. 'Hal, Lynn and I want you to take over Beattie's job as works manager. Will you?'

He stopped. 'I don't know.' He pulled the lobe of his ear in the anxious gesture she had seen him make before.

'You'd be really good. It'd make all the difference to the mill, having you run things. Please say you'll do it.'

He patted his pockets, searching. 'Always eat in a crisis.' He offered the packet of M&Ms. 'It's a bit like a bad joke. I can't have you telling me when we have a row that I slept my way to the top.'

'But that's got nothing to do with it, you know that as . . .' In the middle of the denial, she heard what he'd said. 'We're not going to have rows, are we?' All that day she'd wanted to touch him, to confirm last night had happened. But she hadn't.

'Probably.' He squinted up at the mill. 'Married couples do, you know. Part of life's rich pattern.'

She was instantly alarmed. 'I haven't said . . .'

He looked at her with an odd expression, both resigned and determined. 'I realise you haven't. I'll wait for however long it takes.' He rested his hand briefly on her shoulder, a gesture so restrained it would have revealed nothing to any watcher. 'D'you know which are the hardest words to say?' She unlocked the car door without answering. His voice dropped to a deeper note. 'I love you.' He shut the door for her, and she wound down the window. 'I love you.' He reached in and stroked where the hair grew low on her nape. His tenderness for her was without limit. She could tell he was holding back, not presuming on the intimacy of their night. He was waiting for her move. Her decision.

She drove home so preoccupied with her thoughts, she couldn't remember a moment of the journey. He had said it,

379

but she had not. Not once during all the hours last night. She really hated herself sometimes.

'I'd like you to meet Miss Summers . . . This is the gentleman from Daimaru in Tokyo. The buyer from Odakyu . . .' Over the buzz of interpreters, Walter Street's reassuring rumble ushered in the trade delegation. Anna and Lynn – both dressed in Lynn's most elegant suits – shook proferred hands, smiled warmly, dutifully repeated Japanese names: Mr Yonezawa, Miss Hara, Mr Miyata. The man from the Ministry of Trade was clipped and grey and spruce as a furled umbrella, worrying at the edges of the crowd of foreign buyers, fifteen of them at least in the mill's cramped entrance.

'Thank God the heating's back,' Lynn whispered. It was sleeting again and the overcoats piled on chairs had whitened shoulders. 'Where's Daniel Stern? He did know it was today?'

'I told his secretary at least twice.' Anna ran a hand over her hair. They had heard nothing since the scrawled postcard from Ullswater with the curt message: I'll be there.

A middle-aged man in a suit of what Anna's professional eye noted was superb material, beamed at her and at his shoulder the interpreter repeated his words tonelessly. 'This is a pleasure, dear ladies.' A youngish woman with her hair dressed in a formal Japanese bun said politely in excellent English, 'We all look forward to this occasion.'

Anna introduced an unfamiliar Hal, almost conventional ('Didn't know you had a tie,' she whispered), to four bowing, smiling Japanese buyers in hornrims and blue suits. 'Mr Hallam is our manager. He will show you the technical side in a moment.'

While Hal explained the functions of flyer-spinner and doffer-frame, Anna stood at the back with the man from the Ministry and listened to her lover's softly-accented voice warm with enthusiasm. He patted the old polished wood with proprietorial pride, showed the brass plate with the maker's name and date – Hall & Shell, 1926.

At that point, as arranged, she took over, explaining how

their yarns were the nearest possible to hand spun, that in an age of increasing mechanisation, Nightingale Mill products were individual and unique. Pickles had delivered the last of the dyed skeins on time and by working round the clock for thirty-six hours, they were ready and labelled. She had to shout as usual over the roar and stammer of machinery. She, Lynn and Hal had decided it would be a mistake to shut down for the visitors. They'd settled for an air of steady busyness, and compromised by asking the girls to turn off the radios.

As she paused for the interpreter – though the Japanese had a good deal of English, the man from the Ministry explained, they liked technicalities in their own tongue – she noted the improvement in the workroom. The cleaning up had been prodigious and everyone had helped. Dust undisturbed for years had been swept away, windows cleaned for the first time since anyone could remember. Why had it taken the fire to make them undertake such an obvious task? There had been no time yet for painting, but Lynn had driven over to the Wool Marketing Board in Clayton and bought dozens of their posters. Huge photographs of sheep almost hid smoke-blackened walls: Herdwick and Suffolk, the horned Jacob and the wild curls of the Teeswater. And it had been Lynn who suggested the 'girls' be given bright check overalls to wear. Looking round, Anna saw with amusement that all the old hands – Edna, Viv, Dawn – had their hair tucked into flowering scarves tied at the front, as usual, but they were new. Rene, catching her glance, winked broadly and made a V-sign.

Anna just hoped her confidence wasn't misplaced. As she had anticipated, only half a dozen of their English wholesalers had expressed interest in taking the new products. They'd liked them, that was clear enough. But the message had been the same everywhere: in this economic climate women wouldn't buy expensive yarns. So if the Japanese didn't bite, Nightingale Mill could not carry on: they had come to the end of their credit.

After the tour, Anna ushered everyone back to the Managing Director's room. Peggy insisted she refer to it as 'her' office.

('I'm putting your bits and pieces in there and no arguing. Working in that cubbyhole like a clerk, it's ridiculous.') She was in there now, brisk as ever, handing out trays of sherry and snacks. She was too pale beneath her rouge and she had a blue silk scarf bound round her head over her frizzed-off hair, but she refused to stay away. Lynn was doing a superb job with earnestly smiling Japanese buyers, showing the glass-fronted mahogany cabinet displaying samples of their yarns dating back nearly a hundred years.

'Went off a treat, girlie. Well done.' Walter Street had secured a tray of cocktail biscuits. 'They seem impressed. And I don't think that bit of fire damage bothered anyone.' He nodded across to where Hal was talking to a couple of the younger men. 'That chap did you proud.'

'Thanks, Walter.' Anna touched his hand in gratitude. 'But we're not there yet. I won't be happy till orders are on the books.' She was conscious of a lull in the talk. 'Time to give out the packs.' She showed him the kit they'd put together: transparent zipped folders containing the narrow folded card of samples threaded by the nuns with Sister Peter's sketch of the mill on the front, the words *Natural Spinning Company* stamped in black letters. The leaflet with the same cover giving the history of Nightingale Mill, and folded hanks of yarn, one of each type, in different colours. The neat labels attached to these had the same sketch again, and detailed the origins of the wool and mohair, silk and linen. Anna and Lynn distributed them to the delegates, listened to their approving comments.

'Your products are admirable, Miss Summers. Mrs. Summers.' Mr Tagaki's tight shirt collar made a fleshy concertina of his neck. 'We have seen such yarns in Italy.' He turned to the black-clad woman beside him. 'You have met Miss Masui?' She was easily the most impressive of the delegates. Delicate and somehow tough at the same time, with skin of matt cream, she must have been in her late forties. Hair without a touch of grey was cut short and smooth with a heavy fringe. Her suit was clearly couture, her smile gracious.

'We buy for a large chain of stores across Japan. And we are very much interested in your product.' Anna felt Lynn's touch on her back. 'Before we place orders with you, however, we have to be certain there will be continuity of standard, quality, colour.'

Anna had to keep her voice from rising with excitement. 'Of course, that goes without saying.' She almost began to relax. It looked as though they'd done it.

'And there would seem to be a problem.' Anna felt Lynn tense beside her. 'We have heard there are difficulties with your mill.'

Anna couldn't manage a word. Beattie must have been talking – but who to? Lynn said swiftly, 'Oh no, you must be mistaken.' The interpreter finishing passing on Lynn's remark. As she did so she heard Lynn mutter, 'Where's your blasted banker?'

'Our information suggests otherwise,' the smooth Miss Masui continued. 'We understand the head of the company has died and you are in charge only recently.' She waited for Anna's reply.

'It's true I've been here just a few months.' She felt she could stretch a point. 'But it was my father's mill and I've been involved in yarnspinning all my life. On a smaller scale, of course.' She knew the admission was a mistake even before Miss Masui's polite smile. Damn.

'I meant, financial difficulties. Cash flow problems. We noticed you carry very small amounts of the yarns you are promoting, for instance.'

The large Mr Tagaki nodded confirmation beside her.

'We appreciate the cost of stock-piling too much is prohibitive.' The interpreter was speaking for Mr Tagaki. 'But it is necessary to be realistic. We owe it to our company to be assured of your ability to deliver considerable amounts without any problems. We must put the best goods on Japanese shelves.'

He paused. Miss Masui looked round the room. 'You will appreciate, on all the evidence your productivity may be insufficient for our demands. We are a very large company.' This time, she spoke Japanese – a bad sign, Anna thought, even before she heard the translation, which the interpreter delivered without inflexion.

'You probably saw we had a small fire. That was last week, and the builders are already at work. We lost some stock then, but that is a temporary problem.' Although the woman nodded, her expression did not change.

'I don't wish to interfere, Miss Masui.' Walter Street had been listening, his face heavy with concern. 'But it might put your mind at rest to know Nightingale Mill has the backing of a big firm of private bankers in the City. That's right, isn't it?' He appealed to Anna, giving her the opportunity she needed.

But she couldn't take it. She could not bluff her way through as he would have done. Trained for so long to relentless honesty, she could not lie even for Lynn's sake. For a painful pause she said nothing, then: 'We believe we have Maynard Gideon behind us.'

Well, she hadn't been told they had withdrawn their loan, it was no more than a fib. At his side, Walter Street's thumb twitched the signal of his annoyance. 'If you could bear with me for a couple of days, this will be resolved, and I can let you have confirmation of our financial viability.' She didn't know what she would do, but there were other banks. Someone would help them if they had the certainty of big foreign sales.

Anna waited for the rapid translation, searching the woman's face for a hint of her reaction. There was none. Anna and Lynn barely heard the words of polite regret. 'I am sure you will understood, all business must be concluded before we leave the country in two days time.' Miss Masui put her fingertips together and made a slight bow. It was incongruous, the stylised obeisance from a woman dressed in the height of Western fashion. 'It has been my pleasure to visit. Thank you.' She turned away with a politician's finality.

Walter Street blew out his cheeks in a sigh. 'Eh, well. We're for the off, then. Time for lunch.' The man from the Ministry caught his eye and began his shepherding activities again, setting down glasses, offering thanks. Anna tried to hide her dejection, smiling and chatting, but she didn't succeed well enough to fool Hal. He looked at her face and mouthed the question.

'No go?'

'No backing. No security. No chance.' Anna smiled at him to keep what she was saying from the people around them.

'Bugger.' Under his breath, the first expletive she'd heard from him. She suddenly acknowledged desperate tiredness. It had been long after midnight when she got to bed and from old habit she had still risen at five. Modern nights and medieval mornings didn't mix.

'There's nothing more to be done,' she told Hal. 'They'll be leaving any minute. I'm going to get coats.' She walked into the hallway just as Daniel Stern came through the door.

Immaculate in striped three-piece banker's suit, briefcase in hand, Stern was full of graceful apologies about driving difficulties in the bad weather. He handled the situation as if he rescued people from financial disaster every day of his life. He handed out his card, flourished pages of financial projections and explained that Maynard Gideon were committed to the expansion of Nightingale Mill.

'We are convinced their carefully planned development will be successful. The directors have at their disposal all the funding they need to realise their potential.' He looked round the room as the interpreters followed his words. 'And you have my assurance that it was not my intention to make this last minute appearance. I hope you – and Miss Summers – will forgive my late arrival and any confusion I may have caused.'

'*May* have caused indeed,' Peggy muttered not quite audibly at the back of the room as the meeting broke up for the second time. Beside her, Lynn nodded, watching Miss Masui and Mr Tagaki moving purposefully towards Anna.

When the last of the visitors had gone, ushered away by a complacent Walter Street, Daniel Stern looked at the debris of glasses, chose a chunk of smoked salmon on black bread and asked, 'Any chance of a cup of coffee?' Two weeks ago Anna would have hurried to make it for him. Now she leaned against the glass fronted cupboard with its collection of yarns and folded her arms. Peggy offered and disappeared to her office. Hal excused himself, with a meaningful look at Anna, and vanished upstairs.

Lynn eyed Simon's chair as if seriously considering it, then chose to perch on the edge of his desk. She swung a leg thoughtfully and contemplated Daniel Stern as he looked through the presentation pack in its plastic case. 'This looks great. I'd like to take half a dozen to London with me.' He examined the labels carefully. 'Who did the drawing of the mill?'

Anna explained about Sister Peter and the way the nuns had prepared the samples. 'I'm going over this weekend. I promised to tell them what people thought.'

'Tell them it was an unqualified success. An order that size must be almost enough on its own to see you through till summer.' Anna noticed that although he took no sugar, he stirred his coffee. Another habit he was trying to kick.

'Yes. We'll have to be careful, though. It's not a good idea to be too dependent on one outlet.'

Lynn nodded. 'We're going really hard after the European market next. They take a lot of English wool and silk suitings, we're sure they'll like our yarns. Anna and I are going over ourselves.'

'It's good to hear you getting involved.' He gave her a nice smile. 'And you're looking very well indeed. Tell me, how's your small daughter?'

Lynn left five minutes later, shaking hands warmly with Daniel Stern. 'Thanks again – for everything.' She smiled back over her shoulder as she went out of the room. 'Even if you did leave it pretty damn late to send in the cavalry.'

Anna added, 'She's right, you know. I honestly thought you were going to withdraw our loan.' She'd imagined herself saying something like this many times, with every graduation of emotion from faint hostility to furious anger. Now she was actually doing so, it was with gratitude that he so obviously hadn't.

He stopped drinking. 'What are you talking about – that was never a possibility.'

'We'd no word from you. Or the bank.'

His forehead creased. 'But we talked at the Victoria Hotel the evening the baby was born. We'd already come to an arrangement.'

She could hardly believe his bewilderment was genuine. 'There was nothing in writing. I couldn't draw on resources without proper confirmation. And besides, I was afraid you – '

'Are the kind of man who wreaks financial vengeance on women who reject his favours,' he finished for her. 'Thanks for the character reference, but I'm not. Sometimes these things work out. More often they don't, in my experience.' His tone was light.

She thought; I got it wrong again. He wasn't bothered one way or the other. It only seemed a big deal to me.

'When we first met,' he went on, 'I'd just got back from a spell with a firm of New York investment bankers. Salamons, ever heard of them? Their high-flyers are called BSDs.' He paused.

'No idea.'

'Big Swinging Dicks.' He grinned at the expressions that mingled on her face, his own crinkling. 'I decided then and there I wasn't one: too exhausting. I believe business relations should be civilised, and we're business associates now. Next time, for goodness sake, just call me if you have problems.'

She heard that as criticism and snapped, 'All very well to say but how was I supposed to know where you were?' She tried to keep the shrill note from her voice.

He frowned. 'My secretary was meant to tell you.'

Anna spread her hands wide. 'She said something the other day about leaving me a Lorton number, but no one took it.'

'Someone did.' His face set with annoyance. 'So that's what happened. Stan Beattie came to see me. I thought at first you'd sent him.'

'*What?*'

'Turned up while Sam and I were having tea in Crummock Water. Shared a few of his thoughts with me.' He repeated the gist of the conversation.

'And you said?'

Stern replied easily. 'As little as possible, while implying that if he kept out of your way, he'd end up running Nightingale Mill.'

Anna's expression was icy. Stern said, 'Hold on there, I don't deserve that. I'd no intention of even speaking to him again. But I couldn't think of another way to keep him quiet and out of your way. He didn't quite threaten to make sure you failed, but his meaning was clear enough.'

'He had a damn good try.'

'That might be my fault. I wrote and told him nothing doing.'

'And I sacked him.'

'Splendid.' He gave her a wry look. 'Though as it turned out, a rather expensive gesture for both of us.'

'But not without satisfaction.' She felt suddenly light-hearted. 'It looks as if things will work out, doesn't it? As if we'll pull the mill through.'

'Better than that, if I'm any judge.' He put down his coffee cup. 'I expect a great deal from you.' Anna waited. 'Regular reports,' he went on. 'Export figures. Samples of your new colours. Your company when you're in London.'

She was deliberately demure. 'That sounds highly acceptable.'

'When you get around to that European trip, you must come and see me. We've offices in Paris and Madrid and contacts in most cities who could be useful. You'll need interpreters and so on.' He put down his cup. 'Perhaps you'd have dinner with me. No sandwiches, though.' He added, as though he hadn't noticed till now, 'You're not wearing your habit.'

'I've left the convent. Definitely, this time.'

'That's a major move. It must be really strange, leaving all that.' There was an uncertain pause. She waited to see where he was prepared to take the conversation: this was his opportunity to make some reference to that amazing night they'd spent. She had half-anticipated some kind of suggestion or advance: some positive response. She busied herself taking empty glasses left on top of the filing cabinet beside her and putting them on a tray.

Daniel Stern stood up, came over to her and put the glass she was holding with the others. He took hold of her hand and she felt a ridiculous relief that she used handcream now. 'You've done a great job here. You're to be congratulated. I mean it about that dinner: we'll go somewhere really good, celebrate.' He pressed her fingers.

'I'd like that.' She took back her hand with dignity. She understood the incident in Lynn's lounge, so earthshaking and extraordinary for her, for him had been an interlude. He liked her – more than that, had desired her – and if something developed between them, well and good. He would not pursue her, that wasn't his way. And if nothing further happened, then those shared hours would be part of their friendship; they would keep an affection for each other. She did not know how rare that is.

It came as a revelation that she was able so dispassionately to understand her emotions and his. Daniel Stern would let her into his life – into a neat compartment. He might even come to love her, but he was self-contained and he had been hurt once already. Love would not be allowed to overwhelm him. She would never feel, as she did with Hal, that she held his happiness in her hands.

She stood with him at the door facing onto the mill yard. It was sleeting again, sharp grey daggers striking the cobbles. She buttoned Lynn's suit high round her throat while he put on his overcoat.

'You'll phone and tell me what's happening.'

'Of course.'

His car was outside. 'Hate to rush away like this but you know how it is.' He held her lightly, a gloved hand on her shoulder, kissed her cheek. He was cordial, warm, slightly distracted. He turned up his collar against the rain. 'Don't forget we're having dinner.'

She waited there as the car pulled out of the mill yard into Nightingale Street. And the mill cat, sitting on Peggy's window-sill among the sprawling spiderplants, watched her.

24

She stood alone in front of the convent, just like her first day, staring across the wide valley where three rivers of beaten metal coiled over ruckled green silk.

Mother Emmanuel had sent a curt note to Bradford two months ago: Your rescript has arrived. We will need you here to accept formally and sign. Anna had been putting off this visit for weeks. There were always excuses: they had been frantically busy at the mill, Jamie had been ill. But it was something else, a vestige of uncertainty, that made her reluctant to take this last irrevocable step. She'd finally forced herself to a decision that morning when, as always, she woke at five o'clock. Only Lynn knew where she was; she'd not even made her customary telephone call to the convent before catching the train.

Inside the ever-open front door of the house she set down her bag, half-blind in the shady hall after the brightness outside. At the far end the enclosure door waited with its massive lock, the antiquated machinery of the 'turn' which brought in their supplies, the panel which slid back to reveal the wire grille. She pulled the old-fashioned bell for Sister Rosalie to let her in.

No answer.

On an impulse she went back out into the sunshine. Dense rhododendrons edged the path outsiders took to the chapel. No one would be there at this time: she anticipated the consoling silence, the incense and snuffed candles.

But as she pushed open the door, she saw they were still

alight. The chapel was filled with the waiting hush before someone continued speaking.

'Your love, Lord, reaches to heaven;
your truth to the skies.
Your justice is like God's mountain,
your judgements like the deep.'

Sister Thomas à Becket was reciting the psalm as Anna moved quietly into the chapel. The priest stood before the altar, his vestments made by the nuns gleaming as he moved. In front of him several lay people were seated: a youngish couple, two elderly women who lived in the nearby village and regularly visited the nuns, a middle-aged man in a formal suit. What was going on?

'My God, the sons of men
Find refuge in the shelter of your wings.'

The pure voice of Sister Louis gave the answer. She understood now why they were there, when normally they would have been at their afternoon tasks, and the skin pricked on the back of her neck. She moved forward until she was almost level with the wrought-iron grille separating the nuns' choir from the open chapel.

Behind it, on a white-sheeted bier facing the altar, the body of a woman lay clothed in the full habit. Grey scapular over white cowl, the cord at the waist with the silver crucifix and three knots of the three monastic vows. White band and heavy black veil. Anna did not need to see the swollen feet to know who it was and her throat tightened with grief.

Sister Godric lay in the choir where for so long she had prayed seven times every day and once at night. The great Paschal candle, symbol of eternal light, burned steadily in its carved holder above her head and her illumined face showed only peace. There was a wreath of fresh flowers like a crown above her white linen band, for death is part of life.

Two nuns were in their stalls, one either side. Sister Vincent and Sister Louis would have kept watch all day, reciting psalms. Two more would have been beside her through the night. Their dead sister would not be left alone before her God.

The candle-flames shivered through her tears. *When thou shalt pass through the waters I will be with thee, and the rivers shall not cover thee.*

She experience a sudden violent jealousy for the nuns who'd been here to say goodbye. They would have answered the warning call of the wooden rattle in the cloister when death approached Sister Godric. They would have hurried to the infirmary for the anointing by the chaplain, for the responses and the psalms, the prayers that the saints intercede for her soul. And when the end finally came, they would have waited quietly outside the room for an hour, so that Sister Godric's soul could go gently.

Sun struck blue and purple patterns through the stained glass. Anna sank down on the nearest seat. She bent her head and folded her hands and searched for a prayer.

The nuns took Sister Godric away. The strongest of them, three and three, lifted the bier onto their shoulders and carried her out of the choir. As they left Anna moved forward, grasping the heavy grille to steady herself, watching the departing backs of Sister Peter and Sister Rosalie. She knew the route they would take, through the ante-choir and the cloister while the rest of the community followed, singing their sombre Gregorian chant. They would go past the quiet rooms, the refectory and the library, down the long corridors for the last time, pausing for a moment at the statue of St Joseph. They would pace slowly through the inner courtyard beneath pale blue wisteria and out into the summer evening.

Anna paused long enough to kneel and cross herself before the altar. She almost ran out, scrambling through the undergrowth, pushing through to the door set in the stone wall. It was used on the rare occasions when the tractor needed servicing and had to be taken outside the enclosure. The key was in its place, tucked behind a loose stone. Once inside, she hurried past the greenhouses and strawberry frames, the runnerbeans and blackcurrant bushes.

Just beyond the beehives, the rows of raspberry canes and sweet peas, stood one of the old grilles the order had brought with them from France, black and heavy as a barred gate. Sister Godric used it as a frame for a perfumed mass of golden Peace roses. This year, the petals the old nun collected for pot-pourri were scattered on the paved walk.

By the time Anna saw them, the procession had reached the private walled cemetery where even in death the nuns keep their enclosure. Half-hidden beside the flower-hung grille, she watched the priest bless the ground and hallow it with incense.

Then they lowered Sister Godric into her grave, bearing the weight of that frail body on wide bands of unbleached linen. For she would lie uncovered in the earth like all their order.

Everyone knelt, touching the ground with their knuckles in the old way, taking part in the changeless ritual. Behind her grille, Anna knelt too. Three times they begged that God have mercy on her soul, voices rising in the most plaintive and poignant chant of the church. Then two and two the nuns performed the final service for their sister, and with their bare hands dropped soil softly onto her still body.

Anna saw Lis go forward to scoop up a handful of moist earth and her face was bright with brief elation. Sister Godric was gone, but this was a joyful occasion. There is no death. Only a change of worlds.

Anna walked away, back up the long garden, along the covered way round the inner courtyard. Every summer, the stock she had planted would sweeten the whole convent, and the nuns would catch their perfume as they went about their work. She moved slowly, not caring any more if anyone should see her there, caring only for the old woman she had loved.

She mounted the stairs of the cool and silent house. The door of the linen room which was the prioress's office was open as always. On Mother Emmanuel's large, untidy desk were the usual collection of bills held in a clothes peg, an assortment of letters and a pile of slim cardboard files. Holding her breath, Anna flipped through these. Charitable donations; Concessional Relief . . . she went faster . . . Medical; Rome; Sister Gabriel. She pulled the blue file free and opened it. Inside, two sheets of heavy paper with the raised insignia. She scanned the top one and found the sentence she wanted, the words black and important. *Reduced to secular state.*

She picked up Mother Emmanuel's pen and in the appropriate place signed her name. One for the papal archives. She picked up the second copy, folded it and stuck it into her skirt pocket.

Then she pulled the silver wedding band off her left hand and dropped it on top of the blue file. It left, after all those years, a narrow white depression at the base of her third finger.

She could hear the nuns returning to the house as she reached the foot of the stairs. She slipped into the library and stood out of sight behind the door. When they'd all gone through to the refectory for a glass of wine in Sister Godric's honour, she would go past the visitors' parlour, and let herself out through the enclosure door.

A sound made her glance towards the library window. It was a room darkened by the old-fashioned conservatory beyond, where once palms had flourished and now only a sickly vine trailed up the broken panes: the nuns used it as a shortcut to the refectory. Someone was doing that now, and it was her low humming Anna had heard through the open sash.

It was Lis. The tune was Sister Godric's favourite. 'Put on some speed, Oh how I need, someone to watch over me.' Lis had her head high and her shoulders straight and she didn't see Anna standing in the shadows. She looked more contented than she had for months, her eyes calm and steady.

She disappeared from sight and Anna, looking after her, discovered even in her sorrow she had been given an unexpected present. Lis was happy, she hadn't been hurt so much after all. And in her absence, Lis would make the altar breads and sew the winter habits. Nothing would change here.

A nun is like a pane of glass. When one breaks, you put in another.

She ran at last, out on the gravelled drive, past the lodge spouting smoke at the gate where old Mr Dunbabbin sat over the fire he lit winter and summer.

She started down the hill towards Welshpool, no hurry now. She was coming down from the mountain, released from her promises. She had her chance all over again, to make another choice, take a different road.

The world lay in front of her. Sister Julian had understood after all. It was enticing, mysterious, unknowable. She wouldn't think now of what she was going to do, what might happen to her. All that was in the future.

For almost the first time in her adult life, she had no idea what tomorrow would bring: she was in the palm of God's hand.

Anna kept her eyes on her valley, where three rivers made their endless journey.

High above her head, a bird called out of limitless lavender sky.

A List of Film and TV Tie-In Titles Available from Mandarin

While every effort is made to keep prices low it is sometimes necessary to increase prices at short notice. Mandarin Paperbacks reserves the right to show new retail prices on covers which may differ from those previously advertised in the text or elsewhere

The prices shown below were correct at the time of going to press

☐	7493 0942 3	**The Silence of the Lambs**	Thomas Harris	£4.99
☐	7493 1416 8	**Wayne's World**	Myers & Ruzan	£4.99
☐	7493 1345 5	**Batman Returns**	Craig Shaw Gardner	£3.99
☐	7493 3601 3	**Rush**	Kim Wozencraft	£3.99
☐	7493 9801 9	**The Commitments**	Roddy Doyle	£4.99
☐	7493 1334 X	**Northern Exposure**	Ellis Weiner	£3.99
☐	7493 0626 2	**Murder Squad**	Tate & Wyre	£4.99
☐	7493 0277 1	**The Bill (Volume 1)**	John Burke	£3.50
☐	7493 0278 X	**The Bill (Volume 2)**	John Burke	£3.50
☐	7493 0002 7	**The Bill (Volume 3)**	John Burke	£3.50
☐	7493 0374 3	**The Bill (Volume 4)**	John Burke	£2.99
☐	7493 0842 7	**The Bill (Volume 5)**	John Burke	£3.50
☐	7493 1178 9	**The Bill (Volume 6)**	John Burke	£3.50

All these books are available at your bookshop or newsagent, or can be ordered direct from the publisher. Just tick the titles you want and fill in the form below

Mandarin Paperbacks, Cash Sales Department, PO Box 11, Falmouth, Cornwall TR10 9EN.

Please send cheque or postal order, no currency, for purchase price quoted and allow the following for postage and packing

UK including BFPO   £1.00 for the first book, 50p for the second and 30p for each additional book ordered to a maximum charge of £3.00.

Overseas including Eire   £2 for the first book £1 00 for the second and 50p for each additional book thereafter

NAME (Block letters)

ADDRESS

☐ I enclose my remittance for

☐ I wish to pay by Access/Visa Card Number ☐☐☐☐☐☐☐☐☐☐☐☐☐☐☐☐

Expiry Date ☐☐☐☐